A Southie Memoir

by
Brian P. Wallace

Copyright 2014 by Brian P. Wallace
All Rights Reserved Worldwide.

Also by Brian P. Wallace:
Final Confession
Night Runner
For more information, visit Brian's Facebook Profile:
http://www.facebook.com/brian.wallace.33483

Book Design by Y42K Publishing Services:
http://www.y42k.com/bookproduction.html

Table of Contents

Chapter 1 - Why Southie? 5
Chapter 2 – Early Politics 8
Chapter 3 – The Smoke Bomb Incident 10
Chapter 4 – Driving The Swim Instructor Crazy 14
Chapter 5 – Hopping Buses 18
Chapter 6 – Mayor of Boystown 23
Chapter 7 – Southie Nicknames & Tommy Hearns 28
Chapter 8 - Chumpy & Bill Yee 33
Chapter 9 – The Night My Dad Died & Irish Superstitions 35
Chapter 10 – The South Boston High Years & BC High Dances 41
Chapter 11 – Basketball & The New Manager 70
Chapter 12 – The Boston Garden Years, Haystack & Popcorn Charlie . 91
Chapter 13 – Sully's Revenge 137
Chapter 14 – Sully vs. Mooreso 144
Chapter 15 – What's The Holdup? 148
Chapter 16 – Beware of Blazing Salads 152
Chapter 17 – Assorted Weirdos, Perverts and Pimps 156
Chapter 18 – DJ's Hot Dogs 160
Chapter 19 - Watch Out For That Rug 167
Chapter 20 – What's Under That Turban 171
Chapter 21 – Rats on Beverly Street 178
Chapter 22 – Garden Antics and Arrests 183
Chapter 23 – Fight Night At The Garden 196
Chapter 24 – The Boston Celtics & Red Aurebach 205
Chapter 25 – Wilt Chamberlain and the Philadelphia 76'ers 214
Chapter 26 - Sox, Yankees and Mickey Mantle 219
Chapter 27 – An All Star Game To Remember 224
Chapter 28 – Joe Crowley, Ray Flynn and Pat Flaherty 227
Chapter 29 – Hold Deese Line 230
Chapter 30 – Meet The New Boston Patriot Ball Boys 236
Chapter 31 – Navy's Joe Bellino 243
Chapter 32 – Sully Takes On Jerry Williams 251

Chapter 33 – Johnny Most 253
Chapter 34 – Confirmation Debacle 259
Chapter 35 – Where Is The Catholic In Catholic Schools 264
Chapter 36 – Hanging With The Mafia 268
Chapter 37 – Flirting With Danger 276
Chapter 38 – Get A Hit Or Get A Casket 282
Chapter 39 – Getting Back To Whitey 285
Chapter 40 – Meet Chuckie Fuller 288
Chapter 41 – The Boys Club And The End Of An Era 296
Chapter 42 – Who Was Sully And Where Did He Come From? 315
Chapter 43 – Sully's Dad - Swanny Sullivan 317
Chapter 44 - A Pimple Ball And City Games 331
Chapter 45 – Too Much Meat 339
Chapter 46 – Donna's Boyfriend 347
Chapter 47 – Sully's Brother Jimmy 351
Chapter 48 – Bubba Cahill – A Car And A Wedding 354
Chapter 49 – Chumpy's Wedding 359
Chapter 50 – Confessions With Fr. Maury 361
Chapter 51 – We Weren't Rich But We Got By 364
Chapter 52 – Paul Brack And Mother Ranking 370
Chapter 53 - A Weekend At The Kennedy Compound 375
Chapter 54 – Time To Grow Up 382
WHERE ARE THEY NOW 384

Chapter 1 - Why Southie?

You might have seen Good Will Hunting. If you didn't see it, you would have had to live on another planet not to have heard about it. Will Hunting, played by Matt Damon, in the movie, lived at 247 E Street in South Boston. That address might not mean anything to you, but that address, was the house, or more appropriately, the doorstep, where we hung out. One of my friends EJ Flynn lived on the second floor and Timmy Murphy lived on the third floor, of the house that Matt Damon made famous. I met Matt Damon and Ben Affleck on a number of occasions, as they sat in local South Boston bars, trying to capture this elusive thing called Southie Pride. Cliff Robertson tried to capture it when he filmed "Charley," in the shadow of Dorchester Heights, in the late 60's. Paul Newman was next, when he came to our hometown to film "The Verdict"[1] in the early 70's. Robin Williams spent three months in Southie, with Damon and Affleck in 1997 and he too tried. Donnie Wahlberg and Rose McGowan filmed a movie in South Boston in the late 90's but they changed the name of the movie, from 'The Brass Ring,' to ' Southie.' Jack Nicholson, Leonardo Di Caprio, Martin Sheen, Mark Wahlberg, Alec Baldwin, and Matt Damon, Titus Welliver were back with "The Departed" and don't forget Clint Eastwood, Kevin Bacon, Sean Penn, Tim Bobbins, Laurence Fishbaum, Laura Linney ,Kevin Chapmen, Amy Madigan. Marcia Gay Harden, filmed Mystic River in Southie and they did a good job thanks to some great dialect coaching from Southie's Jay Giannone and for once they didn't sound like members of the Kennedy family. "Gone Baby Gone" followed with Ben Affleck back for his second bite with Edward Harris, Morgan Freeman. Casey Affleck, Michelle Monaghan and Sean Malone. Cameron Diaz was seen shooting two movies in Southie, The Box with James Madigan and with Tom Cruise in "Knight and Day." Affleck, it seems, can't get enough of South Boston. He was back yet again with "The Town" which was a mixture of Southie and Charlestown. Mark Ruffalo, Ethan Hawke, Donnie Wahlberg and Amanda Peet did one of the best jobs of looking and sounding like true South Bostonians in a sleeper movie called "What Doesn't Kill You" which was the best film ever made that went straight to video. It also starred and was produced by South Boston hometown boy Brian Goodman which is probably why it was so realistic in every way.

Brian P. Wallace

And now there are four separate television shows either being filmed or planned to be filled in South Boston. Robert DeNiro and Showtime are filming a series in Southie called "The 4th Reich" while "The Housewives of South Boston" "Southie Pride" and "Southie Rules" are all scheduled to be filmed in Southie. Combine that with the up and coming Whitey Bulger trial and there will be no doubt that South Boston has the eyes of the nation, once again, focused right on them. For 35,000 people we sure do get more than our share of publicity, whether wanted or not. But, until now, nobody has really taken the time to see the other part of Southie; the characters, the nicknames, the generosity, the loyalty, the bond that has always held this proud community together. This is that story.

The fascination with South Boston is kind of funny, to us who grew up there, although there was nothing funny about growing up there. It was a tough, hard- nosed place where a 14- year old kid was playing stick ball with us one minute and robbing a bank the next. That actually happened to me. The kid came back to the corner with a bag full of hundreds. The next time, however he never returned. He was killed by his accomplice after an argument about the money they stole from the bank. This fascination about Whitey Bulger is so far over the top it is ridiculous. I can remember sitting on the Santa Monica Pier one afternoon in 2008 with Hollywood producer Ron Shelton who produced such great movies as "Bull Durham" "White Men Can't Jump", "Tin Cup" "Blaze" "Cobb" to name a few of Ron's great movies. The Departed had just come out and Ron asked me if his friend Jack Nicholson had captured Whitey Bulger in the movie. Little did we know at that time that Whitey and was living less than two blocks from where we sat that day on the Pier.

"No, he played him all wrong," I said naively, shocking some of the Hollywood types who had joined us for lunch that day. They all looked at Shelton as if I had offended him. I didn't realize at the time that Shelton and Nicholson were so close. Instead of being insulted Shelton laughed his head off and pulled his phone out of his jacket.

"Will you tell him that?" Shelton laughed, punching in some numbers.

"Tell who?" I asked.

"Jack," he smiled. "I told him he didn't get it right." I almost swallowed my beer. "You want me to tell Jack Nicholson that he misplayed

Whitey Bulger?" I waited for a few minutes and Jack's answering machine went on. Thank God. I got a reprieve but I had to explain why Jack did not play Whitey correctly in "The Departed".

"Too loud," I said, hoping that would suffice, it didn't.

"What do you mean?" Shelton asked. I took a deep breath and looked around the table and saw that I had everyone's attention.

"It's simple," I started "Whitey never showed emotion in public. If he was mad, he never showed it in public.

I was sitting down the Boston Athletic Club one night, and Whitey came in by himself and sat with his back to the oval bar. One of my friends, who had way too much to drink, started getting on Whitey.

"What's wrong Mr. big shot got no gang tonight, you little pussy." my friend yelled at Whitey from across the bar. I almost had a heart attack. Whitey paid no attention.

"No gun on you tonight Whitey? For once you might have to fight with your hands," my friend laughed. He was the only one in the bar who did. Whitey looked at him, and had a drink of his club soda. I had enough. I got up to leave, Whitey looked at me and pointed an imaginary gun at my friend. He had gone too far. Nothing good was going to happen that night. I could hear my friend still yelling across the bar at Whitey as I left. Whitey never said a word or changed his expression. Two weeks later they found my friend in the alley behind Triple O's beat to a pulp. He was unconscious and barely breathing. That was Whitey's payback. And I can guarantee Whitey had an alibi the night my friend got pulverized. Lesson learned but never repeated.

Why is Paul Newman, Jack Nicholson, Martin Scorcese, Cliff Robertson, Robin Williams, Cameron Diaz, Tom Cruise, fascinated about South Boston? What is Southie Pride? I can tell you that it is a lot more than a slogan on a movie billboard, or a bumper sticker. Southie Pride is a way of life. None of those major movies, or the countless other movies, set in South Boston, or made about South Boston have succeeded in capturing the essence of South Boston. What makes South Boston so special? Two words. The people.

Brian P. Wallace

Chapter 2 – Early Politics

This book is about those people, real Southie people, not made up in a screenplay or book or characters on the big screen. This book is about real life people who made growing up in Southie so special and fun. It's about two best friends, who grew up in the turbulence of the 60's and the 70's and how they interacted with the world around them. It's about good guys and some bad guys. It's a behind the scenes look at a community that has captured the imagination of an entire nation from Whitey Bulger to school busing. It's about Sully, and it's about me.

There are 35,000 people in South Boston. Why, Matt Damon and Ben Affleck picked the house, we used as our official whist table, amongst other things, to immortalize, forever on the screen, is ironic. It is also kind of ironic, I guess, that I was introduced to two of the most important things in my life, on the very same day, I had just turned six years old and was very deeply involved in my first political campaign. Politics is something you inherit in South Boston. Politics is passed down from grandfather to father and on to the sons and daughters. You don't become part of politics in South Boston; politics becomes part of you. And so it was on a warm September afternoon, in 1955, that a young, Irish, bespectacled, excited kid stood outside his first polling place passing out poll cards. I was working for my first candidate but certainly not my last. His name was John Powers and he was a candidate for the State Senate. Johnny Powers was a good friend of my father's and had asked me to help him in his campaign. I took that responsibility very seriously and from day one I worked my little tail off. I would pass out flyers and deliver campaign literature. I would pass out bingo dobbers at the dozen of bingo games that each church had during the week. At one point South Boston had more churches and bars per square foot than any other city in America. I would go to the parking lots and affix bumper stickers. I wanted to learn everything about this new and fascinating world, and I worked hard at it. While most kids my age were playing hide and go seek I was putting cards in mail boxes. I was like the campaign mascot and I loved it. I did everything from getting coffee to holding the ladder while my father stapled signs onto houses. The closer it got to Election Day, the more excited I became. There was a certain electricity building and I like that feeling. It was almost addictive and it has kept me addicted, election after election. Finally, on September 15, 1955, after three months of hard work, it was Primary Day. By 8:30 PM that night we would know if all that hard work had, in fact, paid off.

I couldn't wait to get out of school that day and I kept looking at the clock every ten minutes. The nuns used to tell us a lot of things, most of which I found out later in life to be untrue. But the one about, the more you look at the clock the slower it will move, was true that day in 1955. Finally, it was 2:30, and before the bell had sounded the second time, I was sprinting toward the Bigelow School or Ward 6 Precinct 3, where I would pass out John Powers cards until the polls closed at 8 o'clock that evening.

It was about 4 o'clock that afternoon when a kid about my age approached me. He was kind of a roly- poly kid with a red face and a scaly cap. He took one of the cards with, John Power's face embossed on the front, looked it over as if deciding on whether to vote for him.

"Why are you doing this?" he asked. I was kind of caught off guard.

"My father asked me to," I shrugged.

"You do everything your old man asks?" he continued. I just stared, not really sure what to say. Unfazed, he continued his interrogation.

"How much they paying you?" he asked looking around at all the poll workers.

"Nothing," I replied, kind of offended. He continued to survey the card. I still didn't know his name. All of a sudden the card had been magically transformed into a neat airplane and was headed in the direction of my father. It landed at his feet as he shot me one of those 'wait till I get you home' looks. I looked at my father and then back to the little roly -poly ball of trouble. His expression never changed.

"Boy did they suck you in." he said, and walked away. I stared in disbelief. It would not be the last time that I would stare in disbelief at this chubby little kid, who would play such a major part in my life. The rest, as they say, is history.

Chapter 3 – The Smoke Bomb Incident

The second time that I ran into this chubby little ball of destruction proved to be a whole lot worse than the first. It was about two weeks after John Powers victory It was early October, and early October in Boston is a teasing time of year, holding both summer and fall in opposite hands while cascading the landscape with its' wonderfully colored foliage. It really is a special time of year. It is also football season. Doing my very best Johnny Unitas imitation with a friend named Billy 'Bull' Gannon, who was doing his best Raymond Berry imitation, I heard a voice calling for a pass. The voice sounded vaguely familiar but I couldn't place it right away. A second later my worst fears were realized. It was him; Mr. Trouble. Just as he had two weeks ago, he seemed to appear out of nowhere.

"Hey, Mr. President," he yelled.

"Your boy Powers almost lost" he said, even though that was far from the truth. I ignored him and threw the ball to Gannon. He persisted.

"Come on, Senator, throw me the ball." I turned and just looked at him. He really was Unbelievable. He looked like one of the dead end kids, with the scaly cap and a dirty face.

"What do you want?" I finally asked.

"Hey Senator, have you ever seen a smoke bomb?" he asked. I hadn't, and I was duly impressed, forgetting for a minute who I was dealing with. It was actually pretty exciting. Everything is pretty exciting to six year-old boys, I guess. six -year-old boys have their own agenda on life. What is exciting, and important at six, may be unimportant at seven. But at six it's pretty damn important. And so was this mysterious smoke- bomb.

"Come on in this hallway," he said, as clandestine as he could muster. I still, at this point, did not know his name. As if reading my mind;

"By the way my name's Sully," he said" That out of the way, I followed my new friend Sully into the hallway. This was an adventure. I could just feel it. Sully brought the smoke bomb out of his grass stained dungarees as if it contained enough nitroglycerine to blow up the entire town. I had no idea what a smoke bomb looked like, but I was disappointed in this small, black, gumdrop looking thing. I guess that I was expecting a more ominous looking device. This was a smoke bomb? To make matters worse, we couldn't get it lit.

"This is a tough little sucker to light," Sully said, as attempt after attempt produced nothing but frustration. We were growing impatient. Six year old kids also have very limited attention spans. There is always something else more exciting to do if one grows bored, and we were quickly growing bored. Again, as if sensing our frustration, Sully perked up.

"I have it," he said, as he moved deftly and much quicker than I thought he was capable of doing. He brought back a stack of old newspapers, which he lit very quickly on fire. Once the papers were lit we finally got the smoke bomb to light. And I can tell you, it was well worth the wait. A huge plume of thick black smoke rose instantaneously from where we knelt on the hallway floor. We were so enamored with the amount and the thickness of the black smoke that we completely forgot about the old papers we had lit. They were now burning out of control in the back corner of the hallway. The paper fire had risen from its base and had now engulfed the wall and was starting to catch onto the stairs by the time we realized what was happening. I quickly surmised that two little kids were not going to be able to put the fire out. It had grown so fast. It's funny what goes through your mind in a time like that. I remember being very scared, but not for myself. The hallway we were in was located at 247 West 5th street. I lived at 249 West 5th street. My immediate concern was for my house, and my family. I knew that I had to do something real quick or this house was going to burn down. In a flash we were out of that hallway. We ran like characters in a fast motion cartoon. We ran to the fire alarm box located on the corner of corner of F Street and West 5th Street. I got there first and pulled the alarm as quickly and as forcefully as I could.

Within a minute we could hear the fire engines speeding to our rescue. I started to breathe a little easier. The fire station was located at Dorchester Street and West Fourth, which was only a block away. The engines whizzed by us and toward the thick black smoke emanating from 247 West 5th street. They had no way of knowing that the smoke they were seeing was not from a fire, but from Sully's smoke- bomb, and we weren't about to tell them. All they saw as they swung onto West 5th street was the smoke and they simply reacted. They thought they had the start of a major conflagration. What they had, in actuality, was a smoke bomb gone awry. The firemen hit the ground running, even before the truck had stopped. A large crowd had gathered as they usually do when there is the possibility of witnessing a tragedy. The only tragedy in this story was what my father was going to do to me when I got home. There was still an outside chance that we wouldn't get caught. That chance disappeared forever when I saw my nosy neighbor talking to the fire captain and pointing in our direction. She was looking out her window, as usual, and had spotted us running out of the smoking house. She couldn't wait to tell anyone who would listen. And from where I stood the fire captain was certainly listening. A fireman came out of the house holding what remained of our smoke bomb in his big rubber gloves. He actually had a smile on his face. My father who had been called over to the conference with my nosy neighbor and the fire captain did not have a smile on his face. In fact, his face was getting redder by the minute as the talks went on. He looked over to where I was standing and gave me a look that I had never seen before in my long six years on this earth.

"I think I am in serious trouble." I said to Sully.

The fire captain and my father both started walking over to me and Sully. I got a good lecture from one and a good beating from the other. To make matters even worse, my Uncle Ed, who lived in the top floor of my house, was a fireman. He was sleeping, because he had worked the night before. He knew all the firemen who were all looking at the remains of the smoke bomb, and he was even more upset than my father when he learned the true origin of the situation. My uncle was a cool guy whom I had never seen upset in my entire six years on God's earth. Well that certainly changed that day. My father must have felt that God had dealt him a handful of jokers. His six year- old kid, who at this point in his short life, had shown no visible signs of being a major criminal or any other psychotic behavior, was all of a sudden lighting houses on fire. Good start. My uncle said to my mother, who was his sister.

"How am I going to face those guys? My uncle said to my mother who was his sister. "My nephew is a suspected arsonist and he's only six years old." My mother just cried. My older and only brother Eddie, however, loved every minute of it. He had a huge smile on his face as I was getting a tongue-lashing. He was the one that was usually in hot water, but not that day and he loved this role reversal. "Most kids your age can't even cross the street by themselves and you're lighting houses on fire. What are you going to do when you are twelve, kill the President?" my father yelled. I had never seen my father so mad. I had really screwed up this time. Fires were a whole different category of punishment. This, I knew, was not going to be one of those, ' just go to your room' offenses. I was contemplating what punishment they could conjure up that could possibly fit the crime, when the front doorbell rang.

"Who is that the FBI?" my father said as he headed to the door. Better, it was Sully. My father opened the door and just looked at this eight year- old dead end kid. My father stared, my brother smiled, my mother cried and my uncle continued to shake his head. "Can I help you?" my father said very coldly.

"Are you Brian's father?" Sully asked.

"At this moment I'm not quite sure," my father shot back.

"I'm extremely sorry Mr. Wallace, but Brian had absolutely nothing to do with today's unfortunate incident. It was totally my fault and I accept full responsibility for it." My father's mouth dropped open and he just continued to stare at Sully, who stared right back. My father didn't even bother to answer. He closed the door and turned to my mother.

"My six year old son lights the house next door to us on fire and he's hanging around with Baby face Nelson, to boot." He looked like he was in shock. He turned to me. "Where did you meet that little con man?" I didn't know what a con man meant but I knew it wasn't good. I wasn't about to add lying to my offenses, so I told my father how I had met him and how today's events unfurled. He seemed a little calmer after hearing that I wasn't the instigator of the fire. He couldn't get over Sully however. He always talked about Sully using the word incident rather than the word fire every time he would recount the story, which was often. My father really got a kick out of Sully couching his phraseology at eight years old. That however was years and years later.

Brian P. Wallace

Chapter 4 – Driving The Swim Instructor Crazy

Unfortunately, for me, the only kick I got was a kick upstairs to my room where I was grounded for a whole month. I also received very strict orders not to hang around with Sully, who in my father's eyes was Jimmy Cagney, Edward G. Robinson, George Raft and Al Capone all rolled into one little roly- poly package of trouble. They had no idea just how right they were. They also had no idea just how tough it would be to stay away from Sully.

I had to stay in the house for a month, after the smoke bomb incident. I was actually back in circulation for a couple of weeks, after my sentence, before I ran in to him again. It's hard now to imagine how I avoided him for even two weeks. We lived about two blocks from each other and we both hung out at the boys club, which is precisely where our next encounter occurred. One thing that I really liked at the club was the swimming pool although I hadn't learned to swim just yet. I was also kind of shy. That would change, but it would take a little while. The only thing that I didn't like about going swimming at the club, was that we all were naked. It took a little while to get used to it, but once I did it seemed perfectly normal. Although I'm quite sure they would be put in jail if they tried to make 100 kids swim naked together, in today's society. I was in the big shower room, with about 100 other naked kids, getting ready for the group 1 swim, when I heard that unmistakable voice again.

"Hey Commissioner, you're back on the streets, huh." I turned and there he was, smiling that conspiratorial smile.

"Yeah," I said. No thanks to you."

"I can't help it if your father has no sense of humor, it was only a small fire." Later, as we grew into manhood Sully and my father would become very close and the mere mention of Sully's name would bring an instantaneous smile to my father's face. But that was then and this was now.

That day in the shower I was only seven and Sully was nine. Manhood was still a far off place in a strange and distant land. The exuberance we felt that day, so many years ago, was reserved for the giddy anxiety all young kids feel at the site of a gleaming placid swimming pool. As we approached the pool Sully nudged me and whispered.

"This instructor is a real jerk." By the look on the instructor's face, when he saw Sully, I would dare say that the feeling was more than mutual. The instructor checked every boy, before being allowed in to the pool. I was in line just in front of Sully. When it came my turn I showed him my hands, both sides, and lifted up my feet, which he took a cursory look at, and signaled me into the pool. Sully was next. He went through the same ritual as I had just done. The instructor, however, did not wave him into the pool.

"You're supposed to use soap, now go back into the shower and pick up a bar." I could see that Sully was livid. As he turned to go back to the shower a blonde kid, whom I had never seen before, pointed at Sully.

"No grubs in the pool," he laughed" A couple of days later I saw that same kid with a huge black eye. I never asked Sully about it, I didn't have to. We were all in the pool and killing each other as Sully made the long walk from the showers to poolside. He, again, lifted up his feet and showed the instructor both sides of his hands.

"Not good enough," the instructor said as a fuming Sully turned, once again, and headed for the showers. He looked for a second like he was going to say something but thought better of it and retreated to the showers. A spotless Sully re-appeared a couple of minutes later, passed inspection, and was immediately drowning kids and creating all sorts of havoc. Group 1 consisted of kids from six to ten years of age who didn't know how to swim yet. We had the pool every day from 3:00 p.m. - 4 p.m. At 3:30, every day, a whistle would blow and we were required to get out of the pool and sit on the side of the pool with our feet dangling in the water.

First, the instructor, whose name was Joe Lynch, would read all the things that we were not to do, while in the pool, all of which Sully had been doing since he entered. I must have heard that monologue a thousand times and it never varied one syllable.

"There will be no running, pushing or wrestling on the walks of this pool. If you have candy or gum you will kindly deposit it in the receptacle outside the swimming pool area." Since this was only my third time in the pool I was relatively new to the spiel and I was listening very intently. Joe Lynch, was a former Marine, if there is such a thing, and he treated us as if we were all Marine recruits at Paris Island instead of young kids at the boys Club.

Sully, naturally, sat right next to me, as we took our places on the 'walks of the pool,' as the instructor called it. As he was going through his monologue Sully was mimicking him to the letter and sounded just like him. It was really funny and I started to laugh. The instructor turned and looked directly at me.

"You think this is funny son?' he said looking directly at me. I almost died.

"No sir." Was all I could manage to say.

"Well then keep your little mouth shut. Is that asking too much?" he asked.

"No sir," I blushed. He then turned his attention to another subject, thank God, and forgot about me. From my left I heard a whisper.

"I told you he's a jerk." I didn't even bother to acknowledge it. The instructor, in his best Marine voice, then shouted.

"OK ladies I will say this once and only once. I will call out an age if that is your age you will raise your right hand and once I have finished counting I will nod and you will put your hand down. Do you all have that?"

"Yes sir," we all shouted.

"OK," he started, "I want all the six year olds to raise your hands."

"OK, seven year olds." This time I raised my hand and so did Sully.

"OK eight year olds," he shouted. Once again, Sully's hand shot up like a bullet. The instructor counted all the hands, wrote the number on a piece of paper and then shouted.

"All nine year olds." Sully's hand was, once again, up in the air. I couldn't figure out what the hell he was doing.

"Any ten year olds?" he asked. There were none. Once he had finished this routine he began figuring the numbers on his sheet. He shook his head and began turning a deep shade of red. He didn't say a word. He started counting heads. When he finished he looked back at the paper on his clipboard and screamed. "Someone doesn't understand instructions ladies." His face was now crimson. "You only raise your hand when you're particular age group is called, is that clear?" His voice had risen an octave.

"Now we'll do this again." Sully sat stone-faced.

"Ready now, all six year olds please raise your hands." Sully leaned over to me.

"I'll drive this jerk crazy," as he again raised his hand as a 6 year-old. He again raised his hand as a seven year-old and an eight year-old. When the instructor added up the numbers he went absolutely crazy. His voice reverberated throughout the pool area. as if we were in the Grand Canyon.

"I don't care if you ever go in that pool again," he bellowed.

"We will do this until we do it right." I leaned over to Sully.

"Come on cut it out, I want to go back in the pool." I said.

"OK" he said," I think this jerk has learned his lesson." I couldn't believe it. I would later learn over and over and over that this was vintage Sully. Don't piss him off or you will pay in the end. When the instructor did it the third time, Sully only raised his hand when the nine years-olds were called. That was how I learned how old he was, amongst other things. Sully's revenge. It was not always as swift as that day but it was as certain as death and taxes. Later on I will talk about a couple of my favorite Sully revenge stories. One has to do with a famous wrestler. The other has to do with a famous popcorn seller at Boston Garden. Both have to do with the Boston Garden, our home away from home when we were teenagers. That afternoon at the pool, however, was my introduction to the revenge factor. I know that blonde kid with the shiner knows all about Sully's revenge.

Chapter 5 – Hopping Buses

After that day at the club swimming pool I walked home and sat down for supper with my family. It was the first time in a couple of weeks that I actually felt that things were finally getting back to normal at home. My father had started treating me like a normal kid again. The fire incident was beginning to go away, Thank God. My father never mentioned Sully and I never brought up the subject. He didn't know that I had been seeing Sully at the Club, and I wasn't about to tell him. It was about a month after the swimming pool incident when Sully did it to me again. That morning, at breakfast, my father asked me what I was doing that day. I told him that I was in the finals of the club's pocket pool tournament. He liked that, and he wished me luck. My father's American Legion Post, the McDonough Post, had a pool table and my father fancied himself a pretty fair pool player, so he liked that I was pretty good myself. You know the apple and the tree thing. I walked the block and a half to the club and my first shot at the Club's pocket pool title. I was feeling pretty good about myself and about life. I ended up getting my clock cleaned in the tournament by a kid named Ronny Delverde. Ronny Delverde was a big kid who would be in to the Fonzie thing long before Fonzie was a thought on anyone's script. He was two years older than me and about a foot taller. Ronnie would later be one of the twenty five South Boston kids who died in Viet Nam. But on that day Ronny Delverde kicked my ass. I got a trophy for my second place- finish and headed over to West 7th street for a dill pickle and a Pepsi. Nice combination, huh. Pregnant women and kids have an excuse to eat anything without regard to consequences.

Sully was in the store called Tilly's, driving the lady behind the counter crazy. He was buying twenty five cents worth of penny candy as if he were Donald Trump purchasing four blocks of Atlantic City. Only Sully could make buying penny candy into an all- day affair. Basically he was just bored and wanted to aggravate someone. The poor lady, behind the counter, unfortunately for her, happened to be in the wrong place at the wrong time. He brightened up when he saw me.

"Mr. pool shark, got your butt kicked I hear." I always marveled at how fast he got his information. I had lost only ten minutes before, and he already knew all the details. He had a string of informants that would make the CIA, jealous. When he turned to talk to me, the lady behind the counter ran, to get away from him. She did not return. He had his bag of candy in his hand as we headed out of the store. I had my pickle and my Pepsi.

"Delverde kicked your butt huh," he said as nonchalantly as he was asking what time it was.

"He's good," was all I could counter with.

"Way too good for you pickle head." I don't know if he was being nice or just didn't know how to be nice. He was just so matter of fact. No bullshit, just the facts, as Joe Friday would say. I wasn't even mad when he said Delverde was much better than me. It was the way he said it. He wasn't trying to hurt me. That was just the way he was.

We left Tilley's and walked the block to the club, when he got that look on his face. I had seen it in the pool, and at the fire. I called it Sully's "let's get in trouble" look. I didn't know it that day, but I would see that look many more times in my life. This particular day was only the third time I had seen it, but even then, I knew I would be smart to go in the club and get away from Sully. But, I didn't. While we were sitting on the club stairs a couple of Bay View buses went by. The bus stop was directly in front of the club at F and West 6th street. It's funny that I had never paid any attention to the Bay View bus before that day. I had seen kids hopping the buses before, but paid no attention to them. I had no idea how to hop a bus. Those buses were huge. Out of the clear blue, Sully said.

"Let's hop the next bus."

"No way," I said shrinking a little. But I guess my face must have said it all. Sully started singing mama's little baby loves shortening, shortening, mama's little baby loves shortening bread. All the kids were laughing at me and it made me very uncomfortable.

"I'm no baby," I responded in my most macho voice. "I just don't understand why you want to hop the bus in the first place," I said to Sully.

"Because it's fun," he said, turning away to face his audience. I still wasn't convinced.

"What if I fall off?"

"Come on," Sully said, trying to regain the upper hand.

Brian P. Wallace

"Nobody ever falls off a Bay View bus, it's never happened." He hadn't told the truth since I met him a month ago. Why should I believe him now?

"I don't even know how to hop a bus," I said.

"Just follow me," he smiled. I would hear those words again, many more times in my young life. And like a fool, I would follow them again and again. Before I had time to squirm out of my predicament.

"Come on," he shouted. Here comes a Bay View bus now." It was too late. I was caught between a Bay View bus and being a chicken. He flew down the stairs. I followed, like a sheep.

"Just do what I do," he said, as we ran to the bus stop and tried our best to look inconspicuous. The bus came to a full stop as a couple of ladies got on. Like a professional hopper, Sully was affixed to the back of the bus in a millisecond. He could really move fast when he wanted to. He waved to me.

"Come on slow poke hurry up." I had a much harder time getting a grip on the back of the bus. I was starting to panic when he reached over and pulled me up, as the bus started to move. I, like Sully, was glued to the back of the bus. I had done it. I felt like a big shot and I had a big smile plastered all over my kisser, as the bus gained speed and headed down West 6th street. I really liked the feeling that I was getting away with something, as kids going to the club pointed to us with admiration, as they walked up West 6th Street. I liked the feeling. The bus stopped at E street, picked up some more passengers, and made a right onto West 7th street. I had a big smile on my face as the huge bus began its trip to Broadway Station.

"I told you that you'd like it," Sully said, as the wind swept through our hair. The bus came to a full stop at the intersection of D street and West 7th street. The bus had picked up a more passengers and waited for the light to change. A horn beeped behind us. We paid no attention. It beeped again. Sully without turning around yelled, "Hold your water, pal it's a red light," Sully yelled. The horn beeped again. This time, Sully took one hand off the bus and turned his body so that he could better confront the aggravating motorist. I on the other hand had both hands and both feet firmly planted.

"Oh shit," I heard Sully say as the bus closed its doors. "Get off, quick," Sully said in a tone that I'd never heard before. By now, the bus was picking up a little steam.

"Are you crazy?" I asked, looking down as the bus picked up speed.

"As soon as this bus stops we're getting off," Sully said, and this wasn't a request this was a command. I nodded. The bus came to a full stop and we both jumped. I had miscalculated the height, and fell flat on my back. I looked up at Sully expecting to see him laughing. He wasn't. I stopped laughing pretty quickly when I saw who was standing directly behind Sully. My father.

"Oh shit," I said, inadvertently. I couldn't believe it. My very first time hopping a bus and I got caught. If it weren't for bad luck I'd have no luck at all. My father's face was crimson color. This was becoming a habit.

"What did you just say?" he yelled.

"Nothing, nothing," I whispered. He was as mad, if not madder, than he was with the smoke bomb.

"Going on a trip?" he said angrily.

"Dad I was just."

"Save it he said, cutting me off in mid -sentence. I had risen to my feet on wobbly legs, and just stood there as all the project kids came out to see what the commotion was all about. The last thing I needed, in my humiliation, was witnesses.

"Get in the car," My father said, pointing to his brand new 1955 Ford. Head down, I marched over to his new pride and joy. Sully had mysteriously disappeared. We drove the four blocks to my house in total silence. It was the longest four - block ride in my life. This was strike two, in less than a month. I knew I was going to get the strap for this offense.

My brother and his friends Ronny Lescinskas, Tommy Conley, Vinny Crowley, Skippa King, Frankie Crowley and Wally Ambrose were in front of my house, when we pulled up. My brother took one look at my father's face and knew instantly that I had screwed up again. He now had new ammunition, which just made his day.

"What happened dad, what did he do this time?" he managed to say in between smiles. My father never answered, or even looked at him. My mother hearing all the turmoil was waiting just inside the door.

"Do you want to know what your little son did today?" he said to my mother. It was funny, whenever I did something good, I was his son, but whenever I screwed up, I was my mother's son. Go figure. I didn't say a word, that day. My mother, who never liked confrontations, just stood there staring at me and my father.

"Tell your mother what you just did." My brother loved every minute of it.

"I hopped a bus," I whispered.

"Louder" he commanded.

"I hopped a bus," I repeated with tears welling up in my eyes. I knew that my mother didn't have a clue what hopping a bus meant although she knew it was something that I probably shouldn't be doing, by my father's tone and my tears. My father broke in.

"And he was with that little juvenile delinquent to boot." Even at six years old, I wondered where my parents got their expressions, How about this classic.

"Don't keep running in and out of here like a blue ass fly." Now what the hell was that supposed to mean A blue ass fly? And we were either gallivanting or traipsing depending on the situation. My father would say to me something like, "Don't be out gallivanting tonight and don't think you're going to come traipsing in here after midnight." Traipsing in after midnight? It was going to take me that long to figure out what gallivanting meant. I knew that day I got caught hopping the bus that I wouldn't be gallivanting or traipsing anywhere for a long time. My mother started to cry, my brother started to laugh, and my father continued to yell. I just stood there praying this would end.

"Did God put him on this earth to get you in trouble?" my father asked.

"God put Sully on this earth to make Brian laugh,.." my friend Ricky Calnan used to saymany years later. In reality they were both probably right. There was nothing funny about that night however. I got killed and got another jail sentence in my room. It was a full month before I even smelled the street again. They wouldn't even let me run errands,which was about as bad as it got in my house. This time Sully did not come by doing his Eddie Haskell routine. He was completely out of my life for a month. That would be the only month that he would be out of my life for the next 12 years.

Chapter 6 – Mayor of Boystown

Approximately three years after hopping the only bus that I ever hopped in my life, a friend of mine named Billy Barrett talked me into running for Mayor of Boystown. Billy had been the outgoing Mayor and could not succeed himself as Mayor. I had just turned ten years of age which made me eligible to run for Mayor. I had been elected to the Mayor's Council the previous two years and running for Mayor was the logical progression anyway. The problem was that I had no idea who was going to run against me for the coveted Mayor's spot. After talking to Billy Barrett I decided to seek the office regardless of who was going to run against me. Billy was backing me and I did have a lot of friends in the club, especially Sully who I knew could get me some votes. I just had no idea how many or how he would get them.

I had a meeting at my house with a lot of my friends and they were psyched that I was going to run and promised to do all they could to get me elected. My father and Uncle Ed got some stock to make posters to hang all around the club. Sully was at my house when we were deciding to make the posters but were fishing around for the right slogan or theme.

"What about your glasses?" Sully asked.

"What about them?" I asked in return.

"You know the professor thing going on," he said, as my father and uncle looked at us as if we were speaking some kind of foreign language. In a way we were. One of the teams we played basketball against, was called the Emmanuel House from Roxbury. They had nicknamed me the professor because of my rather large glasses. Many of those same kids, like Johnny White, Kevin Tarpey, Kenny Lamberti Marty Foley, Jacky Dooley, Dukie Buckley would eventually become very good friends of both mine and Sully's, but back then we were rivals.

"Hey your boy, the professor can really pat the pill." Kevin Tarpey said one day to Sully after we beat his team by 20 points. Sully agreed, not having a clue as to what Kevin had just said. To break it down, I was the professor and patting the pill meant dribbling the ball. The Emmanuel House is also where I met a Dead End Kid, by the name of Guy Guy Rindini, and if my father thought that Sully was a gangster, he should have met one twelve year old real named gangster named Guy Guy Rindini who held court at the Emmanuel House, which ironically enough was run by nuns.

The first time I met Guy Guy, I was playing basketball for the South Boston Boys Club against the Emmanuel House. As I entered the Emmanuel House gym that day, I was also twelve and I was leading the BOB league in scoring.

"Hey professor. I need you in my office," Guy Guy yelled out so that everyone n the gym could hear him. This little kid wore a pure cashmere overcoat, which had to have cost at least five hundred dollars. He had on another three hundred dollars in jewelry on him and a diamond pinkie ring. He motioned me in to the locker room.

"Now I understand that you're the man Professor," he said, as he took a drag from his cigarette, right under a sign, which said No Smoking. I had no idea, who he was, or what he was talking about. He then reached in to his expensive pants and pulled a wad of money out that would choke a horse. He waved it in my face.

"If you lose this game, this is yours," he waved the wad of money under my nose.

"What?" was all I could manage to get out.

"Come on Professor, you know the game, I can make a lot of money if I have you on my side.," he smiled.

"Who would bet on a kid's basketball game," I laughed. He didn't.

"It's not just any game it's the championship game and I have a lot of people who would lay some action on a game like that. No names of course."

"Of course," I said sarcastically? I couldn't believe it. This twelve year-old gangster was trying to bribe me to throw the game.

"I can't do that," I said."

"You're loss Professor. We both could have made a lot of money, and if you tell anyone about our little talk you'll never make it back to your precious little Boys Club" he smirked. I followed him out of the locker room still in shock. I'll never know if he was for real, or just trying to throw me off, which he did. My friends all tell me he was for real, The money and jewelry were certainly was real. I always wondered whatever happened to Guy Guy! I found out that his father owned a couple of trip clubs in the infamous Combat

Zone in Boston and was tied in pretty good with the Mafia We won the game that day, but the nickname stuck.

But Sully had hit on something that day in my cellar even if I didn't agree. My father and Uncle, however, immediately, liked his idea, so we went with it We made 10 large posters that day down my cellar and hung them all up in very strategic locations around the club.

Each of the posters had a huge pair of glasses and underneath the glasses were the words "We See Brian Wallace As The Next Mayor." I wasn't particularly thrilled with the signs but the kids loved them and they certainly got the message across. Each candidate had to get fifty signatures to get on the ballot. The kids running for Mayor's Council had to get twenty five signatures. I gave one of the signature sheets to Sully and went down to the gym. By the time I had showered and changed Sully has acquired enough signatures to get me on the ballot.

"How did you do that?" I asked, kind of shocked.

"Easy," he said "I threatened them." I laughed, I thought he was kidding. He wasn't. Election Day finally arrived and I was as nervous as I had ever been at any basketball game.

I couldn't believe it when I walked in to vote. Sully was the kid handing out the ballots.

"How did you pull this off?" I asked, after I had been handed my ballot.

"Shut up," he whispered "Santapaul doesn't know that I know you." In actuality Larry Santapaul, the Boys Club Director, hardly ever left his office and he didn't know any of the kids, so I wasn't surprised that he didn't know that Sully and I were close friends. Sully conned Santapaul into letting him escort the voters into the voting area and give them their ballots. I had no idea, whatsoever, that he was doing this. He did it all on his own. Honest.

The voting was held on a Saturday from 10:00 AM. until 5:00 PM. It was the longest day of my life. I waited outside the junior room, passing out my campaign literature for seven straight hours. Finally the doors closed and Larry Santapaul came out and told us that the ballots were now being counted and the results would be announced within the hour. Now that really was the longest hour of my life. Me and my campaign workers were all feeling the strain as we waited outside the Junior games room while Larry Santapaul counted the ballots. The room was packed with candidates and their supporters. There were about twenty kids running for the nine Council seats, so the room was pretty crowded. Larry Santapaul did the Council candidates first, which took about twenty minutes. Then it was time for the big one, the Mayor of Boystown. Not one person had left the room, The stage was now set.

Larry Santapaul took the microphone and asked all the candidates for Mayor to come up to the stage. Sergei Wassilew, David Tremblet and I all trudged up the five stairs to the stage. I could hear Sully and all my friends chanting.

"Brian, Brian, Brian." I was pretty psyched. Santapaul kept checking the sheets which drove everyone crazy, Sully yelled.

"Hey Larry how about before midnight," which cracked everyone up, except the fat Director. There was a strict rule, in the club, that we always addressed the Director as Mister Director or Mr. Santapaul, but never Larry. But, Sully was born to break rules and set new standards. Santapaul stared into the crowd with an evil look on his face.

"I want to congratulate all the candidates who had the courage to put their name on the ballot. In all my years as Director, I have never seen such an incredible plurality." None of us knew what plurality meant, but he went on. "The new Mayor of Boystown is Brian Wallace." The place went bananas with Sully leading the cheers. The final vote was Wallace 249 votes, Wassilew 6 votes, and Tremblett 3 votes. Santapaul was shocked. He said to me.

"Great job, you got 249 votes and there were only 258 votes cast." He kept shaking my hand. "Wow the kids must really like you," he said over and over. And you know what, he was absolutely right, some of the kids did like me, more however were afraid of Sully. It seems that Sully not only handed out the ballots, he also handed out a very stern warning to everyone who voted that day.

"Who ya voting for?" he would ask each voter breaking every rule in the book, as he led them into the voting room.

"I'm voting for Brian or I'm voting for Wallace," Sully would pat them on the back and tell them what good boys they were. If, on the other hand, a kid said.

"I'm voting for Sergei or I'm voting for Tremblett," Sully's admonition n to them was quite different.

"You're voting for who?" Sully would ask in a very threatening manner. A little bit taken back, because of Sully's reputation and his close proximity to their body, the kids would quickly change their minds and ask Sully.

"Why who should I vote for?" Sully would then very politely say, something like.

"I would strongly urge you to vote for Brian Wallace and remember I will see your ballot after you vote and I will see you outside some other day if you vote for anyone else." He would then smile, pat each voter on the back and lead them into the booth as they voted for me. Once the kids had voted and were heading out of the room, Sully would shake their hand and say.

"Remember now this is between us, OK."

"OK, Sully," was the usual reply. No wonder I got almost all the votes. When I asked him about it the next day, he didn't deny it.

"It was no big deal, they were almost all voting for you anyway. Are you mad because I threatened them?" He asked. I had to laugh, because in Sully's world he honestly felt he did nothing wrong. He knew how much I wanted to win, so he helped it to happen., Simple as that. He didn't seem very happy, however, with the final outcome and I asked him about it.

"What are you mad about we got 249 votes out of a possible 258."

"I'd just like to know who those nine kids were who lied to me," he said, dead seriously.

Chapter 7 – Southie Nicknames & Tommy Hearns

I don't know how or where he learned the street life so quick, but there was absolutely nothing that got by him, even at nine- years old. And he would do anything for a laugh. He was never vicious or malicious although there were times that he pushed the envelope to the limit. But his intent was not to hurt anyone it was just to make us laugh and it always worked. I was, by far, his best audience and he knew it. He never liked school, but he had the quickest mind of anyone that I have ever met. I have some close friends who are very talented comedians. A few of them have appeared in movies and on, Jay Leno and the David Letterman show but most of them could touch Sully's sense of what was funny or his quickness. I can recall an incident, which happened at my house, which is indicative of Sully's quick wit and his sixth sense of what is funny. A group of my friends were at my house watching the Sugar Ray Leonard - Tommy Hearns fight. My brother, who is a Boston Police officer, had just gotten off duty and he brought a few of his police friends to the house to watch the fight. We didn't know any of these cops other than my brother. At that time my brother's partner was one of the nicest guys that I had ever met. He was also one of the biggest. He weighed close to 400 pounds. This was the first time he and Sully had met.

Out of the clear blue Sully said to my brother, "Hey Eddie how can you're partner be so fat and still be a cop?" The timing and the sheer audacity of the question caught everyone off guard. It put my brother on the defensive, which is not a place he is too familiar with. My brother blurted out, "He wasn't always that heavy, when he was in Vietnam he weighed 165 pounds.

"What did he get shot with a helium bullet?" Sully said without missing a beat. I just about fell out of my chair. There was an instant of indecision, however, as everyone looked at my brother's partner to see his reaction. He was laughing harder than me. It was a classic line, quick, funny and a knock out.

That same night one of the announcer mentioned that Tommy Hearns was an auxiliary police officer in Detroit. Again, not knowing any of the other seven cops in the room Sully blurted out.

"Wow he must be the only cop in the world who can fight without a billyclub." Again, silence and then all the cops started laughing. Thank God.

Another time, we were getting my mother's cleaning up the street from my house. The owner had just taken the clothes off the rack when a kid about our age walked in. I didn't know that he was the owner's son until he said.

"Hey dad can you give me a buck?"

"Give you a buck?" the guy said. "When I was your age I was earning my own money, I never had to ask my parents for money." The kid seemed deflated, but Sully quickly came to his rescue.

"When Kennedy was your age he was President," Sully said to the father. The guy reached into his pocket and gave the kid five bucks. It was classic. Every time I went into that store I thought about that line. It was the same with the helium bullet line. It just came out of nowhere and leveled everyone in the room." He didn't mean to be fresh, just funny. But, how do you tell a room full of cops, who were drinking, that this roly-poly kid, whom they didn't know, was just trying to be funny. You don't. You simply laugh and hope to God that everyone follows suit. Luckily they did. But that was Sully. He would say anything to anybody regardless of their status, title, or position in life. In that sense he was totally undiscriminating.

Teacher, cop, even priests were not safe with Sully. Which brings me to an incident that occurred the night my father, Coleman 'Bubby' Wallace passed from this life. My father's real name was Coleman Anthony Wallace, but to everyone from Dublin to Farragut Road, he was simply known as 'Bubby.' He had a heart as big as Galway Bay and we all loved him very much. I honestly think that South Boston should be called the nickname capital of the world. Just about everyone, in Southie, has a nickname, or has someone in their family that has a nickname. Some nicknames are given to a person because of their profession. Firebox Higgins was a fireman. Meathead Murphy was a butcher. Every Campbell family had a 'soupy'. Every Owens family had a 'poison' although I'm not really sure why. There were particular parts of Southie where nicknames were the rule rather than the exception. One that particularly stands out is the Old Harbor project where every body had a nickname. You could always tell if a kid came from Old Harbor because of the particular nicknames they had. For example, Walter Mahoney was known as

Brian P. Wallace

Waz, Jerry Lynch was called Jaz. Tom Flynn was Taz, Franny Fraine was Fraz, Janice Cavanaugh was Caz, Larry Tobin was called Laz. You get the idea. The kids at Old Harbor were very industrious when it came to giving their friends nicknames, as well. Joe Flaherty was forever known as Maury but I had no idea why. Maury Wills, who played for the Dodgers, was the fastest runner that I had ever seen. Joe Flaherty, on the other hand, was one of the slowest runners that I had ever seen, hence, he was known as Maury. That happened a lot, a kid would get a nickname that was diametrically opposite his name or his ability. Billy Miles was forever known as 'Inches.' One of the kids, had real bad teeth growing up so he was called, of course, 'Smiley.' One kid, who never smiled, was called 'Jolly'

And then were nicknames for particular traits. Billy Elliot always screwed things up so he was called 'Boob.' A kid named Danny Buckley was so feminine you would have thought he was a girl. His nickname was 'Spike'" John Flaherty, no relation to Maury, smoked three packs of cigarettes a day, he was known as 'Weed.' Jimmy Dolan, who was very heavy as a kid, was 'Chumpy.' Bobby Fisher had a great hook shot on the basketball court, so he became known as 'Hooker' Fisher. Jerry Higgins committed a lot of fouls playing basketball so he became 'Hacka' Higgins and all of his brothers, from then on, were called' Hacka', whether they played basketball or not. Then there were nicknames that nobody could explain. Bob Flynn who would later run for the United States Congress, was known as 'Peaches,' although nobody was ever sure why. When Peaches ran for Congress he had a little peach emblazoned on every sign. There was one family down Old Harbor where every son had a nickname. The Joyce family had four sons Thomas, Francis, Richard and William although not many people in Southie would know them by those names. They will always be 'Jabber' Joyce, 'Sleepy' Joyce, 'Dukie' Joyce and 'Duba' Joyce. Again, every name that I have mentioned either lived or hung down the Old Harbor project. And there were, of course, nicknames, which, were offshoots of real names. Most of the time I never really knew the kid's actual name. Kids like B.L. Linehan, J.L. Linehan., R.L Linehan who were all brothers.

But you knew you had made it in South Boston when you only one name to be identified. Southie legends, such as, ' Wacko,' 'Injun,' 'Snuffy,'

A Southie Memoir

'Satch,' 'Tuffy,' 'Mocha,' 'Stretch' and 'Happy.' And if I had a dime for every Sully, Obie, Murph, or Walshie in South Boston, I would be a very rich man. Some of my other favorites were 'Rabbit' Adams, who, owned the a tavern called the Rabbit Inn, which became famous in 1974 when the Tactical Police Force raided the place during the busing controversy. They came in to the Rabbit Inn, with masks and other disguises and beat up the patrons of the tavern because they had been harassing police that afternoon as the buses rolled up to the High School. Rabbit got his fifteen minutes of fame during that national story. 'Beefy' Boyle whose real name was Billy was a damn good football player at Southie high who put on a lot of weight after he graduated, so he went from 'Porky' Boyle to 'Beefy' Boyle. 'Slinger' Argo developed his nickname because he was a bullshit artist. 'Sailor' Curran had been in the Navy. 'Killer' Crowe was a very good fighter. 'Wacky Jacky' Callahan, after a few beers, became just that and 'Juicehead' Calnan drank like a fish. 'Jumbo' Catusso weighed over 300 pounds. 'Hook' Coyne was a longshoreman and every longshoreman carried their own hook, which was a major part of their job. I can vividly recall my father's hook, which we were never allowed to touch. 'Lank' Carter was 6"5'. Another family like the Joyce's was the Dillon family. The father was 'Snuffy,' the older brother was 'Snoopy,' the younger brother was 'Chopper' and their uncle was called 'Monk,' because he resembled one of those monks with a pot belly and a little bald spot on the top of his head. 'Count' Davis was one of the biggest bookies in town and had a lot of money to count. 'Happy' Flaherty always had something wrong with him. He was also called 'Mr. Negative.' My friend Leo Mahoney used to call people who were negative "books of hate. There were a lot of them, too many if you ask me. 'Fingers' Farrell, was my uncle, and he played the spoons with his fingers. He could actually play very well. 'Bannana' Hayes had a little scar right under his right eye in the shape of a banana. 'Runt' Ingemi was small. 'Twilight' Kelly is credited with holding the very first night baseball game. 'Line Drive' Lunt always threw a line drive to the basket, much like Tommy Heinsohn. "Honk" Marsney had a big nose. 'Knuckles' McNeil loved to fight. 'Shaper' Manning was a great football player who did everything so effortlessly it looked as if he were shaping it up. 'Flash' McCann talked so fast you could barely understand him. 'Whitey' McGrail had blonde hair.

Brian P. Wallace

'Doughnuts' Norton obviously liked a few honey dips. 'Tuffy' O'Hare was always looking for a fight. 'Pinhead' Richardson had himself a tiny little head. Well you get the idea.

But then there were some nicknames, actually a lot of Southie nicknames that I don't have a clue where they came from. Here are a few examples 'Super' Curran, 'Puddy' Curran, Coolie Comeau 'Yogi' Cummings, 'Gypo' Curtis, 'Ninny' Carter, 'Bib' Curran, 'Puffy' Driscoll, 'Tassles' Driscoll, 'Dumpy' Driscoll, 'Mooney' Devin, 'Chinky' Degrandis and his wife 'Shoo Shoo' Degrandis, 'Lupa' Doherty, 'Olive' Doyle, 'Hunky' Estabrook, 'Giggles' Flaherty, 'Dada' Flaherty, 'Salts' Flaherty, 'Mudso' Flaherty, 'Hokey' Farrell, 'Champ' Foley, 'Dudley' Frechette, 'Audy' Ford, 'Harpo' Flannery, 'Booma' Gaston, 'Bulky' Gallagher, 'Tinka' Gaughan, 'Gasha' Gerharty, 'Tinka' Higgins, 'Yacka' Harrington, 'Hucka' Harrington, 'Spooky' Hayes, 'Wacko' Hurley, 'Monkey' Howell, 'Hammie' Hynie, 'Shagga' Hogan, 'Bunka' Imbruglia, 'Noonie' Ingemi, 'Poison' Kane, 'Flappa' Lyman, 'Looney' Linehan, 'Lappa' Larvey, 'Harsey' Larvey, 'Lopsie' Lydon, 'Bummie' Lydon, 'Muff' Murphy, 'Cupcakes' McDonough, 'Touchie' McDonough, 'Smacka' McCarthy, 'Windy' Mahoney, 'Mucka' McGrath, 'Slip' Moran, 'Boo Boo' McAlese, 'Ducky' Mullvaney, 'Bunny' McGarry, 'Cat' Morris, 'Stinky' McGuire, 'Wimpy' MacInrod, 'Boom Boom' Nee, 'Bazo' Norton, 'Dago' Nebbs, 'Oil' O'Connor, 'Tarz' O'Connor, 'Oggs' O'Toole, 'Zutch' O"Toole, 'Hoppa' Prendegast, 'Pluto' Pluff, 'Scudda' Ridge, 'Blubber' Ridge, 'Packy' Ridge, 'Spot' Ryan, 'Rimo' Ryan, 'Toppa' Rodgers, 'Shinna' Sullivan, 'Sniffa' Shea, 'Nardo' Scheffler, 'Deacon' Statsky, 'Nino' Sances, 'Plink' Shaugnessy, 'Tucka' Tinlin, 'Donkey' Walsh, 'Moley' Walsh, 'Joba' Walsh, 'Bird' Walsh, 'Stinger' Walsh, 'Tucky' Woluski, 'Yeodi' Yeoman's and 'Zaggy.' Now that is quite a list of nicknames. It is by no means complete. There are a few hundred more out there, especially amongst the younger kids who are now growing up in Southie. Those nicknames are in and of themselves another whole entirely different book and someday I'll write it. But the nicknames remind me of a good Sully story that went like this.

Chapter 8 - Chumpy & Bill Yee

I was about fourteen years old and we were hanging down the Old Harbor project. Sully was living there then and they had some great basketball players down there. A combination that drew me like a moth to the fire. We were sitting in Sterling Square when Jimmy Dolan approached with a Chinese kid about our age. Jimmy told us that the kid had just moved into his building and Jimmy's mother, Mae, asked Jim to bring him around and introduce him. Jimmy started the introductions and the Chinese kids' mouth seemed to drop. He looked around and then looked back at us as if not comprehending what he was hearing. You get so used to calling your friends by their nicknames that you don't think twice about it. Jimmy said to the Chinese kid, whose name was Bill Yee, "I want you to meet my friends, Cully, Monster, Fraz, Waz, Jaz, Boob, Weed, Sully, Harzy, Smiley, Maury, Moslem and Brian. The poor kid looked at Jimmy, as if he were speaking some kind of foreign language. It was Old Harborspeak. The kid just nodded to each of us as Jimmy introduced us. The funniest part, however, was when Sully asked the Chinese kid what his name was.

"My name is Bill Yee," he said with a very heavy Chinese accent. "I know your name is Billyee," Sully said, "But what is your last name." The kid looked puzzled and repeated.

"My name is Bill Yee." Sully, doing his very best Abbott and Costello impersonation said.

"Listen Billyee, do you have a last name, we know you're first name is Billyee, but Billyee what?" Jimmy Dolan jumped in.

"Come on Sully his name is Bill Yee, you know what he's talking about."

"That's what I asked" Sully playing the misunderstood mar try.

"I just want to know his last name."

"I told you my name three times," the Chinese kid cut in. I was wondering how far he could take this. Now looking directly at Bill Yee, Sully said, "

I don't mean to offend you I'm trying to be friendly but why won't you tell me your last name. Are you ashamed of it?" The Chinese kid, to his credit, stood up and yelled at Sully, "

YEE, YEE, YEE, YEE."

"Is that some sort of a Chinese chant?" Sully asked. I was actually on the ground laughing, by that time.

"That my name. Yee, Bill Yee."

"Oh now I get it," Sully said, as if he just realized the kids name.

"Your name is Bill Yee." Yes that is my name, Bill Yee." "Well why didn't you say that in the first place," Sully said as he started walking away. The poor Chinese kid didn't know it but he had just been Sully'd. Bill Yee lived in the Old Harbor project for about a year. He was a real nice kid and he and Sully, despite their first meeting, got along great.

Chapter 9 – The Night My Dad Died & Irish Superstitions

Everyone in Southie knew who Bubby Wallace was. I'm not sure why but I never inherited the nickname His brother John was called "Cubby'. His brother Mike was called 'Tubby" and he was Bubby. Many times a father's or brother's nickname will be passed down to the son or brother. Thank God that didn't happen in the Wallace house. The only one who ever called me 'Bubby' was my friend Joe 'Maury' Flaherty. Well the night my father passed away is certainly a night that I'll never forget because of the circumstances but also because of Sully. I was up M street park waiting for my friend Bobby Lerro to finish his softball game and we were off to our summer cottage in Mashpee. About twenty minutes after I had left the house my father had a massive heart attack and died. He was sixty two years old and had been bedridden for at least four years. The guy who owned the corner store, Jim Harvey was dispatched to get me up M street park, which he did. To this day I don't remember driving from M Street to my house, but by the time I got there a few neighbors were already inside with my mother. There's nothing like a death in an Irish family to bring people together. There's an old saying that the difference between an Irish wedding and an Irish wake, is one less drunk. I had gone up to see my father's body and stayed with him for about fifteen minutes. It was very emotional. He and I were very close and his death affected me greatly. By the time I returned downstairs, after saying my good-byes to Dad, the place was filled with relatives, friends, neighbors, and even some people that I didn't recognize. Word spreads very quickly in an Irish neighborhood, especially about deaths. I'm really not sure why but the Irish are preoccupied with death. I call the obituary section in the paper the Irish sports section. It is always the first page any Irish women, worth her salt, will turn to. My mother had this habit of waking me up at 6 O'clock in the morning to tell me that someone we knew was dead. I used to tell her that the odds were pretty good that the person would still be dead when I woke up at 8:30. That never detracted her. There seemed to be some sort of vicarious thrill in being the first to know who died in your town especially if the death was controversial or otherwise unexpected. I'm sure that most of you have lost a relative. Isn't it funny the terminology the Irish use Lost a relative! Does that mean we'll find them again?. No it means they're dead, but the Irish always avoid the dreaded word 'dead' It's as if saying the word was somehow contagious. Another way that the Irish will get around the word is by using the word buried. This happened to me about three weeks after my father's funeral. My brother and I were up Broadway and an old Irish friend of my father approached. He had a brogue that you could cut with a knife. He said to me.

"Brian, is it true you buried your father?" Always the wise guy, I responded.

"We had to Pat he was dead." My brother was bullshit at me. I was just having fun, but I used the dreaded word, dead, which sent Pat quickly on his way less he be contaminated with my bad karma. The Irish are real superstitious about all aspects of death but they love the ancillary events surrounding the death. The wakes and the parties after the funerals are legendary. I, like most of you, even with my Irish heritage, am never really comfortable at wakes. It's human nature and I'm sure most people feel the same way. What are you supposed to say at a wake?

"Oh, he looks great." He doesn't, he's dead. But you will always hear people say how good the corpse looks The other thing is, that no matter how much of a jerk the corpse was in life, now in death, he or she is absolved of all previous indiscretions. People who hadn't talked to the dead person for 25 years would invariably say to the widow.

"Oh, he was a good man and I'll miss him." BULLSHIT. The good men do oft lives after them the bad is oft interred with their bones. That should have been an old Irish proverb rather than a Roman one. But the best part of Irish wakes and funerals are the parties that follows. These post funeral parties usually end up in a brawl, after a couple of days. That's right, DAYS. The party after my father's funeral lasted three days and three nights. A major part of these parties is telling stories about the deceased. Many, if not all of these stories are told in public for the very first time. It's like a clandestine death ritual. Now that the person is buried the stories can be told. You can really find out a lot about the deceased at these bloodletting sessions, especially if the whiskey has been flowing like the blood. Most times however these stories are of a humorous and lighthearted nature. Most of the time. Sometimes you find out more than you want to know and that is usually when the fight starts. I must say, however, that there were no fights after my father's funeral or on the night he died. There were a lot of laughs that June night in 1979 thanks to Sully.

My Mother was one of the most superstitious people that I knew, especially about death, but her superstitions encompassed everything. And everything, according to my Mother and her friends, happened for a reason. If someone had an itchy nose, they were looking for a fight. If someone forgot what they were going to say, it was probably a lie, according to my Mother. Vacations brought nothing but bad luck. I was afraid to take a vacation until I was in my twenties. My mother and her Irish friends, were convinced, beyond a reasonable doubt, that going on vacation could prove hazardous to one's health or one's family's health. I can't tell you how many times I heard my Mother ask her best friend Sis Joyce, "How did Thomas go?" which means how did he die.

"I don't know," Sis Joyce would reply.

"All I know is that he was on vacation, when he went."

"Sure enough, there's your reason," my Mother would say, as I sat dumbfounded in the parlor. Neat and tidy. Everything had a reason and there was a reason for everything. And if two friends of my Mother died, then there most assuredly be another death in the very near future, because every Irish woman, worth her salt, knows that death always travels in packs of three. When I was real young I would be extra careful if two of my parent's friends died, because I knew, for a fact, that the death guy was lurking around somewhere, looking for that third one, and it wasn't going to be me. My good friend Steve Sweeney, who is a well- known comedian, always says that growing up Irish Catholic gives you something to work out for the rest of your life. Boy is he right.

One of my Mother's biggest fears was being in the last car of a funeral procession. Every Irish woman knows that the person, who rides in the last car, in any funeral procession, is destined to be the next one to "Go." My Mother called me early one morning and asked me if I could give her a ride to a friend's funeral. I told her that I had a few things to do, but I would meet her at O'Brien's Funeral home, when I got through. The Funeral Mass was scheduled to begin at 10:00 a.m. I arrived at O'Brien's Funeral Home at 9:45 a.m. and I saw my Mother standing in front of the Funeral Home waiting for me. I parked the car, and ran to get her. She was mad that I was so late, and she started to give me a hard time. As we walked to my car, she stopped as if she was shot by a sniper.

"You're the last car," she said horrified.

"I know I was running late," I apologized.

"But you're the last car," she repeated herself. She stood like a statue on Dorchester Street, refusing to even go near my car. She then spotted two friends of her, Mary, and Josie Breen, and she scampered in to their back seat, leaving me standing on Dorchester Street, all by myself. I chased after her.

"Ma are you going to the funeral?" I asked.

"Yeah, but not with you," she replied, as Mary or Josie, I never knew which was which, opened the back door of their already crowded car. Jackie O'Brien, a great guy, who owns the Funeral Home was standing up the street, watching this whole scene play out. He was laughing as I approached him.

"Last car?" he asked. I just shook my head.

"I've never had an Irish woman in that last car in forty years," he laughed.

"Well you're not getting an Irish boy in that last car either," I laughed. "I came here to drive her, I don't even know who's being buried," I told Jackie. I went back to the end of the line, started my car and went home. I just wonder how long it took the person in front of me to die. Living with an Irish Mother could be quite a challenge.

The night my father died, Sully was sitting in my father's favorite chair holding court. I had to laugh when I came down the stairs, from my father's room, and saw him.

You're lucky he's dead," I said to him. He would kick your ass for sitting in that seat."

"He was all talk," Sully shot back. Not everyone had reverence for the dead. I had to laugh and I know my father would have as well. My father, after a pretty rough start, had become Sully's best audience, even surpassing me. The mere mention of Sully's name brought an instant smile to my father's face. The two still acted like enemies but it was all show. By the time I had reached twelve Sully had gotten to my father, like he got to most people. He had become an unofficial member of my family but God forbid either he or my father ever say so. They kept up this, on the surface, adversarial relationship. My father would always mention the fire incident when I was six.

"Grow up it was only a little fire," Sully would say.

If my mother got to my father through corned beef and cabbage, which we had every Sunday, Sully got to him through humor. More specifically, Italian jokes. My father was a sucker for a good Italian joke and Sully knew more Italian jokes than anyone I had ever seen. Sully would try out all his new material on my father. If my father laughed for a minute it was just fair material. If he laughed for two minutes it was pretty good material. When he laughed for three or more minute, Sully had prime material. For all those years my father never understood that he was nothing more than Sully's laugh meter. I know that my father would have gotten a kick out of Sully jumping in his chair before his body was even cold. That was a no no, in my house, and Sully was well aware of it. Nobody sat in my father's chair, nobody. Sully would even set up some of my friends, who had never been in my house before.

"Sit here Brian's father doesn't mind," Sully would say to the unsuspecting kid. We would all wait until my father came home and he would hit the roof and scare the shit out of the poor slob who was sitting in his seat. The priest, who had given my father the last rites the night of his death was a very thin man with what we call a stingy stash, which in effect means he was trying to grow a mustache but wasn't having very much luck. It looked like a skinny version of a Hitler mustache and it was not very becoming. The priest came right over to me after he left my father's body. As he entered the room suddenly everyone became eerily quiet. He proceeded over to where I was sitting and said.

"Brian if there is anything I can do for you please don't hesitate to call." In 1979 I was working in the Boston City Council and had been able to do a few favors for the parish. It was nothing major but it seemed to have an impact on this priest. He went on.

Brian P. Wallace

"We really appreciate all that you have done for us, so I repeat, if there is anything that I can do for you please let me know."

"Father, forget about Brian, do yourself a favor and get that stupid moustache cut off," Sully said in his Irish whisper." I almost joined my father. Again there was that split second of indecision, whether to laugh or cry. I laughed and so did everyone else in the room, including the priest. My father would have probably laughed the hardest. It certainly relieved all the tension in the room. It was also vintage Sully. Never know what to expect but always expect the unexpected. Nobody was immune from the slings and arrows of Sully, not priests, politicians, family, or teachers. All were fair game. Well that isn't entirely true. I would have to say that teachers were a bit higher on Sully's hit list than anyone else alive.

Chapter 10 – The South Boston High Years & BC High Dances

Teachers and Sully were like oil and water. I honestly think that to this very day there are teachers out there who feel that Sully was put on this earth as a curse to all who entered the teaching profession. To say he was never considered a teacher's pet is to understate the case a bit. Sully felt as if teachers were some kind of pets, to be played with or toyed with, but never to be taken seriously. I wouldn't be at all surprised if Spielberg got the inspiration for his movie Gremlins after talking to Sully's home-room teachers. And I'm almost positive that some segments of Animal House were certainly based on Sully's high school antics. School for Sully was a place to be with his friends from 8:30 until 2:30, eat a couple of lunches, play a little basketball and harass as many teachers as humanly possible. He was by no means dumb, in fact he was a lot smarter than most of the kids in school. Sully just wanted to have a good time which he did pretty much all of the time. If his teachers didn't appreciate his humor that was their problem. Students at South Boston High School attended an average of 3 years. The majority of students came to Southie High after attending a Junior High, now called a Middle School. They would attend Southie for the 10th, 11th and 12th grades. Sully attended for four years. He had a sophomore year, 2 junior years and a senior year The funny part was that he was kept back on purpose It might sound strange, but it is the truth. You see all of Sully's friends, including me, were scheduled to graduate in 1967. Sully was scheduled to graduate in 1966. You have to remember that in 1966 the Vietnam war was reaching its height. A lot of kids from Southie were joining the service to go to Vietnam. Sully always wanted to be a Marine and he wanted to go to Vietnam. He just didn't want to go alone. Just about all of our friends had made a deal to join the service after graduation. Sully liked that idea. He wanted to join with his friends, most of whom were graduating in 1967. If he graduated in 1966 he would be drafted and would be off to boot camp by himself. No way. So he hung around Southie High for an extra year and made life unbearable for every person who called himself or herself a teacher, he also made life hilarious for the rest of us.

Brian P. Wallace

By the time we got to high school I was perfectly aware of the shenanigans and mischief that Sully was capable of creating. It was unfortunate that the rest of the world wasn't. Unfortunate, for them that is. He came at teachers like a Roger Clemens fastball. He was constantly giving aliases to unsuspecting teachers, when he'd get caught doing something that he wasn't supposed to be doing, which was most of the time. He was always doing something that was against the rules, he just never got caught a lot. There was one teacher who taught the whole 4 years that Sully was at Southie who thought that Sully's name was Peter Hawkins, one of his more common aliases That poor teacher only found out on graduation night that Peter Hawkins was in actuality the infamous Sully. Sully also had a proclivity for calling teachers by their first names, which he knew drove them crazy. They never understood that, that was exactly why he did it. There was one teacher, above all others that Sully absolutely drove crazy with this first name thing. His name was Mr. Coughlin and he was a new teacher to the school, fresh out of College. He thought he was God's gift to teaching, until he met Sully that is. It took Sully exactly two days to find out that Mr. Coughlin's mother and father baptized him with the name Daniel. That was all the ammunition Sully needed. The very next day in class when Mr. Coughlin was calling the roll, he called Sully's name.

"I'm here Danny." Sully shot back. You could hear a pin drop in the classroom. Mr. Coughlin, his face getting redder by the minute, looked up from his class list.

What did you call me?" he looked directly at Sully.

"You called my name and I called yours," Sully said nonchalantly.

"I didn't hear you say Mr. Coughlin," the furious teacher replied.

"How could you," Sully shot back. "I didn't call you Mr. Coughlin. I said "I'm here Danny." The class burst into laughter.

"Down the office," Danny Coughlin yelled. Sully anticipating the command was already headed down to visit our Headmaster Mr. Reid before Danny got the sentence out of his mouth.

Danny Coughlin had shown Sully his Achilles heel to Sully. Mistake. Mr. Coughlin just got sick of reprimanding Sully, every class he attended, which wasn't many to begin with, so he just gave up. This was in 1966, which was Sully's second junior year, and it was by far when he was at his worst. I remember walking into Mr. Coughlin's class one winter morning and Sully was sitting in my seat. Trouble.

"Screw," I said as he laughed.

"Aren't you glad to see me?" he smirked as he moved across the aisle.

"Thrilled" I deadpanned. Just then Mr. Coughlin entered the room and looked directly at Sully and his smile disappeared, but he said nothing. That particular day Mr. Coughlin was reading off our marks for that semester. He read all the marks and never mentioned Sully's name. I didn't care I got an A. Sitting down the back, legs propped up on a desk Sully yelled.

"Hey Danny, you forgot me." Sully shot his hand up.

Mr. Coughlin spun around, "Believe me I could never forget you."

Now that was an understatement. Sully was just beginning and only I knew what he was truly capable of.

"Wallace got an A, what about me am I getting an A, is that what I'm getting?" Mr. Coughlin looked horrified.

"An A, you've only been to class 5 times and each time you were here I had to send you to the office, and you think you deserve and A."

OK, Danny, fair's fair, maybe you're right I probably only deserve a B." Mr. Coughlin just shook his head.

"All right Danny, I'll take the C but I'm not too happy about it," he kept on. Mr. Coughlin just stared. Sully kept on prodding.

"Danny, my boy, don't tell me you're giving me a D?" Sully said, sounding Surprised. "Even a D, is too good for you," the angered teacher shot back at a pouting Sully. Then he said a line, which I will carry to my grave. "Do you know what you're getting" he challenged Sully. Sully stared back defiantly. "Do you know what you're getting," Mr. Coughlin repeated, as out of control as I had ever seen any teacher. "No but why do I have the feeling you're going to tell me," Sully said, laughing.

"You're not getting an A, you're not getting a B, you're not getting a C and you're not even getting a D" Now he was staring directly at Sully.

"You're getting a fat E." he shouted. Sully was on his feet in a flash and was heading toward the teacher. I froze. With lightning speed the chubby

Brian P. Wallace

Sully, at 5'5" and 185 pounds, was approaching the startled teacher, with a full head of steam. He grabbed Mr. Coughlin by the tie.

"Don't you ever call me fatty." Coughlin didn't know what was happening. But you could tell he was stunned by Sully's reaction and head-long charge. We were all laughing out of control.

"I said you're mark was a fat E, I didn't call you fatty," Coughlin said. Sully let go of the tie and headed out the door. His exit was met with a cacophony of cheers and whistles. Coughlin, defeated, sank back in his chair, his head in his hands. The class was now totally out of control. Sully 1 Danny Coughlin 0

Sully had an incredibly quick wit, which turned a simple word or phrase in to a joke. One day we were in a spuckie shop near the Boston Garden. The place was packed with lunch-time customers, none of whom we knew. The two guys making the subs were working their asses off making the subs and selling them at a non-stop pace.

"I got a large tuna back here," a guy yelled. A guy came out from the crowd, grabbed the sub, paid, and left.

"I got a small Italian back here," the other spuckie maker yelled. Before I knew what was happening, Sully jumped over the counter.

"Where is that small Italian, I'll kick his ass." He yelled. Now you have to understand we were in the North End, which is almost 100% Italian. Everybody in the place was Italian, except me and Sully. The guy, who made the sandwich, stopped, looked at Sully and burst out laughing, as did everyone else in the spuckie shop. I thought we were going to get our asses kicked. Outside, I said to him.

"What in the world possessed you to say that in the middle of the North End/" I asked him when we got outside.

"I don't know, he laughed, but it was funny wasn't it." That was his motto.

I was by no means the best student but I at least went to class. I got by, but no thanks to Sully, who spent more time roaming the corridors than the custodians did. After a while he would get bored with this routine and would improvise, which usually meant trouble. One afternoon I was sitting in my Latin class daydreaming about the girl sitting two seats in front of me, (no names) when the door flew open and in walked Sully. I knew the minute he walked through that door that I was going to be in trouble. The teacher to make matters worse was a substitute teacher. She had no clue as to what was in store for her. I did. He walked into the classroom as if he owned it. He slowly walked over to where the young teacher was standing.

"Is Brian Wallace in this class?" The teacher hadn't even taken attendance yet.

"I don't know, is there a Brian Wallace here?" I didn't say a word.

"There he is," Sully said pointing directly at me.

"The basketball coach wants Wallace down the gym immediately," he barked.

"Do you have a pass?" she said, turning to face Sully. He glared at the overmatched teacher, who was undoubtedly fresh out of some fancy College.

"If the coach wants Wallace down the gym, he goes down the gym." I just slunk down in my seat in a vain effort to prove I wasn't part of this mutiny. It didn't work.

"Mr. Wallace isn't going anywhere until you produce a pass." She shot back. She had some balls.

"You want a pass?" Sully said pulling a pen out of his pocket and grabbing a piece of paper from the desk. He bent over the paper scribbled something and passed it to the stunned teacher.

"Here's your pass," he said handing it to her. She was beginning to take the heat.

"What is your name?" she barked at Sully.

"My name is Peter Hawkins, what's yours?"

The flustered teacher stammered, "That is none of your business. I am a duly appointed teacher assigned by the Boston School Committee," as if that were a panacea that would make Sully deathly afraid. He laughed.

"The School Committee is a bunch of crooks and phonies and anyone they appoint is probably a phony as well." She was speechless. He was winning. I was still slouching.

"Furthermore," he went on. "I think the students are sick and tired of phony and incompetent teachers that are appointed by the School

Committee." He then conducted a spontaneous poll amongst the students, while the incredulous teacher stood next to him with her mouth open.

"How many kids want me to be the teacher?" Just about every hand, in the room, shot up. Sully turned to the awestruck teacher. "You lost, I'm the teacher now." This was the stuff of which legends were made. He turned to face the class.

"All right now class what page did we leave off at?" Someone in the back of the room Yelled.

"Page 121, teacher," and Sully quickly flipped through the book to find the appropriate page.

The teacher just stood there ashen after having her first class commandeered.

When he found page 121 he got a puzzled look on his face. "This is Latin, I can't read this crap. I thought this was English."

"What's the difference, Sully," one of my friends yelled you can't read English either." The class was, by now, totally out of control. Sully turned back to where the teacher was standing.

"You can have your class back now," he said as if nothing had ever happened. He gently placed the book on her desk and nonchalantly sauntered out the door to continue roaming the corridors and creating havoc. It took a while for the shaken teacher to compose herself. When she finally did she said, in a very weak voice.

"Who was that boy?" Nobody said a word. As Billy Joel once said we were living by a code of silence. She repeated.

"I demand to know that boys name, she sternly said." Total silence. She took a different tact.

"Mr. Wallace he seemed to know you very well, would you like to tell me his name?"

"Peter Hawkins," I said quickly.

"Well you can tell your mysterious friend that he will be suspended before the day is out," she said. I don't know if she really believed it, but she felt better for having said it anyway. Why he did it only God and Sully know and I'm not so sure about the former.

A Southie Memoir

It certainly added to the legend of Sully at Southie High. It did nothing, however, for me. When my basketball Coach, Mr. Ray asked me what happened in Latin Class.

I just shrugged. "Ask Sully."

On another occasion Sully told a teacher that unless he passed his course he would flunk out of school.

"If I flunk out, he went on, "I will have to go to Vietnam." The teacher, a rather effeminate man, who years later would become the editor of a gay Boston newspaper, just stared at this brazen young man who was standing before him, in essence threatening him.

"What you do with your life, my friend, is of no great consequence or concern to me," the teacher shot back at Sully. The teacher obviously unimpressed with either Sully's attendance or his threat of demise at the hands of a Vietnamese patrol, simply went on teaching his class. Sully however remained standing, almost as if the teacher were speaking to a student in a different classroom. A ripple started somewhere in the back of the classroom, as the teacher turned and had begun writing on the blackboard. Sully remained standing. The teacher, who continued writing, was totally unaware that Sully was still standing. I could feel trouble fast approaching. To this day little did I realize the extent of it.

"I mean it," Sully yelled. Everyone in the room jumped, especially the teacher.

"I'd rather die right here in South Boston, than in some jungle in Vietnam," he said very loudly. I couldn't believe this. I knew that he had planned to go to Vietnam once he graduated, if he graduated, but I had no idea what this act was about. Finally, he winked at me. I should have known. He was just putting on a show.

"Don't be such a clown," the teacher intoned "And cut the dramatics." He once again turned towards the blackboard. We were in biology class, which was in room 319.

"I'll show you who is a clown," Sully said, as he got out of his seat. He quickly headed for the old fashioned windows, which curse every old school building in Boston.

Brian P. Wallace

Now a little annoyed, the teacher barked, "That is quite enough now either sit down or jump out of the window. It really doesn't matter to me what you do."

To everyone's horror Sully opened the archaic window and jumped to his apparent demise some sixty feet below. Everyone just froze, especially the teacher, who was high strung to begin with. He totally went to pieces. He shouted, "O my God," about six times and then just ran out of the room and out of our lives. We never saw him again. He never taught another class at Southie High. I don't know if he ever taught again, anywhere.

I wasn't thinking about his career options at the time. I was pretty freaked myself. I was the first one to the window. I quickly looked down expecting to see a crowd gathering around a roly-poly dead person, some sixty feet below. I saw a roly-poly person, but he wasn't dead, by any means, and he wasn't sixty feet below either. He was precariously perched on a ledge approximately three feet below the window looking up at me. He saw the look of outright panic on my face and quickly moved to lighten the moment.

"Did I get him?" he excitedly asked. I still couldn't speak. I just shook my head. By now the entire class was looking out the other windows, expecting as I did, to see a corpse on the sidewalk.

"Sully you are absolutely crazy." I stammered. He just laughed as did everyone else in the room, once it became obvious as to what just had transpired. He reached his hand up to me to pull him back into the window. He was loving it.

As he was set to pull himself into the classroom, he looked at me. "It was pretty funny though, wasn't it?"

"I should really push you off," I said, still upset, but relieved nonetheless. He really did scare the shit out of me that day. He looked kind of bewildered.

"What's your problem, everyone laughed didn't they," he said to me.

"Yeah, they all laughed," I said. "And they probably would have laughed just as hard if you really fell." Having said that, I just turned and walked away, still shaken. I couldn't believe that he had purposely planned this whole scenario. He had intended to create that sort of havoc.

It is funny now. It wasn't all that funny forty years ago. I still get a little shiver every time I think about running over to that window. Sometimes I think about that teacher and what he was thinking as he ran out of that room and ultimately out of that school. I wonder if he ever told anyone about the incident, other than a psychiatrist. I wonder if he knew Sully was all right, and I use that term loosely. About a week after this incident I asked Sully why he didn't warn me that he wasn't really going to jump. He said that it would've ruined the effect. Well, as you can imagine, after that incident, the legend of Sully just grew and grew. He was a celebrity. There were more Sully stories now floating around that I never knew which were factual and which were just part of his ever-growing legend And he had only begun. After the window stunt Sully seemed to intimidate some teachers merely by his presence. His presence intimidated students, as well, a lot of students.

My senior year he started to change his attitude about school. He realized that come June all of his friends would be graduating and he would be left behind. I knew that if we graduated and he didn't, he would never get his diploma and he knew it as well. He actually started attending classes on a regular basis, well almost on a regular basis. Not that he wanted to attend, but he did. None of us were honor roll students but Sully was worse. He had been thrown out of five different home rooms and no teacher would take him as a home room student because of his reputation. No teacher in his or her right mind wanted to deal with him first thing every morning. Sully had to report to our headmaster every morning and wait outside his office until the bell rang for first period. I'm quite sure that he was the only student in the history of the school that had to report directly to the headmaster instead of a home-room. Sully didn't mind. I think he kind of, liked it. Our headmaster, Dr. Reid was a gruff old dude whose bark was much worse than his bite. But his bark could certainly scare you into a different time zone. But he was fair and treated Sully with respect. I think that deep down they really liked each other although neither would be caught dead ever saying that. I have served on a few Boards with Dr. Reid, whom I respect greatly, and every once in awhile would ask me how Sully was doing. But if Dr, Reid was fair, he was also a no-nonsense type of guy and Sully knew it. Dr. Reid would never put up with the stunts Sully had pulled on other teachers and he knew it. He also knew that he had reached the end of the line. His next home-room would be in Paris Island. He never had one bit of trouble with Dr. Reid. That didn't hold true for other teachers however. Five homeroom teachers in one year was also a record. He also holds the record for having his name carved on more desks than anyone in the storied history of the school. But those pale in comparison to his next accomplishment. He is the only person that I had ever heard of who got thrown out of the shop course. Nobody gets thrown out of the shop course. There's nowhere to go after shop, other than maybe Walpole State Prison or the Marines. But he managed, and how he managed is hilarious.

    I was in the College course while Sully was in the shop course. The shop rats, as they were often called because the shop classes were in the very bowels of the school, didn't socialize with those in the College course. Sully, of course, was different, he socialized with everybody. Sully liked the shop course because he could get lost in the shuffle easier in the shop than you could in any other curriculum, and Sully took full advantage of that. Boy, did he take advantage of that. He was constantly roaming the corridors and going into classes where he didn't belong, especially mine. It wasn't as if he did nothing else but wander the corridors, he did spend some time in the shop. But like everywhere else, he got in trouble there as well. I didn't know anything about the shop course then, nor do I now. Sully never really talked about it but I got the feeling that he didn't care much for the shop course or its teachers. One teacher really drove Sully crazy, his name was Mr. Melch, who was Sully's welding teacher. It took a lot of guts just to be in the same room with Sully when he had a white-hot torch in his hand. And it didn't take Mr. Melch long to find that out. Melch had assigned a kid named Paul 'Rocco' McDonald as Sully's partner in the welding class. Each student was paired up with another student and they worked together in a little cubicle. Melch's first mistake was teaming these two together. Rocco was also from the Old Harbor project. He came from a very large family and was more than a little bit unstable. I really liked Rocco. He weighed about 110 pounds and after four beers, he thought he was the toughest kid in Southie. Rocco had gotten the shit kicked out of him more than a few times because of his propensity to tell anyone who would listen, just how tough he was. He had this thing about beating up Jimmy Ridge, who was in fact one of the toughest kids in town. Rocco would get a few beers under his belt and say.

"Where's Ridge now? I'll kick his ass if he comes by here." The two never fought, luckily for Rocco. Ridge was a kid who knew how tough he was but never beat up kids like Rocco, no matter how much they provoked him, again lucky for Rocco.

Rocco had one other distinction in life, he was the only kid in history to be thrown out of the Boston College High dance for dancing. If that sounds funny, you should have seen him dance. Rocco didn't have any heroes in his life and then he saw Mick Jagger. That was it. Rocco became Mick Jagger. At least he thought he was Mick Jagger. He was the exact same height and weight as Jagger, and he studied Jagger's moves like a Chinese kid studies for a calculus test. The Stones were just starting to catch on in the United States back in 1964-1965, when Rocco became Mick Jagger. He knew every move that Mick Jagger ever made or was going to make. He would talk incessantly about Mick Jagger to the point where we would just walk away, which brings me to the night that Rocco became famous. Every Friday night Boston College High School or BC High would hold a dance in their gymnasium. Kids from all across the City attended and it was a great way to meet girls. These dances were huge and were a major part of our teenage years. We would all meet at the underpass at diamond two a couple of hours before the dance. Those kids who got their courage up by drinking would inhale the necessary six pack of Schlitz, or a bottle of thunderbird or whatever it took to get them to get enough courage up to ask a strange girl to dance. Not everyone, however, drank. I never did, but Rocco certainly made up for me and for everyone else who didn't drink. For a skinny guy he could really pound them down. After finishing the stash we would all head over to "The Dance."

I was standing with the Southie kids, one Friday night in 1965, waiting for my girlfriend to show up, when Knuckles, all out of breath came running over.

"Come on Brian, Rocco is putting on a show." Knuckles wasn't one to get excited about anything, so I knew instinctively that this had to be good. I was wrong. This wasn't good it was great. There was a huge crowd in the middle of the gym as the Stones "Satisfaction" blared loudly from a multitude of speakers in all corners of the gym. People were clapping and going crazy as we made our way to the front of the crowd. There was Rocco. His face had contorted into a Jaggerlike scowl. He had taken off his sport coat to reveal a black leather vest on underneath. No shirt, just a skin tight black leather vest. He looked like a toothpick wrapped in leather. Sweat was pouring down his face, H was in a zone and didn't seem to even notice the crowd. Rocco had become Mick Jagger. He strutted, he grunted, he wiggled, he split, he wiped his face with an imaginary handkerchief. He had an invisible microphone in his right hand as he sung every lyric as Mick would do on stage. He was dancing all by himself as the crowd grew larger. It was wild. Rocco had turned into Jagger right before our eyes. The best part was that none of us knew that Rocco could dance. Oh we knew he loved Jagger and all that but we had never seen him be Jagger. He had turned into Mick, right before our eyes. The more he wiggled the more the crowd cheered and the more the crowd cheered the more he wiggled. The priest came running over thinking that there was a fight. They pushed their way through the crowd only to find a gyrating Rocco. A tall priest grabbed Rocco by the arm and began pulling him out of the circle. Everyone booed.

"Stop it, stop dancing" the tall priest screamed over the loud noise of the amps and the crowd. Everyone froze. Then everyone looked at each other and began laughing. Rocco had come out of his jagger induced stupor by now and had a very quizzical look on his face.

"What's the problem" he asked the priest. "You can't dance like that in here," the priest responded. "Oh I'm sorry," Rocco said, "For a minute I thought I was at a dance." The crowd wencrazy. That had to be Rocco's all-time best come back and everyone was laughing at the priest which didn't make him too happy.

"This is a dance," the priest said, trying to retain a little bit of dignity. "But what you were doing son was by no means dancing."

Rocco looked shocked. He looked directly into the eyes of the priest. "Don't you know Mick Jagger?" The priest obviously didn't know Mick Jagger from Mickey Rooney.

It was at that moment that the crowd, led of course by Sully, started to chant. "Rocco, Rocco, Rocco." It became a deafening roar, as every one of the four hundred or so kids picked up the chant. "Rocco, Rocco, Rocco."

The priest seeing that he was losing control pulled Rocco out of the circle and out of the gym, with the crowd still chanting, "Rocco, Rocco, Rocco."

A couple of real cute girls came over to me and Sully. "Do you know that kid?"

"He's my best friend," Sully replied, again instantly sizing up the situation. "I actually taught him a few of those moves," he said lying through his teeth.

Thanks to Rocco we were now big shots. About twenty minutes later the D.J. announced that he was playing a new song by the Rolling Stones. Sully and I looked at each other and laughed, thinking that Rocco was probably halfway home. We were wrong. He came running into the gym, with the Stones playing in the background, all in one motion he slid on his knees, taking off his vest as he swept across the floor and again produced the imaginary microphone, without missing a beat. He was so skinny he looked like a poster child from Biafara. I was laughing so hard I thought I was going to be sick. Rocco, now naked from the waist up, was once again Mick Jagger. He was even better than before. The kids in the gym, who had seen Jagger perform, were going absolutely wild. Rocco was really good. Those who hadn't seen Jagger, yet, were getting a look at the closest thing to Jagger that they would see. And all of a sudden the chant changed. "Mick, Mick, Mick,." They chanted. Four young priests came running over and picked Rocco up bodily and carried him out. It was unbelievable.

"Mick, Mick, Mick," everyone chanted as their hero was being carried from the gym, no shirt, still singing into his imaginary microphone and a Jagger scowl on his face. It was priceless. Rocco was an instant hero. The priests carried him right out of the building and onto the grass. He never stopped singing. The crowd followed , still chanting. Sully and I followed as well, but we were laughing so hard we couldn't have chanted if we wanted to. Rocco had actually gotten kicked out of a dance for dancing. Start the revolution. The BC High dance would never be the same. It had lost its' innocence. The staid and vanilla era of the 50's was now gone forever. replaced with the British invasion. long hair, hallucinogenic, Vietnam, hippies and yippies, easy rider, Bob Dylan, Timothy Leary, Woodstock, Kent State and Rocco. He had, single-handedly, changed the tenor of the BC High dances forever. Within a month kids at the same dance were doing their own Jagger impressions, growing their hair a little longer and replacing their madras sport coats with CPO jackets and dingo boots. The times, as Dylan said, were a changing. About a month after getting thrown out, Rocco returned to a hero's welcome. A month before we were doing our best to lose him in the crowd, now we were telling all these girls that we were Rocco's closest friends. And it worked. We were big men on the BC High campus, at least for a little while A white kid from Columbia Point, named George Chadwick, showed up a few weeks later dancing like James Brown and knocked us from our lofty perch. Hey, fame is fleeting. We had our fifteen minutes, thanks to Rocco.

Rocco might have been famous at BC High but that didn't cut any slack with Mr. Melch, his welding teacher. In welding, Rocco was just another shoppie, albeit a skinny one. The only thing that set Rocco apart from every other kid in the welding class was his partner. Sully. Welding can be pretty dangerous and Mr. Melch was a nut about safety precautions in the welding area. He insisted that every safety precaution was observed and they usually were. Usually. Melch had a routine that he followed every day for thirty years at Southie High. When he wanted to check on a student's work he would step in behind that student and gently tap him on the right shoulder. The students were all wearing goggles and masks and were told not to turn around when they felt that tap on their right shoulders. They were told to go right on with their welding as if Melch was not standing behind them watching. Now, as I mentioned this precaution had been in effect for 30 years and there had never been a bit of trouble. But that was BS or Before Sully. It didn't take Sully long to pick up Mr. Melch's patterns and habits. Now Rocco was a good kid, he wasn't going to get any scholarships to Harvard but he was a good kid nonetheless. But Sully played trick after trick on Rocco, usually in shop but not exclusively so. After about a month of Mr. Melchs' class Sully got bored, which is a very bad combination for those who happen to be around him at the time. And Rocco was around him at the time. It all started with 5th period welding class. Melch would give an assignment and each student was to go into his little cubicle and do whatever the teacher assigned them to do. Rocco and Sully were at the very end of the lab, so usually the teacher would not get to them until the very end of the class. Sully checked out the situation and acted upon it. After Melch had given the days assignment, Rocco and Sully both put on their goggles and masks and went into their respective work areas to complete the assignment. After about 20 minutes Sully would put down his iron and slip quietly into Rocco's cubicle. As Rocco was intent on his work, Sully would lightly tap him on the right shoulder, pretending he was Mr. Melch.

    The students were told over and over again never to turn around because they had that red- hot iron in their hands. So when Rocco felt the tap on his shoulder he would meticulously and painstakingly weld his project with the finest care, thinking that the teacher was behind him and grading him on his project. He had no idea that it was Sully behind him. Melch's MO was to tap the student, a second time, which meant that he was leaving the cubicle. So after 4 or 5 minutes standing behind Rocco, Sully would tap him on the shoulder, a second time, and leave. Rocco, now thinking that he was all set, would relax and screw around with his welding and then the real Mr. Melch would come by and Rocco would get screwed. This went on for a couple of weeks. Rocco told one of his friends that he must be flunking welding because he was the only one that Melch checked on twice a class. The kid finally told him that it wasn't Melch but Sully who was doing the checking. Rocco went crazy but didn't tell Sully that his game was up. He went to the next class as if nothing had changed. By now the whole class knew about Sully's impersonation of Melch, except Rocco, he thought. Everyone would watch as Sully quietly slipped into Rocco's cubicle and tapped him on the shoulder. They would be hysterical as he floated out of Rocco's cubicle after four or five minutes. That particular day Mr. Melch went down the far end off the shop and would work his way back toward Sully, so Sully took his cue and slipped in behind Rocco. He proceeded to tap him on the right shoulder. Rocco nodded and continued to work. As Sully's hand was resting on Rocco's shoulder, Rocco quickly brought the red hot iron up to shoulder level and placed it right on Sully's hand. The pain had to be intense as Sully ran out of the shop and upstairs to the nurse's office, where he was treated for second degree burns.

Sully told Melch that the iron had slipped and landed on his hand. But everyone, except Melch, knew the true story and that drove Sully crazy. And Rocco finally getting the upper hand, literally, was acting like a big man, which really drove Sully crazy. Sully laughed it off and told Rocco that he got him good, no hard feelings, but I knew Sully and I knew that this was far from over. A couple of weeks later, again in welding class, Rocco left the shop to go the bath room which was located outside and to the right of the shop. Sully noticed that Rocco was gone and asked Jimmy Ridge where he had gone. When Sully was quite convinced that Rocco was in the bathroom he went into action. He fired up his welding iron and headed towards the only door that allowed access or egress to the welding shop. He knew that Rocco would be back any minute so he quickly welded the doorknob until it was white- hot. Sully figured that Rocco would come through the door any minute and get the shock of his life, not to mention the burn of his life. A minute later they heard a blood curdling scream. Everyone, especially Sully, went crazy laughing at Rocco's revenge. They waited for 10 minutes for the doorknob to cool off and Sully, with a glove on, opened the door. There was nobody there. The bell rang and they all went to their next class. Sully's next class was a study class, which to me was an oxymoron for Sully. He was telling some of his friends about how he burned Rocco when Rocco turned the corner and came right over to Sully. Eddie Mack, who was there, told me that he thought Rocco was going to whack Sully and everyone kind of backed off. But Rocco just smiled.

"Are you all right?" Tommy Gill asked him.

"I'm fine," Rocco smiled but Mr. Melch is on his way to the Mass General,"

"Why?" Sully asked, as if he hadn't a clue.

"It was the craziest thing, Rocco related. "I was heading back to the welding shop and I saw Mr. Melch, open the door And scream bloody murder."

"What happened to him," Eddie Mack asked.

"His hand was burned to shit," Rocco said, "I helped him up to the nurse's office and they immediately called an ambulance to bring him to the

Mass General." Sully's mouth just dropped, but he didn't say a word. Mr. Melch was out of school for a week. So was Sully. Melch, however, was out on sick leave, Sully was out on suspension. Rocco's Revenge II.

Sully, after his week's suspension apologized to Mr. Melch, who against his best judgment agreed to take Sully back. We later found out that Dr. Reid had personally intervened and had Sully reinstated. As I mentioned there was nowhere else to go. Dr. Reid was just a caring guy who knew that Sully could not keep up with the college course, mainly because he hadn't been exposed to the curriculum before. His only chance of graduating, and it was just a chance at that point, was as a member of the shop course. So Sully marched back into the shop and Mr. Melch, I'm sure cringed. And he actually behaved, for a while. He still owed Rocco and I knew that regardless of what he said or how he acted, he would get even. After a couple of weeks of perfect conduct, Sully hatched a plan with Jimmy Ridge as his co-conspirator. He had Ridge convince Rocco that Sully was now fair game to prank because he had to continue his good conduct or be thrown out of the shop. Rocco liked what Ridge was proposing, never dreaming that the plot was Sully's to begin with. So the next day Rocco, as Sully had done to him, slipped quietly into Sully's cubicle and tapped him on his right shoulder. Sully nodded and continued to work on his welding project. After a few minutes Rocco tapped him again and was gone. Rocco was ecstatic. He told everyone in the shop that he had finally got Sully and would do it again the next day. Sully acted as if he knew nothing. The next day was Friday and Mr. Melch gave out his assignments and headed into his office. Sully headed into his cubicle and Rocco did the same. After about 10 minutes Sully received a tap on the shoulder, but this time he was waiting for it. Before the hand could be withdrawn, Sully's white- hot soldering iron came up and rested on the hand. You could actually smell the skin and hair burning. Sully whipped off his glasses and quickly turned to see the expression on Rocco's face. The eyes were wide the mouth was still frozen in a prolonged scream and that is exactly what Sully had hoped to see. He had hoped, however, to see the grimacing face of Rocco McDonald and not Mr. Melch. Too late. Melch turned, and once again, ran to the nurse's office and once again to the Mass. General Hospital. Sully, this time, didn't even wait to be summoned to the office. He got his hat and coat and simply walked out of the building. He returned, again, a week later and his homeroom was now Dr. Reid's office. He remained in the shop course, except for welding. Melch threatened to resign if Sully set a foot inside his shop. Melch had a huge bandage on his right hand and a smaller one on his left hand. It was actually kind of funny, not to him, but to the students and most certainly to Rocco who became an instant trivia question, as the only person to get Sully twice. The story that immediately spread throughout the entire school was that Sully purposely burned Melch, which only added to his already burgeoning legend. Even though he was the butt of Rocco's joke, he still somehow turned it around to his advantage and the story of Rocco's Revenge II, was never told, it took a backseat to a larger story called "SULLY BURNS THE TEACHER." And the legend grew. Rocco died about fifteen years after high school and nobody knew of his greatest triumph. He got Sully not once but twice in a period of a couple of weeks. Some people would have killed for that opportunity, although not many got it and fewer ever took it. Rocco was a good man.

Thanks, once again to Dr. Reid, Sully had a chance, but a final one, to graduate. He did, however, have one major problem. Now that he was getting an incomplete for welding and it seemed that he was going to flunk math, he was going to be ten points short of the needed one hundred and twenty points to graduate. Dr. Reid had saved him from being expelled, which we all appreciated, but Sully desperately needed those five points from welding, which he was never going to get. He had been placed in a study class as a fifth period instead of welding, which was fine with Mr. Melch. I prevailed upon the goodness of our basketball coach, who was a great guy, named Charlie Ray. He knew all about Sully, which was a major problem. But, he like Dr. Reid, I felt, liked him. I was hoping against hope that was the case. I had nothing to lose, so I laid out my plan. I asked Mr. Ray to get Sully put in my English class. He looked at me as if I had two heads.

"Half the school year is gone," Mr. Ray said looking confused, "I can't expect a teacher to pick HIM up now." He said the word him with extra emphasis. "It wouldn't be fair to the other students."

"The other students don't care," I begged, "They all like Sully."

"I'm sure they do," he smirked, "But show me an English teacher who likes him and you've got a deal." I just smiled. He fell into my trap.

A Southie Memoir

"Mr. Kennedy." I had already run this by Jack Kennedy, my English teacher, and he said it was fine with him if Mr. Ray approved it, and now he had. Mr. Ray tried to look mad but couldn't pull it off.

"You conned me Wallace," he said, "I don't think your future is in basketball, I think politics will be a better vehicle for you," he laughed, as he signed Sully's transfer papers. Little did he know that I would spend my entire adult life in politics. So I started a bit young, nothing wrong with that.

That was what I loved about Southie High. People like Charlie Ray, Dr. Reid and Jack Kennedy. All of them were professionals. All of them were from South Boston, and all of them had common sense. They knew that Sully wasn't a bad kid. Mischievous, different, maybe a little crazy, but harmless. They also wanted him to graduate, so they went that extra mile and I'll always be grateful, to them, for that, as will Sully. All three of those men have become very good friends of mine and all are highly successful in their professions. Now I, at least, had him in the class. You know he never had one problem nor did Mr. Kennedy ever have one problem with him. He really liked Mr. Kennedy, and he showed him a great deal of respect in and out of class. There were, however, some others that he didn't always see eye to eye with, other than Melch. One was Mr. Gurry. I didn't like him either. He thought he was a tough guy, which he wasn't, and he tried to belittle Sully. We had a student - teacher basketball game that year and Sully covered Gurry. It was great. Sully was in his shirt. He couldn't move and he was getting real frustrated. The more frustrated he got the closer Sully got. They actually had a shoving match right at the end of the game. Gurry ended up with no points. Sully somehow managed to get five points in the game. Getting five points in Gurry's class, however, as going to be a different story for Sully. He knew that if he flunked Gurry's history class, there was no way he was going to graduate in 1967. We both knew that if he didn't graduate in 1967, he would never graduate. I remember that we were having a history test one day, which normally wouldn't have bothered Sully because he would just skip the class. But the new and improved Sully realized that he was on his last leg and his time was quickly running out. He needed these points to graduate.

"Did you study for the test?" I asked, realizing that this was the first time I had ever talked about academics to Sully. I could see that he wasn't exactly comfortable with the subject either.

"I left my books over the Arena," he said very quickly. I couldn't believe it.

"You have no history book?"

"Well I did up until yesterday," he smiled.

"At this rate you'll graduate with my grandchildren," I said angrily. He just shrugged.

As we approached our history class he just stopped. I realized that I was now walking by myself. Sully had different levels of looks. The look on his face that day was strictly trouble. I had seen it before and my heart nearly stopped. I had no idea what was rummaging around that brain of his, but I would soon find out. He had this glazed look on his face as he just stared straight ahead. I looked into the direction he was staring at and all I could see was a door that said 'Teacher Lounge.' What was the big deal? Mr. Coughlin and Mr. Woods came out of the door and headed to their next class. They said Hi, as they passed and I just waved. Sully now, with that trouble look in his eyes, began to walk towards the Teacher's Lounge. He knew that students weren't allowed in there so I couldn't imagine where he was going or what he was doing. He approached the door as if he were going to enter but didn't. He stopped short, about three feet from the door and he just stood there. He was actually standing to the left of the door, as it would open. Within a matter of seconds the door sprung open and Mr. Tenny and Mr. Stone came through the door. Sully had positioned himself, as I said to the left and behind the door. Stone and Tenny never saw him. As the door swung open all you could hear was this tremendous bang. When the door was pulled back, Sully was lying on the floor as if he were dead. Then I knew. I had seen him pull this trick a hundred times but never as good as that. Sully would position himself so that the door would hit his foot or he would actually kick the door as it swung open, he would then grab his nose all in one quick motion. The unsuspecting person, who opened the door, would hear this big bang and see Sully lying on the floor as if the door had just hit him in the face. He had perfected this technique to an art form. There were times when I knew he was going to do it and he stilled fooled me because he made it look so real. He would do the same thing, with poles, telephone poles, stop sign poles etc. I had seen him, a couple of times, pull this stunt when 13.000 people were exiting from the Boston Garden. He would tie up traffic for twenty minutes as he lay on the ground holding his shattered nose, which mysteriously would heal if a police officer came to the scene. Sully could fall better than most stunt men in Hollywood.

You would think that there were snipers around the way he hit the ground so fast. And he didn't just simply fall. No way. He would slap the ground with his open hand as he was approaching the ground, which intensified the noise and the impact. It always worked. I could tell however, as he lay on the cold marble floor, that there would be no miraculous recovery today, even if a whole cordon of police showed up. Sully was in this one for the long haul, I could feel it. The two teachers, who had opened the door, looked dumbfounded. Sully couldn't have picked two better stooges, more on that later. They looked at each other as Sully lay writhing on the ground.

"My nose, my nose, Oh God you broke my nose." Sully was screaming loud enough to be heard at Charlestown High. I couldn't believe it, although I should have known better by then. A large crowd began to gather, which only made Sully scream even louder. The larger the crowd got the louder the screams got. Robert DeNiro would have been proud of this performance. Sully was in total control and he knew it. So did I. One of the teachers who had, had the misfortune to open the door, ran down to get the nurse. By that time Sully should have been nominated for an academy award. I was even starting to believe him. Our nurse was a buxom, gray hair lady who demanded respect and got it. She pushed her way through the crowd, with the universally accepted.

"Give him air," as she approached her patient, Sully was rolling on the floor, holding his nose as if it were going to come apart in his hands.

"OK son now what seems to be the problem," she growled.

Sully, now really going overboard, "My nose is busted."

She bent down, which was a chore in itself for her. "Let's have a look." she said, reaching for Sully's hands. Sully reluctantly, and ever so slowly, began the arduous task of removing his hands. The crowd, after all his histrionics, was expecting to see the elephant man. They didn't. All they saw was Sully. No cuts, no swelling, no blood, just an Academy Award acting performance. Even though he wasn't permanently disfigured, he had convinced the multitude of onlookers that a stay in the Mass General would probably be necessary.

I watched all of this as if I was outside my own body. The nurse, realizing that he was in no immediate life-threatening situation, regardless of how Sully acted, began dispersing the crowd. The bell had rung about five minutes before, but nobody had gone to class. They were all too curious as this scene was being played out before them.

"Everyone to class now, come on everyone to class," the old nurse barked. And finally people began to disperse. She then ordered a few guys to help Sully to her office. This was the best part. Sully protested in feigned horror.

"Please Miss Bowman, I have to get to my class, I have a test." Now I understood. He started to walk and almost fell back down as if he were dizzy, as the teacher who had started this whole charade simply by walking out of the door ran to his assistance.

"Take it easy son, you go in the nurses office and lie down and don't worry about the test, I'll speak to your teacher." As if he had ever worried about a test in his life.

"Oh thank you sir and I'm sure I'll be all right." Sully said weakly. The distraught teacher leaned over to Sully.

"And what room is your class in." He always had to go too far. He looked puzzled.

"I can't remember, but Brian is in my class," he said pointing directly at me. "I'll take care of everything," the teacher said and accompanied me to room 309 where he explained to Mr. Gurry what had happened. Sully was excused from taking the exam. Unbelievable. He had done it again. I don't know if the teacher feared a lawsuit or not. I do know, however, that Sully never made up that test. I saw him later that day down the gym and looking none the worse for wear.

"How'd ya do on the test," he said in between jump shots.

"Fine," I said, Mr. Gurry really missed you." He laughed.

"Maybe, but Mr. Stone certainly didn't." We both laughed and life went on.

Before I go on, I have to tell you about the two teachers who unsuspectingly and unwittingly became pawns in Sully's drama, Mr. Stone and Mr. Tenny. Sully, as I had mentioned earlier, had attended Southie High for four years. Mr. Stone taught at Southie for the last three of those four years. Sully had immediately given him the name Rocky, which of course stuck to him like glue. From that day on he was Rocky Stone. He was nice enough but he just didn't belong at Southie High. He was very skinny, wore thick black glasses and looked as if he would fall over when he walked. If you looked up the word gullible in the dictionary, Rocky Stone's picture would appear beside the definition. And, Sully instinctively knew that for as long as he was a student at Southie High he could con Rocky Stone for as long or as often as he wanted to. And he did. Sully's alias was Peter Hawkins. Whenever I heard that name, in any context, I knew immediately that it was Sully. I don't know where or why he got Peter Hawkins and I never asked. In the four years that Rocky Stone taught at Southie High he had Sully, in class, twice. Both were study periods. It wasn't until the night we graduated that Rocky Stone found out that Peter Hawkins was in fact the infamous teacher baiting, trouble making, hall-walking Sully. When Dr. Reid called out Sully's name and he finally, received his diploma, Stone blanched.

"That's not Peter Hawkins?" But I have to give Mr. Stone credit. When it finally sunk in that Sully had conned him for four years, he laughed as hard as I've ever seen him laugh and went over and shook Sully's hand. It was a great way for Sully to graduate. Actually any way was a great way for Sully to graduate. But Rocky Stone turned out to be a good sport and I liked that and I liked Rocky as well. The other guy, well, I'm not so sure about.

His name was Mr. Tenny and I'm sure that every high school has had their own Mr. Tenny. He made Ricky Stone look like Dick Butkus. He was very effeminate and talked in a high pitched voice. He made Barney Fife look tough. Well you get the idea. Since Sully was in the shop course, Mr. Tenny and he never really crossed paths. That all changed. Tenny had cafeteria duty and he thought he was bad. He would intimidate all the little freshmen and kids who were harmless and then he tried Sully on for size. MISTAKE. I really don't know how it all started, but when I looked up Sully and Tenny were in each others face and going at it pretty good. Sully ended up with three days detention. Tenny ended up much worse. It started slowly.

One day, after Sully had served his detention stint, he walked by Tenny's homeroom, looked in, and walked away. He didn't say a word. The next day as Mr. Tenny came into his homeroom there was a message written in big letters on the blackboard. It said. MR. TENNY DOES IT FOR A PENNY. Everyone in the class thought it was pretty funny. Tenny didn't. It must have hit a nerve. He went absolutely ballistic. Yelling and screaming. Saying that he would find out who did this and when he did they were going to be sorry and so on and so on. That was all Sully had to hear. He knew he had him. The next day in the cafeteria was a home -made sign which was hung up down the back of the cafeteria: MR. TENNY DOES IT FOR A PENNY. Tenny didn't see it until lunch was almost over and when he did he hit the roof again. He tore down the sign and ranted and raved. Everyday from then on signs would appear all over the school with the same message. MR. TENNY DOES IT FOR A PENNY. Tenny was going crazy trying to find out who was behind the signs. It was getting pretty funny and I think it actually gave Sully an incentive to go to school every day. School had ended, one day, and we all started to file out the front door. A friend of mine, named John Coyne, who is now dead, came running back into the school laughing so hard we couldn't make out a word he was saying. I went outside and directly across from the entrance of the school was this huge sign: MR. TENNY DOES IT FOR A PENNY. There was only a few days left before the seniors were to get out so this was like the coup de grace. A final slap in the face. I don't know how Mr. Tenny reacted to that one. Nor do I care. Sully never did a day for his MR TENNY DOES IT FOR A PENNY, sign. There were some teachers that you just liked and some that you didn't. All I know is that MR. TEENY DID IT FOR A PENNY. I know that Tenny and Rocky Stone and a few other teachers were very happy to see Sully got that sheepskin. I also know that they would never encounter another Sully. God only made one.

Long before that glorious graduation night ever happened, a number of factors had to come into play. If Sully passed all of his courses, which was certainly no guarantee, he would have 115 points. That would still leave him 5 points short of the required 120 points needed. And that was the best scenario. But I remembered my brother telling me one night, about a kid, like Sully, who was short a few points. He also explained to me just how they went about getting those points. I didn't listen to my brother to often but for some reason that conversation stuck in my hhead. I called Sully and explained my plan. He got pretty excited. I also explained that this was useless if he didn't go to class and pass all his courses. He promised he would and we were off in the great point chase. The next day we both signed up for the Glee Club, although neither of us could carry a note. 1 point down. Our next stop was to Mr. McGrann's office where we signed up for the Key Club. 2 points down. Now we were 3 short. Our next stop was to Mr. Crowley's office. Crowley was the legendary football and baseball coach who could be quite gruff. Luckily we caught him on a good day. I asked if he had appointed a manager for the baseball team. He said he hadn't. I asked if Sully could have the job. He was apprehensive and I thought he was going to say no. Instead he looked me right in the face and said, "Why?" No time to be coy I thought. I looked him right back between his eyes.

"He needs the points to graduate." Crowley smiled and said to Sully.

"Our first practice is April 9th." Three points down and only two to go. I had hit a dead end, however, after acquiring the fourth and fifth points. I was pretty dejected. I was telling my brother about my predicament at supper.

"What about swimming?" he said.

"What about swimming?" I asked." We don't have a swimming pool at Southie High," I replied having no idea what he was talking about. "There's and old school policy that is still on the books that says any student who requires a swimming test and passes that test will receive 1 point," he went on. Now that was one that I had never heard of. There had to be a catch.

"How many yards do you have to swim?" I asked him expecting to hear some outlandish number, like 2 miles.

"Twenty five yards," he replied. I was shocked. Sully was a very good swimmer, so 25 yards was a piece of cake. I felt a little better. I called Sully and told him about the swimming point.

The next day we went to see Mr. Woods and asked how we could sign up for a swimming point. The teacher was dumbfounded.

"How do you know about the swimming point?" he asked incredulously.

"We get around," I smiled.

"I haven't given this test in about 4 or 5 years." He went into his office and opened up an old book.

"Yeah," he said, not looking up from the book, "1963 I gave this test to Devin and Wallace." Then he looked at me.

Isn't your name Wallace?"

"Guilty," I laughed.

"And is your name Devin?" he said to Sully.

"No sir, my name is Sullivan." I think it was the first time that Sully had given his real name to a teacher."

"OK," the teacher said and scheduled us for a swim test, which they happen to give down the Boys Club. He also asked that we keep it secret. I could just imagine the number of kids who would ask for the test, if they knew. Well they didn't find out from us. Sully passed. Four points down and one to go.

We were racking our brains trying to come up with one more point. We were sitting in the Club's intermediate room when Knuckles came in and asked what we were doing.

"What about the basketball team, you guys don't have a manager, do you?" It was so close that I had never even thought about it. The old forest from the tree's thing. We all began to laugh. We laughed a little too prematurely. As I was walking to school I thought about approaching Mr. Ray with this request. Mr. Ray thought that Sully was crazy and more importantly he thought that Sully was disruptive to the team. This wasn't shaping up too well. The more I thought about it the more I worried. The more I worried the more I thought about it. But we had come this far, now was not the time to throw in the towel. This was going to be a tough sell. Nevertheless I headed down to Mr. Ray's room. Room 109. I knew what I had to do but I was scared to death to do it. I took a deep breath and walked into 109 where Mr. Ray was alone, thank God. He was reading some papers but stopped as I entered.

"To what do I owe the honor?" He smiled, and motioned me to sit down. I felt that I needed to be direct.

"Mr. Ray I would like Sully to be manager of the basketball team." He just stared. The silence was deafening. I stood my ground.

"Did he put you up to this?" he finally asked.

"No sir it was my idea," I told half the truth.

"Well for a smart kid, Brian I don't think this is one of your better ideas." This wasn't going as I had planned. I felt a lecture coming on.

"I don't know who's crazier, you or him," he said shaking his head. Again, silence.

"Personally I like Sully but I've never met a more disruptive force in my life." He did have a point.

"Brian, you above all, know that Sully not only gets himself in trouble but he gets everyone around him in trouble." He wasn't finished.

"I don't want nor do I need those kinds of headaches around my team and neither do you. You can get yourself a nice scholarship with the year I expect you to have. Why would you want to jeopardize that?"

"I don't think I as jeopardizing anything," I said, as he walked over and closed the door. He then reached into a draw and pulled out a handful of letters.

"Do you know what these are," he asked.

"No," I answered a little defeated.

"These are letters from Colleges that are interested in giving you a scholarship. Do you want to throw all of it away?" I was flattered but I thought he was reaching.

"Mr. Ray with all due respect I don't think having Sully on the bench will hurt my game and it might even help it." Before he had a chance to answer, I threw the heavy artillery.

"Mr. Ray you made me captain of this team all I'm asking is that you give me the responsibility that goes along with it." Point for me. His face was getting redder, which was not a good sign. A student opened the door and started to enter. Mr. Ray, very uncharacteristically screamed.

"Can't you see I'm busy right now?" The kid closed the door and almost ran. I really thought this was going to be easier. He turned to me.

"I think that he will affect your focus because he will always try to make you laugh." I couldn't deny that.

Brian P. Wallace

"I think he will do more to loosen us up than anything else," I countered. He could see that I wasn't going to quit.

"OK, Brian enough bullshit" he said a little calmer now. "Why is this so important to you? And I want the truth."

"He needs the point to graduate."

Is this his last resort?" he asked.

"Very last,"

"Have you tried the Glee Club?" I just nodded my head.

"Key Club?" he asked. Again I nodded.

"Baseball?"

"Yes," I answered. "I even got a swimming point,"

"What the hell is a swimming point?" he laughed.

"Don't ask," I laughed. "Mr. Ray if he didn't need this point, I wouldn't be here, believe me." I smiled, trying to ease the tension.

"You really like him don't you?"

"Yeah, he kind of grows on you," I smiled.

"Go tell him he's our new manager, but remember Mister Captain," he said those last two words in a very sarcastic way, "You wanted some responsibility and now you have it. Sully is you're responsibility. "Do you understand me? If he screws up, you're the one who is in trouble." I had won. This adult stuff wasn't all that bad. I was, however, still shaking. I did learn a good lesson from that, however, and it's one I took with me after I left the old high school on the hill. Tell the truth. People respect you more and you feel better about yourself. Now I just had to control Sully. It turned out that Sully really did help the team. Mr. Ray never said it, but he knew it.

I couldn't wait to tell Sully. I figured he would be waiting right outside the school. He wasn't. He must be outside my house I thought. Again, he wasn't. As I got home my dog Joe greeted me, but no Sully. After supper I walked the block and a half to the Club and there he was. He was actually pacing up and down in front of the clubs stairs. I had never seen him so nervous.

"He said no didn't he?" he quickly blurted out. He went on carrying on a conversation with himself.

"I knew it, I don't care, I knew he doesn't like me" he was going on and on just babbling about how he didn't care. I was laughing at this spectacle. I knew how much he wanted it, not even for the needed point but more for the opportunity to be a part of the team. When he saw me laughing he just shut up.

"Sully, can anybody say no to me?" I asked, boastfully. He still didn't get it because he had convinced himself so thoroughly that Mr. Ray would say no. I was smiling from ear to ear.

"You're shitting me," he finally said realizing that he had in fact got the job.

"I don't believe it. He said yes?"

"He said yes. But, under one condition," I teased.

"What condition? I'll do anything. What is it?"

"That you get my lunch every day." We both started to laugh I had never seen him so happy nor had I ever seen him speechless.

"Do I get to travel with the team?" he asked.

"Yes," I said as if it were no big deal. He knew that for the first time in his life he would get to miss class legally. Plus he would get the fifth point he needed to graduate. I thought he was going to kiss me, which really would have worried me. But it was true.

Ladies and Gentlemen, now managing the South Boston High School Varsity Basketball Team, Sully. Things, for the first time, were starting to look up for Sully.

Chapter 11 – Basketball & The New Manager

Little did Mr. Ray, or any of us, realize exactly how important Sully would become to the team, that year. I remember the first day of practice, Sully was more enthusiastic than most of the kids trying out for the team.

"Sully, pull those weights out of the closet." Mr. Ray yelled. Then he shook his head in disbelief as if it just dawned on him that Sully was actually part of the team. But Sully behaved, at least for a while. And he proved his worth right away and in a way that I will certainly never forget.

We had won our first two games in pretty convincing fashion. We beat Somerville Tech By twenty six points and then beat Charlestown by sixteen points. They were good wins but not great teams. In the first game, we scored seventy eight points. Johnny White and I combined scored sixty one of those seventy eight points. In our second game we scored eighty one team points. Whitey and I scored sixty five points combined. At our next practice Mr. Ray was really getting on the rest of the team.

"What if Brian or Whitey get injured or they get in foul trouble? We might as well forfeit the rest of the game." Mr. Ray yelled at the rest of the team. We did have a lot of young players and I think, at first, it was just easier to give me or Whitey the ball. But Mr. Ray had a point, Injuries and fouls are a part of the game. And we found out exactly what Mr. Ray was warning us about when we traveled to Dorchester High to face one of the best teams in the State.

Dot also had one of the top players in the State. His name was Larry Roland. Larry was about 6'6" and could shoot the lights out. The newspaper said that Dorchester would beat us by at least fifteen points. But that is why they play the games on the court and not in the paper. We both came into the game with two wins and no losses, so there would be no sneaking up on Dorchester. Their coach was from South Boston. His name was Joe Mason and he actually played on the only State Championship Basketball Team from South Boston High. They won the Tech Tourney in 1956 at Boston Garden, led by the future Mayor of Boston and United States Ambassador to the Vatican, Ray Flynn. Joe Mason was my Health teacher, two years before that day we came into his gym in Dorchester to take on Roland and company, Mason always wanted to be a head coach in basketball or football. Southie but he had two legendary coaches, Joe Crowley and Joe Callahan in front of him and Mason knew he wasn't going to have a shot with Crowley and Callahan and firmly entrenched in those positions. An opportunity arose for Mason at Dorchester High to be both Head basketball and football coach and he quickly accepted. He wanted nothing better than to kick our butts.

The gym was packed. You couldn't fit another person in that gymnasium with a shoehorn. It was kind of intimidating, especially to the young kids. And I certainly knew that feeling. Three years earlier I had made the varsity as a freshman which was a pretty big deal. Coach Callahan didn't like to put freshmen on the varsity, for whatever reason. I was very small and I certainly didn't look like a varsity basketball player. I was shocked when Coach Cal posted the Varsity and Jr. Varsity teams on the gym bulletin board. I quickly scanned the Jr. Varsity team and my name was on it, as I expected. I didn't even look at the varsity roster which was hanging up next to it. All of a sudden I got a pat on the back.

"Congratulations Mister Varsity," said Tommy Frane, who would later become the Police Commissioner of Quincy. Now I really was shocked. I went back to the bulletin board and sure enough there it was, Johnny White and I were the only 9th grader on the team. Johnny would later star at Tabor Academy and Tufts University. He coached Tufts for eight years and gave a basketball scholarship to a kid named Scot Brown from Wakefield who would later replace Ted Kennedy in the U. S. Senate. I flew home to tell my parents, who knew that I did something good but they didn't really grasp the true significance of their fourteen year old son making the varsity basketball team.

Before our first away game I must have tried on my uniform, sweatpants and sweat jacket at least twenty times in front of the mirror. I was ready. At least I thought I was. We were to play Boston Trade that afternoon. And if I wasn't nervous before I got to the gym, that changed very quickly. Boston Trade is right in the middle of Roxbury, which is almost 100% black, as Southie was 100% white. When we walked in the gym, that day, we were the only white people perhaps for three miles. That never bothered me because I had played against and with black players all my life. Many of them have become my lifelong friends. So I was well prepared for that. What I wasn't at all prepared for was the crowd. Actually, I guess, it was the noise, more than the crowd. We could hear it as soon as we got off the bus. I had never heard anything like it and it scared me. As we got closer it just got louder and louder. There was one big radiator that traveled the length of this old gym. The radiator was just above the last row of the bleachers. The entire radiator had a metal covering, made out of tin. The entire stands were using this metal covered radiator as one giant drum and the noise was not only deafening but quite intimidating. And they never stopped banging. They banged before the game. They banged during the entire game and they even banged after the game. When they saw us enter the gym they banged so loud I thought the whole radiator, as well as the entire wall, was going to come down.

"Don't worry about them," Coach Cal yelled over the noise. He then pointed down the other end of the court, to where the Boston Trade team was performing dunk after dunk. It was very intimidating.

"Worry about them." The first person I saw was a player named Milt Wornum, whom I had heard of, but had never seen. I still wish I hadn't. He was 6'11" tall. I had never seen a player that big. Never mind play against one. Coach Cal was right, the kids in the stand meant nothing, but Milt Wornum certainly meant something. Shaken, we went into this tiny locker room before we were fed to the lions. I put on my school uniform, for the first time and felt pretty proud. I finished putting on my and reached into my gym bag for my sneakers. Nothing. I reached in again, and again, nothing. My heart started to racing and then I realized that this must be some kind of freshman initiation joke. I asked everyone where my sneakers were. All I got was blank stares. I quickly realized that this was no prank. In all my excitement I had simply forgot to pack my sneakers. I was panicking. I was going around to every player and asking if they packed an extra pair of sneakers. I had exhausted half the team when a kid named Johnny Nee yelled that he had an extra pair. Relief. The relief was short lived. Johnny's sneakers were a size 12 and a half. My sneakers, laying at home somewhere were a size 6 and a half. But I had no alternative. I couldn't tell my coach, in my very first game, that I forgot my sneakers. How would that make me look?. But, in retrospect, that is exactly what I should have done.

A Southie Memoir

When we were all dressed, the coach came in and gave us a few instructions, and we headed into that jungle of noise and emotion. It didn't take them long. First I heard them laugh, which grew and grew, each time I took a step. Then they started pointing. My face was so red I could actually feel the heat. Then the radiators began to play a new chant. The chant that we had heard from since we got off the bus had been "BEAT SOUTHIE, BEAT SOUTHIE." As we went through our pre-game drills, that changed to, "WE WANT BOZO, WE WANT BOZO." And I was Bozo. The sneakers were so big on my feet that they made a slapping sound, much like clown shoes do, every step I took. It was humiliating. And they kept it up, all through the warm-ups and into the game. I sat on the very end of the bench and never raised my head. They would stop for a while and I would relax and then it would start again "WE WANT BOZO. WE WANT BOZO." We were getting beat by about 30 points and both teams began to empty their respective benches. This whipped them into a frenzy. They were banging on the radiator pipes and chanting, 'WE WANT BOZO, PUT IN BOZO." Then they began to throw things at Coach Callahan when he wouldn't put me in the game. I have never wanted a game to end so bad in my entire life Even worse Sully wasn't there to help me. The game finally ended and I sprinted to the locker room and tore off the offending sneakers. I was sitting in front of my locker when Jimmy Ridge came by and stopped in front of my locker.

"You'd better hurry?" he said. I looked at him, not knowing the post game routine.

"Why?" I asked.

"Because, Bozo you have a show to do tonight at 5 'O'clock" The whole room began to laugh and couldn't stop. They started throwing the huge sneakers around the room I was, finally, laughing as hard as everyone else in the room. The door opened and Mr. Callahan came in. All the laughing stopped and everyone turned towards the door. He had a real mad look on his face and he finally spoke.

"Mr. Wallace please make sure you bring your sneakers to the Roslindale game," and he smiled. Thank God. Everyone, again, started laughing Tough first game. I figured that it had to get better from here, and it did. But I will never forget Boston Trade and I never watched Bozo again.

Brian P. Wallace

Three years later, things were very different, as we entered a raucous Dorchester High gym, I patted my gym bag to make sure my sneakers were there. It had become a ritual with me ever since that Trade game three years earlier. During warm-ups we couldn't even make a lay-up. The Dorchester team looked as if they were on trampolines, even the little guys were dunking the ball. Each Dorchester dunk brought the huge crowd to another level of frenzy. By game time they were rocking and we were rolling. As we were getting ready to be introduced there seemed to be some type of confusion around the scorer table. It seemed the third referee never showed up or was never scheduled, which often happened in our conference. The third ref was the one who kept the official score book at the scorer table. They now needed someone to keep the official book. Before I knew what was happening Sully had leapt from the end of our bench and was embroiled in the middle of the discussion. I saw one ref point to Sully and then walk over to Mr. Ray. I eavesdropped.

"This kid says he knows how to keep score, do you have any objections?" I don't think the ref even knew he was with our team. Mr. Ray looked directly at me, shrugged and said.

"No, we have no objections."

The refs then escorted Sully over to the Dorchester bench and asked Coach Mason if he had any objections to Sully being the official scorer. Mason had never metSully, plus he thought his team was going to run us out of the gym. He simply wanted the slaughter to begin. He quickly agreed to letting Sully keep score.

"Whatever." Coach Mason replied. Mr. Ray, again, looked at me but didn't say anything. Sully took his place at the scorer's table and we got the game started. Just as Mr. Ray had talked about that week in practice, Whitey got into immediate foul trouble. Beating Dorchester was going to be hard. Beating Dorchester without Whitey, was going to be impossible. I was having a pretty good game and Stevie Flaherty was playing the game of his life against Larry Roland. Whitey was his usual brilliant self but was playing tentative due to two early fouls. We were tied at half-time and we were behind by two points after the third quarter ended. I was so totally immersed in the game that I had completely forgotten about Sully. At least he was behaving himself. One minute into the 4th quarter Whitey was called for a charging foul. The Dorchester coach, Joe Mason, immediately jumped to his feet.

"That's five fouls on White, he's out of the game," he was screaming at the top of his lungs. I knew that Whitey had picked up a couple of early fouls but I had lost count since then. Whitey, who was one of the smartest players that I had ever played with or against, simply stood near the foul line as if nothing had happened. He was also street smart and he wasn't leaving the game until told to do by the ref. Mr. Ray was himself yelling that it was only Whitey's fourth foul. It was bedlam. I honestly didn't know if Whitey had four or five fouls. Both refs headed over to, you guessed it, the official scorer; Sully.

The gym went from bedlam to total silence. One of the refs said to Sully.

"How many fouls do you have on White?" Very calmly and nonchalantly Sully took his time, counted the fouls in the book.

"White has three fouls." The Dorchester coach went ballistic. He ran over to Sully, took the book out of his hands and began counting the fouls himself. He threw the book on the floor.

"This is absurd," he yelled. I'm getting cheated in my own gymnasium" The fans began to throw things at the scorers bench, books, sneakers, oranges, paper airplanes. One girl threw both of her shoes. Sully never flinched. He acted as if he had been keeping score since the game was invented. The refs didn't know what to do. Sully, however, knew that they had no recourse. He was the OFFICIAL scorer. The refs called time out and conferred with Sully. He was masterful. The refs broke the conference with Sully, blew the whistle, and began play.

Coach Mason was so red I thought his head might come off. "This isn't right, ref, you know this isn't right," he kept yelling at the refs.

I looked over at Whitey and even he had a little smirk. Coach Mason wouldn't sit down so the ref called a time out and went over to him.

"Listen he said, the kid is the official scorer, you agreed to have him keep the official book now sit down and shut up or we're going to throw you are going to get a technical." Mason sat down but the crowd continued to boo for at least five minutes. Mason kept looking over at Sully but Sully never looked his way once. I didn't know how many fouls Whitey had. I did know, however, that without him, we lose the game. So, we still had a chance. Mason was so mad he had forgotten about his game plan and we went ahead by four points with a couple of minutes left in the game. Behind Roland, however, they came back and tied the game with just over a minute to play. Next time down the court Whitey set a pick for me and was called for an offensive foul. Before anyone had a chance to say anything Sully yelled out.

"That's his fourth foul." Coach Mason threw his towel high in the air.

"I don't believe this." he yelled. "That's about his eighth foul." I believed it. I knew Sully.

Sully looked at me and winked. I had to crack up. Nothing bothered him, nothing. I think he liked all the attention. He was in charge and he knew it. The game went into overtime and we won in the final seconds. I had thirty one points and Whitey had twenty nine points. We had pulled it off. As we were jubilantly racing to our locker room I could hear Coach Mason yelling about protesting the game. Sully was sitting there finishing up the book as if nothing happened, which only enraged Mason even more. I asked Whitey in the showers how many fouls he had. He told me that he knew he didn't have eight, as Mason had proclaimed, but he thought he had six. We both began to laugh. Sully had pulled it off When Sully came into the locker room everyone started to clap. Everyone, except Mr. Ray. He sat in a corner with a dazed look on his face. He called Sully over and they talked in very quiet tones. We were all staring and trying to hear what was being said, but we couldn't. In a few minutes they stopped talking and Sully came over to where me and Ricky Calnan were sitting. I couldn't wait.

"What did he say?" Sully was acting real cool.

"Oh he asked me how many fouls did Whitey really have?" Then he paused, I could've killed him.

"Come on, come on," I said. "What did you tell him?" He smiled.

"I told him that math was always one of my worst subjects and that I didn't really know how many he had."

"Did he believe you?" Ricky interjected.

"Probably not," Sully said, but we won the game didn't we. The next day the Globe and the Herald both had big stories on how we beat Dorchester at Dorchester. Whitey and I got all the ink. Sully was never mentioned. Mr.

Ray never mentioned the Dorchester game again. I don't think that he really wanted to know how many fouls Whitey had. I told him having Sully around wouldn't hurt. Even I didn't know it would help that much either.

We were 3 and 0 and riding high on top of the City. But there is no rest for the weary We faced the number one team in the State and the number one player in the State, Russell Lee, next. That was tough, but playing them at Hyde Park made it even tougher. Hyde Park was also 3 and 0 and they were heavy favorites to kick our butts. Russell Lee was a 6'6" scoring machine, who played basketball at Marshall University and then for the Milwaukee Bucks in the National Basketball Association. His brother Gene was the point guard for Hyde Park and he, like Russell, was a very talented basketball player. And the Lee's were complimented with six or seven other top players, all of whom made them the top ranked team in the State. They were about as good a team as I had ever seen at the high school level. They played in a gym that was like a shoebox. Their fans were crazy and were fond of throwing objects at opposing players heads before, during, and after the game. Russell Lee and I played in a number of All Star games and had become pretty close friends. That, however, was all forgotten that cold January afternoon in 1967, as twelve Southie boys walked into the lion's den. I remember thinking how Custer must have felt at Little Big Horn.

There were 700 screaming Hyde Park students crammed into every nook and cranny of the gym and the balcony. They were all screaming for Lee and company to kick our asses, in much harsher terms and language. You have to understand that for as long as anyone can remember, Southie High football teams would just run over all other District and City League teams. My senior year they beat Hyde Park by forty points. So this was payback. It was like that in every gym we went to all across the City. We had to pay the price for a great football program. That particular year our football team had beaten Charlestown by the score of 56-0. The Charlestown team couldn't wait to get us in their gym to recoup some of their lost dignity. We also kicked their butts, which only intensified the rivalry. It is pretty intimidating to fifteen, sixteen and seventeen year old kids. I'm sure it would be intimidating to anyone who was thrown in that kind of situation. When I arrived downstairs for breakfast that morning, my uncle was reading the sports section and he wasn't looking too happy.

"What's in the sports," I asked.

"Oh, nothing" he said unconvincingly. I finally got the paper and read where this writer predicted that we didn't belong on the same court as Hyde Park. The way the game started I had a tendency to believe it. They were killing us. Russell Lee was everywhere. He had 23 points 10 rebounds and 6 assists and that was just the first half. We were behind by 22 points at the half. The crowd, smelling blood, was going absolutely wild. So was Mr. Ray in our makeshift locker room which also served as the cafeteria for the Hyde Park students.

We sat in there dejected, not saying a word. Mr. Ray came crashing in and started yelling as soon as the door was halfway shut. And unfortunately I was the object of most of that yelling.

"Wallace, what the hell are you playing out there, it certainly isn't basketball." Have you been reading to many of your press clippings?" he paced. I was afraid to look up. He continued yelling in my direction.

"If you don't want to play Mr. Captain (he was getting me back for pulling rank with him about Sully) there are a lot of kids on the bench who would give their right arms to play." I quickly scanned the room. Given the talent of the Hyde Park team and the temperament of the crowd, I wasn't as sure as Mr. Ray that a lot of subs would relish the chance to mix it up with Russell Lee. Nobody reacted to my look. Everyone had their heads down, fearing a look from Mr. Ray would transfer his fury from me to them. Christ, I felt bad enough, I didn't need the coach kicking the crap out of me in front of everybody. Hyde Park did a good enough job of that in the first half. I ended the first half with four points. I had been averaging twenty two points a game. Nobody had played well, but I was the captain and he took it out on me, which is fair. I didn't think so at the time, however. But his tirade stopped as quickly as it had started. It was the first and last time any of us had seen him blow up like that. I guess he was reading our press clippings too. Mr. Ray turned to Sully. "Go get the oranges Sully." He said as he slammed the door and left.

Sully flew across the room. We would eat oranges at half-time, it was suppose to replenish the vitamin C that you lost in the first half, or so we were told. Usually I looked forward to the oranges because I didn't like to drink a lot of water during a game and the oranges really quenched my thirst. That day I was looking forward to the oranges for an entirely different reason, so that the coach would forget about me for a few minutes. I watched as Sully hurriedly retrieved a huge Purity Supreme bag, the kind my mother would bring the groceries home in, every Saturday. He brought the bag up shoulder length, and dumped the contents onto a large table. I nearly died. Instead of three dozen nice round oranges, out of the bag flew two dozen huge grapefruits. Nobody said a word, everyone just looked. One of the grapefruits had rolled off the table and Sully scurried after it as if it were gold. By now Mr. Ray's, face had taken on a shade I had never seen before. We froze, as all eyes turned to our coach. He screamed.

"Sully, are you crazy? I told you oranges."

"I said oranges, Sully oranges," You could hear a pin drop in the locker room. Mr. Ray then reached across the table and picked up one of the grapefruits. He examined it. It was like a scene from a movie. He looked at Sully.

"Sully are these oranges?" Now Sully was on stage.

"No Mr. Ray those are grapefruits, but it's like this, I went down the Supreme Market, like you told me. I was going to get oranges, like you told me, and then I looked and saw that these were on sale. And you can ask Brian I could never pass up a sale." Mr. Ray just shook his head, turned around and, once again, looked directly at where I was sitting motionless.

"Wallace he's all yours. I told you this would happen. Mr. Captain." With that, he stormed out of the make shift locker room/cafeteria.

The room became a morgue. I don't know, to this day who started laughing nor do I care. But within a matter of seconds the whole room had exploded in gales of laughter. And I don't know who threw the first grapefruit. But within a matter of seconds, grapefruits were flying all over the locker room. I got hit right in the back of the head with one and it stunned me for a second. Those things were big. Sully, of course was right in the middle of it. Standing on the table and whipping grapefruits and halves of grapefruits all over the room. We were covered in grapefruit juice. Some of the team was actually on the floor laughing. They were laughing too hard to even get up and the grapefruits kept flying. For a few minutes we forgot that we were even in a basketball game. Someone knocked on the door. "Hyde Park is already on the floor," they yelled It still took a few minutes to get ourselves together. Finally we started up the stairs to the gym. Stevie Foley was directly in front of me as we made our way up the stairs. Since I had known Stevie, I don't think he has ever had a hair out of place. We used to call him Stephen Sweetheart. He had the best clothes and all that. When I looked at him, that day, he had grapefruit in his hair, grapefruit all over his warm-up jacket and a big grapefruit stain on his trunks. It just struck me funny and I started to laugh again and I could not stop. We were all laughing and smiling as we went into our two line drills. Mr. Ray was just staring and not comprehending what he was seeing. He had no idea what had just happened in the locker room. Even the Hyde Park players were looking at us like we were weird, as were the fans. We didn't care. We were laughing and slapping five and faking like we were throwing grapefruits at each other. It must have looked pretty weird. We were down 22 points to the top team in the State and we were acting as if we were up 22 points. It was a little disconcerting, I'm sure, for the Hyde Park players.

When the second half started the Hyde Park players seemed unnerved. We were as loose as if we were in practice. They were up by 22 points and we were laughing. It really spooked them and their wheels started to come off. They started making stupid mistakes and thank God I started to find my jump shot. The whole pattern of the game changed. Whitey began picking Gene Lee's pocket and Stevie Flaherty started rebounding like Dave Cowens. Mr., Ray just sat back and watched, probably convinced that his half-time speech had worked. After three quarters we had cut the lead from twenty two points to six points. They actually looked scared. When the third period ended Mr. Ray looked at us. "I don't know what you're doing but please keep it up." We all looked at Sully and laughed. Hyde Park managed to get back on track and when the game ended we had lost by four points and we had them scared to death. I scored 26 points in the second half and ended up with 30, for the game. Whitey ended up with 31 and Stevie Flaherty got his high game of the year with 18 points. Nobody outside that locker room knew what went on during that half-time. They probably wouldn't believe it anyway. It was better that way. Mr. Ray grabbed me in the corridor between classes a couple of days later. "I'm not sure I want to know but what happened in that locker room after I left?" I just smiled and told him to ask Sully. He never did. But I think that Mr. Ray was starting to realize that Sully was good for the team. He knew when to make us laugh at ourselves and at him. He never did hurt that team. We never would have beaten Dorchester without his magical score book. To this day not many people outside those of us who were in the locker room, know that grapefruit story. It was one of those things that you had to be there to appreciate. It certainly was vintage Sully. But more than that, it gave our team a communality of purpose and a bonding mechanism that we didn't have up until that point. We entered that hostile gym in Hyde Park as twelve individual basketball players and we left as a team. Sully in about seven minutes did what took our coaches seven weeks to do. He made us a team.

That however was the high point of our season, injuries killed us. I played our last five games on a badly injured ankle and other kids like Joe Fraser and Stevie Flaherty fought through nagging injuries as well. Whitey was a rock and I really admired his toughness and basketball sense. Even with all the injuries we still had a chance at making the State Tournament. But, and this was a very big but, we had to win our last game of the season to qualify. The game was against our bitter rival, East Boston High School. It was also at East Boston High School. The East Boston High School gym was not meant to play basketball in. Many years later they were serving lunch to the the cast and crew of "Mystic River" in the East Boston High School gymnasium. Dennis Lehane, who wrote "Mystic River," also wrote the foreword for my first book Final Confession". My good friend Kevin Chapman also had a starring role in the movie, which was directed by Clint Eastwood, invited me over to the set and asked me if I wanted to have lunch with Clint Eastwood. At lunch, I told them all about the East Boston High gymnasium we were in, which now acted as an unofficial cafeteria. I told Clint Eastwood that I had already been served as lunch in that place, which wasn't far from the truth. The gym had an overlapping track, which circled the entire gym. The track made shooting shots from the corner impossible. It also gave hostile Eastie fans a great vantage point to hit opposing players with pennies and spitballs, which they continually did. I remember the first time I played at East Boston High, I was a sophomore and Mr. Ray put me in midway through the first period. Eastie scored and Marty Hogan took the ball out of bounds and threw it to me. I started to dribble up court when someone spit on me from the track. Instinctively I reached to my shoulder to wipe off the spit and a kid named Tony Albano, from Eastie, quickly stole the ball from me and went in for an easy basket. Mr. Ray called a quick time out. He asked me what happened. I told him that someone spit on me. He said to disregard the spit and just concentrate on the game.

"You can take a shower after the game," he yelled over the crowd noise. Easy for him to say. But I did, and we ended up winning.

But, as you can guess, Eastie was not one of my favorite places to play basketball. I knew that I would be spit on and I knew that pennies would rain off my head and body. That was what you got at Eastie. I know it sounds disgusting and it is, but at least I knew what to expect. I was a lot more leery of the unexpected, which I knew was in store for us that day at Eastie. It's called payback. Earlier that year, we played Eastie at Southie High. Southie-Eastie games, no matter what the sport, are always big. Southie-Eastie football games on Thanksgiving would typically draw 10,000 to 15,000 fans. That particular basketball game was no exception. The gym was jammed. People were lined up five and six deep on the sidelines and under each basket. I had never seen the balcony so crowded in my life. I kept checking to make sure it stayed up because my father was directly underneath it. I went over to Mr. Ray right before our two lines drill and asked him if we could warm up at the other end of the gym. He looked at me funny.

"We've warmed up at this end for as long as I can remember, why change now?" I pointed to the overfilled balcony.

"Because that balcony is going to come down and I don't want to be near it when it does." He smiled, realizing that I was just kidding.

"You just worry about your 30 points and I'll worry about the balcony." But I was worried, and not because of the size of the crowd, but by who was in the crowd. Living in South Boston, my whole life, I knew a lot of good kids and I knew a lot of bad kids. I was kind of shocked to see a large number of bad kids in the crowd. When I say bad kids, I mean BAD kids. They weren't basketball fans. They knew as much about basketball as I knew about killing people or robbing banks(their professions). It unnerved me as I scanned the crowd and saw a lot of these punks dispersed throughout the crowd. The largest number had positioned themselves right underneath the East Boston basket. I didn't say anything to Mr. Ray, but in retrospect I wish I had.

    I got caught up in the excitement of the moment. The gym was electric. It was like a Celtics 7th game. The game got underway and I completely forgot about everything except beating a very good East Boston team. Midway through the second period I had the ball on a three on two fast break. I had Whitey on one wing and Mike Carter on the other. I stopped at the foul line, like I was taught. and then threw the ball three feet over Mike Carter's head, which is difficult to do because Mike is 6'4." I wasn't that used to passing the ball either. The ball flew into the crowd, which was under the balcony. The ref went over and asked that the ball be thrown to him. And after about ten seconds it was. When the ref went to bounce the ball, it was dead. Someone in the crowd had stabbed the ball with a very large knife. Talk about intimidation. The crowd roared. The East Boston players froze. I quickly glanced over to my friend Eddie Contilli, who was Eastie's star player. He was ghost white. I really felt bad. There was no place for this kind of macho bullshit in sports. These were sixteen and seventeen year- old kids who were representing their school and their community, they didn't need this kind of crap, and neither did we. I knew we could beat this team on our own. We didn't ask these punks to come into our gym and intimidate anybody. I was furious. The refs called a time out and talked to both coaches, which didn't accomplish squat. I had to give the Eastie players credit they were initially stunned when they saw the size of the hole in the ball, but they shook it right off and were ready to play. They, like us, were street kids, and they were pretty tough in their own right. I had two very good friends on that team, Eddie Contilli and Tony Albano, and I knew those two wouldn't back down from anybody. With less than a minute left in the first half, Contilli dove into the crowd, after a loose ball. Eddie Contilli dove after more balls than Madonna. This time, however, he didn't come out whereas Madonna usually does.

Brian P. Wallace

I froze. I knew right away that something was very wrong. There were so many spectators congested in that small area that I couldn't even see Contilli, or what was happening to him. It lasted only about ten seconds but it seemed like an eternity. As if by remote control the crowd, the red sea, began to part. I then got my first glimpse of Contilli and it wasn't good. He was lying on his stomach and he was unconscious. At first I thought he had been stabbed. He wasn't. Thank God. He had been punched and kicked but he was all right, relatively speaking. His face was pretty bloody and he had a couple of broken ribs but I thought it was a lot worse when he didn't come out of the crowd. The EMT's arrived and carried him out on a stretcher. The Eastie coach was livid and he had every right to be. He wanted the game called off and he wanted us to forfeit the game. The refs compromised. They cleared the gym of everyone except the players, the coaches, the refs, the time- keeper and scorekeeper. That was it. It was the first time in the history of high school sports that this happened. Nothing to be proud about. I didn't even want to play. All I could think about was my friend Eddie Contilli. Basketball, at least that day, had become secondary. We did finish the game in an empty gym, which was really weird. No cheerleaders, no noise, no anything. It didn't seem like a real game but it certainly counted in the standings. All the papers wrote about, the next day, were Contilli's injury, and how the gym had to cleared of all spectators. Violence in sports had once again taken center stage. Unfortunately, and once again it was South Boston in the headlines. And oh, by the way, we won the game by three points, again thanks to Whitey.

Now, later that same year, it was time for the payback and I knew it would come. The paper that morning had a story about the leading scores in the City. I was in second place behind Russell Lee. I had a chance to win the title if I had a big game at Eastie. This only made matters worse. I knew that the East Boston crowd did not want a South Boston kid win the scoring title without a fight and that was exactly what we got. Unbeknownst to me, my brother, who had just returned from Viet Nam, and eight of his equally crazy friends traveled through the tunnel to Eastie to watch our game. Nine Southie kids against 900 spitball- throwing Italians. Sounds about even to me. As we came up the stairs from our locker room two things happened. We could hear the large Eastie crowd chanting.

"Here we go Eastie, here we go." I could also, faintly hear, a chant.

"Here we go Southie here we go." I wasn't expecting that. Sully and I just looked at each other.

"Who the hell is crazy enough to come over here and root for us?" I said more in the form of a question than a statement. We looked at each other and both of us said in unison, "Eddie Wallace."

"I thought he was in Vietnam?" Sully said, looking confused.

"Not anymore," I said, "I think he's in a different war now."

"Oh shit," was Sully's only response. My brother was either crazy or he and his friends had a lot of balls. I wasn't sure which. I would find out very quickly though. As we entered the old, smelly gym I noticed two things, the size of the crowd, which was huge, and the number of beautiful Italian girls in that crowd. We didn't see many Italian girls in Southie, which is about 99% Irish. Sully noticed as well. As we were getting ready for our warm-ups, he walked over to me.

"Look at those three girls at half-court, they should be in the movies." I looked, and quickly agreed with my star struck friend.

"Go over and talk to them," I said, "You can talk to anyone go over and get a few phone numbers."

He didn't say anything, but I never put anything past him. As we were shooting around before the game started I noticed Sully walk over to where the three girls were standing. Good old Sully, I thought. He was talking to this beautiful Italian girl with long jet-black hair. She was unbelievable. I saw him pointing to me. Good man, that Sully. A few minutes later one of the balls rolled over near where the girls were standing. I ran to retrieve it. As I picked up the ball I noticed that the girl Sully had been talking to, motioning to me. I remember thinking that Mr. Ray wouldn't be too happy if I walked off the court to talk to a girl, even one that looked like her. She motioned again. I just shrugged helplessly. She got the message and started to walk onto the court. I was standing right at half court and I was praising Sully to myself. I was also wondering what he had told this lovely creature who was sexily making her way to half court.

"Hi, are you Brian Wallace?" I figured that she had probably read the story about me in the paper that day, and I was pretty impressed with myself.

Brian P. Wallace

"Yeah I'm Brian Wallace," I said, in my most macho voice.

"What's your name?" I never found out. She took a step closer to me and then spit right in my face. I was humiliated. The crowd started cheering wildly and she just walked away. It was bad enough that it had to happen in the first place. But did it have to happen in front of 900 people in Eastie? I was frozen to the spot. I watched her walk back to the sidelines where everyone was giving her high five's. I couldn't move. It was only a few seconds but it seemed like an eternity. The place was bedlam. I never felt so foolish in my entire life. I couldn't believe I had been set up. I was pissed at Sully. He, to this day, denies he did anything. He said the girl just asked him where Brian Wallace was, and he pointed to me. "She set you up," he laughed.

"As long as you didn't." I told him. He swore on his mother that he didn't. It was my own fault. I was very lucky that Mr. Ray didn't see it.

The game itself turned out to be the dirtiest, roughest game that I had ever played in. The refs were intimidated by the crowd and let all but flagrant fouls go uncalled. I was getting killed. Every time I drove to the basket, I got knocked to the floor. When I wasn't picking myself off the floor, I was picking spitballs out of my hair. It wasn't a good day. I knew that the players from Eastie did not want me to win the scoring title but this was ridiculous. We were up by t ten points when the refs called a jump ball, right near the spot where I had just been humiliated by the girl. On the jump ball Jimmy Ridge, who was a miniature version of Arnold Schwartzenegger, grabbed the ball for us. At the same time a huge kid from Eastie, who, as a basketball player, made a great football player grabbed the ball for them. They both tugged at the ball. The ref blew the whistle. They continued to tug at the ball. The ref blew his whistle again and they continued their struggle. Both refs blew their whistles. Jimmy Ridge made one final Herculean tug which threw the Eastie player halfway across the gym. The refs just looked at each other and ran. One of the Eastie players took a run at Ridge. There were two distinct sounds, Ridge hitting the kid and the kid hitting the floor. Pandemonium ensued.

The spectators on the floor all ran to where we were standing, at half court. The spectators in the balcony all rushed down the stairs to where we were standing. Both benches converged to where we were standing. It seemed the place to be, if you were looking to stand in the middle of a burgeoning riot.

The refs kept running, right to the locker room. It reminded me of an old movie. Ridge was knocking people out left and right. Bodies were starting to pile up beside Ridge. My brother and his friends were now standing next to Ridge, and doing their share of damage. Sully had grabbed the clock and was hitting people over the head with the clock. I was looking for that Italian girl. Even Mr. Ray was fighting. It seemed like we were fighting the whole East Boston community. When sanity returned along with the police, all the injured East Boston injured were lying scattered in the general vicinity of Ridge, Sully and my brother's gang. Ridge had a pretty bad cut over his eye. Sully's hand was bleeding, I'm sure from giving someone else a cut over their eye. It took about twenty minutes before order was restored. They were yelling threats at us, in Italian and in English, from the balcony and throwing cans and books. It was pretty scary. My brother's crew was now standing next to our bench. They thought it was great. I still couldn't find that Italian girl. We ended up losing the game as well as our chance at playing in the State Tournament. I ended the game with 29 points, which put me 14 ahead of Russell Lee for the title. Lee played, later that day, and scored 51 points. So I not only lost a chance to play in the Garden but the scoring title as well as the girl. Some days are better than others. Sully was all excited. He loved being in a fight that he didn't start. He thought it was great that Mr. Ray was standing toe to toe with us. They wanted to kill Ridge. They had their chance, unfortunately for them Ridge had his chance as well and he made the most of it, He must have knocked out at least a dozen people. Unfortunately thirty years after that fight Ridge killed two people in a drug deal gone bad and will spend the rest of his life in prison. Drugs have ruined a lot of lives and a lot of good people in our town. Fifty one of Whitey Bulger's cocaine sellers were rounded up back in the early nineties and most, if not all, did some prison time. I knew just about all of them.

I found out very early that Boston Public Schools were a WHOLE lot different from the Catholic Schools I had been attending. A lot of the friends that I had in Grammar School were going to private schools like Boston College High, Don Bosco High, Catholic Memorial, and Christopher Columbus High School. I had never, for a minute, entertained thoughts of going to another Catholic school. I had spent the past nine years of my life being taught by Sister of Notre Dame and that was enough. No nuns, no

Brian P. Wallace

uniforms, no nuns, no more first Fridays, no nuns, You get the picture. Not me. I was heading up the hill to fame and glory as a member of the Class of 1967. I was really looking forward to Southie High. It didn't take me very long, however, to find out that there are some major differences between catholic schools and public schools. Actually it was my very first homeroom period that I found out, as Dorothy said.

"I don't think I'm in Kansas anymore." Nor did I think I was in St. Augustine's anymore."

My homeroom teacher was a man named Mr. Pieri, who was a wiry Don Knotts type of guy who usually had his sleeves rolled up to his elbows even before the 8:38 bell rang. He was my very first lay teacher and one that I'll certainly never forget. He was a science teacher, so my very first home- room was in a science lab, replete with all the test tubes, gas jets, microscopes, sinks etc. It was a drastic change of venue from the drab, holy picture filled walls of the Catholic school that I had attended. I immediately noticed another difference, which kind of unnerved me. The age difference. I was accustomed to everyone, in my class, being the same age as me. Surprise. I had turned fourteen two months before the start of my freshman year. The students who were in my first homeroom class ranged anywhere from fourteen to twenty and there was even one guy who was what they call a PG or post graduate. He was twenty four. years old and had already served in the Army. It certainly was a long way from St. Augustine's where everyone is the same age, which is very young. I didn't know what I was expecting but it certainly wasn't that. They all looked pretty tough and I soon found out that they were. As Mr. Pieri was calling the roll, that very first day, in my very first class, there was a real loud snoring noise coming from the back of the room. Mr. Pieri got through most of the roll call when he called out "Mr. McGrath." No answer. He called it our again "Mr. McGrath," again no answer. He stopped, and began to walk toward the slumbering student. All eyes followed his trek. He approached the kid whose head was cradled in his arms and his arms were spread across the desk. Mr. Pieri shook him and called out his name.

"Mr. McGrath." No response. Mr. McGrath." He finally stirred, as Mr. Pieri gently prodded his shoulder. His head rose slowly from his arms and he had a vacant stare on his face.

"Are you talking to me?" he said in a threatening tone that certainly scared me. Years later I would be sitting in a movie theater watching Robert Deniro in a movie called Taxi Driver and in one of the signature lines. "Are you talking to me, are you talking to me, you must be talking to me because there's nobody else here." When I saw Deniro do that scene it immediately transported me back to this first day at Southie High. That day in 1964, Mr. Pieri took a step back, I would've to.

"I was merely seeing if you were with us today, Mr. McGrath." "

"Why the hell were you yelling," the half- sleeping student replied.

"I wasn't yelling," a smiling Pieri said, trying to lighten the moment, That is how all teachers talk to high school students," he laughed. McGrath didn't.

"You knew I was here Pieri, you saw me walk through the door" he said as he remained seated. I was mesmerized. I had never heard anyone talk to a teacher like that. Pieri stood his ground.

"You don't get any special treatment in here McGrath and I won't tolerate anyone sleeping in my classroom." Good for him, I thought. McGrath looked at him.

"I'll do whatever I want in this class because there is nobody in here with the balls to stop me." Wow. This was like a movie. I couldn't believe that I was in school. Pieri still didn't back down but he did make a huge mistake.

"Maybe there is nobody in this room who will stop you but if I call your Parole Officer, I'm quite sure that he will stop you." In a flash McGrath stood up, and stood up, and stood up, and stood up. He had to be 6'6" and 250 pounds. He was absolutely huge. He towered over the skinny 5'6" and 140 pound Pieri. His huge body now blocked my view of Pieri I stood up to get a better view of what was happening and maybe deep inside wishing that I had taken that scholarship to B.C. High. There was total silence in the room. The next thing I knew McGrath pulled a gun from his belt. I knew absolutely nothing about guns then and know probably less about guns now. I found out later that it was a .38 caliber pistol.

With a menacing voice, McGrath screamed into Pieri's face.

"You can call my Parole Officer once Pieri, but I guarantee you'll won't be alive to call him a second time." Unbelievable, and school hadn't even started yet. Pieri didn't say a word and neither did anyone else. Finally Pieri said, in a voice that was a lot calmer than mine would have been.

"Put the gun down, Mr. McGrath before you actually hurt someone." McGrath didn't move. Pieri repeated.

"Please put the gun down , nobody has gotten hurt, let's keep it that way." Slowly McGrath right hand made its way to his side. Now I saw the gun for the first time. I was stunned. A standoff. Thank God. Mr. Pieri quickly moved out of harm's way. McGrath just stood there and finally he put the gun back in his belt and sat down as if nothing had happened. Once McGrath sat down Pieri quickly left the room. What if this nut goes on a rampage I thought to myself. St. Augustine's was starting to look pretty good to me about that time. I kept my eyes forward looking at the blackboard but not really seeing anything. McGrath was back snoring within five minutes. I breathed a little easier. Nobody said a word for the next five minutes. Pieri never came back. The bell for first period, finally rang, releasing the tension and providing safety. I flew out of that classroom. The next day Mr. Pieri returned, McGrath didn't. In fact, McGrath never returned again. I heard from the grapevine that he had been suspended. Suspended. What the hell do you have to do to get expelled, pull a Jeffrey Dahmer. Well he only ate three teachers, so we'll only suspend him this time. If he eats any more teachers we'll expel him. Wow, life was sure different in public schools. One of my friends got expelled at St. Augustines because he called another student an asshole. All in all it was quite an introduction. I knew that I might get roughed up a little in high school but I figured it would be on the basketball court and not in my homeroom. I didn't dare tell my parents what happened that day. They had wanted me to go to a Catholic High School. Worse, they had wanted me to go to a Catholic high school that was all boys. No way. Those 14 year old hormones were starting to kick in and I was looking forward to high school and girls and girls and girls and girls Maybe I would have a little time to play basketball. I ran into the kid I only knew as McGrath many years later. He was still huge but he had found Christ. He was attending AA, had a nice family, and was doing all right for himself. I thought the next time I heard about him would be in the paper and at the end of an obituary column. I was pleasantly surprised. He turned out to be a very nice guy. See some people can change. Not Sully however.

Chapter 12 – The Boston Garden Years, Haystack & Popcorn Charlie

High school was a place where we went five days a week for six hours a day from September through June. The Boston Garden was the place where we went most of the other hours. From the time I was 13 years old, we pretty much hung at Boston Garden from October through April. That was when the Celtics and Bruins playedAnd that is where, if you looked hard enough, you would find Sully and me. The ushers, however, could never find us. As I have often mentioned, basketball consumed most of our passion, at least at that age. Other stuff would consume our passion later, but that was much later The Celtics were Gods. The Pope was close to God, we knew, but Bob Cousy was closer. When I was 13 years old I was hired, through the Boys Club, to be the Celtics ball-boy, water-boy, retriever any or all of those titles will do. The Celtics would take two kids from the South Boston Boys Club, two kids from the Roxbury Club and two kids from the Charlestown Club and hire them as their official ball-boys. It was the biggest thrill of my young life. I, who had worshipped from afar would now get to worship at the very altar where these Gods performed their miracles. What I mean is that I now got to sit on the Celtics bench and if you don't think that was big time then you have completely forgotten what it's like to be 13 years old. The Celtics paid us $5 per game. I would have paid them $20. I was absolutely in heaven. I don't think there is a more prestigious job for a 13 year- old kid, in Boston, during the early and mid - 60's than to be a ball-boy for the Boston Celtics. I was a hero. People who knew I had this job were constantly asking me about the Celtics. What is Russell like? What is Cousy like? Is Red really that tough? Does Ramsey really use that many bandages? How many foul shots does Sharman take a day? Do they talk to you? Can you get us some autographs? It was endless, and I never tired of it. Even the adults would grab me aside and throw a few Celtics questions at me every once in a while. I was never shy to begin with. I loved the attention and notoriety it brought me. I don't think my big brother liked it all that much but we'll get into that later. It was an experience that I'll never forget and I'll never forget the part that Sully played in that experience.

Brian P. Wallace

I had only been on the job for a day or two, and I was still very uneasy being around all my heroes. This particular day I had arrived at the Garden long before my 5 o'clock start time. I was placing each player's uniform in their respective lockers, which really were just hooks on the wall, when the door opened and in walked Bob Cousy. Now you have to understand I had been playing basketball, then, for more than half of my life. My number, on every team that I ever played on, was #14 or Bob Cousy's number. Many years later I was elected to the South Boston Sports Hall of Fame and the ring that I wear, today, on my finger has number 14 on the side. Cousy was my man and everyone from my mother, to the nuns at school, to my coaches knew it.

I turned and there he was. I froze. He kind of sensed it. "Hi, I'm Bob Cousy." He said, extending his hand. Like I didn't know it.

"Brian, I mean my name's Brian." I forgot, momentarily, that my last name was Wallace. I felt kind of foolish, like some hick kid who was in the big city for the first time. Cooz went over to his locker or hook and started to put his sweats on. I started folding towels, just to look like I was doing something.

"Hey kid ya busy?" he called from the other side of the locker room. I looked around and realized that I was the only kid in the room.

"No sir." I replied quickly.

"Good, follow me." Bob Cousy said to me. At that point I probably would have followed him off the empire state building if he asked. He didn't. He asked me, instead, to grab a basketball and bring it out onto the court. I grabbed a ball from the rack and he grabbed two, one in each hand. I couldn't believe the size of his hands, they were huge. We walked out of the old dimly lit dressing room and headed toward the famed parquet floor. I stared in amazement as he began juggling the three basketballs. He handled the balls like a magician, which in a way I guess he was.

I was trailing about three steps behind, as the 'Houdini of the Hardwood' mesmerized me with his mastery.

"Did you see the game last night?" he asked me over his shoulder.

"Yes sir," I quickly replied. I must not been making much of an impression on these guys, I thought. I sat on the bench for the entire game, the night before, and he never even noticed that I was there.

"I missed four foul shots last night," Cooz said, that won't happen tonight." He didn't mention that he had made about seventeen or eighteen foul shots, only that he missed four. That's an average I would have taken any day. We continued through the old building and onto the parquet. The Cooz shot fouls shots and nothing but foul shots for at least forty minutes. He would shoot and I would throw the ball back to him, over and over and over. I couldn't believe that I was rebounding for 'The Cooz.' He didn't miss many. My job was pretty easy actually. After he finished his foul shooting he began to dribble, one ball then two then three balls. It was amazing to watch. He wasn't showing off either, this was one of his dexterity drills. I saw Pete Maravich doing the exact same drill years later. This was great I kept thinking that I wished some of my friends were here to see this, me and the Cooz. They'll never believe this, I said under my breath.

They didn't. Sully did. He had snuck into the Garden early and was up in the stands, quietly watching me and Cooz on the floor. He was hiding from the ushers so he couldn't make a sound or they would hone in on his position. He was a master at hiding and he drove the ushers crazy, because they knew he snuck in but could never catch him. He would usually, but not always, hide in the ladies room until the doors officially opened. Other times he would hide in the catwalk which was about 110 feet from the Garden floor. There was no usher on earth who was going to climb up that catwalk, no matter who was hiding up there. But sometimes he would get bored and sit right in the loge seats, visible to all the ushers, whose manhood was now being challenged. And the chase would be on. Sully loved when the ushers chased him and they never caught him. What these out matched ushers didn't know was that Sully had more hiding places, inside the Garden, than most terrorist organizations had outside the Garden. He used to brag that he had over fifty, places to hide in the Garden and over twenty five ways to sneak into the Garden. I never doubted these boasts for a minute. Neither, I'm sure, did the frustrated ushers. He snuck into every event that was held at the Garden from Celtic and Bruins game to Billy Graham Prayer Congregations to the Circus. He was virtually unstoppable.

We had snuck in to the Garden for something like a hundred ten straight events, and we thought we were pretty much unstoppable. That was

Brian P. Wallace

before the Beatles came to town. The year was 1965 and we figured that sneaking into the Beatles show would be a piece of cake. Boy, were we wrong. I had never seen so many people in my life. And most of them were teenage girls. They were everywhere trying to catch a glimpse of the 'Fab Four'. I had never seen so many cops before. They were everywhere, trying to stop the teenage girls from overrunning the hotel, next to the Garden, where the Beatles were staying. The Garden had also hired private security as well as private K9 units, which made the Garden a virtual fortress. We tried each of Sully's twenty something ways to sneak in. Impossible. We couldn't even get near most of the possible sneak in entries. This had never happened before. We were kind of shocked. Sully was furious. He was determined to get in. He didn't care about the Beatles he did care about being embarrassed in front of his friends. The crowd continued to grow larger. It was getting out of hand and Sully was getting madder by the minute. We decided to try the Hotel Madison as a last resort. This was tricky because we had to jump over an alley, which separated the Hotel and the Garden. The problem was that the alley was eight floors below. We had only used this way once before and for good reason, it scared the hell out of me. We never made it as far as the Hotel.

Somewhere between the hotel and the Garden we got split up. The crowd was just so big that I lost sight of Sully and Knuckles. They thought that I was right behind them. By the time they realized I wasn't, it was too late. They, in turn, got split up themselves in the huge crowd. What started as the three and quickly became on our own, separate and apart. I, like Sully, was now determined to get into the Garden. I, unlike, Sully, however, wanted to see the Beatles. In that split second, amidst a sea of screaming girls, I devised a plan and went into action immediately. I still don't believe what I did. The focus of my plan was to somehow capitalize on the total chaos that was erupting all around me. The gates where the ushers were taking tickets, I saw, were absolute bedlam. I'm sure that these ushers had never seen anything like this in their lives nor did they expect anything like this. The Garden had protected itself and the Beatles by hiring a small army of security. They didn't think about the ticket takers. I did. I would guess that everyone approaching the ticket taker did in fact have a ticket. That wasn't the problem. The problem was the sheer numbers who all tried to get into the Garden at the same time.

A Southie Memoir

They all wanted to be the first to see the Beatles although the Beatles would not be on stage for at least another two hours, although they didn't know that. The ushers were being pushed and shoved. One usher's hat was knocked clean off his head and into the crowd. He made no attempt to retrieve it. I jumped into the sea of humanity. When I got near the door I quickly bent down and grabbed a ticket stub that had already been ripped by the usher. Usually these stubs were all put in a self - contained box that was attached to the door. My hunch was right. Because of the pushing and shoving a couple of the stubs had missed the box and were lying on the floor, just as I thought. Here's where I knew it would get tricky. The noise was deafening. I was next. I handed my ticket stub to the sweating usher. He reached for my stub, and his hand, as if stung by a rattle- snake, quickly recoiled.

"What's this?" he asked, sounding and looking quite annoyed.

"Where's the other half?" he asked.

"You already took it," I responded. He wasn't buying it. But I knew he wouldn't. There was a moment of indecision when neither of us said a word. The crowd howled their disapproval, which I had counted on. I held my ground.

"No way kid," this ticket has already been ripped."

"I know you ripped it. I said, being pushed, pulled and jostled, which I had also counted on.

We both stared at each other neither backing down. The crowd was now almost pushing me into the Garden. I knew that every second counted and I counted on that.

"I don't know what you're trying to pull," the disheveled usher said, "But it's not going to work." The crowd was now screaming to get in. He kept looking at me and then anxiously looking at the crowd behind me.

"Can I see your supervisor?" I asked as innocently as a kid from Southie could. He looked at me like I was crazy. Yeah, crazy as a fox.

"My supervisor?" he screamed above the din of the crowd. I had him on the ropes. In my best little boys voice I said, "I'm not leaving until I talk to a supervisor." He was now totally flustered and the crowd had become really frenzied. They were pushing me into the lobby and we both knew that there was no way I was going back through that crowd. I knew I had won. He shouted.

"Go ahead kid before you get us both killed." A desperate situation calls for desperate measures. I know that I would never have the nerve to pull that off again, but once was enough.

As I scampered by the frustrated ticket taker I heard a band called 'Teddy and the Pandas doing their best to warm up the crowd. They were a great band but weren't having much luck with this crowd who only wanted the Beatles. I really liked 'Teddy and the Pandas', but nobody was paying any attention to them. The place was total bedlam. Girls were fainting, girls were screaming, girls were crying and the show hadn't even started yet. What a scene! I stood transfixed watching this phenomenon. I had been transported beyond the twilight zone. I was now in the Beatlemania zone. I was getting pretty psyched, like everyone else, to see the Liverpool mopheads. I really liked their music. I was kind of sad, however, to be witnessing this phenomenon by myself. I knew that Sully would really be bullshit when I told him about this scene. I worked my way down to the stage, just as 'Teddy and the Pandas' were finishing their last song. The ushers had lost any control they might have had over the crowd. Tickets meant nothing. People were fighting to get down front. I had never heard such a noise in the Garden, it really was deafening. Just then Arnie Woo Ginsberg a DJ for WMEX trotted on-stage and was immediately booed. This crowd might have even booed Bob Cousy, God forbid. He kept waving his arms. He did this for at least five minutes. The noise began to lessen.

"Before we bring out the Beatles," he started, but when the crowd heard the word Beatles, they again went nuts. He waited and tried again.

"We are not going to start the show until we have some order in the building and we are prepared to cancel the show if you don't calm down." That did the trick. The crowd began to simmer down.

I felt a tap on my shoulder and heard a familiar voice. "You want to buy some popcorn, mister?" I spun around, knowing the voice but not believing I was hearing it. There was Sully. Only he looked a little different. He had a white apron a white hat and a huge canvass sack of popcorn. I didn't know whether to laugh or cry. I did the former.

"How do you like this outfit?" he laughed.

"I bet I'll score today." I was laughing hysterically but with the amount of noise in the Garden, nobody even noticed, at least they pretended not to.

"Here have a popcorn on me," Sully said as he reached into his bag and grabbed a couple of boxes of popcorn. We quickly polished off the two boxes. I remarked that somehow free food tastes better. I learned, halfway through our first box, that Sully had gotten totally frustrated at not being able to sneak in and he decided to try going up the employees elevator as a last resort. And believe me going up the employee's elevator was a last resort and for one reason, a guy named Festa. He was bad. He ran the employees concession department and he ate kids who tried to sneak in on HIS elevator. This guy was the bogeyman and Mike Tyson all rolled up into one big fat Italian package. Sully knew that the moment he alighted from that elevator he would be staring at the smelly cigar and the big fat face of Festa. His reputation alone would have been enough to keep me off that elevator. Not Sully.

Festa once beat up two kids from Savin Hill, who had made the mistake of trying to sneak in by using the concession elevator. He's just lucky that it wasn't the Ryan brothers, Danny and Teddy, from Savin Hill, who used to sneak in with us or they would have kicked the shit out of him. He also had three kids from Southie arrested for the same thing. He was bad news. He always bragged that not one kid had ever snuck in through concessions. He would stand at the elevator, clipboard in hand, and check off the names of everyone who entered. If your name wasn't on his list then you were in trouble. Sully's wasn't. Sully told me that he was on the elevator with five other kids and when it came to a stop on the second level the door opened and there he was, like a junk-yard dog. He checked off the other five kids and assigned them their jobs for the night. After he had checked off the fifth kid he looked at Sully.

"Who the hell are you? "You don't work here." Looking as destitute as possible Sully went into his act.

"I know, Sully said anxiously, "But I really need a job and a kid from Somerville told me to take this elevator and ask for a Mr. Festa".

"I'm Festa," he said, softening a bit. Sully could smell a weakness a half block away. Sully was cute. There were about thirty kids from Somerville who worked at the Garden and Sully knew it. He wasn't through his act. In fact, he had just stated.

"Oh I'm sorry sir I can see that you're terribly busy can I come back some other time and fill out an application."

"I oughta kick you're fat little ass right down the stairs, nobody uses that elevator except employees and you're not an employee," Festa growled. Sully looked scared. He wasn't. In fact he should have been in Hollywood.

"I'm sorry sir but the kid from Somerville."

"I already heard the story," Festa broke in, before Sully had a chance to finish his sentence.

"Just stand over there," Festa barked, pointing to a spot near the door. Sully complied as another elevator full of employees arrived and were checked in. Festa waited, as Sully watched two elevators arrive and they were both empty. Festa started counting his list and turned towards Sully.

"This might just be you're lucky day kid," he growled. "It seems I need a few more floor sellers." Sully was trapped. Festa again counted the list and threw a sheet of paper in Sully's direction.

"You know how to write don't you kid." Sully acting indignant.

"I'm on the honor roll at Latin." Well woopdiedo. Excuse me Mr. Latin" Festa said sarcastically.

"We're not used to such high and mighty company around here." One thing about Sully, he knew when to act bold and he knew when to act timid and he never confused the two. I can just imagine Festa thinking that he was scaring the shit out of Sully and never once realizing that Sully was conning the shit out of him. About ten minutes went by and Festa reappeared.

"You're going to sell popcorn tonight, Mr. Latin do you think you can handle that?"

"I learn quick," Sully's replied.

"I know you're an honor roll student at Latin," Festa said, again mimicking Sully. He threw Sully a white hat and an apron, gave him his big bag of popcorn and Sully was employed. Simple as that. I was laughing so hard as Sully recounted the story that I had forgotten all about the Beatles who were getting set to go on-stage.

"Watch this," Sully said, as he began throwing his popcorn to very appreciative teenage girls. To make matters worse he was yelling.

"Popcorn, free popcorn, compliments of Mr. Festa." It was incredible. Sully was always a crowd pleaser. I must have looked a bit worried at this act of unprecedented kindness.

"What's your problem?" he said in between throws.

"What about Festa?" I asked. "Do you think I gave that jerk my right name?" I should have known. Sully had filled out all the employment forms as Peter Hawkins and has listed his address as 230 West 6th street, which just happened to be the same address as the Boys Club. I had to give it to him, he really was something. I can just picture Festa thinking he was intimidating Sully while all the while Sully was planning this caper. Little did Festa realize that he had looked his last upon Mr. Peter Hawkins honor roll student at Boston Latin. It was also the first time, that we knew about, that anyone had burned Festa. Sully kept the hat too.

The roadies were now on stage fixing the Beatles microphones and other equipment when I spotted a former basketball player at the club who now worked on the bull gang at the garden. The Bull gang set up and took down the Celtics floor and got the Bruins ice ready for play. They also worked all the other events like the circus and the Ice Capades and boxing. He was probably in his early twenties and was the guy who sometimes gave us free beer when he worked the Garden beer concession once in a while. He spotted me, the same time I spotted him. He motioned me over to the side of the stage. Getting through that crowd of girls wasn't easy, but it was enjoyable.

"Where you sitting?" he asked over the noise.

"We snuck in, I told him. He laughed and told us to follow him. We moved one of the barriers and we followed close behind.

"Where are we going?" Sully asked. I just shrugged. He parted the curtains and we were instantly backstage. Backstage at the biggest concert ever held in Boston. I remember thinking to myself, a half hour ago I was alone with no ticket, no Sully and now I am backstage and about ten yards from the Beatles dressing room. Both Sully and I were awestruck. It was controlled chaos as our friend tapped us on the shoulder and told us he had to report to his boss.

"Stay right here and don't move. I'll be back in a few minutes, he said as he began a slow jog away from us. I thought we would be thrown right out. We had no backstage pass, no staff shirts on, but nobody seemed to notice. If they did, they were too busy with their own jobs to worry about us.

"Can you believe this?" I asked Sully, who for the first time in my life was speechless. We saw all the photographers before we saw the Beatles.

"I think it's them," Sully said in a voice I had never heard before. He was actually awed by something.

"No shit. I hope we don't get booted," I answered, looking around for ushers or security. Just as I saw Paul McCartney, I felt a hand on my shoulder and I knew it was too good to be true.

"You guys all right?" our Boys Club friend asked.

"We are now," I sighed. He stood right behind us with one hand on my shoulder and one hand on Sully's shoulder and nobody even looked at us. WE were, however, looking right into the faces of John, Paul, John and Ringo who passed within two feet of us to get to the stage. It was pretty awesome and something I have never forgotten. Like little schoolgirls, we waved to them and John gave us the peace sign. And they were gone, just like that. We thanked our friend who asked us if we wanted to watch the show from backstage.

"Not with that many girls out there," Sully laughed.

"I wish I was you age, "he said. "Good luck with the girls and I'll see you guys around, he said as he went back to work and we went out front and saw the entire show no more than five yards from the stage. Sully beat Festa and we met the Beatles all in one historic day. It was a day neither Sully or I will ever forget.

It's kind of ironic that Festa would be gone from the Garden the very next year and Sully would, in fact, get a full time job working in concessions. He was already a hero to many of the kids who worked there. They all hated Festa and they had heard how Sully had conned Festa during the Beatles concert. Sully and I had received many a box of free popcorn from admiring popcorn vendors during that year. Sully never ran into Festa after that incident, luckily for Sully, or maybe luckily for Festa. Festa never came out of his concessions department and Sully wasn't about to go in there.

We literally hung out at the Garden and we knew all the angles. For a 7:30 Bruins game we would arrive at the Garden by 5:00. We would be inside the Garden before anyone arrived. Most employees didn't arrive until 5:30. We would hide until 6:30 when the doors officially opened and then we would reappear and go get our ticket stubs from some guys from Southie who were season ticket holders. They were never asked for their stubs because all the usher's knew them. But this modus operandi didn't last long. It was to tame for Sully. He got bored very easily and needed constant challenges to keep him interested. So we would start coming out of our hiding spots at 6:15 instead of 6:30. Then we would come out at 6:10 and then 6:00.

"Why bother hiding at all?" I said to Sully. I was kidding, but he liked that idea. He always had to live on the edge. The game, now, was not only to sneak in but challenge the ushers to catch us. One night they almost did. It was just after 6 O'clock, and we were in the ladies room in the second balcony, which is at the very highest point in the Garden. Sully was pacing, which was always a bad sign. Pacing meant he was getting bored, which was always a dangerous thing. "This is bullshit," he said to nobody in particular. "Those guys couldn't catch us on their best day." He started toward the door and like sheep me and Knuckles followed. There was still thirty minutes left until the doors opened but Sully was in one of those moods. We walked all the way down to the promenade and sat down.

"This is crazy," I pleaded with him, "They're going to catch us." He shot me one of those 'Who cares looks', and stared straight ahead. Five minutes later the ushers started going to their assigned sections. He didn't move.

"Come on Sully," I pleaded "They're all coming up here now." He paid no attention. From behind us we heard a voice call out.

"You little bastards stay right there." Right. We were City kids. Did he really think we were going to just sit there and let them throw us out, or worse. We looked behind us and this usher had to weigh 350 pounds. We got up, and he yelled again.

"You'd better stay there if you know what's good for you."

"You'd better go knock off the cheeseburgers, if you know what's good for you," Sully yelled back. I couldn't help it, I just started to laugh, and I couldn't stop. Sully and Knuckles were already ten yards ahead of me. I couldn't believe that he told the fat guy to go on a diet. The fat guy was furious as he bounded down the old Garden promenade stairs. He got to within five yards of me before I took off. I knew there was no way he was going to catch me. I caught up to Sully and Knuckles in a few seconds and we left the fat usher in our wake. As we ran down the stairs, we spotted an usher heading down the stairs in our direction. It was none other than our old friend Usher George who hated us with a passion. His eyes were gleaming, This was exactly what Sully wanted.

"Are we sitting in your section tonight?" Sully asked, as we turned and ran back down the stairs.

"You'll be sitting in a police station tonight," George yelled back, as he followed us down the stairs.

"Now we're in trouble." I said to Sully.

"Screw him," he shot back "If we let that asshole catch us, we deserve to be in the police station." And we kept running. We were like Butch Cassidy and the Sundance Kid running from Lord Baltimore.

They really wanted us this time. We would run down one corridor and there would be two more ushers at the end of that corridor. We would head back only to find two more chasing us from another corridor. I didn't know they had that many ushers. We ran down the North corridor to the South corridor to the second balcony to the West concourse with ushers in close pursuit. Sully loved it. I was scared to death. They harder they chased us the madder they got.

"Let's get out of here," I said to Knuckles.

"I've got a better idea," Sully said, and, again, like sheep, we followed him. He led us up a ladder onto another ladder until we were on the catwalk 110 feet from the ground. We had lost the ushers. We caught our breath and wiped off the sweat and just stayed there until there was a half- decent crowd in the Garden. Sully was pumped.

"That was great, that was great." Sully said. He loved the chase.

I was just glad to have survived. I could picture my father bailing me out at the Police Station. I didn't think that was so great. As soon as we were safe, Knuckles yelled at Sully.

"What are you crazy, now they'll be after us every night."

"No way," they had their shot and they blew it, "We're golden now." He was absolutely right. They never chased us again. However, that night wasn't over yet.

After we got our obligatory pizza and ticket stub exchange, we walked slowly past George the usher. He had about five people who were asking him where their seats were.

"Better start working out," Sully said, "The Marathon will be here before you know it." If looks could kill Sully would have been stone cold dead.

"I'll get you one of these nights," George muttered.

Sully pulled out his ticket, "But why Mr. usher we're good paying customers."

George said a bit too loudly, "Screw" as a bunch of people turned and stared at him.

"Why did you have to do that?" I asked Sully. He just shook his head. and said, "I don't know but it was funny wasn't it?" It was like a catch all phrase, never uttered until we were out of danger and then uttered as if nothing had ever happened.

"It was funny wasn't it?" The problem was that most of what he did really was quite funny. When his antics made us laugh, conversely, they had the opposite effect on the individual or individuals for which the frivolity was directed at. I always told him that one of these days his humor and his pranks would backfire. Other than that incident with Rocco, I was wrong. It never happened.

One night the Boys Club received a block of tickets for the Beach Boys concert that was being held at the Garden. I think they were the first legitimate tickets that Sully ever had. That fact didn't escape his attention either, I was to find out the hard way. The day of the concert he called my house, told my father an Italian joke and then asked me to go over to the Garden early.

"Why?" I asked, "We have real tickets."

"I'll be right up." he said, before I could hang up the phone.

"I think Sully's losing his marbles," I said to my brother.

"We have tickets for the concert and he still wants to sneak in." My brother shrugged.

"Sully doesn't have any marbles to lose." Maybe he had a point. What Sully had cooked up in his conniving little mind, however, was far from crazy. There was always a method to his madness. All the way over from Broadway station to North station I tried to talk him out of sneaking in.

"Trust me, this will be fun," was all he said. Trust him, right. So we did what we usually did. We snuck in and hid.

"This is crazy we have tickets, why are we hiding?" I asked Sully.

"Just wait," was all he would say. We waited until 6:20. He kept checking his watch every two minutes and at precisely 6:20 he jumped up and said let's go. I knew that the gates opened at 6:30. I had forgotten, however, that the usher in the West lobby, for whatever reason, always opened up his gate between five and seven minutes early. One of the older kids had told us that a long time ago. I had simply forgotten it. Sully stored the information away, in his devious little mind, for future use and today was the future.

He led the way, still looking at his watch. We casually walked right through the front lobby amid curious stares from some of the Garden employees. We walked directly to the front of the stage and sat down in the very first row.

"Are you nuts?" I said to him. "George is standing right over there." George had his back turned away from us but he was only a few feet away. Sully just stared. I looked around and we were the only people, other than employees in the whole building. I looked back and George was gone. I caught a flash from the corner of my eye. Too late. I felt a hand on my shoulder. It was George. He had a smile from ear to ear.

"I got you two little bastards now." I had never seen him smile before. He had rotten teeth and very bad breath. He grabbed Sully's collar in his right hand and mine in his left as he led us out into the lobby. As we got into the lobby Sully acted scared, which I knew he wasn't.

"What are you going to do with us?" Sully screamed loud enough to get the other usher's attention. I knew he was I still couldn't figure out his plan but it was starting to come in to play. We did have tickets. but George didn't know that. George continued to lead us into the lobby, which was just now letting the crowd in.

"Are you going to throw us out?" Sully whimpered like some scared juvenile. Now, George laughed.

"Throw you out? I wouldn't think of it, I'll let the police deal with you two." My father was all I could think about when he mentioned the word police. Sully looked at me and I guess he could tell by the look of panic, which was written all over my face that this had gone far enough. He immediately went into action.

"The police," Sully yelled as everyone in the lobby turned and looked at him. The whole place seemed to stop what they were doing and head over to where George still had us by our collars. This is what Sully wanted but George had no clue he was being played. Sully now had his audience, which grew by the minute.

"We didn't rob a bank, we only came to see the concert."

"Hey, leave the kids alone." A few people chimed in. George held fast. , "Why are you picking on us we didn't do anything." Sully said, a little louder now. George was now getting a little uptight.

"Shut up," he said, "You're causing a scene." Like Sully didn't know that. This was the major part of his plan.

"Hey you can't talk to those kids like that," a huge guy yelled at George. The lobby was now filled with concert- goers who were streaming in the front lobby.

The head Garden usher managed to push his way through the sea of bodies and looked quite upset at the disruption. He wore a blue blazer while George and all the other ushers wore red blazers. We knew who he was anyway from just being at the Garden so much. By the time the head usher reached us, Sully had stepped up his routine and was now entering phase two.

"Please sir," Sully implored the head usher. "Can you help us?" Sully looked like some poor little kid from the sticks that had lost his parents. He looked as if he were about to cry. George, who at that time still had both of us by our collars, quickly let go. The crowd continued to grow.

"What the hell is going on here?" the head usher said, loud enough to be heard over the background noise of the crowd.

"Sir these are the two kids who sneak in every night and I finally caught them." Sully looked dumbfounded. The head usher looked at both of us trying to get a handle on the situation.

"Let the kids go," someone in the crowd yelled. George began to sweat. Now almost crying, as if on cue, Sully pleaded his case to the head - man.

"Sneak in," he said "I've never been in this building in my life." This was really getting good. The head usher who had never really seen us before just looked at George. More comments were hurled from the crowd.

"He's lying, "George said. "He's in here every night causing trouble. With his gang." He had no idea how much trouble Sully could really cause but he was certainly going to findout.

"Are you sure this is the same kid?" the head- man pleaded with George, who stuck to his guns.

"I'm positive," George shot back. "Ask him for his ticket," George said to his boss.

The head usher looked around, as the curious crowd began to become more vocal.

"Leave the kids alone," someone yelled from the back of the crowd, and everyone cheered.

"Go ahead ask them for their tickets, There is no way they have tickets," George almost yelled. Again, as if on cue Sully pulled out his ticket which had mysteriously been cut in half as if the ticket taker had ripped it, and given Sully his half and threw the other half in the box on the door. Sully was holding his ticket up in the air for everyone to see. The head usher didn't say a word but he looked at George as if he were going to kill him.

"It's a fake ticket," George hurriedly said, "He always has a fake ticket."

"Can I please see your ticket?" the head usher said to Sully. His voice inflection had changed drastically.

"This IS a real ticket," he said looking at George. George grabbed it, out of his hand. "Where did you get this ticket?" he yelled at Sully. He was losing it.

"The guy at the Boys Club gave them to me and all of my friends," Sully said very innocently. George wasn't through with Sully, his job maybe, but he had a point to prove.

"How did you and your friend get in before the gates opened?"?" he again interrogated.

"We just walked in the door and gave the guy our tickets, I know we weren't supposed to be near the stage but I just wanted to see it." Sully was good. He had a rehearsed answer for everything George threw at him. I could see George beginning to get the feeling that he was in trouble, but he was not through just yet.

"The doors weren't even opened yet when I caught you two on the floor explain that," he said and looked at his boss. His boss, in turn, looked directly at Sully for a response. So did I.

"That guy over on the other side of the building let us in around 6:20," Sully said, driving the final nail into George's coffin. The head-man, knowing that the old usher on the West pavilion did, in fact, open his doors a little early, now knew he had some serious fence mending to do. George just looked defeated. Sully had him on the ropes and he was about to deliver the knockout punch.

Now Sully was about to take it to phase three. Sully now was playing strictly to the head-man. He acted as if George were no longer even there.

"Can I call my father, he's a lawyer and he told me that if I ever got into trouble to call him immediately." The head-man, now smelling a lawsuit, quickly moved to defuse the situation.

"You're not in any trouble, son," he said patting Sully on the head as if he were a long lost son.

"This has only been a misunderstanding," he went on. "There's certainly no need to call anyone, everything is fine."

"Fine," Sully yelled, loud enough to pique the crowds interest once again. He repeated.

"Everything is fine? That usher just told us we were some kind of criminals and that he was going to have us arrested and you say that everything is fine." The crowd cheered. Sully was back on stage. Meanwhile I was standing there sweating. All I could think of was the ticket in my pocket.

Brian P. Wallace

It was still whole, not ripped in half like Sully's. If they ever asked to see my ticket we were screwed. But, they never did, thank God. They actually acted as if I wasn't even a part of this production., which was fine with me. Sully was handling things very nicely on his own, thank you. There were about 300 people straining to see what all the commotion was about. The head usher was now just trying to end this confrontation any way he could, without any more disruption or a lawsuit. George was now a rag doll, totally defeated. "

"Is this how you treat all kids who want to come to the Garden to see a concert?" Sully yelled, as the crowd erupted in cheers. Sully was putting on a show. He looked at the head usher.

"This guy, want to put me in jail one minute and you tell me everything is fine the next minute, well I don't think so." Again the crowd cheered. Sully looked directly at me, and I just shook my head in an effort to call him off, before he went too far with this thing. Just then the head usher leaned down. "I'm really sorry that this happened and I'd like to make it up to you." We were all ears.

"Let's talk about it backstage," he said as he started to lead us through the crowd. In a matter of minutes we were backstage and standing five feet from the Beach Boys. We got their autographs and spent the entire night watching the show from backstage, like two big shots. We got free food, five orsix6 tonics, free programs, and Beach Boy paraphernalia. Halfway through the concert I gazed over at Sully, he had pizza sauce all over his chin and he was halfway through a giant Pepsi. I just began to laugh. He looked at me as if I had gone completely insane.

"What's the problem?" he asked in between bites of the Garden's famous pizza.

"No problem," I shot back as "Little Deuce Coupe" echoed through the Garden.

"Then what are you laughing at?"

"I'm laughing at you." He hated people laughing at him.

"Me, why?" What did I do?" he asked defensively.

"You totally amaze me." I said. He just smiled.

"When did you plan all of this?" I asked.

"When we got the free tickets," he nonchalantly replied. He kind of chuckled and said, "But I never thought it would go this good," as we gazed on to the Garden crowd from our backstage perches.

"What do you think will happen to George?" I asked.

"Maybe he'll lighten up," he laughed. "I know he won't bother us again." Sully's revenge, chapter 96.

When there was nothing to do in Southie, there was always something to do at the Garden. Even if there were no games or no events going on there were still the crazy people that hung at the arcade and who were always good for a laugh. One night, after supper, we were sitting on Sully's stairs, bored out of our minds.

"What's going on at the Garden tonight?" Sully asked.

"Nothing," Knuckles answered. "The Celtics and the Bruins are on road trips and the circus just left," Knuckles said.

"Well there's certainly nothing to do here, lets go over to the Garden anyway," Sully replied. We snuck into Broadway Station and were headed to our favorite place. Just the anticipation of going to the Garden had brightened everyone's mood from boredom to excitement. Sully always made these road trips exciting. We got off the train at North Station and were kind of puzzled at the crowd getting off with us. Sully looked at Knuckles. "Hey knucklehead," I thought you said there was nothing going on at the Garden tonight?"

"I just said that the Celts and Bruins were away, I I didn't know if there was anything else here tonight." I examined the people getting off the train and they weren't your usual sport fans. These people were all dressed in suits and ties and the ladies were all decked out as well.

"Looks like they're going to church," Sully replied and he wasn't very far off. Whatever it was there certainly were a lot of people going into the Garden that night.

By that time we were pretty curious, so we did what came naturally, we snuck in. We climbed up two stories, on the drainpipe, which actually was kind of dangerous, but we all managed to make it. Once on the fire escape, our trusty old matchbook had prevented the door from closing and we were inside the Garden in an instant. We took seats in the first balcony and we were all by ourselves. All the people were sitting in the Promenade, the Loge or on the floor. We had never seen this type of setup before. The organ that our friend John Kiley had used to excite the Bruins and Celtic fans was now playing stuff that sounded like church music. I looked at Sully and I could see that he was puzzled.

"What the hell is going on here?" he asked.

"Damned if I know," I shot back. Just then the music stopped and everyone rose to their feet. One man emerged from somewhere behind a curtain and took his place on stage. The crowd began clapping like Cousy had just hit a 40 foot game winner. They clapped for a good five minutes.

"Who is that guy?" Knuckles asked.

"Let's go find out, Sully said, and headed downstairs before the final syllable had tumbled from his mouth. We all ran down the stands and onto the Garden floor, which looked naked without the ice or the parquet. We sat in the second last row from the stage Sully tapped a well- dressed man on the arm.

"Excuse me sir, who is that guy?" he asked very politely. The guy looked at Sully as if he had just landed from another planet.

"Are you serious?" the guy asked. Sully hated to look stupid.

"I know who he is but my friends don't and they won't believe me." He was quick. The guy smiled and looked past Sully at us as if we were some sort of imbeciles.

"That man up there is the great Billy Graham" the man smiled.

"See I told ya," Sully said.

Knuckles said to the man, "How come he's not wrestling?"

The guy now looked at Knuckles as if he, like his roly- poly friend had just landed their spaceship on Causeway street.

"Not Billy Graham the wrestler, he's Billy Graham the evangelist." "

Oh," Knuckles said, looking at me to see if I knew what an evangelist was. I did, but I didn't say anything.

"How much does he get paid for something like this," Sully asked the guy who was becoming increasingly annoyed with us.

"I have no idea," the guy said, and this is not about money."

"Everything is about money," Sully laughed, but he was far from through.

"How much did you pay to get in?" he asked the guy who clearly wanted no part of us by now. The guy was now starting to get mad.

"There was no price for admission, this is a spiritual conclave," he angrily said. "Now if you don't mind I'd like to get back to the sermon." Fat chance.

"You mean it didn't cost to get in here tonight?" he asked the same guy.

"That is usually what no admission price means" the guy angrily shot back.

"You mean you came all the way over here to hear a guy, who's not even a real priest give a sermon, what are you nuts?" We were Catholic kids, and we had never seen anyone preach about God, except Catholic priests. The guy was now losing any of the cool he had left.

"If anyone in here is nuts, I would put my money on you," he said, staring straight at Sully.

"Well at least you didn't give your money to that con man" Sully replied.

"That con man is Billy Graham," the guy exploded.

"He should have stuck to wrestling, at least they charge for tickets, there," Sully said.

"He's not the wrestler," the guy screamed. He is the most famous evangelist in the world, but I don't think you riff raff come from that same world,"' he said, and then got up, and stormed out of the aisle.

'What's he mad about," Knuckles said, "We're the ones who should be mad, we risk our lives sneaking in here, when we could have walked right through the front door." Sully motioned to all of us.

"Let's get the hell out of here, I get enough preaching from my old man." Sully's was mad because the thrill of sneaking in was gone, once we found out that the event was free, it had lost whatever allure it had On the way home on the subway, I said to Sully.

"That must be some kind of record, we even sneak into free events." He didn't want to hear it, but we laughed for a week about that rich guy who called us riff raff.

Brian P. Wallace

Another event that we snuck into was the Lippazanier Horse Show. Knuckles, for some reason was all excited about going to this event. He kept telling us it was like a rodeo and stuff like that.

"How much does it cost to get in?" Sully asked. He would never again be caught dead sneaking into another free event. Knuckles went to the phone and when he came back his face was all flushed.

"It's free huh?" Sully asked.

"Far from it," Knuckles said very slowly. "Do you know how much they're getting for a ticket?"

"No stupid, that is exactly why we had you call to find out," Sully teased. Knuckles, however, wasn't even listening.

"Tickets are fifty bucks a piece," Knuckles stammered.

"Fifty bucks for a rodeo" Sully yelled.

"That's what the guy said," Knuckles replied. Sully was still stuck on fifity bucks a ticket.

"That's great, I've never snuck into something that expensive," Sully said all excited. This was no Billy Graham deal, in Sully's eyes. This was the big time, although we had no idea what Lippanzanier Horses did. But I could tell by the excitement in Sully's voice that we were soon going to find out. Sully kept grilling Knuckles all the way over on the train, since Knuckles was the only one it seemed, who knew even the slightest details about these horses. We walked out of North Station and stopped short at the sight that confronted us. There had to be at least Twenty five limousines stretched all along Causeway Street. All brand new, shiny black limousines. We had never seen that many limos in one place before. Actually wehad never even seen a limo, up close before, at least I hadn't. People in Southie didn't usually use that mode of transportation to and from work. Ridge said he had been in a limo when his sister got married. I, on the other hand, had never set foot in a limo and I was duly impressed.

We were also way out of element. One of the kids with us was Eddie Seale AKA IS. IS stood for 'Irresistible Seale' and was a name given to Eddie Seale by Eddie Seale, who was a real piece of work. He had absolutely no fear and was very quick to show us his fearless nature. Is was always the first kick to jump one hundred feet off the highest rock in the Quincy Quarry or the first kid to hang fifty feet from the club roof into the small grass yard in front of the club. Is was absolutely fearless, maybe not the brightest kid but certainly the bravest. I never seen Is back down from any type of dare and that included some mighty scary dares, usually ones concocted by Sully. Is dove off Anthony's Pier Four Restaurant into the frigid and polluted waters of Boston Harbor on a two dollar bet. Is was dared to walk on the live subway tracks from Broadway Station to South Station, and he did. We were all standing there as Is accepted the challenge and began to walk down the dark, dangerous tracks separating Broadway station from South Station. He was gone about ninety seconds when we heard the unmistakable sound of a train coming into Broadway station from Andrew Station. We just looked at each other in fear and nobody said a word. We all got on the train, which was now speeding over the same tracks that Is had just journeyed off on. I was scared to death and I honestly thought that Is's death was imminent. We arrived at South Station, in about a minute and a half. No sign of Is. Nobody dared say a word. I sat down on the closest bench and everyone joined me.

"What do we do now?" I asked. I looked around and everyone avoided my eyes.

We waited a few minutes and then we heard a voice calling. "Hey Pedroes," which was the name of our gang.

We all jumped up. "It's Is, it's Is," we all shouted in unison.

"Who'd you expect Billy Graham, IS smiled. Was glad to see him. He came running out of the tunnel with a big smile on his face and climbed up the ladder from the tracks to the landing.

"What about the train that went by?" I asked.

"Oh I just ducked into one of the little cubbies when I heard it."

"How close was it to you?" I asked again."

"At least two feet away," Is laughed.

"I bet you'll never do that again?" Knuckles said.

"Are you shitting me" Is said, "I might never take the train again," he laughed. "What a rush." He smiled. He continued to walk the tracks for at least another couple of months. I don't know why he stopped, but then again I don't know why he started or why he did anything that he did. That was IS, one of our gang.

Well that night at the Garden, IS became totally enamored with the limos. He went up to the first one he saw and began to run his hand along the sleek black exterior.

"Excuse me, sir," a guy with a black uniform and a little cap, said to IS.

"Why, what did you do?" IS said back to the gentleman.

"This sir is a $90,000 vehicle," the man said in a clipped British accent.

"Is it yours?" IS asked.

'Hardly, sir," the man answered, again in a very proper English dialect.

"Did you steal it?" IS went on. The guy almost had a heart attack.

"I have never heard such a blasphemous comment. Of course I didn't steal it."

"So what are you worried about?" IS asked. It made perfect sense to him. This wasn't the chauffeur's car, so what was the problem if IS touched it.

"Sir, I am in the employ of the vehicles owner," he said. Once again, Is ran his hand along the shiny chrome of the limo, once again the driver admonished him.

"Excuse me sir." The chauffeur was getting redder by the minute.

"Why do you keep saying excuse me? Did you do something?" IS asked.

"Do, sir, I'm afraid I don't understand.

"Why do you keep saying excuse me if you didn't burp or anything?" IS asked the befuddled driver. Listening to IS and this chauffeur talk was like listening to an Abbott and Costello routine.

"Do you drive the car?" IS asked, totally switching gears.

"That is my job, sir, yes."

"Your job is just to drive this beautiful car? We're do ya get a job like that?" IS replied. He was as serious as a heart attack. "Do you get those cool duds too?" The chauffeur was now totally lost. He just stared at IS.

"I beg your pardon sir." he said, shaking his head.

"First of all, why do you keep begging my pardon and excusing yourself and why do you keep calling me sir?"

"At this point, sir, I really don't know what I'm doing or saying." The guy was totally flustered.

"Can I sit in the car?" IS asked.

"Hardly" the chauffeur said.

"Hardly what?" IS shot back, "Why don't you speak English," IS said as he began following us to the back of the Garden to sneak in. That exchange between IS and the chauffeur was so funny because they were each speaking their own version of the English language and one's language was as foreign as Japanese to the other.

"I don't get that guy," IS said to me as we left the chauffeur much worse for wear.

"That's OK IS, I don't think he gets you either," I laughed.

It was priceless. So wasn't the Lippanzanier Horse Show. Priceless in the sense that I would have paid any price to get the hell out of there. We were surrounded by millionaires who clapped when we didn't see anything to clap about and who clapped rather funny. Talk about oil and water. The Dead End kids meet the Cabot's and the Lodges. The show consisted of a bunch of horses prancing around with their noses in the air, the same as the people in the stands. The horses didn't do anything and the people still clapped.

"When do we see the rodeo stuff?" IS asked Knuckles.

"He just shrugged and we waited and we waited, but there never was any rodeo stuff. No bulls, no clowns, no bucking broncos, no rope tricks, just horses prancing around. It was the most boring day I ever spent in my life. We were all going to kill Knuckles on the way home. IS was the only one who enjoyed himself. He talked about those limousines for weeks. Knuckles heard about the Lippanzanier horse for a lot longer than that.

We saw George the usher the next time we went to the Garden, but he ignored us and we ignored him. In fact, he never even looked at us again. Play with fire and you get burned. I have always wondered what he thought when Sully pulled out that real ticket. I wonder what his boss said to him. Sully had pulled it off without a hitch. Sometimes he really did awe me. We never really discussed the particulars of that incident, which was Sully's way. Once it was over, it was over. But it was priceless, HOW he got George. I wasn't at all surprised that he got George just how he did it, and the lengths he went to do it. He had prepared for that role, and he pulled it off flawlessly. Robert DeNiro couldn't have done any better. This had to be one of his best performances. I really think that he would have been a tremendous actor.

Brian P. Wallace

Actually he was a tremendous actor he just never made any money at it. I wonder what would have happened if we had grown up in Newton or Wellesley and had access to drama courses and real drama coaches? Sully might have made Taxi Driver or Raging Bull. But he really was quite talented. Had all the expressions and mannerisms of a first class performer. Just ask any teacher at Southie High, where he gave some of his best performances. And when he wanted to get eve, he did it in a big way. It was if he were planning a bank robbery. He would have been pretty good in that line of work as well. But he always worked out all the contingencies. He never left one detail unresolved. If he had spent as much time on his homework he would've had a free ride to Harvard and my childhood would have been pretty boring. George was actually lucky he could have ended up like Haystack Calhoun. Now that's a funny story.

It all started off innocently enough. We were in school and Sully asked me if I wanted to go over to the wrestling matches, that night, at the Garden. Neither of us was a big wrestling fan, but we always had a ball with the people who attended these matches. I don't know where some of these people came from but they were really off the wall. Somehow strange people always seemed to gravitate toward Sully and I. We made up nicknames for the most outrageous ones. There was whistling lady, ridey- didey, autograph man to name just a few. I had nothing better to do that night so I agreed to go. We were playing pinball in the arcade, which was located directly underneath the Garden until 5:00 at which time we decided it was time to sneak in.

"Let's use the player's elevator," Sully said as we left the arcade. The player's elevator was usually monitored but it was real early and the Garden personnel usually didn't start monitoring it until the players started to arrive, which was usually never before 5:00 for a 7:30 start. As we were waiting for the elevator, I turned around and saw the biggest human being that I had ever seen waddling towards us. He was huge.

"Look," I said excitedly to Sully, "It's Haystack Calhoun." At that time he was one of the top three wrestlers in the world and we were duly excited. He was going to take the player's elevator, as well, so we waited for him. He weighed 601 pounds and wore dungaree overalls with a huge horseshoe around his neck. He was a pretty imposing figure.

"Hi, Haystack" I said, He looked at us as if we were bill collectors.

"What do you two want?" he said pissed off.

"Nothing," I said back a little bit taken back by his attitude.

"Good," he said "Then leave me alone."

"Nice guy," Sully said, loud enough for the giant to hear. I didn't say anything, he was way too big. The three of us were standing in front of the elevator, not saying anything. I really felt uneasy about this guy. I looked at Sully.

"Let's go," I said.

"No way," Sully replied as he stared at the giant.

He had that look in his eye, and I knew something was going to happen, I just didn't know what. The elevator finally arrived and all three of us piled on. Haystack walked in first and proceeded to the back of the tiny elevator. He made it crowded just by his mere presence. Sully got in and turned to the wrestler.

"What floor?" I felt a little bit better. Maybe I had misjudged the look in Sully's eye.

"Second floor," the giant barked.

"Sorry," Sully said, in his best elevator operator voice, "The second floor is only for athletes." I was wrong. Trouble was also riding in the elevator along with me, Sully and Haystack. The wrestler's face turned redder than a fire engine and he yelled.

"What the hell do you think I am?" I couldn't look. He was towering over Sully.

"You're not an athlete you're just a wrestler," Sully said, very matter of factly.

"Wrestlers are athletes," Haystack screamed." It was obvious that Sully, unknowingly, had hit a nerve.

"I don't have the faintest idea what you are, but I'd give anything to see you run up and down the court," Sully laughed. I couldn't help it, I burst out laughing too, which only made the giant madder. He was screaming about wrestler's getting no respect and about how all wrestlers were stronger than all other athletes. Haystack was really ticked off. Sully never flinched. By the time the elevator arrived at the second floor there were six ushers running to see what all the commotion was. You could hear Haystack screaming, from all parts of the building. The ushers must have died when the doors to the elevator finally opened. You really have to picture this, if you can. I was lying on the floor laughing uncontrollably. I actually thought that I was going to pass out. Haystack, all 601 pounds of him, had completely hidden Sully from their view and was yelling at the top of his lungs.

"I am an athlete, I am an athlete." Sully was staring straight up into his 8 chins and yelling back.

"Cousy is an athlete, Russell is an athlete, you are not an athlete."

"I want these two arrested," Haystack screamed at the ushers. I was still laughing. A couple of the ushers began to giggle which further incensed Haystack. Sully took over. Looking directly at the ushers Sully said, "You can arrest this one for laughing," as he pointed to me.

"He's wanted in 4 States for uncontrollable laughter, which I think is a misdemeanor." Haystack wasn't laughing.

"And you can arrest me for telling the truth." Sully said. He looked at the ushers. And then out of the clear blue Sully turns to the giant.

"How the hell do you take a dump," he asked. That was it for me. I completely lost it and some of the ushers did too,.

"You're all a bunch of assholes," Haystack screamed. Sully was still in total control.

"Why don't you have them arrested too," he said pointing to the ushers. "They should at least get probation for laughing" Sully said as the fat man began to waddle off.

"Screw you, screw all of you," he yelled, as he waddled down the corridor. The ushers tried to compose themselves. A few did, but most of them couldn't. They escorted us back down to the North Station concourse and out of the Garden. They couldn't believe that anyone Sully's size could have such balls. On the way down they told us that they all hated the egomaniacal 601-pound wrestler. They said they always had some kind of problem with him.

"We, now, have a problem with him." Sully said. I was the only one in the elevator who knew what that meant, and I knew only too well. The ushers apologized for throwing us out, which was kind of funny. They told us that Haystack would check to see if they had, in fact, thrown us out. We knew they were only doing their job. We had no problem with them. Haystack was a different story, but that story was to be written another day in another venue. That night we still had to sneak back in the Garden. I don't think that I had ever seen Sully so mad. He kept saying.

"Can you believe that fat jerk?" I knew that Sully was really bothered by the incident with Haystack. He just wouldn't let it go. If Sully did something to you and you returned the favor, fine. That was to be expected, But if you did something to him that was unprovoked. Trouble. What upset us so much that night was Haystack's attitude. We were trying to be nice but he wouldn't let us. I guess we had been spoiled by guys like K.C. Jones, Sam Jones, John Havlicek or Cousy. They were all great athletes and they were all great men. Many a night, KC or Hondo would hand their gym bag to one of us and let all of us ride the elevator to the second floor with them. When the elevator would stop at the second floor, KC, Hondo or Sam, would say to the ushers, "They're OK, they're with me," and we would walk in like we owned the joint. Not only were they great athletes, they were great human beings. Haystack was neither.

I remember the first time I met KC Jones. It was on that same elevator. He got on the elevator just as it was about to close. He was singing a popular song and boy could he sing. He gave us a big.

"How you guys doing?" he asked.

"Fine Mr. Jones," he wrinkled up his face.

"Mr. Jones, do I look like a Mr. Jones to you?" I didn't know what to say.

"KC's the name gentlemen." We got in with no problem that night because there were no ushers waiting as we alighted from the elevator. We were actually getting a bit too complacent, for a while, because we had gotten in about five times in a row by way of the player's elevator. The next night we saw KC was, again, at the elevator. He always had a big smile on his handsome face. He spotted us at the elevator.

"There's my boys,." K.C. said.

"Hi KC," both Sully and I said in unison. His smile broadened.

"Now ya got it," KC said, and we laughed. He was a great guy. As we started to get off the elevator an usher appeared from nowhere and grabbed me by the arm.

"Not tonight, my friends," he said. KC who had walked a few steps off the elevator turned and he no longer had that ever- present smile on his face.

"What's the problem?" he said, looking directly in the eyes of the usher.

"No problem sir', I'm just throwing these guys out," the usher smirked.

"Woah," KC said, "These boys are with me." The shocked usher let go of me as KC passed me his gym bag.

"They're helping me out tonight" he smiled. The usher forced a smile.

"Of course, I'm sorry Mr. Jones."

"Don't apologize to me, "KC said, "Apologize to them." The usher was pissed, but he didn't want KC on his case, so he looked at us.

"Sorry guys, my mistake."

"No harm no foul," KC smiled. "Let's go boys." We all headed towards the Celtic locker room. How do you like that Haystack?

About six weeks later, Sully and I were over at the Boston Arena to watch a boxing match. I hadn't thought about the fat wrestler much because I had a lot of other things to worry about. Not Sully. More than a couple of times during that period he would bring up the incident with Haystack and get all bent out of shape about it. I would just tell him to forget it because the old wrestler wasn't worth worrying about.

"It's over Sully," I would tell him and I hoped that it was, but for some unknown reason, I didn't believe it myself. My fears were justified. The Boston Arena was an old building that had really come under major disrepair. We went there to watch High school hockey mostly but every once in a while they would put on a pretty good boxing show. The boxing shows would feature Southie boxers like Tommy Connors or Bobby Ellis or Cliffy McDonald (the same one who had the milk thrown at him in the great food fight) or Billy Weeks, whom we hung around with. The Arena had no ushers and sneaking into it wasn't even a challenge. We did it anyway, of course. The best thing about the Arena was the french fries. The Arena didn't have much, but the Garden could never match those French fries. Sully and I had just bought some fries and were heading down to the locker room to see Tommy Connors, who was fighting that night. There was a preliminary bout going on between two fighters who we didn't know so we didn't pay too much attention to the match. As we started to go downstairs, Sully stopped dead in his tracks. I almost knocked him over but he didn't even notice. He became excited and began to point. I had no idea what was going on, but that was not uncommon with Sully.

"There he is," he said as if spotting a whale, and in this case it was pretty close. I looked quick and there he was, all 601 pounds of him.

Haystack Calhoun. He was much too large to fit in one of the tiny Arena chairs so he was sitting on the top step of one of the aisles. He had a whole pizza sitting next to him and a coke and some fries and some chips.

"He has enough food there to open his own convenience store." Sully said. I laughed Sully didn't. He was just glaring at the giant. I had no idea what was going on in that devious mind of his, but I knew it wasn't good. It wasn't long, however, before we all would find out exactly what was on that mind. And it is certainly something I will never, ever forget. Without a word Sully started running. Slowly at first and then picking up steam. I was the only one watching him. Everyone else was watching the prelim fight. He gained speed as he got closer to the gluttonous wrestler, who was to concerned with his pizza to notice anything. With a couple of yards to go, Sully raised his right hand way over his head, much like a rodeo cowboy would do, while riding a bunking bronco. The giant never knew what hit him. As Sully swooped down, he brought his right hand down and hit the wrestlers neck, at least a couple of them, with a huge slap. The noise was deafening. It sounded like a gunshot as it echoed throughout the cavernous old building. You have to understand Haystack had about eight chins made up of nothing but fat. What Sully slapped was all that fat. Sully didn't hurt him, he just stunned him. He was way too big to hurt with a single slap. It was the sound it made that made it seem much worse than it actually was. Sully's open palm on all that fat was much louder than I had anticipated. The whole place turned around in unison to see what that sound was. And what they saw I'm sure they will never forget. The stunned wrestler, who obviously had no idea what had just happened to him, or why, was, after a few seconds trying to get to his feet. It ordinarily would've taken him some time to accomplish this task just because of his bulk and the close quarters in which he was sitting. He was however having a much harder time getting up than usual. And this is where it got really funny. Sully was standing directly behind him and he wouldn't let him get up. Every time Haystack would attempt to lift his mountainous frame Sully would put his hands on Haystack's shoulders and push him back down. The best part was that Haystack had no idea, who was behind him, doing this, or why. All the people in the Arena had stopped watching the fight and were all laughing hysterically at the sight of this teenage kid manhandling this giant wrestler. It went on for about a minutes, and by the time it ended the entire Arena audience was going crazy over this spectacle. Haystack was screaming that he was going to kill someone. Problem was, he didn't know who. The fight was now an afterthought. Sully was making Haystack's size work against him. Because of his great girth he also began to tire quite easily and his attempts to get up didn't have the fervor that they did at the start of this insane confrontation. And, unlike the Garden, the Arena had no ushers, to help the big jerk. Finally with one last push, Sully was off. He began running as fast as he could to the other end of the Arena and to one of our hiding spots. Haystack was not going to catch him in a million years anyway. After an additional twenty seconds, Haystack finally managed to get onto his feet. He menacingly looked down the corridor where Sully had disappeared, but he was about nineteen seconds to late. He still had not even seen Sully, who was now long gone and hard to find. A menacing stare now graced his fat face, as the crowd laughter finally began to subside. He was probably wondering why he got suckered in the first place. There's an old saying " Don't throw Southie kids out of elevators". He learned the hard way.

    The quickness at which the whole incident took place also left me, as well as Haystack, a bit stunned. Sully had never said what he intended to do, he just did it. The giant began to look in my direction as he stood trying to save face more than anything else. I prayed that he didn't somehow recognize me, from the elevator. He didn't, thank God. Haystack had finally sat down in the same spot. I waited until he started watching the next fight before I ventured out. I walked quickly passed the giant as quietly as I could, he never stirred. I looked everywhere for Sully. I couldn't find him in any of our usual spots. I finally figured that he probably ran right out of the building once he had whacked Haystack. Wrong, again. I found him at the pizza stand. I was so scared I could barely talk and there he was taking his time enjoying a pizza, with sauce all over his face. He spotted me and broke into a huge grin. Despite myself, I did too. And then all the fright that was bottled up inside of me came out in the form of laughter. We were both laughing so hard that people were avoiding us. We didn't care. They must have thought we were crazy and they probably were right. Sully broke the spell.

"That fat bastard should learn to mind his own business," he laughed with pizza sauce all over his face which kind of made it hard to take him seriously. A lot of people made that fatal mistake. Once, just once.

"If he ever gets you, you won't have any business to mind," I said. As if trying to.

"He deserved that you know." He said, trying to justify what he did. I started laughing.

"Come on let's do it again." He said. Maybe he really was crazy. ` "No way, I'm not going anywhere near that fat man." I said.

"What are you chicken?" Sully shot back.

"Absolutely," I said, I meant every syllable.

"Well I'm not," Sully said. I was trying to reason with him but it wasn't working. Finally he said.

"There is no way he'll be expecting me to come back, and there is no way I'm going to get caught." I knew he had his mind made up, so I didn't say anything. "You coming with me?" he asked." "Nope. You're on your own," I said back to him. That didn't bother him one bit. "You are going to watch aren't you?" he implored. Again I had to laugh. He was incredible. "

Yeah I'll watch," I laughed. Now he was beaming, "

Well here goes," and he was off. I walked up to the balcony so I could see where he was going and how he was going to pull this off. I watched as he ran along the back corridor, on the opposite side of the building from where Haystack was sitting. He looped around the horseshoe until he was on the same side of the arena as Haystack. I now had left the balcony and was standing pretty near to where I was standing during the first attack. The corridor was about 60 yards long. Sully was at one end and I was at the other end. Haystack was about fifteen yards from me. So when Sully began his run he had to travel about forty five yards before he reached the fat man, who was now working on his second pizza. Everyone had gone back to watching the fights and had forgotten about the Haystack incident. I was standing there holding Sully's maroon parka as he started his run. Again, right hand held high in the air, as he began to pick up speed. But a funny thing happened as he got about thirty yards from Haystack I heard a slight murmur, which grew as Sully got closer. With ten yards separating him and Haystack, everyone on the opposite side of the arena stands was standing and pointing to Sully. The people who were sitting on our side of the Arena could not see Sully because he was behind them. and it all happened so quick. Although as he got to within five yards of Haystack some people on our side began to turn around to see what the people were pointing at. I prayed that Haystack wasn't one of them. Right arm raised way above his head he swooped quickly on the unsuspecting giant. This time the noise was even louder than the first time. BOOM. The force of the blow sent Haystack toppling to his left and into a fan, who was sitting in the seat next to him. The crowd was going crazy. This time Sully didn't hang around to see his work. He passed me, going full speed and continued right out the front door of the Boston Arena. We could hear the crowd cheering behind us as we exited the place and kept right on running into Symphony Hall station where we caught a train home. I couldn't wait to get to school the next day to tell the Haystack story. I was like an apostle always spreading the word of Sully. But the kids couldn't get enough of those Sully story. The interesting part of the Haystack story was Sully's reaction. It had really bothered him for a long time that Haystack treated us like he did. I heard him mention the incident at least once a week, if not more, for the six weeks following the incident in the elevator. Once he felt he had gotten even with Haystack he never mentioned Haystackagain. No hard feelings. Just get even. And he always did. Sully's Revenge.

There were a lot of Sully revenge stories like the Haystack incident, but that was my personal favorite. There were many others however. One especially, comes to mind, and it happened, where else, the Boston Garden. Sully had been working at the Garden, for over a year, selling everything from popcorn to souvenirs. He never talked much about his job. The only time he really opened up about work was to complain. The one person that he always complained about was a guy we called, "Popcorn Charlie." Charlie was in his 60's and he had been selling popcorn, I think, since the Garden opened in 1928. He seemed like a decent enough guy to me, but Sully hated him. Charlie it seems was a real company man and was constantly squealing on other employees who were committing such capital crimes as sitting down to watch a few minutes of the a Celtics or Bruins game. A couple of kids even had the nerve to drink a Coke or to have a box of popcorn. You weren't allowed to eat or drink any of what you were selling, at least when you were on the floor. But most kids would partake of what they were selling when not on the Garden floor. Everyone did it and it was pretty much an accepted practice. But not Charlie. He thought you should be fired for that particular practice and he did, in fact, get a few kids fired for that and for other minor indiscretions. If there was one thing that Sully hated it was a squealer. We were brought up that way. It was just something that you didn't do. Never. Sully would talk about Charlie telling on this guy or that guy but he never squealed on Sully. At least that is what we thought. Charlie didn't like Sully and Sully didn't like Charlie. That was pretty obvious because Sully never hid his disgust for, "Charlie the Canary" as he called him. Then one night Sully got called into his boss' office, and the roof fell His boss had a couple of pages of job related violations that Sully had committed since his first day at the Garden. Charlie had kept a list of things that he saw Sully doing. He never said a word. When he had about twenty violations he gave them to their boss. Sully was fuming. He had been suspended and he was as mad as I had ever seen him in my life. He must have ranted and raved for a half hour about Charlie and what he was going to do to him. Sully never went back to work at the Garden after that. I knew that Charlie's day would come. I just didn't know how or when. I didn't have to wait long to find out.

    We had been to the Garden about a dozen times after Sully was suspended. He was very popular with all the other employees and they kept asking him when he was coming back, every time we went to the Garden. He would always make a snide comment about Charlie every time he was asked about his return. We saw Charlie every time we came into the Garden and Sully just ignored him as if he didn't exist. You could hear Charlie all over the

Brian P. Wallace

Garden when he was selling his popcorn. He would shuffle along with the huge canvass bag, which contained his popcorn, slung over his right shoulder. He also had a very distinct and very loud call. His call never changed one iota. It was always the same,.

"Popcorn, red hot popcorn. Popcorn get your popcorn here." Always the exact same. He would say the word popcorn four times in each yell. He would say the same nine words over and over again.

"Popcorn, red hot popcorn here. Popcorn, get your popcorn here." He also had a very distinctive shuffle as he walked. He was an original. He was an asshole but he was an original asshole. Charlie's day was fast approaching I could see it in Sully's eyes. And like most things Sully did, it came totally from out of the blue when I least expected it. But it most certainly was a classic.

Sully, Knuckles Jimmy Ridge and myself met in the school cafeteria that afternoon and we discussed going over to the Garden right after school. The Celtics were playing the Cincinnati Royals and Oscar Robertson. Oscar was one of the greatest players ever to play the game and we never missed an opportunity to see the Big O when he came to Boston. We were pretty excited and wanted to make sure that there would be no problem sneaking in. Anytime that there was a big event we would go over extra early just to make sure we didn't get caught sneaking in. We almost never did but it was better to be safe than sorry, especially when the Big O was involved. That particular day we went home, changed and were already in the Boston Garden by 4 O'clock. We went around and made sure we had at least three doors open and went to Rocco's Pizza Place to get something to eat. Rocco's Pizza place will always go down in history as the first place we heard a Beatle song. That might not sound like an earth -shattering thing to most people, but it was to us. Feeling pretty good about getting back in to see the Big O and feeling even better about Rocco's pizza, I had no idea that this would be the night that Charlie would regret the rest of his life. We headed back to the Garden about 5 O'clock, which gave us a good hour before the gates actually opened and the general public filed in. We had no problem getting back into the Garden. The doors, which we put our boys club tickets in to keep open, were ready for us when we returned from our fine Italian dining experience. We headed for the ladies room up on the highest level of the building. The ushers, for whatever reason, never checked the ladies rooms when they made their rounds. I never understood why they didn't check the ladies rooms. It was not like there was supposed to be anybody in there. There were no female ushers. It was a little trick that was passed down from my brother's friends to us. So every time we snuck in we made a beeline for the ladies room. We always went to the same one. Other than being stupid those ushers were also very lazy. They weren't about to walk all the way up to the highest reaches of the Garden just to check and see if anyone had snuck in. It was too much work for them and it wasn't worth it. We were as good as gold once we had made it to the sanctity of the ladies room. We knew exactly when the gates would open and we would be out of there long before the first lady had to take care of her business. We were in the ladies room that night as Knuckles had broken out the ever- present deck of cards. We would often pass the time playing whist. As Knuckles began to deal the cards, "Don't deal me in." Sully said uncharacteristically, because Sully loved to play whist. But we never knew what Sully was going to do next so nothing he did or said ever really surprised us. Knuckles stopped in mid deal as Sully started towards the door.

"Where the hell are you going?" I asked.

"I'll be right back," Sully answered.

He was gone for about twenty minutes, which worried us all very much. We were checking our watches then checking the ladies room door constantly. The door finally burst open and in strolled a red faced Sully. He had about five boxes of popcorn and a couple of old Boston Globe's in his hands. He also had about five empty boxes of popcorn, which I didn't see until later. We stared at him as he trampled in and threw the papers and the empty popcorn boxes in a heap on the floor.

"What the hell are you doing?" Knuckles asked, looking at the debris on the floor.

"I'll tell you later." Sully answered. He was, all business now. As if to heighten the suspense he yelled, "Come on. Help me we don't have much time."

"Help you do what?" I asked. Sully was already on the ground tearing up the old Boston Globe papers into little balls. We looked at him, and then looked at each other, still not comprehending a thing he was doing.

"Are you just going to stand there?" he said as if reading our minds I knew Sully well enough to know that he was in one of those crazy moods and he wasn't about to stop and explain to us what he was doing or attempting to do.

"What do you want us to do?" I asked, now resigned to our fate. He blurted out instructions as if he were a Marine drill instructor. With machine precision.

"All right we don't have a lot of time, Brian throw all the popcorn, except for one box, down the toilet."

"What are you crazy?" Ridge jumped in. "I'm starved." I looked at Knuckles and we both laughed.

"Give me at least one box to eat," Ridge pleaded. Sully looked disgusted, but agreed. But you have to help," he said, as he handed Ridge box full of popcorn. Jimmy was fine with that, as he inhaled the free popcorn. I still had no idea what he was up to, or where he had gotten the popcorn. I also knew better than to ask. I looked at him as he gave me my instructions.

"Brian, help me tear this paper up." I did. By 5:50 p.m. we had our work done although we still did not know why. We now had five boxes of what looked like popcorn. In actuality what we had were five boxes, which were filled with shredded paper and topped off with popcorn If you didn't know better, it looked like they were all filled with popcorn. After you ate about thirty pieces of popcorn you would have nothing left in the box except shredded Boston Globe. I now knew that this somehow had something to do with 'Popcorn Charlie' although I didn't know exactly what. I knew that I would find out very shortly. And I did. And I will never forget it. Nor will Charlie.

The doors opened at exactly 6 O'clock and we were in the lobby by 6:05. Sully had the five boxes of fake popcorn hidden as if they contained some toxic material. The Celtics, in those days never sold out so we never had any problem getting seats. We usually found very good seats right near the floor. Not this day however. Sully insisted that we sit in the promenade away from everyone else. I hated those seats, but we obliged Sully. By the time the game had started I had actually forgotten all about the fake popcorn. Sully hadn't.

A Southie Memoir

Oscar Robertson was putting on a show and I was really getting caught up in the game when I heard a familiar sound.

"Popcorn, red hot popcorn. Popcorn get your popcorn here." We all turned in unison, now it was the game, and Oscar Robertson, that I forgot about. We all looked at Sully. And yes, he had that look on his face. Sully was getting ready to do battle, although the enemy had no idea that he was about to be taken down. And yet I still didn't know how or when the attack was going to take place. As Charlie got closer, the tension mounted. Sully had now taken the five boxes out of their hiding- place, under his jacket and was ready to spring into action. Again, we heard.

"Popcorn, red hot popcorn. Popcorn get your popcorn here." Now Charlie had slowly shuffled by us, as he kept up his incessant popcorn chant. He had that huge canvass bag slung over his right shoulder as he shuffled by us Sully knew every move the old popcorn seller made. He knew that when Charlie had a sale in the loge seats he would rest the big canvass popcorn box on the top step, take out two or three boxes, and walk down the stairs until he reached the his customer. It was much easier to do it that way than lugging that big canvass bag all the way down those steep stairs. What could happen? Nothing that anyone could have imagined. It was also why Sully wanted us to sit in the promenade section that night. From where we sat we had a perfect view of all of Charlie's movements. Two aisles over from where we sat, Charlie eyed a sale in the loge section and went to work.

He placed the huge sack on the top stair, reached down and brought out three bags of popcorn, and went down the stairs to collect his money. Sully moved with the speed of a cat. Before anyone knew what had happened Sully was now beside Charlie's canvass popcorn sack, which was left unattended as Charlie made his sale. In one quick motion Sully brought out all five boxes from under his coat and deposited all five in Charlie's popcorn sack. He did it so quickly that if I weren't watching him so closely I never would have known what he did. Having completed his task, he turned around and was back in his seat as if nothing had happened. Actually nothing had happened yet, but it most certainly going to. Charlie trudged back up the loge stairs and in one motion, which he had completed thousands and thousands of times, he hoisted the sack onto his right shoulder and began his chant as he walked

Brian P. Wallace

around the ancient Boston Garden. We watched, as if transfixed, as this ancient popcorn vendor continued to sell his wares. We had completely forgot aboutthe game. Charlie had only walked about fifteen yards before a guy held up two fingersCharlie immediately stopped and reached deep into his bag. We held our breath. The guy paid Charlie and returned to his seat. We now forgot all about Charlie and were focusing on the man who had just purchased the popcorn. He gave one of the two boxes to a guy sitting next to him. They both opened the popcorn and reached in. We knew that the top quarter of the box would be filled with popcorn. We also knew what lay under the top quarter. We waited and waited. False alarm. Now we quickly scanned the Garden to find Charlie, which wasn't too hard. He had only walked about ten yards and hadn't sold anymore popcorn. Again, we watched in anxious anticipation. A well- dressed man in a three- piece suit approached. He said something to Charlie who quickly turned and brought two more boxes out of his bag. The man paid and returned to his seat. Again we watched. The man passed the boxes to a boy who was about six years old and a girl who looked to be about ten years old. The man went back to watching the Celtics as the boy and girl both dug into their popcorn. We had a clear view of the two kids. They reached in almost simultaneously and both brought out handfuls of popcorn. They repeated this process again and again came out with popcorn. The third time the boy looked rather puzzled as he brought out a handful of the BostonGlobe all scrunched up. He just stared at the paper as if too dumbfounded to say anything. He simply stared. He turned to the girl just as she was pulling her hand out of the popcorn box. She too, looked totally puzzled. Instead of popcorn her hand was now filled with dirty old newspaper. The boy began to cry. The girl just stared at the newspaper. The father turned quickly toward his son who was now saying something in between his tears. The father realizing what had happened bolted from his seat. Charlie, oblivious to what had transpired was still walking down the aisle selling his popcorn. The guy reached Charlie and began yelling as he thrust the evidence under Charlie's face. He continued to yell as Charlie, continued to look at the contents of the two popcorn boxes, which were still half filled with paper. Charlie was all apologies and quickly reached into his canvass popcorn bag and brought out two new boxes of popcorn, which he handed over to the fuming gentleman. The crowd, which had been watching the game, was now enthralled with this confrontation taking place before them between Charlie and the irate father.

People were pointing and laughing. Me, Knuckles, and Ridge were laughing our heads off. Sully wasn't laughing at all. He had a smirk but was intent on capturing this entire confrontation for posterity. The well-dressed man accepted the two boxes, which Charlie had offered, and headed back to his seat. His kids were now standing watching the scene, which I kind of felt bad about. Once their father returned however they seemed fine, which made me feel a little better. This however was far from over. The father, feeling justified, handed the two boxes of popcorn to his kids. I just looked at Sully.

"No way." was all I could say. He did not reply. Ridge and Knuckles were still laughing as Charlie had stopped selling and was now intently looking in his canvas bag. Sully and I were still looking at the two kids who were now opening their second boxes of popcorn. The girl had eaten a few handfuls without a hint of a problem. The boy was taking his time. "Another false alarm," Sully said to nobody in particular. Just as Sully said that, the kid pulled out another huge handful of paper. The kid just froze. This time he didn't cry. I think he might have been afraid of his father's reaction. It was the girl, this time, who screamed.

"Dad." she screamed. The father grabbed the bogus popcorn box and ran to where Charlie was busy inspecting the rest of his popcorn stash. He was on Charlie in an instant. This time an apology would not suffice. This guy was pissed. We ran to be closer to the scene. Charlie was speechless as the guy demanded his money back. I heard Charlie. "I'm so sorry but this has never happened before." He had obviously never pissed Sully off before. The guy wasn't buying any of it. He was screaming at Charlie, who was frantically reaching in to his money pouch to give the man his money. Charlie kept saying how sorry he was over and over again.

"Don't apologize to me, apologize to them" the screaming father said as he thrust his kids in front of Charlie. The crowd had now totally forgotten about the basketball game. All eyes and ears were now on Charlie and the disgruntled father. The guy was really going after Charlie and Sully loved every minute of it.

"What kind of circus are you running here?" the guy screamed.

"You haven't heard the last of me," he said grabbing the money out of Charlie's hand and going back to his seat. Charlie was in shock. He just stood there without saying a word. People were pointing and laughing, but Charlie was in his own world. After a minute, or two, he picked up his bag and started his chant once again. We followed. We stayed far enough away but close enough to see his next sale. The next two sales were uneventful and Charlie probably thought the bogus popcorn boxes were just a fluke. A hand went up again in the loge section and Charlie, now back on his game, responded as he had done thousands and thousands of times before. This guy who looked like a wrestler ordered four boxes. He had a guy sitting beside him who made him look small. These guys were huge. It looked to me like they were getting two boxes apiece. Sully and I just looked at each other. No words were necessary. Charlie got the money and proceeded on his way. My vision was blocked so I didn't have a clear view of the behemoths as they opened their popcorn. I didn't need to. In a matter of minutes they both were up and out of their seats and chasing Charlie down the Garden walkway. The crowd, once again, started to murmur as the two giants got closer to 'Popcorn Charlie.' You could feel the fury as they tracked down the old popcorn man. They had the incriminating evidence in their hands. Each had a box, which had been stuffed with paper. They were livid. The guy, who bought the popcorn originally, reached Charlie first. He tapped Charlie on the back. As Charlie turned the guy put the bogus popcorn box right in his face.

Is this some kind of sick joke?" he screamed in Charlie's face. "If it is, I don't think it's too funny," he continued to yell.

"This is great," Sully said. Charlie was now totally flustered. The guy was still screaming at him but I'm not sure he even heard them. He was in shock. He, once again, reached into his pouch and gave them back their money. He had probably not given anyone back their money in thirty years and now he had done it twice within fifteen minutes. The guys took their money. They also took two bags to replace the bogus ones. Charlie just looked as they reached into his bag and produced two fresh bags. I know that was a first. Charlie had never let anybody into his bag. He was defeated however and he looked as if they could have taken his entire stock as well as the money in his money pouch. The crowd was really enjoying this sideshow at Charlie's expense. That was it for Charlie. He had enough. He picked up his bag canvass bag and headed toward the concession office. His face was chalk white and his walk a little slower, if that were possible. Sully's revenge came in all forms and shapes and tastes. This certainly was one of the most memorable. Unbelievable. Payback is a bitch.

"I would love to be a fly on the wall in that room," I said to Knuckles.

"Well let's fly," Sully said, already heading for the concession's office.

"Now I know he's crazy," I said to Knuckles.

"Yeah but he's certainly not boring," was Knuckles reply. I had no idea how he was going to pull this one off. I should have known, however, that he had already had a plan and a contingency plan. We all walked into the world of hot dogs, cokes, popcorn and peanuts that is the Boston Garden concessions office. It was a madhouse with kids running in to get their supplies replenished, and kids running out to sell their wares. We were very conspicuous, being the only ones not in uniform. We could hear Charlie even before we entered the room. He was cursing and yelling about a conspiracy and never being so embarrassed and a whole litany of things There were, however, smiles all around from his co- workers who hated his guts for getting so many of them suspended or fired. That was what we entered into. It was actually a couple of minutes before anyone realized that we were even in the room. They were so caught up with Charlie's lunatic ramblings that they never even saw us standing in the back of the room. Finally, Sully's old boss spotted us.

"Sully what the hell do you want?" he barked.

"My friends are looking for a job," he said, which totally surprised the three of us.

"Not now Sully, can't you see we're pretty busy?" "

"Forget it then we'll go over to the Arena," Sully said nonchalantly as he headed for the door. The Boston Arena was a competitor of the Garden and Sully knew that this guy hated the people at the Arena. He knew exactly what buttons to push. And it worked.

"All right all right," the boss said, "Fill out those forms but do it quietly and in that corner." He handed each of us a single sheet of paper and headed over to where Charlie was still screaming.

"You are unreal," I said to Sully, as we headed over to fill out the work forms.

The place was a zoo, and Charlie only added to that atmosphere. The boss had left us, and was now trying to slow Charlie down so that he could understand what had happened.

"I'm not selling any more popcorn," Charlie said loudly.

"What's wrong Charlie?" the boss said to his most productive employee. Charlie went on to explain everything that we had witnessed in the Garden.

"But, that's impossible," his boss said. "Charlie you know yourself that we inspect every box before it goes in the bag."

"Of course I know but I also know what happened to me out on the floor." "I'm not going crazy." And in an attempt to prove his sanity he did a very crazy thing. We were still in the corner. At least three of us were. Sully had disappeared. Charlie picked up the huge bag and dumped all of its contents on the floor. About forty bags of popcorn now lay in a pile at Charlie's feet. He began to open each one. He would open the box and pour its contents onto the floor. He was waiting for a box full of paper to be emptied on the floor. It didn't happen. There was a huge mound of popcorn on the floor when he had emptied the final box. The boss was livid. He tried to control his voice, but it didn't work.

"You will pick up every single kernel off that floor and if I hear any more talk about popcorn boxes filled with paper you will be suspended." Everyone in the room, except Charlie and the boss were smiling. Charlie was even more dumbfounded now than he was earlier on the floor. He began the cleanup amid smirks and catcalls. Sully had returned.

"You missed it," I said.

"I saw it he smiled "I was in the other room." Sully smiled. The boss came over to where we were finishing our applications.

"You ready to come back to work now?" he said to Sully, who might have been a wise guy but he was one of the best sellers in the place and Festa's replacement knew it.

"Not while you have maniacs like him, here," he said pointing to Charlie, who was on his knees picking up the pieces of popcorn. The boss just shook his head and took our applications.

"It seems you're friends want to work here even if you don't," he said looking directly at Sully. He took my application first.

"OK. Let's see, you're Mr. Park? Mr. Thomas Park?"

"Yes I said." I could hear Sully laugh but I kept a very straight face. This guy was weird. He had the other two applications in his hands as he put mine on the table. He looked at one of the two applications.

"And which of you is Ivan Paul Daly."

"I am," said Knuckles. But everyone just calls me I.P." Sully was busting a gut behind his old boss. The boss, who wasn't getting any of it, looked at Ridge.

"Then you must be Mr. Gun?"

"Yes sir, said Ridge, "Raymond Gun." Now most of the employees were trying to hide Their own laughter. A couple of them ran out after Mr. I.P. Daly. The boss didn't have a clue. Thomas Park, I.P Daly and Ray Gun. Talk about aliases. I thought for sure that he would catch on but he didn't.

"OK we'll call you if we have an opening." he said, as we were walking out the door we had to pass by Charlie who was still on his hands and knees.

"You're not going to hire my friends? And you're going to keep this crazy old broken down dime dropper," Sully said, looking at Charlie.

"Cuckoo, cuckoo," Ridge sang as he walked by.

"Screw you," Charlie spat out giving Sully a dirty look. We all burst out laughing as we exited the room.

"Can I get a box of paper popcorn Charlie?" Sully asked. "Paper, get your red hot paper. Paper right here," he said imitating Charlie perfectly. The whole room, even the boss cracked up.

"You probably had something to do with it fatso," Charlie said to Sully. I could see Sully was enraged.

"I didn't have something to do with it, you old asshole. I had everything to do with it. I planned it and I pulled it off to a T. How does it feel? Maybe you should treat people better and not trying to get them fired," Sully said, going in for the kill. He started out and then turned back.

"And if I ever find out you finked on even one of my friends, they will bury you in that popcorn bag." Sully was done and so was Charlie. You could hear cheering all the way down to the corridor.

"I.P. Daly?" I said to Knuckles, "Where did you come up with that one?" He was laughing too hard to answer.

Chapter 13 – Sully's Revenge

Sully's revenge came in all forms and in many different locations. I never knew when it would appear. When it did it was short, to the point and always achieved the desired effect. I knew that there were a few people, when we were growing up that Sully really disliked. They weren't many, which is kind of surprising given the fact that he was always pissing someone off. Oddly enough, most people did get a kick out of Sully. Most, not all. One of the kids that Sully really despised was a kid named Johnny Britt and the feeling was very mutual. They were like oil and water. Johnny hung with us down E street. I got along with him, but for whatever reason Sully couldn't stand to even be in his presence. Johnny had one of those hairdo's which stood up in a DA (Duck's Ass) with the help of about 2 pounds of grease. He had a cousin who hung with us as well. His name was Paul Kersanskas, we called him PK. Sully hated PK a little bit less than he hated Johnny. Might as well keep it in the family, I guess. We were sitting on the Boys Club steps one very hot July day. The year was 1962 and we were waiting for the 3 o'clock swim. It was only about 2 o'clock, so we had some time to kill and we were very good at doing that. Sully was harassing the usual suspects more out of boredom than animosity, when I spotted a kid named Paul Moore slowly walking up West 6th street toward the Club. Paul Moore was perhaps the toughest kid in Southie and that included some pretty tough kids. He was my age, which at that time was 12. His father was a professional boxer. His ring name was Porky Moore. Paul and both of his brothers were boxers as well. His older brother Jimmy had inherited his father's nickname. The Moore brothers could have posed for a body- sculpturing magazine, if there was such a thing back then, especially Paul. He looked as if he was cut from a block of granite and he worked out twice a day, every day, for a couple of hours each session.

    I always got along great with all the Moore brothers, Porky, Paul and their younger brother Billy, who probably could have been the best boxer of the whole crew. He didn't have Paul's discipline however but he certainly had the talent. Paul loved to play basketball but he had too many muscles. If that sound strange it really isn't. His muscles were so tight that it restricted his range of motion. He played all the time and actually made himself a pretty good player as he got into his teenage years. I think that is why we always got along so well. He was always asking me questions about basketball. And I always answered every one carefully and diplomatically. He was a good kid, most of the time. I had, however, seen the other side of Paul Moore, and it is a day I will never forget. To say Mooreso, which was one of his nick-names, had a temper would be like saying the Beatles had a few hits. He didn't get mad, he exploded. And when Paul Moore exploded you really didn't want to be anywhere near him. As I mentioned I had only seen that side of him once but I had heard stories about his explosions and I believed every one. Paul was tough but he was no Rhodes Scholar. He wasn't stupid, comparatively speaking, he just like to hit people more than he liked to hit the books. He and Sully had a strange relationship. There were kind of standoffish to each other. They respected each other but weren't what I'd call friendly. Sully was always very careful around Mooreso, for good reason, and this particular lazy summer day was no different. I said to Sully.

"Uh oh here comes Mooreso, he's really getting fat." It was obviously said in jest. I forgot who I was talking to.

"I'm telling him what you said," Sully said in a very serious tone. I almost died. I probably could have gotten away with saying a lot of things to Mooreso, but that wasn't one of them, and Sully knew it.

"I was only kidding" I said panic-stricken.

Saying Mooreso was getting fat, looked a little heavy or looked out of shape was not something you said in his presence, not if you wanted to see your next birthday. But I never knew when Sully was kidding. This time, thank God, he was. Now Mooreso and his buddy Louie Sasso had reached the bottom of the Club stairs.

"Hey, Mooreso, how ya doing?" Sully intoned.

"Good as long as you're not around" Mooreso replied. Everyone laughed. If Paul Moore said anything even remotely funny, you laughed. It's called being street smart. He and Louie began to climb the stairs.

"No I mean it," Sully said. "Are you all right?" Sully's voice had taken on a very caring tone, but he was still traveling on very shaky territory. I had no idea what he was up to.

Mooreso looked kind of funny at Sully. "Have you've been in the sun to long." Again everybody laughed. "Why don't you go take a jump in the pool," Mooreso said without a smile. Now Mooreso had risen to the same step that Sully was standing on and was about a head over Sully.

"I will as soon as 3 o'clock comes around," Sully smiled. Mooreso kept walking. "I thought you would look a lot worse than you do, actually," Sully kind of laughed. Mooreso stopped dead in his tracks and turned, now a couple of heads over Sully, he looked down.

"What are you babbling about now Chubby?" he asked.

"Oh nothing," Sully said as turned away. I still had no idea what he was doing. It's funny how some things remain in your memory long after more important things have long vanished.

This is one of those times. I remember the St. Augustine's bell chiming out its' 3 o'clock declaration as Mooreso's face started to turn red, which wasn't a good sign.

"Forget what?" he barked. He's gone too far this time, I thought. Nobody moved toward the swimming pool although it was 3 o'clock. Actually nobody moved, except Mooreso, who took a threatening step toward Sully.

"I was just walking by Billy the Tailor's," Sully began as everyone on the steps strained to hear. "And I was talking to Johnny Britt." He stopped, heightening the suspense as only he could do. Mooreso just stared. Mooreso was waiting like everyone else for the rest of the story. Sully waited. I knew that Sully and Johnny Britt hadn't talked in over a year but I didn't know where he was heading.

"So you talked to Britt? What do you want a medal or a chest to pin it on?" Mooreso said and he waited for everyone to laugh. We did. Street smarts, remember. A couple of kids headed to the pool, thinking that this was just a false alarm. I knew better. Sully didn't do false alarms. The last false alarm he pulled was when I was six years of age with a smoke bomb.

"I just didn't want to embarrass you in front of all these kids," Sully said. Uh oh. If fat was one word you didn't use when talking about Mooreso, embarrass was another, especially with him standing three feet from you. The migration to the pool stopped dead in their tracks, and everyone turned around.

Brian P. Wallace

"You've got a lot of balls Sully, but not to many brains," Mooreso steamed. Silence. Sully acting scared, the optimum word here is acting.

"Johnny Britt told me that he kicked your ass last night down D Street and I thought you were hurt pretty bad, that's why I asked you if you were all right, that's all. You don't have to get pissed at me" Sully sulked. Everyone, especially Mooreso stared but nobody said anything. Sully had set the hook, now he was taking his time reeling it in.

"Johnny Britt said what?" Mooreso asked said in amazement. Sully repeated the story only this time he slowed it down considerably, for effect. This time he told the story more emphatically, almost as if he had witnessed it himself. And he added to the story, he said.

"Personally I didn't think Johnny Britt could kick your ass." Mooreso interrupted, as Sully said the word 'ass'. The veins in Mooreso's head were now showing and his face was a deep red color. He actually began to shake.

Many years later I watched a TV show called the Hulk in which Bill Bixby turned into this enraged monster, called The Hulk, when provoked. They might have based that character on Mooreso that afternoon on the Club's stairs. Sully had reeled him in.

"Where is he?" was all Mooreso could manage to say. Nobody said a word. He repeated himself, only this time he yelled.

"Where is he?" Sully, now nice as pie, said I saw him down E street about 40 minutes ago. That was all Mooreso needed. He started walking down West 6th street toward E street, which was only a block away. Everyone who was waiting to go swimming had now eschewed those plans and was now following Mooreso. All except Sully and me. (Good title for a book, huh). Undaunted, Sully waited until the entourage had disappeared, turned and headed to the pool. I did the same.

"The pool won't be too crowded today," he laughed as we were getting our towels. I looked at him. "What the hell was that all about? Mooreso is going to kill him." He smiled.

"I know," was all he said.

"Are you crazy," I said, " Mooreso might really kill him, dead." He looked me right between the eyes.

"Yesterday when my mother was coming home with some shopping bags Johnny Britt gave her a real hard time, and I can't let him get away with that." He was as serious as a heart attack. I was still a little dumbfounded. "But you could have gone after Britt, why didn't you just kick his ass yourself?" I asked. "Sure I could kick his ass" he said, smiling for the first time "But nowhere near as good Mooreso is going to kick has ass." "I don't feel one bit sorry for Britt, he's a real jerk" he finished. I wasn't.

"When did you plan all this?" I asked.

"Actually," he said, "I was going to go after Britt myself, but when I saw Mooreso the idea just popped into my head." "Britt is just going to deny he said it," I continued. Sully just laughed.

"You saw Mooreso when he left the stairs, Britt ain't going to have time to say anything." We both headed down the ramp towards the deserted pool. Sully in that split second had choreographed this whole scene and had played Mooreso like a fiddle. To this day I never knew what Johnny Britt said to Sully's mother, if anything. I do know, however, that Johnny Britt did get a beating from Mooreso. And I do know that Sully was exactly right, Mooreso never gave Britt time to deny the charges. Mooreso pummeled Britt in a matter of minutes. Sully's motto.' don't get mad get even.' And he did much to the dismay of one John Britt.

About 25 years after that incident I walked into the Quietman Pub in South Boston and saw Johnny Britt sitting at the end of the bar. I hadn't seen him in over 20 years and those years didn't treat Johnny any better than Mooreso had done that day He looked terrible. Actually I didn't even recognize him at first. I actually recognized the voice, before I recognized the face. I bought him a couple of beers and we talked about the old days. But, unbeknownst to Britt I did have an ulterior motive. Not that he would care as long as I was buying him beers. After the fourth beer I started talking about tough kids in Southie.

"Paul Moore was probably the toughest of them all," I said slyly.

"Tell me about it." was all he said in between gulps of his free beer.

"Oh, that's right you fought Mooreseo one time," I said, feigning ignorance He gave a weird little laugh.

"I never fought Mooreso, I never had a chance. He just kicked my ass." Here came thequestion which I had been contemplating for over 25 years.

Why did Mooreso do a job on you?" He looked at me through half seeing eyes.

"How the hell should I know, you know Mooreso, Brian, he was just crazy." He never knew that his old nemesis Sully was behind the mysterious beating. Never even suspected it.

"Whatever happened to Mooreso" he asked?

"He's in jail," I said realizing how easy it was to say, because so many of the kids we grew up with, were, in fact either in jail or dead.

"Good," he said, smiling now, for the very first time and exposing a mouthful of broken, cracked or missing teeth. He was staring to get a little tipsy. I had no idea how long he had been in the bar before I arrived.

"Ya know, he said "I hope Mooreso gets his ass kicked in the joint." I smile.

"He might but I kind of doubt it." And out of the clear blue.

"By the way, what ever happened to your fat little friend Sully?" I embellished a little bit and enjoyed it more than I figured I would.

"Oh, Sully's doing all right, he's one of the top men in the Edison, he's making over a hundred grand," I said. His mouth dropped when he heard Sully's salary.

"No shit," he said. Then a smile lit up his face.

"Well good for him that fat little shit." I had to laugh.

"Do you see him at all" he asked.

"Yeah, a couple of times a year," I said.

"Well the next time you see him tell him Johnny Britt was asking for him. I couldn't wait.

"What if I see Mooreso?" I teased. "What do you want me to tell him?" He gave me a funny look.

"Tell him I'm dead." We both laughed. I guess the old saying is true, "Time heals all wounds." Someone, a few years later told me that Johnny Britt died from a heroin overdose. I was sad but not very surprised. His cousin PK has turned into a street person. I see him every once in a while picking up cans or bottles. He used to ask me for change but I don't think he even recognizes me anymore, which is fine with me. Mooreso just got out of jail, He was one of Whitey Bulger's top guys. He went into the Federal Witness protection Program, for a few years but returned to South Boston after all the dirt came out on Whitey. It's funny how life turns out.

Brian P. Wallace

Chapter 14 – Sully vs. Mooreso

About 6 years after the Johnny Britt incident Sully and Mooreso hooked up again. We were all playing Park League football for a team called the South Boston Monks. We had a pretty good team and we were tied for first place with a team from the Neponset section of Dorchester. I played halfback, Sully played one end and Mooreso and Paul Carter alternated at the other end. We had just beaten a very good O'Brien Club, the defending champs, and we were down Columbia Park the next night for practice, which happened to be Monday night. During the O'Brien Club game, the day before, our quarterback Boob Elliott threw a perfect 30 yard strike, to Mooreso, who had beaten his man, in the end zone, Mooreso let the ball hit his pads, rather than his hands, and the ball fell harmlessly to the ground. No catch, no touchdown. Nobody said a word, of course. Luckily we went on to win, and everybody forgot the missed catch. Well, almost everybody. As we were changing into our equipment that Monday night at practice, Sully began to imitate Mooreso dropping the ball in the end zone. Dangerous move! Sully was throwing the football high in the air and saying, as an announcer would yell. "Ladies and gentlemen, Paul Moore is all alone in the end zone, it looks like a sure touchdown." And when the ball would come down Sully would drop it.

"Oh no, Paul Moore drops a sure touchdown pass, I can't believe it." Believe me I couldn't believe it either. Nor could anyone else. Everyone looked to where Mooreso was dressing. He said nothing, so Sully did it again. This time as the ball was coming down Sully made an exaggerated try for the ball before falling on his face.

"Oh no Mooreso misses it again," he yelled as he hit the ground. Everyone was stunned. Our coach, a guy named Peaches Flynn, who would later run for the United States Congress against Joe Moakley, was uncharacteristically late for practice that night. Mooreso had just put his cleats on and looked over to where Sully was still lying on the ground.

"Don't do it again Sully," he said, quite emphatically. I felt kind of relieved and I thought, Sully, now that he had Mooreso's attention, wouldn't do it again. Sully got up, dusted himself off, went over to get a drink and everyone just relaxed, figuring it was over and that Sully had lucked out. All of a sudden, in a voice that could be heard for a couple of city blocks.

"Ladies and gentlemen, Boob Elliott back to pass, he sees Paul Moore all alone in the end zone, Elliott throws," And with that Sully threw the football high in the air, and began to mimic an announcer once again.

"Moore is wide open it looks like a sure touchdown,. As the ball got to his hands he yells. "But oh no Paul Moore drops it again."

Now you could hear a pin drop. All of us knew what Paul Moore was capable of doing. All eyes turned quickly to Mooreso, who was watching this whole scene with his helmet in his right hand. Sully was still on the ground. Mooreso didn't move.

"OK Sully you've had your fun, and if you say one more word I'm going to knock you out." Paul Moore turned his back and started to walk away. Good I thought, he's in a pretty good mood. Sully, for sure, would stop antagonizing him now. Antagonizing Paul Moore. It evens sounds weird. Nobody in their right mind would antagonize Paul Moore. Sully got up slowly and walked over to our equipment bag, he reached in and brought out a new football. I had my back turned away from Sully because I was watching Mooreso. Unbeknownst to me Sully had already thrown the ball high into the air.

"Ladies and gentlemen Paul Moore is wide open in the end zone." I couldn't believe it. What the hell was he doing? Mooreso obviously couldn't believe it either. He just stood there for a second, and then he charged. The ball was still in the air as Mooreso reached Sully. At the very last second Sully stepped back and put out his foot. It was too quick for Mooreso to react and he went head over heels onto the ground. There was a gasp from all of us watching this proceeding. Sully was like a cat. As soon as Mooreso hit the ground Sully was on top of him. He had Mooreso pinned to the ground and he had him pinned pretty good. Mooreso couldn't do anything, which further infuriated him. The harder he tried to get up the more pressure Sully exerted. We were all dumbfounded as we watched this scene play out. "Let me up Sully," Mooreso yelled. Now I knew Sully was crazy but he wasn't stupid.

"Take it easy Mooreso, I was only fooling," he said, as Mooreso further attempted to free himself in a fight. It was probably the first time in his life that he was on the ground in a fight. He looked bewildered.

"I'll let you up if you'll just calm down," Sully said. I couldn't believe this.

"I'm going to kick your ass when I get up," Mooreso yelled.

"If that's your attitude then you just won't get up," Sully yelled back. Someone started to laugh and it became infectious. I mean the scene was right out of the twilight zone. Our laughing made Mooreso even more mad, if that was possible. He was now so mad he couldn't even think straight.

"What the hell is going on here?" we heard our coach yell as he moved to separate the two combatants. Peaches Flynn was about 6'4" and 230 pounds. He lifted Sully off Mooreso like he weighed nothing at all.

"That's enough," he yelled. "Now I don't know who started this but I know it ends right here, do you hear me?" I had never seen Mooreso so mad. He wouldn't even look at Peaches.

"We have a championship game this Sunday and we don't need any fighting amongst ourselves," Peaches went on.

"I'm sorry coach," Sully said, "I was only kidding with Mooreso and he went crazy, you know how he is."

"What do you have to say Paul?" our coach asked.

"I have nothing to say," Mooreso said, "But I am going to kill him.

"Not tonight, and not here, you're not," Peaches shot right back.

"If you two want to fight after Sunday's game that is your business, but if you fight any time before Sunday, then neither one of you will play in the Championship game," he looked at Sully and then at Mooreso.

"Do you understand?" he asked. Sully quickly nodded his head, Mooreso didn't. Peaches waited and he asked Mooreso again.

"It's up to you Paul, either shake hands or give me your uniform." Mooreso wanted to kick Sully's ass but he wanted that championship a lot more. He shook Sully's hand.

"Good now let's get some practice in while we still have some light," Peaches yelled and turned his back on both Sully and Mooreso. Sully quickly ran beside Peaches. I told you he wasn't stupid.

We beat Neponset that next Sunday for the League Title. Mooreso had the best game of his career. He caught 5 passes and 1 was for a touchdown. Every time Mooreso caught a pass the first person over to help him up was, you guessed it, Sully. After the game we were all in a pretty good mood, especially Paul Moore who really played well. Everyone was hugging each other and drinking champagne like we had seen the pros do on TV. Sully made his way over to Mooreso's locker and put out his hand. Mooreso hesitated but finally shook Sully's hand. I breathed a lot easier. Sully was incredible. He knew that everyone in that locker room was watching, as he approached Mooreso. Knowing Mooreso, I really didn't know if he was going to shake Sully's hand or kick his ass. As soon as they shook, Sully turned to face the rest of the team.

"He's lucky he shook or I was going to kick his ass again." I couldn't believe it. Everyone just looked, and a couple of players started laughing, thank God. Pretty soon the whole locker room, including Mooreso, was laughing. Sully had pulled it off. On the way home that night he said, "Mooreso's a piece of cake, I knew I could kick his ass." But even he couldn't keep a straight face on that one. We both laughed and held onto our trophies. A couple of years later, we were having a few beers down the square when the fight with Mooreso came up.

"Why did you want to get him mad?" Boob asked. Sully got real serious.

"At first I was only kidding and I was only going to do it once, but he never said anything so I kept doing it."

"But why did you do it even after he told you to stop?" Knuckles asked. Sully laughed that wretched laugh that always hid a secret.

"The last time I did it, I saw Peaches car pull up and I knew he wouldn't let us fight.

"But what if he didn't get there as quick as he did?" I asked.

"Well I guess I would have just had to keep kicking his ass all over the Park," a brazen Sully replied. Maury turned around just then, said, "Speaking of the devil, here comes Mooreso." Sully almost had a heart attack. Maury got him and we all had a laugh at his expense for once. But the legend lived on, the only man ever to beat Paul Moore.

Brian P. Wallace

Chapter 15 – What's The Holdup?

As I mentioned earlier Sully's revenge came in all sizes, shapes and forms. Nobody was excluded, if he felt you had done something to discredit, disturb, dismay or upset him, you had better be prepared for his wrath. I never knew when it was going to appear. There were times when I was sure that a certain person was going to feel that wrath but Sully would laugh and just walk away. Other times, little things would set him off and the next thing I knew I was embroiled in the middle of a confrontation. Again, a good motto was, "Never expect anything but always be prepared for the unexpected." I cannot think of a better example of that, than a hot summer day in the summer of 1966. Sully and I were both working that summer. I was working for the City of Boston and Sully was working for his Uncle. His uncle was the unofficial sawdust king of Boston. He made Sully look tame by comparison and was a legend in South Boston I met Sully one hot summer day for lunch. Lunch was a tuna spuckie from Pete's and a bottle of tonic. We both had received our pay-checks and were going to go to the South Boston Savings Bank after our gourmet lunch, and cash the checks. He was in a very good mood that afternoon as we headed up Broadway to the Bank. He didn't stay in a good mood for very long.

The Southie Savings Bank was by far the most popular Bank in the community. That Friday It seemed like the entire community had decided to do their banking business at the same time. The place was jammed. To make matters even worse the air conditioner was not working that steamy afternoon, and tempers were beginning to rise with the temperature. It was a circus. We only had about 25 minutes to cash our checks and get back to work so we decided to wait in line and brave the crowds and the heat. We headed for the shortest line, which was an oxymoron, in this case. We knew all the girls who worked at the bank and they were really sweating and didn't look too happy. We took our place at the back of the line and decided to make the best of a bad situation. We were probably about 18th in line. Within a minute a guy, wearing a 3-piece suit fell in line directly behind us. Right away he started bitching and moaning.

A Southie Memoir

"This is totally ridiculous," he said, A minute later he said, "I'll never come back to this bank." And he kept it up. "I can't believe the air conditioning isn't working," he said loud enough for half the bank to hear him. The guy was a real pain in the ass. Worse he had on a 3- piece suit, which for some reason, to Sully, is like a red flag to a bull. I don't know why or what precipitated this behavioral pattern, but it was a definite pattern. Sully just didn't like guys with 3 piece suits. Maybe it had something to do with his childhood, I don't know. But, I had seen him react to 3- piece suit wearing dudes in very strange and inexplicable ways many times before. I could see Sully getting very upset with this guy's constant bellyaching. Sully didn't say anything but he didn't have to. His face was getting redder by the minute and it had nothing to do with the oppressive heat. But, it did have everything to do with the guy who was standing directly behind us. He kept it u.

"You gotta be kidding me, why don't they open more teller windows," he said, again loud enough to be heard a block away. The line was moving extremely slow but this guy was getting way out of line. Another five minutes went by and we were about 10th in line.

"Come on will ya, some of us have places to go today," he shouted at a teller, who was a very close friend of ours. Now Sully was boiling mad. He still had not said a word to the well- dressed man. He hadn't even turned around to look at him. Then the man said something that he will probably regret for the rest of his life. It would have gone unnoticed by anybody else, but Sully was not just anybody else.

The guy said, again in a loud voice, "What is the holdup?"

As soon as he said it, Sully reacted. He raised both hands high in the air over his head and screamed, "HOLD UP." He quickly dropped his hands and began pointing directly at the bewildered 3- piece suit, who seemed to have no idea what was going on.

Sully screamed at the top of his lungs, "This guy is holding up the bank." When people heard the word holdup, they began to run for the exits, which really created a panic situation. Some people still weren't sure what was going on and stayed in line, but, not for long. Sully pointed directly at the guy and literally yelled, "help this guy is holding up the bank." The guy froze, as people now began to run out of the bank and the tellers simply walked away from their windows.

"No no," the guy pleaded "I just said what is the holdup." But Sully was on his game. As soon as the guy said the word holdup, Sully jumped on the ground, on his belly with his hands outstretched and began yelling.

"Holdup, hold up please don't hurt me." The more the guy tried to explain the louder Sully yelled and every time he tried to explain that he had just said, "What's the holdup," Sully would focus on the word holdup and yell.

"He said it again. He said holdup." It was incredible. The bank was now nearly empty as two Boston police officers, with guns drawn, had the guy against the wall, legs spread and searching him for a weapon. I watched this whole thing develop and I couldn't believe how Sully had manipulated this incredible scene by using just 3 words, "He said holdup." The cops were all over the guy. They didn't know. They saw everybody run from the bank yelling, "There's a holdup." They then saw Sully laying on the floor and pointing to this guy. What would you think? The guy wasn't complaining anymore about the air conditioner or the size of the lines, at least. He was trying his best to explain what happened, but he wasn't really sure himself what happened. By now, the Bank was full of Boston police officers who got a call that the Bank was in the process of being robbed. As they pulled up they saw everyone running out of the front door, and as they entered the Bank they saw two fellow cops with this guy up against the wall. They thought it was the real McCoy. After about five minutes they realized that this guy was no John Dillinger. The Bank President, Alfred Archibald, had come running over to where the police were interrogating the guy. He looked rather disheveled and worried. The South Boston Savings Bank, in its' 50 year history had never been robbed, and Archibald was duly concerned. He needn't have been, but he didn't know Sully. He talked for a few minutes with the police and walked away. As he was walking by us he motioned to the tellers to get back to their windows, which they quickly did. And guess who was first in line? The police had now escorted the 3- piece suit guy out of the Bank and into his car. He never did cash his check. I seriously doubt if he ever returned to the bank. I know I wouldn't have. We had already cashed our checks and were outside the bank when the cops and the guy came out. His face was ashen and he fumbled with the keys of his car as everyone pointed to him as the robber. I wonder what the guy thought as he drove away. More importantly, I wonder if he ever told anyone the story. Hey guess what I was in a bank today and...

"Oh, never mind you wouldn't believe it anyway." It all happened so quick. It was, again, vintage Sully. I told you he hated 3 piece suits. It was, however, one of those incidents that I think about from time to time. He had no way to plan something like this. He just reacted to a situation. And he reacted that way because the guy was a real jerk, who paid in the end for his loud and obnoxious actions.

As the police were starting to disperse, Sully went over to one of the cops. and "What happened?" he asked. The cop, wiping sweat off his face, said, "just a false alarm, everyone thought some guy was robbing the bank."

"Was he?" Sully asked.

"That's the strange part," the cop said, "Nobody seems to know why they thought he was robbing the bank."

"I thought I saw a gun," Sully said acting real concerned.

"Where?" the cop asked, concerned.

"Inside the Bank," Sully said as the cop got out of his car.

"Maybe he ditched it," Sully said. Now the cop was out of the car and heading back into the bank.

"Let's get the hell out of here, before they find out what really happened." I said to Sully.

"No way," Sully laughed as a group of police officers re-entered the bank. I pulled him down Broadway.

"Haven't you done enough for one day?" I asked. He had almost caused a riot. He almost had a guy arrested for bank robbery, all in the space of five minutes and he wasn't satisfied yet. He laughed and we walked down Broadway, and back to work. Just another lunch hour with Sully.

Chapter 16 – Beware of Blazing Salads

It could happen as quickly as it did that day in the bank, or it could be something that he had thought for a long time, like Haystack, but you never knew. One thing I do know, however, is that he never changed. About 15 years after the hold up incident in the South Boston Savings Bank, we were in Blazing Salads in Quincy Center. We had just finished playing racquetball in Randy Vataha's Club in Braintree and were looking to have a light lunch. Sully had beaten me pretty good in racquetball and he was in a very good mood. Actually he was an excellent racquetball player. It was just that most people flat out refused to get into a confined space with him while he had a racquet in his hand. He couldn't wait to tell Ricky Calnan that he had beaten me. He was married and living in Braintree at the time. I was working at the State House. He looked really good. He had dropped about 40 pounds and was in the best shape of his life. We were looking for anything, other than McDonalds, when we agreed on Blazing Salads. He was really rubbing it in all the way from the racquetball club. I was glad to get out of the car. It was about 12:30 in the afternoon and the place was packed. We weren't in any hurry since we had both taken the afternoon off, so we settled in at the end of a long line and began our wait. I could see that it was going to be a longer wait than I thought. He started right away.

"What were the scores of the games?" Like he hadn't memorized them! Then he started asking total strangers to ask me if I had ever played racquetball before and stuff like that. He was having a ball at my expense. It was harmless stuff and everybody in line was laughing. Sully said to a girl who was in the opposite line.

"Excuse me, which one of us looks like an athlete to you?" The girl just laughed. He was having fun, at my expense, and he loved it. As we got closer to the front of the line we heard this guy, who was obviously the store manager, and guess what he had on? A 3- piece suit. This guy was a bigger jerk than the guy in the bank. He was bossing people around, yelling at the kids, who were making the salads, and just making life miserable for everybody.

"What's his problem?" Sully asked me.

"I think he's just an asshole," I said as we got closer to the front of the line. There was a young girl, about 18 or 19 years old, who was three places ahead of us. When she got to the front of the line the manager was there to wait on her.

"What do you want?" he said, in a very fresh manner. The girl said "I'm thinking," and she continued to look at the daily specials. He waited about 30 seconds.

"I don't have all day lady." Sully looked at me, but didn't say anything. The girl was a little flustered.

"I'm sorry," she said.

"You're sorry" he said, "That makes two of us." Sully was now getting really mad.

"I hope he says something to me I'll punch the shit out of that little jerk." The girl ordered her salad and left. When it was our turn, there was no confrontation. Sully did ask him if he were the manager. He said he was, and that was it, or so I thought We got our salads and looked around for a place to sit. No luck. The place was really crowded so we decided to go to Sully's new house, which was only 5 minutes from Braintree Center. And we almost made it. As we were coming out of the store a car was just pulling out of its' space which was directly in front of Blazing Salads. Now anyone who has ever lived in the city knows how rare a good parking spot is in any downtown location. This was prime real estate. We watched as two cars competed for the one space. One driver felt the quickest way to get into the space was by putting his car in reverse and speeding in backwards. The other driver felt he would be better served by pulling in frontwards. They both had the right idea but terrible timing. The other car whacked the car going in reverse. Both drivers jumped out of their cars and began swearing at each other. to put it mildly. Their screaming and swearing began to draw a crowd of curious on-lookers. We were still only a couple of feet from the Blazing Salad's door. We, like everybody else, were watching these two guys go at it. Sully's eyes lit up.

"Watch this." He said. He had that devious smile on, which always meant trouble was just around the corner.

I turned just in time to see the manager, in his 3- piece suit, push open the door of Blazing Salads, obviously to see what all the commotion was about. As the glass door flew open, I heard two distinct sounds, the door hitting Sully and Sully hitting the ground. As he hit the ground, the scream that he let out froze everyone in their place. Even the two guys, who were arguing, now paused to see who had been killed. The store manager didn't know whether to shit or go blind. I think he chose the former. Sully was now on the ground screaming that his nose had been broken. I had seen this act before but each time he added a new twist. That day he faked a severe head injury. At Southie High it was his nose that was broken. He certainly was never boring. He tried to get up, by himself and fell down. Everyone was now watching Sully, even the two combatant motorists.

"I didn't mean it, I didn't mean it," the manager kept saying over and over. Sully continued to roll on the ground, saying he was badly hurt. The manager was really panicking and Sully loved every second that the jerk squirmed. After a couple of minutes the crowd began to disperse and Sully was helped to his feet. He said he could stand but he felt as if his nose was broken.

"What's your name?" Sully asked, looking directly at the manager. The guy obviously smelling a lawsuit and the loss of his job asked why he Sully wanted to know his name.

"You almost killed me," Sully said to the sweating manager.

"But it was an accident," the guy pleaded.

"I'll let my attorney be the judge of that," Sully said as he began to walk away. The crowd was now totally gone. There was only me, Sully, the manager, and two store employees left on the sidewalk.

"I'm really sorry sir," he said trying his best to stem any tide of a lawsuit.

"I have to go," Sully said and began walking to his car. One of the store Employees blocked his progress.

"Sir you really should sit down for a while." The manager shot the kid a dirty look but did pick up on the subject.

"Yeah," he said, "Come on in the store, we'll get you something to drink."

"No I have to go," Sully said, and he began to walk to the car. But he walked as if he were totally drunk. He staggered from side to side and nearly fell off the sidewalk. The manager was now really panicking.

"Come on, you really might have a head injury, he said"

"I'm all right" Sully shot back, as he opened the car door and got in to drive. We were about 20 yards from the front of the store where the manager and his two employees were standing and staring. Sully started the car and then proceeded to drive on the sidewalk right through the heart of Braintree Center. The manager and the two employees were chasing the car.

"Stop that car, the driver he has a head injury." They were yelling, "Get out of his way he has a head injury, he has a head injury." Sully was doing his best to support their theory, as he went weaving down the sidewalk as startled shoppers jumped onto the street or into storefronts. He drove about 30 yards, all the way on the sidewalk. Finally he saw a cop and said, "Let's get out of here." He drove off the sidewalk and out of danger. I was laughing so hard I almost threw up my just purchased salad.

"Taught that jerk a lesson," he said, as we headed to his house for lunch. Some things never change. After a few minutes driving, he turned to me.

"Don't tell my wife, she thinks I stopped all that stuff." I didn't tell his wife, but I told everyone else that Sully might have gotten married but he's still the same old Sully. Still quick as a cat. One minute we were talking about racquetball, at least he was, and the next minute he's lying on the ground a heartbeat away from O'Brien's Funeral Home. But in all those years, and all those flops I never seen him get caught once. Never. He did it so completely that you had to believe it was for real. He had every aspect of his dive totally choreographed from the time the door hit him in the hell of his hand, which was directly in front of his face, until the time he left the startled onlookers wondering what had just happened. It was always an academy award performance whether at Southie High to get out of a test, in Boston Garden in front of 13,909 or in a small salad bar in Braintree. The Oscar always went to Sully. Always.

Chapter 17 – Assorted Weirdos, Perverts and Pimps

We met all kinds of weirdo's in our travels, especially, as I mentioned at the wrestling matches, and more specifically at the Arena, than the Garden. They came out of the woodwork for wrestling. I once told Sully that we should turn our chairs around and watch the audience, rather than the wrestling matches. The audience was a much better show, believe me. One night we were at the Arena and once again, Sully spotted a weirdo staring at us. We went over to him.

"What's your problem?' Sully asked. "Why are you staring at us?" The guy told us that he liked one of our friends, named Faz.

"So what do you want me to do?" Sully asked.

"I just want to be alone with him for ten minutes," the guy, who was in his 30's, said.

"And do what?" Sully, again acting as chief legal counsel inquired.

"I just want him to swear at me," the guy said.

For how much?" Sully asked.

"Fifty dollars," the guy unabashedly said.

"Let me see what we can do, Sully said, "We'll be right back." He walked over to Faz and they were immersed in deep conversation. Faz kept shaking his head, no, and finally Sully went back to where the weird guy was standing and I saw the guy reach in to his pocket and give Sully a single bill Next thing I saw was Faz and the guy, go beneath the stands.

"What is that all about?" I asked Sully.

"We're just trying to make some money here, that's all," Sully said.

"What's this we shit, since when are you French?" I asked.

"Come on , lighten up. The guy only wanted Faz to swear at him."

"Are you crazy, you have no idea what that guy wants," I said. "The guy's harmless," he laughed.

"Do you think I would put Faz in danger? Come on, the guy's a wimp."

"Let's go, make sure he's all right," I said, as we ran down the old Arena's stairs. Faz was fine. He was actually walking upstairs to meet us.

"You all right?" I asked, concerned.

"I'm fine," he laughed. 'What did the guy want you to do?" I asked.

"At first he just wanted me to swear at him. But then he took out his thing and began to play with it, as I was swearing.

"You're kidding," I said. "What did you do then?" Sully piped in.

"I split, it was the easiest 25 bucks I ever made." I looked at Sully, who had one of those You caught me, looks on his face. Sully, under the guise of a french fries attack, hurriedly left Faz and I standing there. On the way home, after Faz had left, I said.

"That guy gave you 50 bucks, didn't he?"

"Well, yeah," Sully said. "But I had to take my commission," he smiled.

"A hundred percent commission?" I asked.

"You heard Faz, it was the easiest 25 bucks he ever made."

"Did Faz know that you got 25 bucks?" I asked.

"I don't think it ever came up," Sully smirked. I'm sure it didn't," I laughed.

I have to laugh when I think of how my father would have reacted if he had any idea that we were dealing with such weird people at 14 years of age. None of us ever got hurt. In fact none of us ever got touched. That was a rule, which we lived by. We only went with them a few times, and we all felt it was way too weird, even if the money was good. I could never figure out what the swearing thing was all about. "Swear at me." "Throw things at me." Give me a break. I knew a lot more about life than my parents did, even at that early age. I can remember sitting at home one Sunday night, with my parents, watching Ed Sullivan. Liberace came out and performed a few songs on the piano.

During the commercial my father said to me, "I think that guy is queer." I just looked at him in amazement. He took the look for bewilderment.

"Do you know what a queer is?" he said, in my only face to face parental sexual education lesson.

"Yeah Dad," I blushed, "But I think they liked to be called gay, now." He never missed.

"No shit Sherlock. If Liberace was any more gay he would have a woman. I think it was the furs that gave him away. That was my one birds and bees talk, with my father. Gays we had no problem with. Gays gravitated towards us for some reason. We never bothered them. One guy who was gay, not as bad as Liberace, but most definitely gay, was a guy named Willie Hackett. We met him down the Old Harbor project when we were about 13 years old. He had an apartment in Old Harbor and he used to invite us up there all the time. Willie Hackett was way too smart to try anything on any of us. He was also black, which didn't always go over too well in Southie during the 60's and especially during the 70's after forced busing. He was entertainment to us. We had never really met anyone who was so out of the closet. And, Willie Hackett was way out of the closet. He was outrageous, and he flaunted his homosexuality, which we found fascinating., even if it was a bit disconcerting. He would always say to us.

"Boys, now remember. Don't whack, just come see Hackett." We would laugh like hell, and he would get the biggest kick out of making us all laugh. Another guy who took to us, was a piano player at the Colonial Room in Southie. His name was "Paul the Fag." Swear to God. Nobody ever knew his last name. He was just "Paul the Fag." He was a cross between Liberace, Paul Lind and Peter Gabriel. He was a very talented piano player, who would make up the lewdest lyrics to popular songs. We met him when we about 18 and he loved to see us bound up the Colonial Room stairs. He would squeal, "Oh it's my tough little Southie boys." One night we went up the Colonial Room and Paul was sitting in the back booth crying. We all went over and asked him what was wrong. He told us that a gang of kids, where he lived, broke in to his house and terrorized him. We left the Colonial Room, and went down to the corner where these kids hung. We told them that if anyone ever bothered Paul again, we were coming back and would kick their asses.

"What's your problem," one of them said. The guy's a fag."

I said, "Yeah, but he's our fag."

I didn't mean it like that, but as soon as it came out, I knew I was in trouble. Boy did I get shit for that comment, for years. Someone told Paul the Fag, what we had done, and more specifically what I had said, and he cried. He told us it was the greatest thing that anyone had ever done for him. But, I got more shit for that one line, "Yeah, but he's our fag," My friend Jimmy Ridge, who was with us at the time told me that he had never laughed so hard in his life. Jimmy is doing double life in prison now and will never get out.

We never feared either pedophiles or homosexuals. Pimps, however, as they said in the Wizard of Oz, were a horse of a different color. Those guys killed people for a lot less than we were accustomed to doing. They played for keeps and they didn't care how old you were. A good friend of mine named Andy Popoulo was killed in the combat zone. Andy was a great athlete from the North End. He was attending Harvard and had brought some of his classmates down the combat zone for a night on the town. Andy ended up getting stabbed by a guy that both Sully and I knew. Andy died, and with him, a lot of the combat zone did as well. I often remarked to Sully that we were lucky that we never got killed or beat up for some of the stunts we, more like he, pulled. He would laugh and say we were to smart for that. I thought Andy was too. The owner of the Intermission liked us and would let us in to check out some of new talent, even though were about 5 years too young to be even near there. And I don't mean girls when I say new talent. The Intermission was a place that had great music and very talented performers, unlike a lot of the other strip joints that only provided two things, strippers and watered down drinks. Our favorite Intermission performer was a guy named Roy Pace. This guy was as good as James Brown. The difference was that he was white, but that was the only difference. Well, maybe their paychecks were a little different. Roger Pace was bad. He would open up his set by singing, "My name is Roger Pace and if James Brown is here he better hide his face." The manager of the Intermission would let us come in, during the day, when Roger was rehearsing. We would run and get him cigarettes and coffee and stuff like that. But it was always a special thrill to sit there and watch him perform. He might rehearse the same song 30 times but we didn't care. It's funny, but I never stepped foot in any other strip joint in my life other than the Intermission.

Chapter 18 – DJ's Hot Dogs

Dealing with loan sharks, prostitutes, pimps and drug dealers was not something that all kids in Southie did on a regular basis. It was kind of exciting nonetheless. We didn't see the downside or we didn't want to see the downside, maybe. Most of the time we would hang out in front of Dirty Johns AKA DJ's. Dirty John made the best 15- cent hot dog in the world. He was also the most abrupt, ill mannered, dirty, filthy, foul-mouthed man that I had ever met. That was also part of why he was a legend. The other part was that you could get 2 hot dog and a coke and get a dime change on a half a buck. That was key. So you put up with a little grief for such a deal. It was all part of the ambiance. I can remember the first time I ever went to DJ's. I was 11 years old and pretty unsure of my surroundings. Sully, who was a lot more street smart than me, or anyone else I know for that matter, was right at home with DJ. This wasn't Sully's first time. He yelled into the open window.

"Hey John my man, how bout fixing me and friend up with a couple of barkers." Dirty Johns was just a storefront window, no seats, no anything, just a window.

"Not you again," DJ said as he turned around and saw Sully. "Now my day is complete," the old Italian said to some of the bookies who hung outside his hot dog stand.

"What's a matter you John, you no sella hot dogs today," Sully teased, in his very best broken Italian accent." John leaned to where we were standing. I could smell garlic mixed with a heavy dose of cigar.

"Hey kid, why you allaways gutta bust my balls."

"You don't gutta any balls," Sully shot right back.

"I getta hold of you and there be balls rolling down Washington street, ya little bastard," DJ said, as he made a fake attempt to jump over the counter.

"Get back in your cage," Sully yelled, "Only humans are allowed on the street." Nobody even raised their heads or stopped to take a look at the two nuts that were yelling at each other. I later learned that this was how you talked to DJ, if he liked you. The more DJ ranked you the more he liked you. He obviously liked Sully. But I didn't know that then. I was scared to death. I thought this guy was going to kill Sully. But that was how their relationship worked. The more they ranked each other the more they liked each other. Go figure.

"So whada you say, you just come by to busta my balls or you gotta some money today." DJ yelled over the counter. Sully smiled and impersonating DJ to the letter he yelled back.

"Holda your water pizano I gotta some scratch." Sully pulled out a $5 bill, which looked like it had been in his pocket since he made his First Communion and waved it at DJ. Dirty John smiled, showing yellow decaying teeth.

"Whatta you just rob some bum on the common."

"You're the only bum I know." Sully shot right back.

As if signaling an end to the pleasantries, if that's what they were, DJ became all business and barked out his famous yell, "OK how many?" You could hear DJ yelling that phrase all the way up Washington street, "OK how many?"

"Give me two and run them through the garden," Sully yelled as DJ turned his back to us and began the task of fixing our hot dogs. As if by magic two steaming hot dogs piled high with mustard, ketchup, relish and onions appeared directly in front of Sully.

"Tonic" he said to Sully.

"Give me a bud," i5 year old Sully responded.

"Ya cheap piker, you wouldn't know what to do with a bud." Then he looked directly at me.

"How many, four eyes?" I was very intimidated. It seemed that he and Sully had their own vocabulary and I had missed that course. I didn't answer right away which was a major no no with DJ. Everything he did, he did fast, talking, walking, serving. He was not a man to be kept waiting. Many years later I saw an episode on Seinfeld about the Soup Nazi. That was Dirty John to a tee.

"Two hot dogs sir," I managed to blurt out. He looked at Sully.

"Sir?" now why you no call me sir, fatso?" Sully laughed, in between bites of his huge hot dog.

"Because I know ya, he doesn't." He quickly turned his back and yelled over his shoulder to me, "Ya want mustard and relish?" I again hesitated.

"No." I said as he turned around with my two hot dogs piled high with mustard and Relish.

"Too late, you gatta mustard and relish." Sully started laughing.

"Don't wait on DJ or you get whatever he decides you get."

"I guess," I said looking at the mustard and relish overflowing onto my hand.

"Tonic?" he growled in my direction. I was too afraid to say anything.

"No." I managed to squeak out.

"Ya cheap piker," he again growled and walked away to take care of a few hookers who had just shimmied up to the window.

"He's something else," I said to Sully. He just laughed.

"Looks like you'll need a couple of napkins," Sully said very innocently. I waited until he had come back to where we were standing.

"Excuse me John can I get a couple of napkins?" You'd have thought I insulted he and his entire family.

"Napkin? Whatta you think, this is the Hotel Statler. Getatta here ya bum." I wasn't expecting such a volatile response to such a simple request and I almost jumped into the street. He was ranting and raving.

"These kids, they buy a 15 cent hot dog and they wanna napkins." I didn't know what was going on until I looked at Sully.

He was almost pissing his pants laughing and pointing at me. Then I knew that I had been had.

"What was that? " I asked.

"John has a thing about napkins," he laughed.

"So you set me up?" I said trying to act mad.

"Absolutely," Sully smiled. It wasn't the first time nor would it be the last.

That was my introduction to Dirty John. I would spend many happy hours at DJ's over the next couple of years. He was always good for a laugh, and we made the most out of that situation. We would bring kids over to DJ's, telling them how great the hot dogs were, and how cheap they were. Our friends would really be psyched up as we walked up Washington Street toward the storefront. Sully would order and then tell the kid or kids we brought to order.

"I'll be right back. I have to go to the bathroom at the Intermission." He would ask one of the kids to hold his hot dogs until he got back and just as he was leaving he would say.

"Oh by the way, don't forget to get me a couple of napkins." He would then hide around the corner as the kid ordered. Everything would be going along great and then the kid, innocently enough would ask, "Can I have a couple napkins?" DJ would explode and Sully would magically appear from out of nowhere. It was always funny, and we got a lot of kids with the old napkin trick. It was especially funny when tourists stopped to buy a cheap hot dog. I'm quite sure that those kids had never seen anything or anyone like Dirty John before. I remember a bunch of kids, who had on Andover jackets, stopping at DJ's. Sully and I were waiting there for some of our friends to join us, and we were talking to one of the biggest bookies in Boston. He absolutely loved Sully, and he was always trying to recruit him to be a runner. There was a lot of money in it, but Sully never even considered it. Too many of the cops, in downtown Boston, were from Southie and knew our parents. We talked a good game but that was about it. This bookie's name was Fat Vinny and he looked like he ate everything in sight. He was huge and he was always wearing diamond rings and other fancy jewelry and flashing huge wads of money. I read in the paper, many years later, that they found Fat Vinny shot in the back of the head in a gangland killing. But that was in the future and Fat Vinny was very much alive that day as we waited at DJs for our boys. DJ's was always our meeting place, whether we lost each other or whether we had to meet each other. There were about six kids from Andover who approached DJ's that afternoon. They looked about as much out of place as Madonna in a convent. They walked up to the window, which was really packed that day and waited in line. Johnny had been on a roll all day. He was like Sully. He performed better infront of a large crowd. The first kid ordered two hot dogs.

"Where you kids from?" DJ asked, very politely. They answered in unison.

"Andover."

"Is that near the Dover street bridge?" Johnny asked. The kids looked at each other, totally without a clue.

"We don't think so

"Johnny's on a roll, watch this," Fat Vinny whispered to Sully.

"You have a flowers and trees in Dover," he again politely asked. They were all smiles.

"Lots of them," the obvious leader of the group answered, "But it is Andover, not Dover."

"That's a nice," Johnny smiled and then went right back to business. "OK how many?" The first kid, again, ordered two.

"You like a garden?" John said to the kid. Thinking that John was still talking about flowers and trees, "Oh yeah, my mother has one." Johnny turned to get the kid his hot dog and when he turned again he deposited two hot dogs in front of the wide eyed kid, who just looked at the onions, ketchup, mustard and relish that were now falling all over the counter.

"I wanted mine plain," the kid finally said.

"I aska you if you likea the garden, no?" John said looking at the overmatched suburbanite.

"Yes you did, but."

"Well that is what I do, I runna it through the garden." Most people would say put everything on it but not DJ. He had his own language and if you didn't know it too bad. The other five kids began to walk quickly away, not really sure that they really wanted hot dogs in the first place. They had however experienced DJ and I'm sure they never forgot it. DJ's closed a couple of year ago. Johnny started to look really old. but the fire was still there and I would stop by and say HI when I was in the area, which wasn't too often. Unfortunately.

The last time I was there he was really glad to see me and he even said so, which really blew my mind. He always asked for Sully.

"Howsa that little juvenile delinquent doing?" he would ask.

"He's no juvenile now," I would say to John, but he didn't want to hear it. Johnny, like a lot of people who get old, would rather think of people as they were, in the good times. Sully would always be fifteen years old to John and maybe that was good. That last time I stopped by his stand, I knew that the handwriting was on the wall for the famous DJ's. There were no customers and the place had really become run down. The combat zone was all but dead, and so was DJ's business. Time had passed him by and he knew it, even if he didn't want to admit it. Andy Puopolo was not the only combat zone casualty. DJ AKA Dirty John was another. I never knew his last name and I have no idea if he is alive or dead. He was a part of the very best time in my life and I wish I had told him how much he meant to me. That last visit I paid to DJ, before he closed, he said to one of the last bookies.

"Look at this," John barked trying to act mad, "Look whosea come slumming."

"Come on John," I said actually feeling a little guilty that I hadn't been back before.

"I seea your picture ina da paper" he said. "Hey ya know Figgy" he said to his old friend, "Our boys a bigga shot, no wonder he no comea back to see his old friends." "John if you're trying to make me feel bad, you're doing a very good job." I said. His mood changed instantaneously and he was the old DJ again.

"See Figgy" he yelled he stilla can no take the jab." We all laughed.

"You hungry?" DJ asked. "No thanks I just ate," I said and knowing that as soon as I said it that it was the wrong thing to say.

"But I always have room for a DJ barker." His old face lit up and he went to work. "Mustard and relish,?" he yelled "No" I said, already knowing the game. He turned around and produced two steaming hot dogs piled high with mustard and relish.

"Too late you gutta mustard and relish." Again, we all laughed. There was that old twinkle in his eye and I felt a little sad, knowing that this would probably be the last time I would have a DJ barker. More importantly, I had a gut feeling that this would be the last time I would be in the company of my old friend. Unfortunately I was right. But the game, that day wasn't over yet. I took one bite from my barker.

"Hey John would you happen to have a napkins?" Instead of screaming, my old friend smiled and produced two napkins from under the counter. I cracked up.

"Ya gutta change with the times," he said and we all had a very good laugh. Our last.

"I have to go," I said, delaying this scene for as long as I could.

Brian P. Wallace

"I know, I know you're a busy man now with your picture in the paper, hey Figgy did I tell ya that this schmucks picture was in the paper."

"Yeah, you told me" Figgy said turning to his racing form. We shook hands and I was about to get on my way, when he got real serious.

"Hey, Wallace you take care of yourself and that goes for your fat little fresh friend too, OK." I just shook my head, afraid that my voice would betray me. I waved goodbye to DJ and to a part of my childhood that day and walked up Washington street to the Mayor's Office and to my new world and my new friends. Thinking as I walked about a lyric from a Simon and Garfunkel song, "Preserve your memories there all that's left for you." John died three months after that day, and a part of my childhood died right along with him Thanks for the memories, my friend.

Chapter 19 - Watch Out For That Rug

One day we had annoyed DJ as much as humanely possible and we were walking up Summer Street toward Washington, to the Paramount Theater. The Paramount was a majestic old Theater. It hadthose high ceilings and overhanging balcony lofts. It had seen better days, however, and was now only a shell of its' former grand stature. Knuckles was walking backwards, which is again something that only young kids could get away with on Washington street. He was facing Sully and me, and we were all talking as we walked. Behind Knuckles I spotted two guys coming at us quite fast. They were holding an 18 foot oriental rug and, as my mother would say, "They were hell bent on election," whatever that means. All I knew was that these guys were about six yards from Knuckles and they looked like they had no intention of stopping. One guy was holding the front of the rug while the other guy had the back end of the rug. I didn't know if they stole it, or not. All I knew was that Knuckles was going to get creamed in a few seconds.

"Knuckles look out," I yelled. At the last second Knuckles jumped out of harms way as the two rug merchants or whatever they were went barreling by.

"You idiot stay the Christ out of the way." The lead rug carrier said to Knuckles. The guy at the back end of the rug just looked at Knuckles and said, "Asshole."

Now you can tell from what you have read that we were no angels and we oftentimes instigated situations. This time, for once, we did absolutely nothing wrong. This time we were provoked.

"What did you call him?" Sully demanded of the guy holding the rear end of the rug. Sully was now walking alongside the rug carrier.

"I called him an asshole," the guy said, obviously underestimating Sully because of his size.

"You shouldn't go around swearing at people," Sully calmly said.

"Get lost you little dirtball," the guy said to Sully, as they came to a stop in front of Kennedy's. where we had just left. Sully was through talking. He just stood there and stared at the two guys each holding an end of the 18 - foot rug. When the light changed a few other things had changed as well. Now there were three people carrying the rug instead of two. There was a guy in the front, a guy in the back and Sully directly in the middle. Sully started to turn the rug. The guy in the front had no idea what was going on because he had his back to Sully. The guy in back saw what was happening but couldn't do anything about it. The rug was now totally out of control, as pedestrians, on Summer Street, ducked out of the way as the rug began going in circles. The guys were Greeks and they began swearing at Sully, first in Greek and then in English and finally in a mixture of both languages. They were livid but they couldn't do anything about it because they each had to hold on to their end. Within a matter of seconds Sully had steered the runaway rug onto Summer Street, directly in front of Jordan Marsh. Every shopper, and there were quite a few, had was now watching this show. Sully in the middle steering the rug in any direction he wished and the two irateGreeks screaming at the top of their lungs. They were now right in the middle of Summer Street and traffic had come to a standstill. Cars were beeping their horns, people were pointing, the two guys were swearing and we were on the ground laughing. There was a cop directing traffic about a half a block away at the intersection of Washington and Summer Street. He couldn't figure out what the hell was tying up the entire downtown area. I looked at the cop. and said to Knuckles, whose father was a policeman.

"Do you recognize that cop?" I asked Knuckles. His father was also a cop. Knuckles froze thinking that it was his father. It wasn't. It was Jimmy Dolan's stepfather, Johnny Murphy. Jimmy wasn't with us that day, but he was with us almost every other day.

Sully, by this time, had the entire area in gridlock. Cars were honking their horns. People were screaming out of their car windows and the rug just kept going round in circles. I watched as Johnny Murphy started to walk down to where Sully was manipulating the two Greeks. Finally the one on the back end put his side down and started to come after Sully, who was already halfway into the crowd. The guy looked around, as if he were restoring his dignity, picked up his end and told the guy in the front to go. They started to walk down Summer Street AGAIN, but in a flash Sully was back. The crowd began cheering wildly as Sully took up his position in the middle of the rug. It was hilarious. The Greeks didn't hesitate this time. They both immediately put the rug down and began to chase Sully. But Sully was long gone and hard to find. He darted into the large crowd and into Filenes before the guy had any idea where he went. They chased him as far as Filene's and then realized that they had left their precious rug unattended on Summer Street. They looked at each other, as if what they had done, had just dawned on them. They made a mad dash back to the spot at where they had dropped the rug. It was gone. They went nuts, jumping up and down, and swearing at each other in Greek. It was like something out of a movie. When they ran after Sully, we had quickly grabbed the rug and hid in on Chauncey Street, which bordered Summer Street. Finally after 5 minutes, Ridge said, "Hey assholes." The guys turned. "You shouldn't go around swearing at people." The guy gave Ridge a nasty look and began pointing at us and saying that we had stolen his rug. Johnny Murphy, who was directing traffic up the block, came over to us.

"What did you do now?" We laughed and told him. Johnny was cool, he wasn't like some parents who would be mortified at what we had just done. Johnny just laughed.

"Did they deserve it?" was all he asked. We assured him that they did and that was the end of it.

"Where is their rug?" Johnny Murphy asked, and we told him. He walked over to the two Greeks and took them down Chauncey Street where they retrieved their rug. By the time Johnny got back, without the Greeks, Sully had returned. Johnny politely asked us to find another place in Boston to hang out, at least until his shift was over.

We are going to go now," I said to Johnny. He smiled and said, "Thank God."

Johnny was working that same detail a few years later when he chased a robber into the Washington Street station. As he got closer to the robber, the guy turned and fired fourshots at Johnny. Two of the shots found their mark and Johnny's career as a police officer was history. He died a few years later. He never fully recovered from those gunshots He was a good guy and didn't deserve to go out like that. After hanging with Sully that day, James Bond seemed tame. I remember eating at Sully's house that night. His father asked him if he did anything exciting that day.

Brian P. Wallace

"No just the usual." Sully replied. The funny part was that this was usual for him. He got Ronald and the Rug merchants in the same day, actually, in the same hour. What a day! Both hoped that they never ran across Sully again.

Chapter 20 – What's Under That Turban

And finally my favorite Sully revenge story. Others were funnier and others had been better planned. Maybe that is why I liked this one so much. It was totally spontaneous and the sheer audacity of it was unreal. There were a lot of factors in this particular story that were almost incomprehensible. Sully took it as far as it would go, then further and then further and even further still. Actually it was more scary than funny. But once we were out of danger, and I thought about the sheer nerve that it took to pull it off, I couldn't stop laughing for a good ten minutes.

It all began at a place called the Bayside Mall, which was located just on the outskirts of South Boston. It was some kind of an experiment to see if a major shopping center could survive next to a low- income housing development. The development was called Columbia Point and it was about 75% minority. Well let's just say it was a good try. I will say that the Mall, while it lasted, did employ a lot of local kids and it did give people another alternative to shop. It also broke the the world's record for most shoplifting in one mall. My girlfriend, whose name was Anne Marie, got a job working, after school, in one of the department stores. She worked from 3 to 11 , Monday through Thursday. I was playing in a basketball league in the Columbia Point project and I would stop in to see her on the way home after my game. One day Sully decided to come over and watch our game and he accompanied me as we went in to see Annie. Annie liked Sully but she thought he was crazy. I wonder why? We were standing at her counter and just talking, when her face lost all of its color and her eyes went trancelike. I looked at Sully and I just shrugged.

"What's wrong?" I asked. She tried to downplay it but we wouldn't let her. Finally she told us that a guy just came into the store unnerved her. She told us that the guy always hit on her and made lewd remarks. I was getting very mad as she continued to speak.

"Where is he?" Sully asked. She pointed to a man who had a turban on. Sully and I both laughed.

"A towelhead?" Sully laughed "A towelhead has been bothering you?". She nodded. I told you that Sully didn't like 3 piece suits. He liked towelheads even less. As soon as I saw that the guy was a towelhead, as Sully called them, I knew there was going to be trouble, so did Annie.

"Please guys," she implored "I need this job, please don't do anything to get me fired."

"I'm just going to have a little fun with him," Sully laughed as he headed over to whetowelhead was standing.

"What's he going to do?" Annie asked me, close to tears.

"I don't know," I said. And I didn't. "Please go with him and make sure Sully doesn't hit him," she asked.

"OK" I said, feeling pretty confident that he never would hit a guy like him. I knew that he just wanted to have some fun. But I also knew, that could mean anything.

"Excuse me sir but could I talk to you for a second?" he asked the guy as he approached. I had hurried over to make sure things didn't get out of hand.

The guy looked a little annoyed. "Why?"

Sully brought his hand to his back pocket and quickly retrieved his wallet. He flashed some sort of a badge that I had never seen before and put the wallet back into his back pocket. The guy had looked at the badge but obviously didn't have time to read it.

"My name is Peter Hawkins and I'm with store security," Sully said in his best Joe Friday voice. 'Now can we have a little chat?" Sully said a little more forcefully.

"About what?" towelhead countered. Sully went into a routine as if he had been doing it every day of his life, instead of making it up as he went along. Now, remember he is just seventeen years old at the time.

"Sir we have been inundated with shoplifters since we opened this store three months ago. We have identified the ringleaders of this shoplifting gang and I was told to bring him in as soon as he steps foot in our door."

"What does all that have to do with me?" the towelhead finally broke his silence.

"You sir, have been identified as that ringleader. The blood drained out of the guys face.

"Identified by who?" he exploded.

A Southie Memoir

"One of our clerks has positively identified you, from pictures, and she has just made a positive personal identification." Oh no I thought he's going to bring Anne Marie into this.

"What clerk?" the towelhead said very loudly.

"You will have your chance, in court, to meet your accuser," Sully went on undaunted.

'This is wrong," he said, very loudly.

"It could be, sir but we have reason to believe that you have stolen property on your person right now." "

You're crazy," he screamed.

"Sir we don't get a whole lot of people in here wearing turbans," Sully said.

"What the hell does that mean," towelhead asked.

"It's just that the man we have ID'd wears a turban."

"So don't a million other people," he screamed. His voice was getting real loud and a crowd was beginning to form. I was starting to get a little uneasy with this whole situation. I was also wondering how and when Sully was going to get out of this sensitive situation.

"Do you stop every person who comes in here wearing a turban?" the guy protested. I thought Sully was getting in over his head. I should've known.

"Yes sir we do." The guy went nuts.

"This is nothing but religious persecution, this is a violation of my civil rights and my first amendment rights," and on and on he ranted and raved Sully never wavered.

"Shut up," Sully yelled right in the guy's face. The force and tenor of Sully's voice, startled the guy for a second, which was all Sully needed. The crowd was growing by the minute. Sully did his very best Clint Eastwood impersonation, long before we knew who Clint Eastwood was.

"Listen here you little puke" Sully started. The crowd was silent. "I'm sick of you and people like you, who come to our Country and break our laws and blame everyone else when you get caught. You know what Mister religious persecution. I don't even know what religion you practice and I don't care. All I care is that you have stolen from this store, not once and not twice but over and over and over. Well you will steal no more because you are going to jail. Now how do you like that Mister Civil rights." The towelhead and the crowd were speechless. So was I.

"You have no proof," towelhead stated.

"I have a clerk right over there," Sully said pointing in the direction of Anne Marie, who has signed a deposition identifying you as the person who has been systematically stealing everything in this store that is not tied down." The crowd was now growing even larger. I spotted Anne Marie on the fringes of the crowd. I wondered what she was thinking. Sully was really getting into this. I honestly felt that Sully was just going to fool with the guy but the guy really pissed him off. I don't know if a towelhead slept with Sully's camel in another life or something. I do know that he didn't like this guy and was now taking this charade all the way, whatever that meant.

"Calm down, you're starting to draw a crowd," Sully said as more and more shoppers and some employees came over to see what all the commotion was about.

"I'm drawing a crowd?" the guy screamed. "You're the one who started this."

"No sir, you started this the minute you stole something from this store. Would you mind emptying your pockets." The guy didn't move. "You can do it here or you can do it at the police station, it's your choice" Sully said very calmly. The guy looked around and went into his pockets and put the contents on a display table in front of him. I couldn't believe he was getting away with this charade. He was a fat little roly- poly seventeen year old who was acting like he had been a police officer for thirty years and he was getting away with it.

"See, there's nothing there," the towelhead smirked at Sully.

"We're not through," Sully said. I wasn't ready for the next thing Sully said and it floored me.

"OK take off the turban." Sully said calmly. There was complete silence. The guy just looked at Sully and asked.

"What did you say?"

"Take off the turban."

"I will not," towelhead shot back.

"Fine," Sully said, and looking directly at me. "Go call the wagon." Now if Sully looked a little young to be a detective, I looked young to be a junior detective. But the rouse worked because the guy never even looked at me.

"I will take this off, and then I will sue you and I will sue this store, do I make myself clear?"

"Never mind the speeches, take it off," Sully coldly replied. And he started to unravel it. I couldn't believe it. I looked at Anne Marie and her face was ghostly white. "What do you expect I have in my turban?" he asked coldly, as he continued to unravel it."

"We'll soon find out. Won't we?" Sully replied. The whole time he was unraveling the turban he was babbling about political persecution and religious persecution and on and on. Sully said nothing. "You will be sorry for this my friend," the half-towelhead replied.

"I am not your friend. Do you get that," Sully shouted. Now the scene had over fifty onlookers and I was starting to panic a little. Sully never wavered. I was watching out for the real store detective. He never showed up. No wonder the store was being rifled every day. The towelhead had half the turban unraveled and wrapped around his hands but he never stopped telling Sully about all the things that were going to happen to him and the store. Finally the entire turban was removed.

"Are you satisfied now, you pig," he spat at the seventeen year old store detective. Sully's expression never changed.

"I want your name," the untowelhead said very loudly.

"There must be some mistake," Sully said, for the first time taking a back step.

"A very big mistake," the former towelhead said.

"That clerk has positively identified you and has signed a deposition to that effect" Sully blurted out.

"What clerk?" the towelman demanded.

"I will go get her and let you confront her, right now" Sully said acting mad.

"I'm not going anywhere, you get her and I will sue her as well," the disgruntled towelhead yelled.

Brian P. Wallace

"I'll be right back," Sully said as he made his way through the crowd. I followed. But instead of looking for a clerk, we went out the side door and onto Day Boulevard, through Columbia Park and into the Mary Ellen McCormack project. We were out of breath as we ran into Knuckles and Maury at the statues.

"What happened?" Knuckles asked, as we approached them totally out of breath. I looked at Sully and we both burst out laughing. We laughed for at least five minutes. Knuckles and Maury just stared. They didn't believe the story.

"Even Sully couldn't pull that off," Maury said and they walked away. It was only later that week when Anne Marie verified what happened did our friends believe this incredible story. The best part, however, happened after we left. The guy waited for ten minutes for us to return, and became more belligerent every minute. Finally the real store detective showed up when the commotion got way out of control. He showed the guy his badge and the towelhead kept repeating, "No the other store detective."

"There is no other store detective," the store manager was called and he kept repeating. that the store only had one security detective. The towelhead was ranting and raving so bad that the manager called the Boston police to the store. It turns out that one of the police officers, who answered the call knew the towelhead. He knew him under a different name however. The towelhead was actually a felon who had jumped bail and was wanted by the police. He was wearing the turban and the robes as a disguise, which is why he didn't want to go to the police station with Sully. He ended up being dragged out of the store in handcuffs, kicking and screaming all the way into the police cruiser. When Anne Marie told us the story we were shocked, at least I was.

"I knew it." Sully said smugly.

"You're full of shit," I said "How could you have possibly known that guy was dirty."

"How many towelheads have you seen hit on girls, or even swear for that matter?" he asked.

"I don't know any towelheads personally," I responded.

"Neither do I," Sully said. "But I do know they keep to themselves, not like that jerk."

"So you knew all along that the guy was dirty?" I asked.

"Not at first," Sully explained, "but as we started to get into it, I just had a feeling that the guy wasn't the real deal."

"When did you know for sure?" I asked.

"When I mentioned going to the station, I could see the look in his eyes. He wanted no part of the police station, so I just had a feeling that this guy was shady." I looked at Anne Marie who was just astounded at what she just heard.

"You should be a cop, Sully" she said.

'No thanks," he said "I'd rather be a bounty hunter." With that over, we all laughed and went on to our next adventure. I have no idea what ever happened to the towelhead.

Brian P. Wallace

Chapter 21 – Rats on Beverly Street

If downtown was a place to hang out, meet some people and have a little fun, it was merely a diversion from our number one place, the Boston Garden. I have some very fond memories of that Grand old building and I was very sorry to see it torn down. The Boston Herald did a big story entitled "Growing Up With The Garden" on September 17, 1995. The story, written by Peter Gelzinis, was about my memories of the old Garden. There was a particularly poignant opening paragraph that Peter wrote that started out," 65 or 70 years from now, when Billy Bulger's grandson hammers out a controversial deal to build a bigger and better Fleet Center, I wonder if there'll be someone like me to record the memories of Brian Wallace." I was fortunate enough to do play by play for one of the final events at the old place. It was called "Give it a last shot." It was a corporate 4 on 4 tournament on the storied parquet. It was the second time that I had the opportunity to announce at the Garden. I did a Division 3 State hockey final there in 1991. It really was a special treat for me because the place always meant so much to me and because of all those childhood memories that hang somewhere in the hall. I only wish my good friend Johnny Most was still alive to see me announcing basketball in the Garden. I know he would have gotten a kick out of that. But the night I said good bye to the old place for the final time was pretty emotional. And yes I did go see the elevator that Haystack threw us off. That certainly lightened the mood. But no matter where we were or what we were doing we always gravitated back to the Garden.

As I mentioned we had so many ways of sneaking in that it was almost impossible to get caught. Not all of them worked all of the time, however. There might be an usher patrolling a door that we would ordinarily use, or a door we thought we had left open was locked. Things like that happened all the time. That is why it was so important to have so many backup plans. If one means of entry was closed we simply went to another or another until we finally got in. And we always got in, eventually. Some nights were more difficult than others and some night were far more memorable than others. Which brings me to the Beverly street story. We had arrived for a Bruins game relatively early but had fooled around for too long in the arcade. When we looked at the clock, we knew we were going to have some trouble getting in. The later we tried the harder it became because all the ushers were in place and all the security guards and dogs had taken their places as well.

"Great," Sully said, "Why didn't we just wait until the game started?" We were shut out at the first seven or eight places we tried. And it was really getting late.

"Beverly Street," Sully said excitedly. "I think our matchbook is still in the door." and we began running up Causeway street. Beverly street was the street that the very end of the Garden bordered. There was one door on Beverly Street that fed into the back storage room in the Garden. It was very dark and extremely spooky, which is why it wasn't always one of our first priorities. It was pretty far down on the list but we were getting desperate. Beverly Street, other than being dark and spooky, also had some other drawbacks. First, the door had to be open or we were completely out of luck. We always kept a matchbook in the door, which kept it open, not enough to be visible to the naked eye but enough for us to crack open the big steel doors when he had to. And that night, we had to. The other drawback was once you were inside the door you still had to get by a bunch of workers who worked in storage for the Garden and then get by some more ushers who were located just outside the storage area doors. It was a lot of work, with way too many chances for something to go wrong. Beggars, however, can't be choosers, and we were now down to our final means of entry.

We hadn't tried Beverly street for over six months and had no idea if our matchbook was still intact. It was. We opened the door a crack and were inside in a flash. There were four of us me, Sully, Knuckles and Ridge. I was kind of caught off guard by the total blackness that enveloped us, as we stood silently just inside the door.

"Sure is creepy," Knuckles said.

"Quiet," Sully whispered.

"Listen to the voices upstairs and see if we can determine how many are up there." I said. Nobody disagreed. I had the willy's. We could hear voices right above us but it was hard to determine just how many there were. The total darkness was very creepy and disorienting.

Brian P. Wallace

"Let's wait and see if they go away," Sully whispered. I didn't want to spend any more time in this hell-hole than I had to. We waited for about five minutes and the voices started to recede.

"Good," Sully again whispered "I think we're going to be all set." Just as he finished saying that, a guy started whistling and he sounded as if he were beside us. In fact he was right above us, but the sound carried very well in that cavernous space. "Shit," Knuckles said, "I can't stay in this place too long." We couldn't see each other, but we certainly knew each other's voices well enough to know just who was saying what.

"Don't be a baby," Sully said, "There's nothing down here except us and maybe a few spider webs." It was again deathly quiet up above us.

"What's that scratching noise," Ridge said.

"I don't know but I've been hearing it for a few minutes," I said in return.

"Shit," Knuckles screamed. "Something just grabbed my leg."

"Mine too," Ridge yelled. Then I felt something against my foot and I jumped. "Something's in here," Knuckles said. We only have a couple of minutes to wait, come guys hang in there," Sully said while bringing out his cigarette lighter.

"Let's get some light on the situation," he laughed as he struck a flame. When the bright flame illuminated our surroundings I thought I would die. There were at least 1,000 rats all around us. They were everywhere, and when the light when on they began to scatter. They ran over our feet and through our legs. It was the scariest moment of my life. Even Sully was scared. It looked like the floor was moving. I heard Ridge scream at the top of his lungs as a rat ran up his pants leg. That was it for me. Sully's cigarette lighter went out and we ran like characters in a cartoon, up the stairs and in to the back of the Garden storage area. We were sweating and brushing our clothes and scratching ourselves. We were out of the rats nest, but not out of the woods, yet.

Years later I was sitting in a movie theater watching, "Indiana Jones and the Temple of Doom," and they threw Harrsion Ford into a pit where the floor was made up of squirming snakes. My mind immediately flashed back to a night long ago in a dark cavernous pit on Beverly street. I guess I must have shuttered. The girl I was with said I didn't know you were afraid of snakes." I shuddered again.

"I'm not, it's rats that I'm afraid of." I said remembering Beverly Street. She looked at me as if I had two heads.

It's a long story," I said, and left it at that. Indiana Jones, as usual, turned out to be a hero. There were no heroes present that night as we scampered out of that rat infested basement to safety. I'll always remember that squealing noise as the rats ran over each other to find shelter from Sully's light. You just don't forget things like that, ever. After a couple of minutes we got our composure back, a little, and realized we still had to get by a whole slew of Garden ushers before we were safely inside the Garden. We were still in the very back of the Garden, where they store the hockey nets and the Ice Capades equipment and the piles of stuff that the Garden has accumulated over the years. In order to get into the Garden lobby we had to open a door and walk directly past where all the ushers congregate, which wasn't going to be easy. We were trying to figure out a plan when Sully jumped up.'Screw it let's just walk past them like we own the joint." Maybe the rat scare had re-scrambled his brains, I thought.

"They'll see us as soon as we open the door," I said. Sully laughed.

"So what, is that going to be any worse than what we just went through?" We all looked at each other and laughed, realizing that he was right. So what if they threw us out. That paled in comparison to what we just went through. It was a pretty good lesson. We all headed out the door and into the arms of about 25 Boston Garden ushers.

Just before we got to the door, Sully stopped.

"Remember we own this joint." And with an air of invincibility we opened the door , waved to the ushers like they were some of our best friends and walked right into the Garden lobby. The ushers just looked around figuring that we were waving to some ushers that we knew. They all waved back. Sully was right. Look like you own the joint and you will. It was an old three stooges trick. I knew watching all those Stooges shows would come in handy one day. We watched the Bruins lose, as usual and as we were heading toward North Station.

"Come on," Sully joked. "Let's go put the matchbook back into the Beverly street door."

"Let's not and say we did" I said, using one of my father's favorite expressions. My father had another expression that was also applicable to the situation that night.

"If it doesn't kill you, it will make you stronger." I never knew what he meant by that, until that night with the rats. For obvious reasons we never used the Beverly Street entrance again. But we did learn a few of life's valuable lessons that night. So it wasn't all bad, except when I dream about the rats that night, and I still do.

Chapter 22 – Garden Antics and Arrests

That night, as I mentioned the Bruins lost. That was not unexpected. While the Celtics were almost unbeatable, the Bruins were eminently beatable. Bobby Orr was probably just trying on a new pair of skates that he found under his Christmas tree in Prarie Sound Ontario. Derek Sanderson was probably still in detention for beating up the entire 5th grade class. The names Johnny McKenzie, Phil Esposito, Gerry Cheevers, Ken Hodge, Wayne Cashman, Don Awrey, Dallas Smith, Teddy Green, Eddie Westfall and Harry Sinden were still some years away from gracing the cover of the Boston papers and every sports magazine around the Country. The big bad Bruins were still years away, these were just the bad Bruins. They had some pretty decent players but were never quite in the hunt for the Stanley Cup. I remember players like Leo Boivin, Bronco Horvath, Jerry Toppazinni, Bobby Leiter, Doug Mohns, Orland Kurtenbach and Fernye Flamin. We would still sneak in to watch the games, but we went more to see Gordie Howe, Bobby Hull, Stan Mikita, Maurice Richard, Gump Worsley, Jacques Plante, Johnny Bower and Glen Hall. It was great watching these big names come into the Garden. We would wait by the elevator and get their autographs and talk to them. We found out, very quickly, that hockey players were real good guys. They weren't prima dona's, the way some other athletes were, and they were always approachable. I couldn't believe some of the scars they had on their faces. This was long before players wore helmets or goaltenders wore masks. Jacques Plante was the first goalie to wear a mask in a real game. But masks bothered some goalies, like Gump Worsley and Johnny Bower. None of the skaters wore helmets. Those were some very tough dudes. We saw Gump get hit in the face one night. He took a wicked slap shot off the stick of Bronco Horvath right in the forehead. His head was split wide open and blood was all over the ice. I thought he was dead. He wasn't. He came back into the game after being stitched up and got the win.

My favorite player was the Golden jet, Bobby Hull. If there was a marquee player in the NHL it was certainly Bobby Hull, at least until #4 came around. He had golden blonde hair and a great smile, when his teeth were in, and he had a slapshot that broke the sound barrier. He was excitement on skates. In those days there were only six teams in the NHL. Today there are so many that I've lost count. But with only six teams, we knew just about every player in the league. Not personally, but it was much easier to keep track of who was playing in the NHL, back then. And the best part was that the teams played each other a lot more than they do today. There were more rivalries and the fans were more into individual match ups. I never missed an opportunity to see Bobby Hull when the Chicago Blackhawks came to town. Sully knew that I loved Bobby Hull so there was never any doubt that if the Blackhawks were in town then we would be at the Garden. This one particular game, occurred in 1964. Again there were four of us who snuck in. Me, Sully, Knuckles, and Ridge. Knuckles loved to watch Hull as well. Knuckles also had this hat on, that to put it as nice as I can, wasn't flattering. It was some kind of alpine hat with a feather in it. As soon as I saw him that night I knew it was going to be a long night. We would all meet at the Club and get the bus there, the same Bay View bus that my father caught me hopping years before. Only now, at 14 years of age, we paid our dimes and rode inside. As soon as Sully turned the corner he started on Knuckles's hat. "Did you lose a bet?" he asked Knuckles. "No," Knuckles replied, "Why?" "Then why else would you wear that stupid looking hat?" Sully laughed. Knuckles got mad, but I knew he was in for a very long evening. We quickly forgot about the hat as we started talking about Bobby Hull and Stan Mikita. We were pretty excited and had no trouble sneaking in. The ushers never bothered us anymore, especially George. We kind of had the run of the place. Sully, from working at the Garden, knew just about everybody in the place, from ushers to beer concession workers. The old club guy who got us Backstage at the Beatles concert also worked the beer concession from time to time. Sully would tell him Italian jokes and other stories. The guy thought Sully was hilarious. There was a method to Sully's madness, which we would find out that night.

We plunked ourselves down into some pretty good seats as the two teams had a pre game skate. Getting good seats, especially for the Bruins was never a problem. Sully said he was going to the bath- room and left a few minutes before the National Anthem. A few minutes into the game he came back with two large Cokes and took his seat.

'Why'd buy two cokes?" I asked.

A Southie Memoir

"It's cheaper that way," he said.

"Sully's a math major now," Knuckles said as we all laughed.

"I might not be good in math, but least I know when people are laughing at me," Sully said back to Knuckles, as he pointed to Knuckles's stupid hat. I was sitting in-between the two and I didn't want Coke spilled all over me so I tried to stop anything before it started.

"Let's just watch the game," I said to both of them. They did, Thank God. The Bruins were quickly behind by three goals and the way Glen Hall was playing in the Blackhawks net, it was going to be a very long night for the home team.

"I got dibs on that tonic," Ridge said to Sully. ('Dibs' was a City term, meaning that the person who bought the tonic, ice cream pizza, or whatever they had to share some of it with the first person who called 'Dibs')

"Get your own" Sully said back to him. "Ya got two of them for Christ's sake, and I called dibs" Ridge said a little offended at being rebuked.

"I called dibs," Sully mimicked Ridge in a very sarcastic voice.

"Don't take too much," Sully relented, as he passed Ridge the coke. Ridge took a big swig and his eyes almost bugged out.

"This is beer," he said in amazement.

"Why don't you say it loud enough for the cop up there to hear you," Sully said, taking back the coke cup, which didn't contain an ounce of coke. We all looked at each other. I learned a long time before not to ask Sully any questions, so I kept my mouth shut.

"Let me have some," Knuckles piped up.

"You didn't call dibs," Sully said, again making fun of Ridge. Finally Sully handed Knuckles the cup.

"You?" he said offering me the cup. I had never had a beer in my short 14 years, and I politely refused. Sully downed the remains of the first and then started on the second beer.

'Where did you get the beer?" Knuckles inquired.

"That guy form Southie put them in these cups for me," he said as he swigged down the second beer.

The first period was history as Sully disappeared again. Twenty minutes later he was back with two more Coke cups. This time, he even had a cigar. It's funny how much we, as kids. try to act like adults which is what Sully was doing that night. He was starting to get a little drunk and the cigar stunk. We started to rank him about the cigar and he got really mad.

"I don't know why I hang with you, you're just a bunch of kids," he said. That made us laugh even harder and he got madder and madder. His face was now very red either from the beer, and the cigar, or because he was so mad. He took a big gulp from his beer, finished the cup, and threw it on the ground.

"I'm outta here," he said as he pushed past our legs and into the aisle. He was a little wobbly on his feet and we laughed at him again. He left in a huff.

"He's really mad," I said to Knuckles.

"He'll be all right as soon as he sobers up," he said and again we all started laughing.

The second period began and we quickly forgot all about our drunken, cigar smoking friend. But, not for long.

What happened next stands out in my mind as vividly as if it happened yesterday? There was a little over five minutes to play in the second period. The game was a blowout, as usual. There was a face off to our left, which was in the Bruins offensive end. The ref had called time out and was skating into the face-off circle to drop the puck. As the ref started to drop the puck the door on the Chicago side, which was directly opposite from where we sat, opened. Guess who decided, at that moment to make his NHL debut? Me, Knuckles and Ridge just looked at each other as if trying to comprehend what we were seeing at the Chicago bench. It was like a moment frozen in time. I heard Knuckles, as if he were somewhere in the distance.

"I don't believe this." He put into words exactly what we all felt. Even for Sully this was a bit much. As the puck hit the ice so did Sully. It took a few seconds for the crowd to realize what was happening. Nobody had ever seen this happen before. Not in hockey. Not on the ice. You see that kind of thing all the time at Fenway Park or even during a Patriots game, but never during a Bruins game. It just doesn't happen. until Sully made his NHL debut. The play continued in the Chicago end. The refs had their backs to Sully. Stan Mikita tried to clear the puck out of the Bruins zone but a Bruins defenseman stopped

A Southie Memoir

the clear out pass and fired a shot at Glen Hall, who made a kick save as the puck went sliding into the corner. While all this was happening, Sully had managed to slowly get about halfway across the ice. The crowd was now howling as Sully fell on his ass right in the middle of the Bruins insignia. He was lying on the ice and trying to get up when Bobby Hull retrieved the puck deep in his own end and started a rush Sully had just managed to get to his feet as the teams started skating towards him. As the Bruins defensemen scurried to get back into their zone, one of them skated withintwo2 yards of Sully was still near the Bruins emblem on the ice as the refs skated backwards toward the Bruins zone. They stopped and looked at each other, not knowing what to do. Bobby Hull had now picked up a head of steam and was screaming through center ice and heading right at Sully. I was afraid to look. One of the refs, however, blew his whistle stopping play and stopping Hull's end to end rush. The crowd was going crazy and pointing at Sully. I couldn't believe this was happening. The refs had blown the play dead as Sully was just reaching the Bruins door. The players were all standing around laughing, as they watched Sully slipping and sliding across the ice. Just as he was about to reach out for the door, two Boston police officers had arrived at the same door and awaited his arrival with open arms. Sully saw the cops and tried to stop, but again fell on his ass. One of the cops reached for him and he fell on his ass as well.

The Garden crowd was now in hysterics, as both Sully and the Boston cop were on the ice. Sully got up first, and scrambled to his feet. He turned around and started back across the ice in the same direction that he came. The players were still standing around watching all of this and nobody moved, on the ice, except Sully. The cop, feeling embarrassed, went back to the safety of the Bruins bench. As Sully made his way across the ice the fans started to cheer. He fell, got up, and fell again. Every time he fell, the crowd cheered louder. The Bruins hadn't heard an ovation like that in years. As he approached the Chicago bench two more Boston cops were standing by the door waiting with open arms. By now, Sully was totally exhausted. Playing in the NHL was tough. He almost fell into the cops arms. The crowd was now booing the police with as much resolve as they had been cheering Sully. As soon as one of the cops dragged him off the ice, the crowd began chanting.

"Let him go, let him go." I looked at Knuckles."

"Fat chance of that." Knuckles said. W nodded our heads in agreement. This was the big time. This was, as Knuckles's said "an arrestable offense," and in all matters that concerned the police, we deferred to Knuckles because his father was a police officer.

I still couldn't believe he had done it. He must have known that once he was on the ice there was no way he was going to escape.

"What if they put bail on him?" I asked. "Can we bail him out, or do his parents have to bail him out?" Knuckles hadn't taken that course yet.

"I don't know, but let's see how much money we have just in case." Knuckles answered. We emptied our pockets in the lobby of the Garden. We have four dollars and twelve cents, combined. That wasn't going to get us anywhere. We looked at each other and began running down the maze of ramps that led out of the ancient building. Halfway down one of the ramps. Ridge began to laugh. I had never seen him laugh so hard. He fell against the wall and finally he fell onto his butt. He was laughing so hard he could barely catch his breath. I looked at Knuckles.

"Forget about him," I said. "Let's get to the police station." We left Ridge and continued down the ramp, past the penny arcade and out the doors onto Causeway street. I crossed the street first, as a fast moving car heading down Causeway toward Nashua street stopped Knuckles in his tracks. I looked back at Knuckles, but kept on running. I heard Knuckles yell.

"Brian, Brian." I stopped short and quickly turned around. Knuckles had crossed the street, and was standing at the North Station entrance, about ten yards from where I stood.

'What' I yelled. I was, upset that he had stopped me from getting to the police station.

"He's over there," he pointed.

"Who's over where?" I angrily asked.

"It's him, it's Sully," Knuckles quickly and breathlessly exclaimed. I couldn't believe it. I ran back to the corner and immediately spotted Sully. I also spotted the big Irish cop who had a pretty tight grip on Sully's collar. It was the same cop who had embarrassed himself on the ice. I looked around and didn't see any cop car or wagon, which surprised me. We had seen a lot of people get arrested at the Garden, and all of them were transported to the station by some sort of police vehicle. Just as that thought was going through my mind, the big cop spun Sully around and gave him a hard kick right up his ass. I was stunned.

"The next time you pull a stunt like that you'll get a lot more than a kick up the ass," the cop said in a thick heavy Irish brogue. Knuckless and I just looked at each other in amazement.

"And I had better not see you in the Garden again," the cop said, as he let go of Sully, who turned and faced the cop.

"Oh, you'll see me again, and the next time you had better watch out or I just might kick you in the ass." The cop looked was livid.

"You fresh little bastard," he yelled as began to chase Sully down Causeway street. They never even saw us standing there. Sully was running his fat little ass off and the cop was in close pursuit.

"He'll kill him when he catches him," Knuckles said.

"He'll have to catch him first," I said, knowing how deceptive Sully could be. People always underestimated him because of his physical makeup. And, like the Irish cop, they all learned from their mistakes. Sully, for a kid his size, was quick as a cat, and had very good foot speed. By the time they had gotten to the end of the Garden Sully had opened up a ten yard lead and was adding to it quickly. I turned to Knuckles.

"Case closed," I grinned The cop slowed and then came to a full stop as Sully picked up even more speed and left the disgruntled policeman in his dust. The cop yelled.

"Don't worry I'll see you again, and you won't be so lucky next time," the cop yelled. Sully now knowing that he could outdistance the cop, stopped, turned and yelled back.

"You couldn't catch me on your best day, go have another doughnut."

"He always has to push it," I said, as Ridge finally caught up to us.

"What the hell is going on?" Ridge asked.

"You wouldn't believe me if I told you," I said. The cop picked up his hat, which had come off during the chase, and slowly started to walk back to the front of the Garden. We had crossed the street, by then, and were also standing right outside the Garden front door.

"Do you know that kid?" he asked, still a little bit out of breath.

"I think his name is Peter Hawkins," I said. The cop took out a small pad of paper and wrote the name down.

"Do you know where he's from?" he asked.

"Charlestown." Knuckles said, without a bit of hesitation. He wrote that down as well.

"What did he do officer?" I asked, taking a page out of Sully's book. Now it was the cops turn.

"You wouldn't believe it if I told you," he said, mimicking exactly what I had just told Ridge. The cop continued to walk down Causeway street toward Beverly street, still shaking his head.

"He's definitely crazy," I said as Knuckles and Ridge shook their heads in agreement.

"He's also pretty funny," Knuckles added. And all at once, it hit us, and, we all began to Laugh. The sight of him running his little ass off, down Causeway Street with the big cop chasing him was priceless. All he had to do was walk away, but no, not Sully. He had to get the last word in, always.

"What happened to you, anyway?" I asked Ridge.

"I was running down the ramp," he said," And all of a sudden I pictured Sully running across the ice and all the cops waiting for him, and I lost it."

"We thought you had a heart attack." I said, as we were discussing the night's events, I heard a familiar voice, but I didn't know where it was coming from.

"Brian over here, behind the car." It was him.

"Is the cop still around?" he whispered.

"He went back into the Garden," I said, speaking to a person I still couldn't see. He still didn't know that we had witnessed the entire incident with the cop.

"Where did you go?" I asked.

"That Irish cop was chasing me," he said, looking all around.

'Get out of here," Knuckles interjected, "We didn't see any cop."

"Well how did you know he just went into the Garden?" Sully asked, as he walked over to where he stood. You couldn't get anything past him. He had the mind of a great detective. One slipup and he had you. I watched him do it hundreds of times and he never ceased to amaze me. All at once, the whole absurdity of the night hit me and I began to laugh so hard I thought I was going to piss my pants. Knuckles, Ridge and Sully followed suit and the four of us stood in front of the Garden laughing like maniacs. "Did you see the cop chasing me" Sully asked as our laughter died down.

"Every minute of it," I said.

"Eat another doughnut?" Knuckles said as we all started laughing again.

'Let's go home," I said because I really couldn't take much more in one night.

"No way," Sully almost yelled, "I still have a score to settle."

He began to walk away, and as usual we followed.

"Where ya going," Ridge asked.

"Hotel Madison," was all he said. That was one of the ways we snuck in to the Garden. Within 5 minutes we were back inside the Garden. There was about five minutes left to play.

'What if that cop sees you?" I asked him.

"There are no ifs about it, he's going to see me," he said. We all got a pizza and started munching in the Garden lobby. The crowd was already starting to pour out, even though there was still a lot of time left in the game. A couple of those leaving were pointing at Sully and laughing.

"See your famous now," I laughed.

"There's your buddy," Knuckles said. In the distance we could see the big Irish cop walking towards us. He hadn't seen us yet, but he would any second. Sully took off in a flash.

"He's all talk," Ridge said. I was shocked. I had never seen him back down before, from anyone. The cop spotted us, and kind of did a double take, but he didn't say anything. We just acted as if we belonged there, which was a lesson we learned in 'Sneaking in 101'.

"Oh my God," I heard Knuckles say. Sully had run around the entire length of the Garden, and was now fast approaching behind the cop. The Garden is an oval shaped facility and he had done an entire loop, and was now almost back to where he had started, right at the pizza place. The cop never saw him, but we saw the entire incident unfolding right before us.

He came up on the cop and goosed the cop, in front of a couple of hundred fans who were leaving the Garden. The cop didn't know what to do. By the time he knew what had happened, Sully had continued running out of the Garden towards North Station. Everyone, in the lobby, was laughing and pointing at the red-faced cop. To add insult to injury, I said to him.

"Wasn't that the same kid you were chasing before?" He shot me a look that could have killed, a lesser teenager, and walked right out the door. He had been Sully'd and he didn't like it. Welcome to the club officer and go have another doughnut.

After the policeman moved on, we knew exactly where Sully would be. Like DJ's, Ricco's pizza place was our designated meeting place when we were at or near the Garden. Ricco's was famous, to us, for two things. The first, as I just said, was because it was our designated meeting spot. We might not have been the brightest or the best dressed but we always had a plan. Sully would have it no other way. The second reason it was important was that it was the first place we ever heard a Beatle song. To kids of our generation that was equivalent to where you were when you heard JFK was shot. It was something you always remembered. It was 1964 when we walked into Ricco's, ordered a few slices of pizza and Sully put a quarter in the old juke box and played there songs. We were fooling around and not really paying attention to the music until this new song came on. It was a song called "I wanna hold your hand," by a group called the Beatles. I had vaguely heard about this group of mop top singers from London who were creating quite a stir across the pond. Now that I had heard them, that day in Ricco's, music, as we knew it, would never be the same. The Beatles changed everything, starting with music and spreading to fashion, hairstyles, mores and culture. The Beatles played a very big part in our teenage years and had a profound effect on most kids our age. That first day, in Ricco's, when we heard "I wanna hold your hand," we stopped fooling around. We even stopped talking, as we all listened to the entire song. This was different. This wasn't Elvis. This wasn't Motown. This wasn't the Beach Boys and it certainly wasn't Sinatra. We didn't quite know what it was, but we knew we liked it. And we knew it was going to be big. It was the only time that Sully was quiet. Once the song was over Sully went over and put another quarter in the slot and played the same song three more times. We listened intently and we knew that something, we didn't know what, had changed. It turned out the whole world was changing and we were right in the middle of it. Just where we wanted to be.

As we approached Ricco's that night after Sully ran his little ass up Causeway Street we were still laughing about him goosing the policeman , when we spotted him. He was sitting on his favorite stool, drinking a cup of coffee. He was the only teenage kid I knew who drank coffee. When he saw, us his face lit up. We got our pizza and listened to Sully's play by play of his short- lived NHL career.

"Did you hear the crowd cheering?" I asked.

"Yeah but I didn't know it was for me," he said.

'Who did you think they were cheering?" I went on.

"When I saw all those cops I didn't have time to think," he laughed.

"Why did you tell that Irish cop that you were going to kick his ass?" I laughingly asked. I pictured in my mind the cop chasing Sully, and I began to laugh so hard that Ricco threw us out. We walked out of Ricco's toward North Station and people were avoiding us because we were acting like maniacs.

"That cop was really mad," Knuckles said to Sully.

"That tub of lard," Sully said, "He thought he could catch me." As we turned onto Causeway street, I yelled, "Look out, it's the Irish cop."

Sully turned, and was ready to take off, when he realized I was fooling. "You asshole," he said to me as Knuckles, Ridge and I continued to laugh. And laugh was the optimum word that evening. I don't think that I ever laughed as hard, in one night, as I did that night. My stomach actually hurt for the next two days. And the night wasn't even over yet. We snuck into North Station and people, who were at the hockey game, were pointing at Sully. He loved it. You know fifteen minutes of fame and all that stuff.

"That's him, that's him," a little kid said to his father as he pointed to Sully. The father tried to shush the kid as he looked at us. He probably thought we were all as crazy as Sully. Sully was in his glory.

We were waiting at Washington Street station, later that night, for a train. Sully was again acting up, as usual. He and Knuckles had gotten into a mother - ranking contest, which started with Knuckles's stupid looking hat. Somehow, and I don't know how or when, Sully talked Ridge into throwing Knuckles's hat onto the train tracks. Knuckles went after Ridge, which was a real mistake. They began rolling on the filthy subway concrete. Ridge was probably the second toughest kid in Southie after Mooreso. He wasn't trying to hurt Knuckles though. He was just playing with him, Thank God. Sully loved it. For once someone else was fighting eve if he instigated it. I broke them up, but Knuckles was really pissed.

"Come on Knuckles that hat made you look like a geek, you should thank Ridge, he did you a favor," Sully said. The train, which had pulled into the station, had crushed Knuckle's hat under its massive wheels. Knuckles never believed a word Sully said but he did trust me.

"Was the hat that bad?" he asked me in confidence.

"Worse than bad," I said quietly. Knuckles smiled.

"I knew that, I just wanted a chance to kick Ridge's ass." We both laughed as Sully and Ridge stared at us, not knowing what was said, but thinking we were conspiring against them. We got to Broadway Station and took a Bay View bus. Sully and I got off at E Streett, Ridge got off two blocks later on Dorchester street and Knuckles got off at the next stop which was 8th street. Sully and I waved good-bye to our two friends and headed down E Street.

"Are you through now?" I asked him. He looked at me like he had no idea what I was talking about.

"What do you mean?" he asked.

"You almost got killed on the ice, then you almost got arrested then you got us thrown out of Ricco's and then you had Ridge and Knuckles killing each other," I said, in rapid succession. He thought about what I had said and then he smiled.

"Hey wait a minute, you got us thrown out of Ricco's."

"Maybe I did," I laughed, "But what about all the other stuff. Do you at least plead guilty to all of that?" He thought a minute.

"I'll take the Fifth, on those charges." He smiled. We arrived at his house, just as he was taking the Fifth. He said good bye and went in to his house to obviously torment his family for a few hours before he finally went to bed. Just a day in the life of Sully.

Chapter 23 – Fight Night At The Garden

There was nothing happening at the Garden for a week, which does happen periodically, when the Celtics and Bruins are on extended road trips and nothing has been booked to fill in the dead time. Usually the Ice Capades or the Circus will fill that time, but not this time. I don't know if I could have taken another night like the last one anyway. My stomach had recuperated and the legend of Sully continued to grow. Actually when I arrived at school the day after Sully ran across the ice, a couple of my friends were a ready waiting for me, on the High School stairs, to find out if what they heard was true.

"What did you hear?" I asked. They said that a kid named John White, not the basketball player, was at the game with his father and saw Sully running back and forth across the ice while the game was still going on.

"Did he really do it?" they anxiously asked, in unison. I tried to keep a straight Face.

"Come on, you know Sully do you think he would do something like that?"

"Absolutely," Tommy Lyons said. And the legend continued to grow, even without my help. It had taken on a life of its own. I was sitting in my fifth period class, that afternoon, when I spied the living legend peering into my class. He spotted me and began motioning me to get up and leave the class. Sully just figured that everyone was like him, and that they could come and go, as they pleased. He looked very excited, but I wasn't about to walk out of Joe Crowley's math class, because it would have been the last class that I walked out of. I motioned to him that I would meet him down the gym. Dejectedly he left. When my last class was finished I went directly down to the gym. I was wondering what had him so excited. As I entered the cavernous old gymnasium I saw him down the far end of the court playing 21 with some chump. Sully wasn't the fastest runner in the world, although he could motor when he had to especially when being chased by Irish cops. He could, however, shoot the basketball, especially from the foul line, with more than average accuracy. He made a lot of money playing 21. As I approached he said.

A Southie Memoir

"Come on don't break my concentration I'm up 19 to 5." He said as I approached. I walked away as he sunk the winning basket and collected the $2 bet. As he was walking over to me he was beaming.

"Someday Wallace I'm going to take you too."

"Let's go right now," I challenged right back.

"I said someday," he laughed, as he pushed his hard earned $2 bill in his well- worn jeans.

"What's up?" I asked, knowing that he had something he couldn't wait to tell me.

"Did you see the paper today?" he asked excitedly. I hadn't.

"Did you know that there was a fight tonight at the Garden?" he asked.

"Yeah but it's just Tom McNeeley, no big deal," I replied.

"Not McNeeley the other guy." He was so excited I didn't know what the hell he was talking about. We had seen Tom McNeeley fight a number of times. He was a great guy but just a journeyman fighter. His claim to fame was that he once fought for the Heavyweight Championship of the World. At least it started out as a fight. McNeeley fought Floyd Patterson, who was the reigning champ. In the first round McNeeley caught Patterson with a straight right hand, which sent the unsuspecting champ quickly to the canvass. All Boston was amazed. McNeeley was probably more amazed. But Patterson got up and he was pissed. He knocked McNeeley down seven times in the next round and a half. The ref mercifully stopped the fight. And that was the apex of Tom McNeeley's career. His son Peter,was the sacrificial lamb who fought Mike Tyson, when he first got out of prison. I'm losing track of how many times Mike Tyson has got out of prison. Peter McNeeley lasted all of ninety seconds against Iron Mike in Las Vegas, but he had his fifteen minutes of fame, much like his father did against Floyd Patterson. The McNeeley's have been involved in some strange fights. One night Tom lost a decision and the entire McNeeley family charged, and entered the ring and beat the other fighter, the referee and the other fighter's trainers. It was bedlam and would have went viral in this day and age. The fight Sully was talking about that day in the gym was against we went over to see Tom McNeeley fight a guy named Duke Sabedong and it turned out to be one of the strangest nights that we ever had at the old barn on Causeway Street.

Brian P. Wallace

Sully had picked up the paper, in the bathroom, where else, and was captivated with the guy that McNeeley was fighting. Duke Sabedong was a native Aborigine who was from a lost tribe in Australia. The story said that this was his first time in a City and that he spoke some ancient aboriginal language. The papers hyped this guy up pretty good and Sully fell for it hook, line and sinker. It did sound intriguing. It also sounded a little too hokey. Nothing that was run by Sam Silverman was completely on the up and up. Sam Silverman was a white Don King without the hairdo. We were at one of Marvin Hagler's early fights, one night at the Garden, and we were waiting and waiting for the first preliminary fight to start. The fans were starting to get a little restless. We had snuck into seats that were in the second row from the ring and were anxiously awaiting the Marvelous one. There were five guys sitting next to us who looked like they were boxers or more appropriately had at one time been boxers. They all had noses that were spread over a good 60% of their faces. And they were all in great shape. We got talking to them and found out that they were from Lowell. They all had boxed in the golden gloves, which was their boxing claim to fame. They were all friends of Marvin Hagler and were there to see Marvin knock out his opponent, which he usually did, with incredible regularity. Some guy came to the microphone and thanked the crowd for their patience and promised that the first fight would be underway shortly.

We decided to get a slice of pizza and get back in time to see the first fight. We ran out to the lobby got our pizza and coke and were back within 10 minutes. The fighters had still not entered the ring. The crowd was now hooting and hollering and, of course, we joined in the yelling. Within a couple of minutes one of the fighters was in the ring as the crowd quieted down. A couple of minutes later the second fighter entered the ring. Both fighters had towels draped over their heads and white terry cloth robes. We weren't paying to much attention until Sully began to laugh.

"What's so funny?" I asked, and he just pointed into the ring. I was shocked. One of the fighters, in the ring, was one of the guys who was just sitting next to us before we went to get our pizzas. His friends were all laughing as he shadow- boxed around the ring. He actually looked pretty good as he bobbed and he and threw a number of combinations. He was only fighting air, but he looked good doing it. We were kind of in shock as the two fighters went to their corners to be introduced. The announcer went to the center of the ring and grabbed the microphone.

"Ladies and gentlemen our first bout tonight is a four round contest between two up and coming welterweights.". The crowd, was anxious for a fight, any fight, and they cheered wildly as the announcer continued.

"In the red corner fighting out of Philadelphia with a record of 18 wins and only 3 defeats, let's welcome Willie Munroe." The crowd again cheered. And then the announcer turned to face our new friend, who was still throwing combinations against an unseen opponent.

"Ladies and gentlemen and in the blue corner, he comes to us by way of New York City and he has a professional record of 13 wins and 2 defeats, let's welcome Tough Tony Cannazalli." His friends were pissing themselves laughing, as the fight began. It was a boring fight, which went the distance. Munroe got a unanimous decision, and our friend from Lowell, returned to his seat, next to us, $250 richer, and with a nice shiner. His real name was Tom something but Sam Silverman changed it, and even gave him a nickname and a bogus professional record. We later learned that the guy who was scheduled to fight Munroe on the under card never showed up. Silverman was on the spot, so he grabbed this guy Tom out of the audience. He promised him $250 to fight. He never said anything about the shiner. He also never said anything about changing his name or making up a won-lost record, however. We learned a good lesson that night, one that stuck with me, but obviously not with Sully. As we were heading over to the Garden that night I asked Sully to remember that we were dealing with Sam Silverman and that things, With Sam, things aren't always what they seemed to be. I reminded Sully of the incident I just wrote about. But, Sully had already made up his mind and he didn't want to hear any more from me. Sully wanted to see this Aborigine, who was from a lost tribe somewhere in Australia and who spoke no English at all. I don't know what he was expecting to see, but he was surely fired up as we got off the train at North Station.

"I wonder if he wears war paint?" he asked. I just shook my head. But he was far from through.

"I wonder if he'll freak out when he sees all the people," he went on.

"This is a Tom McNeeley fight, there probably will be more people at Amrhein's," which is a famous south Boston restaurant.

"I want to get right down near him, when he comes out." Sully excitedly said. This immediately set off a series of warning bells in my head. Thinking of our venture at the Garden and his trip across the ice.

"Wait a minute, no crazy stuff tonight." "Yeah, yeah, yeah," he said. "Never mind the Beatle bullshit, yeah, yeah, yeah, I mean it Sully. I don't want to have my father come to Station 1 and get me out." I said forcefully.

"Relax, I only want to see the Aborigine," Sully said, trying to lighten the mood. And then he said, "But if that savage goes nuts I want to be near the ring." Most people, under those circumstances, would want to be as far away from the ring as possible. Not Sully. He always had to be in the eye of the storm. Come to think of it, most times he was the storm. As we got near the Garden I had no idea who or what, Sully expected to see that night. Maybe he expected an 8 foot behemoth, dressed up in war paint to come flying out of the dressing room., chanting some incoherent Aborigine chant and proceed to bite Tom McNeeley's head off and spit it into the crowd. Maybe that's what he hoped to see, and he wanted to be close enough to catch the head if and when it came flying out of the ring.

We were very early that evening so we had no trouble sneaking in. I did, however, have a great deal of trouble with Sully.

"Let's sneak into the locker room," he said. I tried to reason with him, but he was way beyond that.

"If we go into that locker room we are going to get caught and miss the fight," I said. He had already had his mind made up.

"I have an idea," he said as we walked, in plain sight, toward the fighter's locker room. We snuck into the locker room through a small window in the back.

"This is really crazy," I said to him, but he was in a different world. This Aborigine really intrigued him. We found ourselves in the very back of a completely dark locker room, which gave me the creeps. I couldn't help thinking about the rats at Beverly Street.

"Let's get up high," I said as I began to climb on some boxes and we actually got a better vantage- point of the entire locker room. Now, all we had to do was wait. We waited for about an hour in the pitch black. This was crazy.

"Do you think he even wears shoes?" a voice, which I recognized as my infatuated fat little friend, came out of the dark.

"Shut up," I shot back. I didn't know if he was putting me on, but I would soon find out as the locker room door swung open. We both held our breath as the lights bathed the room in a fluorescent glow. Four men walked in. Three of the men were obviously trainers or managers and the fourth was the Aborigine. He was pretty big., I estimated about 6'5" and maybe 270 pounds. Not anywhere near the 7 foot 359 lb. wild man that Sam Silverman and the newspaper story, said he was. And instead of beads and war paint the big guy wore a Brooks Brothers suit. Sully was deflated. I almost laughed, until I remembered where I was. The Aborigine looked more Italian than Aborigine. They all walked to the back of the room. We were no more than ten feet from them as we hid behind a bunch of boxes. The littlest guy, who was obviously the manager, spoke first.

"Sit down," he said pointing to the huge boxer. He did as he was instructed.

"You ain't gonna step a foot outside this dressing room until we see some money," the manager exploded. The Aborigine said nothing.

"See he can't speak English." Sully said.

The manager was building up quite a head of steam.

"Every friggin time I come to this dump it's the same bullshit." Sully and I just looked at each other, but said nothing. The little manager was just starting his tirade.

"Every time, they try to screw me out of money. Not once not twice, every friggin time." The huge boxer sat like a stone and never even changed expressions. The manager looked at one of the trainers, "You can go tell that cheap bastard Silverman, no way, not this time no way no how no money no fight."

The guy got up and left the room, which was becoming quite hot, literally and figuratively. The manager then let go with a string of expletives that would have made Andrew Dice Clay blush. I was starting to get a little scared. The door opened, once again, and in walked Sam Silverman and a few of his henchmen. Silverman was very red and looked exasperated.

"What is all this shit about?" he screamed at the disgruntled manager. The manager, who was swearing a blue streak just minutes ago, was now very calm.

"We're not fighting," he said calmly.

"Kiss my ass, you're not fighting," Silverman's yell could have been heard back in Southie.

"We have 8,500 fans out there who say you are fighting." There was a moment of silence as both of the war worn old promoters sized each other up. The Aborigine's manager broke the ice.

"Unless we get the money we agreed to, my fighter is not leaving this dressing room." Even redder now, Sam Silverman screamed, "I told you that you would get every cent of your moncy after the fight." The manager began to laugh.

"Just like the last time huh Sammy, and the time before and the time before. Not this time Sammy." Everyone looked at Sam.

"No, no, last time I had to pay a lot of people off, I had a lot of expenses to cover."

"What about the time before that?" the old manager asked.

"Same thing," Silverman grunted. 'Well, tonight will not be the same thing Sammy, tonight will not be the same thing. Tonight your expenses start with us, you can cheat someone else, but you're not going to cheat us again." Now Sam became indignant.

"I never cheated anybody in my life," he screamed. But even some of Sam's own people were smirking at that line. Finally the huge Aboriginal fighter stood up. He stood a good foot over Sam Silverman. The room became eerily quiet. Leaning down so that he could look at Sam.

"If you don't have my money in here within TEN minutes I am going to kick your fat little ass all over the Garden. Do you understand that you little weasel," the Aborigine roared.

"That sounds like pretty good English to me," I nudged Sully. Silverman and his entourage stormed out. The manager turned to his fighter.

"You really scared the shit out of him Jim."

"Jim?" Sully said. "I thought his name was Duke." This was getting to be to much, even for me.

Within five minutes Silverman and his troops were back with a bag full of money.

"Now that's more like it," the manager smiled. Sully and I were justmesmerized, staring at all that money, which the manager had spilled on to the training table, not trusting Silverman. I had no idea how much was there but there was a lot of $100 bills.

"Now get that asshole into some trunks," Silverman, now back in charge, demanded.

"And you'd better make this look real," Silverman said as he was leaving the room. He peeked his head back in.

"If the crowd don't buy this Aborigine bullshit, you're giving all of that money back." Silverman said, closing the door.

"Fuck you," the big Aborigine in the Brooks Brothers Suit screamed at Silverman.

"Wow, he's got those English swears down pretty good," I said to a crestfallen Sully. I felt like a peeping Tom. As soon as Silverman had closed the door a few of the people in the room began to frantically scurry around. There was a big white bag in the corner of the room, which they had quickly opened and were taking objects out of the bag. We stared in fascination.

"How ya feeling big guy?" the manager said, as he slapped the big fighter on the shoulder.

"I'm OK," he said, as he started to unbutton his shirt. "They're just lucky they came through with that dough or I would've crippled that fat little cigar smoking asshole" he said.

"Pretty good English to me," I whispered to Sully." As he continued to undress I really felt like a peeping Tom. He was standing there in just his jock strap when one of the guys approached him.

"Ready." The big guy just shook his head. The trainer took out a jar of white cream or a creamy substance and began to apply the gel to his chest. He next took out a different colored substance and began to apply that, as well, to the fighter's chest.

Brian P. Wallace

"This shit is cold," the fighter bellowed. "What is this stuff anyway?" he asked.

"Some Aborigine," I said to Sully, who for once said nothing. Within 20 minutes he was transformed from a Brooks Brother Italian boxer to a non-English speaking, savage Aborigine. His white skin had now been transformed into a golden color, almost like the color someone would get if they applied QT all over their body. It was quite amazing to watch this transformation right before our eyes. As the stuff was drying on his chest, they began applying the same gel to his face. And as one guy was doing that another was braiding his hair. His hair was long, but he wore it in a way that kind of hid how long it really was. Now his hair hung down and was braided with beads and other stuff. He put on leather moccasins and loincloth trunks a big head dress, a huge tribal blanket and the transformation was complete. The guy who had entered that room forty minute before, looking like an Italian businessman on his way to a Wall Street meeting, was now leaving that same room as a savage Aborigine from some lost tribe in Australia. I was fascinated. Sully was bullshit. It was like he just found out that the Easter Bunny wasn't real. It struck me funny how a kid, who was so street smart, was taken in again by Sam Silverman. But, he wasn't alone. Everyone in the Garden, that night, was taken in as well, except McNeeley who knocked the big stiff cold in three rounds. Silverman had his big pay- day and from the looks of it so did Duke Sabedong or whatever his real name was. Everyone was happy, except Sully. It was a good lesson for both of us. Never believe what you read or maybe believe half of what you read. When you're dealing with boxing, and Sam Silverman believe absolutely nothing.

Chapter 24 – The Boston Celtics & Red Aurebach

Boxing, wrestling, the Circus, the Ice Capades and even the Bruins were all great, but the Garden really meant only one thing to us. The Boston Celtics. I mentioned earlier about meeting Bob Cousy and working on the Celtic bench. I actually started late in the 1963 season and worked the 1964 and some of the 1965 seasons. By the time I began working for the Celtics Bill Sharman, one of my favorite players had already left and the Cooz was in his last season. Some people thought that once Cooz was gone the Celtics would be in trouble Those people obviously didn't know a red head from Washington D.C. by the name of Auerbach He would prove to be the best coach that the NBA had seen or probably will ever see. He did have some help though. Starting with a center from the University of San Francisco named Bill Russell and a line drive shooting forward from Holy Cross, named Heinsohn. Not a bad nucleus to start with. Personally I think the best draft choice the Celtics ever made was in 1962. The basketball world was turned on its' head over a superstar named Jerry Lucas who was playing College ball at Ohio State. Lucas, no doubt was the real deal. He could do everything on the floor. There were a couple of other players on that team, however, who played in the very large shadow of Lucas. On a trip to Ohio State to see Lucas in person, Auerbach left the gym extremely pleased about the performance he had just witnessed.

Oh yeah, Lucas was good too, but the Redhead came back to Boston talking about a 6'5" forward named John Havlicek Red, on the same scouting trip also saw a scrappy little guard named Larry Siegfried and both would ultimately end up in Celtics green. Not a bad scouting trip. Havlicek sat and learned from the very best sixth man in basketball, Frank Ramsey. When Ramsey retired in 1964, Hondo was ready, willing and able to step in right away. Ramsey was a great guy and his presence was certainly missed in the locker room after he hung up his sneakers. He was a real southern gentleman with a Kentucky accent you could have cut with a knife. Ramsey looked like a walking mummy when he was on the floor. He had bandages everywhere. I always thought it was to psyche out the other team. They would see this guy, who didn't look much like a basketball player in the first place, hobble out of the dressing room looking like he should be in a hospital rather than on a basketball court. Opponents first instinct would be to let down a little. And that was a mistake. Ramsey could shoot the lights out on any given night. He was a great basketball player and more important, he was a great guy. People will argue about Ramsey's greatest contribution to the Celtics. There is no argument as far as I am concerned. Ramsey taught Havlicek the fine art of being an effective and immediate impact player, coming off the bench. A lot of big ego players would never be able to adjust to not starting. Hondo and Ramsey knew the importance of their role, to the team, and changed the face of basketball. Red Auerbach has said a lot of profound things about basketball. One of my favorites was, "It's not who starts the game that's important, it's who finishes the game." I always remembered that quote and it always reminded me of Ramsey and Havlicek.

But the Celtics were changing after Cooz and Sharman and Ramsey had waved good bye. Red was eyeing retirement and the league seemed to be catching up to the aging Celtics. That was the atmosphere that we walked into that 1964 season as Celtic ball-boys. Owen Noonan, George Piano, and me. The Roxbury Club also had three ball-boys but they were changing all the time so we never really got close to any of them. The Charlestown Club had a kid named Alfred McLaughlin who was, like us, a basketball junky. The four of us were constants during the 63 and 64 seasons. Sully, although not officially a ball-boy did fill in when any of us couldn't make a game. Whether he worked the game or not, Sully was at every game. We had a lot of fun those two years and I have some very great memories of the Celtics. I also have some not so pleasant memories of the Celtics. As I mentioned we started late in the 63 season, so we didn't really get to know any of the players or even the routine until the next year. The 1964 Celtics were awesome. I remember sitting on their bench and getting bored because they never lost. Most games were over before half-time. I think in the 64 season they lost only three or four home games all year and they played maybe forty home games that year. They were simply better than every other team that came into the Boston Garden. A loss for the Celtics at home was indeed a rare occurrence. That first year I worked strictly on the Celtics bench, which is exactly where I wanted to be. I had a chance to sit beside Tommy Heinsohn, John Havlicek, Bill Russell, KC Jones, Sam Jones,

A Southie Memoir

Larry Siegfried, Satch Sanders and Red Auerbach every night. I thought I had died and gone to heaven. Some of the older kids, who had been at the Garden for a few years wanted no part of the Celtic bench. At first I thought they were crazy. Yeah, crazy like a fox. I looked at it this way, the Celtics were paying me five dollars a game to sit on their bench. I would have paid them five dollars to sit on their bench, if I had the money. I saw absolutely nothing wrong with the situation. That however would change. I worked for Buddy Leroux that first year I sat on the Celtics bench. He had the personality of a rock. It was very hard to get close to the guy. He was good at his job but he seemed to have difficulty relating to other people, especially other younger people. All the kids, who worked there, hated Buddy Leroux. He treated everyone as if he was better than them. He might have been richer than us but he was certainly no better. Buddy later went on to own the Boston Red Sox and he opened a very lucrative clinic somewhere in the suburbs. He was not one of my favorite people. He was one of the reasons why the older kids did not want to work on the Celtic bench.

There were other reasons, the biggest being money. When you worked the Celtic bench you could be almost guaranteed two things. First, the Celtics would win and second, Buddy Leroux would yell at you whether or not you were guilty of anything. That's just the way it was. I knew it, and I accepted it. The alternative was to be watching the game on TV or in the stands, or not at all, which was no alternative for me. About twelve games into the season I found out why all the older kids wanted to work the visitors bench, other than dealing with Buddy Leroux. The visiting trainers usually, if not always, tipped the ball boys. Some teams tipped better than others and team's that beat the Celtics tipped very well, although it didn't happen that often. But one of my friends got tipped $20 from the Lakers trainer, one night when the Lakers beat the Celts. Now you have to understand we didn't come from rich backgrounds. My father was a custodian and worked at a liquor store and as a longshoreman to make ends meet. Sully's father worked for the railroad and worked as many as 4 side jobs so his family had food on the table. So getting $20. from the Lakers was a pretty good deal. The other reason they wanted to work the visitor's bench was to meet players like Oscar Robertson, Jerry West, Elgin Baylor, Bob Pettit, Richie Guerin, Wilt Chamberlain and others. Those sounded like were pretty good reasons to me. So the next year 1964-65, I put in for, and received, my assignment to sit on the visitor's bench. I knew I would miss some of the Celtics like KC, Sam, Satch and especially Hondo who really treated us with respect and dignity. He was a class guy and everyone who ever worked for the Celtics will tell you the same thing. I knew I wouldn't miss Russell at all. Don't get me wrong, Russell was one of the greatest basketball players to lace up a pair of sneakers. I admired him every time he stepped on the court. I despised him every time he stepped off the court. He treated us like dirt. Russell didn't like anybody. Sully hated him more than I did. Sully had worked a couple of night when Owen couldn't make it and he was assigned to work the Celtics bench with me.

    One night, just before I was leaving the house to go to the Garden, I got a call from Owen. He said he had the flu, and he asked me to call Sully and see he if he could work for him. Sully jumped at every opportunity to work the bench, especially when both he and I were working the same bench. That particular night, we were both assigned to the Celtics bench. The game went along as usual with the Celtics wining without any problem. The problem would come later. I was already in the locker room by the time the team came running in. A major part of our job was to have the locker room all set up before the players arrived. That meant that with three or four minutes left in the game, I would take all the sweat jackets and pants, that weren't being worn, and take them back to the locker room and hang them up in each player's locker. We would also break out the beer and orange juice and place one of each in front of everyone's locker. The rest of the beer and the orange juice would be left on the trainer's table, for everyone to help themselves. The worst part about doing this was that I never got to see the end of a game. Usually it didn't matter because the Celtics always had the game well in hand long before the 4th quarter even started. First, back to Sully. There was nothing unusual about the Celtics game, the night that Sully filled in for Owen. The Celtics ran out to a big lead and just coasted the rest of the way. I had the locker room all ready as the happy victors came jogging in. The Celtics locker room was a fun place, when they won, which was almost always, as I've said. When they lost, there was no joy in Mudville. After a Celtic loss I always tried to be as inconspicuous as possible. I would do my work and get out of there as soon as possible. Those guys didn't take too kindly to losing, especially Auerbach. Red was all smiles after a win, but his face would take on a whole different look after they lost. Even the reporters treaded lightly with Red after a loss. He looked like he was just waiting to take someone's head off and it wasn't going to be mine. I always steered very clear of the redhead on those occasions. The players, after a loss, would just sit in front of their lockers and sulk. They were like giant little kids, when they lost. Before the game, there was always a lot of practical joking going on and some guys were really funny. I remember working the Knicks bench one night when a guy named Jim Barnett put on a show that could have been headlining in Las Vegas. He sang and did impressions. He was great. Another night I was working the Lakers bench when Elgin Baylor walked into the locker room, jumped up on the trainer's table, and removed his sweat pants. The trainer came over to him and pulled out a huge needle. The size of the needle shocked me. As the trainer approached, Elgin, he let go with a real loud scream. Everyone in the locker room just froze.

"What's the matter Elgin, I haven't done anything yet," the trainer said, surprised.

Elgin smiled. "I'm just practicing."

The whole locker room cracked up. It was amazing the things some of the players had to go through to play. Elgin got that needle before every game. I don't know if they were taking stuff out of his knee, or putting stuff in his knee, I just know that I might have thought twice about playing every night if I had to go through that before every game.

The Celtics had their own practical jokers. Jungle Jim Luscutoff and KC were always doing something. KC could really sing too. He could have had a career as a singer, I bet, if he wasn't such a great basketball player. They were always getting on Larry Siegfried as well. I guess Larry liked to party. And from what I had heard the girls at these parties were a little on the younger side. After one game, I was sweeping up the tape and a journeyman guard, who I really liked, named Johnny McCarthy, asked, "hey Brian, how old are you?"

"I'm 14," I said, not really knowing why he even cared.

'What are you doing later?" he asked.

"Nothing," I responded warily. I had no idea what he was doing or where he was going with this.

"Larry's having a party after the game and all the girls will be your age, why don't you come by." Everyone in the locker room cracked up, except Siegfried, who said something about Johnny McCarthy being too old to party. That was how it was in the locker room and I always enjoyed it, when they won. Most teams hated coming into the Garden to play. First they had to play the best team in all of professional sports, and second they had to deal with Red Auerbach.

Red was a master. No, make that, Red was THE master. If the Celtics were playing the Detroit Pistons on December 14th and the temperature outside the Garden was ten degrees, Red would turn off the heat in the Detroit locker room until minutes before the Pistons bus pulled up on Causeway Street. The Pistons would be freezing as they entered the Garden. They would go directly to their locker room and it would be almost as cold in there, as it was outside. They would go berserk. I know, I was there on a number of occasions when the coach would demand to see Red. I always knew where to find him. He would be in the Celtics locker room.

"Coach," I would say "Coach Schausse would like to talk to you."

"Tell them I'll be there in fifteen minutes." I would relay the message to the freezing, frustrated coach, which would just get him madder. Thirty minutes later you could smell Red's cigar long before you saw him. He would come in the locker room bigger than life.

"Hey coach how ya doing?" The visiting coach would be fit to be tied by this time.

"How am I doing?" he would yell "I'm freezing my ass off." Red would go over and put his hand on the radiator, which had gotten hot in the past twenty minutes.

"It's this old building, I don't know why it's so cold in here the heat is on. Come on over here and feel it." He would then have the visiting coach feel the hot pipes and continue his harangue about the old building. He was amazing. I watched this happen maybe a dozen times and each time it amazed me. He would reverse the procedure when the weather got warm. When the playoffs were played in late April and May and sometimes it would get pretty hot outside, the visitor's locker room would be like a sauna bath. I found out, the hard way, that the heating pipes worked just fine then. I arrived early one day for a playoff game between the Celtics and the 76'ers. It was unseasonably hot for that time of year. It was probably in the- high 80's as I opened the visiting team's locker room door. A rush of hot air came rushing out of the door and almost knocked me over. It had to be 120 degrees in that room. There were no windows and the heat was oppressive. I went over to the heating pipes and placed my hand on one of them. I recoiled from the pain. The pipes were scalding hot. I just laughed and went to get some salve for my burned hand. Red was at it again.

I remember another incident similar to that. I got to the Garden right after the 9 o'clock Mass. Again, it was unseasonably warm and I knew the Garden would be like an oven. I walked into the Lakers locker room and I was almost overcome by the heat The radiators were going full blast. I walked out of the room and didn't come back until the Lakers had entered the building. The room, by that time had cooled off to about 105 degrees. Freddie Schausse, the Lakers Coach went crazy. He was yelling and screaming about Red this and Red that. It was pretty funny to watch. Red used every ploy in the book and then he even invented some to gain an advantage. He was great. Every time the opposing coach confronted him, he would blame "This old building."

"Red these conditions are ridiculous." The Laker coach yelled at Red. Red would nod his agreement.

"I know, our locker room is just as hot." The truth was that the Celtics locker room was roughly 72 degrees with fans blowing all over the place. There was not one fan in the Lakers locker room. Another thing he would do was to shut off the hot water in the visitors shower room. Teams would go crazy. The Celtics would have just beaten then by twenty points or more and after the game they would come back and be faced with a freezing shower. By the end of the day they just wanted to get the hell out of Boston. Which is exactly what Red wanted them to be thinking about. They would hate to come back to the Boston Garden, which is exactly what Red wanted. He had them thinking about the cold water and the locker room temperature, long before they stepped into the building. He was playing mind games with them, and he always won. Always. He would get us in trouble because the players or the coaches would yell at us, figuring that we had something to do with the shenanigans, which we didn't. It was just little things but they drove the opposing players and coaches wild. After each game Red would give us two six packs of beer and twelve orange juices for the visiting team. The visiting teams had twelve players on their roster, so they got exactly one warm beer and one small orange juice. Not one beer or orange juice for then for the coaches. They would yell at us and we would always play Mickey the dunce. The Celtics, at the other end of the Garden, would have two cases of beer andtwo2 cases of orange juice to split between their twelve players and coaches. Soap was another biggie. The visiting team never had any soap in the shower room. They, again, would yell at us to get them some soap. I would go down to the Celtics locker room and tell Red that the Knicks or the Pistons or the Royals wanted soap. He would give me 1 bar of soap. One. It was also one of those little bar of soap, which you got in every hotel room across the country. I would bring the tiny bar over to the other locker room where they were already taking cold showers. By that time they just wanted out of Boston, soap or no soap, beer or no beer. They were all seeing red as they got on the team bus.

I remember one time when the St. Louis Hawks were in town. These two teams justdidn't like each other. I went to the Hawks locker room and had everything ready by the time the team arrived. I helped the trainer with the tape as he did everyone's ankles. They told us we had five minutes before they took the court. I went into the closet to get the bag of balls. They were gone. I panicked. I went to the coach and told him that the teams warm up balls were missing.

"Well go get another bag," he said in a Southern drawl. I went to the Celtics locker room looking for another bag of basketballs. There were none. Now I was really panicking. My friend Owen was working the Celtics bench and he saw that I was pretty perplexed. When I told him what was happening, he went in to where Red was sitting and came out a few seconds later with a set of keys.

"Red said there are some balls in the back in storage room three," Owen said handing me the keys. I ran to the very back of the Garden in search of basketballs. I ran right by the Hawks coach, who just looked at me and shrugged. I went into the dark recesses of the old building and began my search. I was scared to death. This was the area where we had encountered the rats and that was very much in the front of my mind as I began looking for storage room #3. It was also freezing back there and there were no lights on which made it very spooky. I found Room #3, grabbed a bag of balls, in the dark, and was out of there in a flash. The Hawks were waiting for me, when I finally arrived. They couldn't take the floor without any basketballs, and they weren't too happy about the delay. The coach saw me, with the bag of balls, and motioned me over to where they had already lined up, to take the floor. I ran ahead of them, and got to the court just as the Hawks were entering the arena. The crowd began to boo as they ran to where I was standing. I had one ball in my hand and I threw it to their captain Bob Pettit who was running at a good clip. He caught the ball and threw it on the ground in a dribbling motion. Only the ball didn't bounce. It hit the floor like a rock, and never moved. It was frozen. The crowd began to howl laughing as Pettit stared at me like I had done it on purpose. I hadn't, but I had a good idea who had. All of the balls were frozen so we had to borrow two from the Celtics. Red had a big smile on his face. The next game the old bag of balls was back in the closet. Now I wonder who masterminded that little sabotage. Two guesses and Sully wasn't even there.

Chapter 25 – Wilt Chamberlain and the Philadelphia 76'ers

Some of the players took all of these shenanigans in stride and laughed about them.

Not all, but a few. And we all had our favorite player or players, for one reason or another. One of the people that the fans in Boston loved to hate, was Wilt Chamberlain But, for me, Chamberlain was one of the players I loved to see come to the Garden. Beside his awesome physical ability, Wilt was a good guy. This might sound kind of sacrilege a kid from South Boston who liked Wilt Chamberlain and disliked Bill Russell, but as my friend Jimmy Brett, who ran for Mayor of Boston, would often say," the proof is in the pudding." Chamberlain treated us well and Russell didn't. Simple as that. I remember walking into the Philadelphia 76'er's locker room and seeing, Wilt, Billy Cuningham, Hal Greer, Luscious Jackson and Chet Walker and I knew the Celtics had some trouble. That was a very talented basketball team and my favorite team to work for. They were a bunch of characters. Hal Greer was the most superstitious player in the league. He had all these little idiosyncrasies that he went through before, during and after each game. He had to be the last one to get his warm-up jacket during a time-out, he would have a half piece of gum. He would be the last person out of the locker room and on and on and on. It was a full-time job just trying to keep up with his superstitions. There were a lot of superstitious players in the league but Greer was the most superstitious of the lot. He was a hell of a player as well. Billy Cunningham reminded me a lot of John Havlicek. He always talked to us and asked us our opinions of certain players. He always asked us how we were doing in school. Some players get caught up in their own importance, Cunningham was not one of them. And he could play too. And then there was Wilt. I was afraid of him when I first walked into their locker room. I guess I believed a lot of the propaganda in the Boston papers about how mean and tough he was. And I'm sure he was on the court. But off the court Wilt was funny and caring. I often thought how the Boston papers made Wilt out to be the bad guy and Russell the good guy. If they only knew. My first game with Wilt, he called me aside, which was unusual for every other team except the 76'ers.

"Are you working our bench tonight?" he said, leaning way over. I was kind of intimidated.

"Yes sir," I quickly replied.

"Can you do me a big favor" he asked.

"Yes sir" I quickly relied again. Wilt bent over and produced one of the tiny little Dixie cups, which we used to give the players water during time-outs or between periods. He held the cup up for a few seconds.

"Do you see this little cup?" he asked.

"Yes sir." I said wide-eyed, even to be talking to Wilt Chamberlain.

"Now how many of these little cups do you think it takes to fill me up?" I looked at the tiny little cup and then back at the giant sitting next to me.

"Quite a few," I answered.

"That's the point," he said. "During a time-out I don't have time to drink 10 little cups of water," he went on, "And you don't have time to just wait on me, right?"

"Right," I agreed.

"Here's what I want you to do," he said, leaning over and whispering as if he were telling me his innermost secrets.

"Go out to the concession stand and get a beer cup, fill it with water and I will use that during the game rather than these little cups OK" he said, again producing the 2 ounce cups that every ball boy had used since basketball was invented.

"OK," I said and I was immediately off to find the nearest concession stand. But it wasn't that easy. I went to two concession stands before the guy behind the counter would believe me.

"Why do you want a beer cup?" the first guy asked.

"It's not for me it's for Wilt Chamberlain," I said boastfully.

"Yeah kid and I'm Oscar Robertson," he laughed." The same thing happened at the next concession stand. But by the third one, I had smartened up.

"Excuse me sir," I said, as I wormed my way in between beer buying customers, could I buy one of those cups?" I asked, pointing to the large beer cups.

"Yeah give me a dime," he answered. I did, and I was back in the 76'ers locker room in no time flat. I produced the cup for Wilt, who smiled and patted my head.

'Thank you my man", he smiled. From then on Wilt and I were on good terms.

I started getting ready to go out, now that Wilt was satisfied, when Hal Greer stopped me.

"Hey kid ya got a minute?" Greer asked.

"Sure," I said walking over to the jump shooting foul shooter. He proceeded to give me a list of things that he wanted me to do, which I briefly mentioned earlier. After he got finished, he looked at me.

"Now you got all that?"

"Yeah" I said trying to assimilate all the things he told me, about his warm-up jacket, about only wanting a half cup of water and a half piece of gum. This job was starting to get complicated. But I remembered everything, and I got Wilt his large cup of water and the 76'ers even beat the Celtics that night. I was in the locker room after the game picking up tape and cleaning up, when Wilt came over and stuck a $20 bill in my hand.

"Thanks man," was all he said, and he was out the door. I was surprised because no player had ever given me any money before. I continued cleaning up, when Hal Greer walked by and threw me another $10 bill. He just smiled and didn't say a word. I couldn't believe it thirty bucks. I told Owen on the way home. He had worked the Celtics bench and hadn't gotten a cent. He was pretty jealous, but he was also very resourceful. The next time the 76'ers were in town, guess who all of a sudden was working the 76'ers locker room with me. Owen. I was glad to see the 76'ers come back, for a number of reasons. First, they were fun to watch, and I knew they would play the Celtics tough. Secondly, because I was hoping to get $30, although I now had a rival for the money in Owen.

I almost died when I saw Owen in the 76'ers locker room when I came in. He just smiled. I cracked up. This was the first time that Owen had worked in any locker room other than the Celtics locker room. We were talking to Billy Cunningham when Wilt came strolling in. He was a pretty awesome sight. Owen turned and just stared, and so did everyone else. All the reporters, who were talking to, or interviewing other players, stopped in mid sentence, and looked at Wilt. His mere presence demanded that kind of attention. Wilt could take over a room, not only because of his tremendous size but because of his manner. Everyone knew when Wilt was in the room. His booming voice and high- pitched laugh was unmistakable. He gave me a wave.

"Got my cup?" I was well prepared, and I withdrew a huge beer cup from my bag.

"My man," he laughed. Then he said, for everyone to hear. "I told you these Boston kids liked us." Everyone in the room laughed as I turned red. Hal Greer, who was sitting in the corner, came over and asked me if I remembered his instructions. I recited them one by one, he smiled and slapped me five. Wilt was visiting with everyone, telling stories, and just kind of fooling around. He worked a room better than any politician I have ever seen. He finally made his way over to his locker, which consisted of 1 hook, and began to undress. The locker room was very noisy. The Boston reporters covered the 76'ers and the Lakers more thoroughly than any other teams, when those two came to Boston. You could count on the 76'ers and the Laker's locker rooms to be crowded with Boston reporters, looking for an angle for their stories. The 76'ers knew they were good and it showed. They were very loose before a game, which was unusual. Most teams were very quiet and tight before a game, including the Celtics. But the 76'ers locker room was noisy and loose and I really liked that. I had been helping the trainer with taping the player's ankles and I kind of lost track of where Owen was. I made sure the balls were good. I did learn my lesson from the St. Louis fiasco and when I turned around Owen was standing beside me. He was dumbfounded at the atmosphere, which existed in the room. He was used to the Celtics locker room, which was usually quiet before a game and boisterous after a game.

"These guys are crazy," he whispered, as they continued a series of practical jokes.

"No, there just having fun," I said and went on to another task.

Owen, who was usually one of the best workers, of all the ball-boys, was just standing around kind of mesmerized at the convivial atmosphere in the room. I went over to him, and we began talking about who was going to do what during the game. He was talking to me, but he was looking beyond

Brian P. Wallace

me at something, the way that some politicians do when they shake your hand. I turned, just as Wilt had begun taking off his underpants. The room was still pretty boisterous. Wilt was now completely naked with his back toward us. Owen was still staring at him. What happened next seemed like it was in slow motion. Wilt had his jock strap in his right hand and he turned to face us as he began putting on his jock. Owen in a voice that was much louder than he wanted it to be said, "Holy shit, look at the size of his dick." The problem was, that when he said it, the room had momentarily quieted down and when Owen said, "Look at the size of his dick," it could be heard in every corner of the room. Everyone turned to look at Owen and then at the object of Owen's fascination. I was never so embarrassed in my entire life. I can't even imagine how Owen felt. He turned so red I thought he was going to explode. He turned and ran out of the room. The room became deathly quiet and then someone started to laugh, and the whole room followed, Thank God. Owen never came back. He told Buddy that he was sick and went home. I worked the bench by myself that night and got my $30 bucks even though the Celtics beat them that night.

Chapter 26 - Sox, Yankees and Mickey Mantle

Our pro careers weren't just limited to the NBA either. We loved all sports and we went wherever the home teams were playing. Fenway Park was even easier to sneak in than the Garden. We would buy one ticket for $1.50 and one of us would go in, and open the men's room window on the right field side of the Park, and we would all squeeze through. It was a tight fit and one, which I couldn't even attempt today, but at 14 years old I only weighed 110 pounds. Sully had a little more trouble than I did, so he was usually the one who went in and opened the window for the rest of us. We never got caught and I bet we went to about 40 or 50 home games a year. The Red Sox stunk but we loved baseball. Like the Bruins we went to Fenway Park, most days, to watch the opposing team. Ted was in his last years but he could still hit the cover off the ball, but he was about the only good player the Red Sox had. It's funny though, how you remember so much about the games our youth. I can remember so many things about the Sox from the early 60's that are permanently implanted into my brain. I remember particular games and numbers and small little things like who hit what, when and against who. Why do I remember that Tommy Brewer wore #23 or Ike Delock wore #14 or Bill Monboquette wore #27. Why will I never forget names like names like Jim Pagliaroni, Pumpsie Green, Bob Tillman, Billy Goodman, Frank Sullivan, Ted Lepcio, Frank Malzone, Pete Runnells, Chuck Shillling, Don Schwall, Eddie Bressoud, Dick Gernet, Dave Morehead, Don Buddin, Lou Clinton, Gary Geiger, Sammy White, Gene Stephen's, or Mike Higgins? Each of them, in their own way, played a part in my childhood. They were my heroes. And they were regular guys, not like the millionaire prima donna's that play today. These guys didn't make a whole lot of money, but they loved the game and so did I. One day we were getting the train at Broadway to go to Fenway. Sully tells me that his uncle, knows Bill Monboquette. "How?" I ask skeptically.

"He works with him," Sully shot back, "Come on" I said "Bill Monboquette doesn't work, He's a baseball player."

"Swear to God," Sully said. "My uncle works with him." I didn't believe him. I thought that ball players just played ball. There's no way they actually worked. We got seats in the bleachers and we immediately went down to the first row.

"There's your buddy Bill Monboquette," I said mimicking Sully.

"Hey Monbo," Sully shouted at the top of his lungs. Monboquette turned around and waved. Not satisfied, Sully motioned the right-handed pitcher over to where we sat. Monbo shrugged and jogged over.

"Do you know Tim Sullivan?" Sully quickly asked. Monboquette brightened.

"Sure, I work with him, how's he doing?" He was telling the truth. Monbo came over to us and talked with us for about ten minutes and then gave us each a baseball. It was great.

Things were different then. Very different. We had some great times at Fenway. One of my favorite days, of all time, occurred early in July, 1961. Our doorbell rang that summer morning and I heard my mother's voice calling me downstairs. I had no idea why I was being summoned from the sanctity of my bedroom. I knew I hadn't done anything yet, it was too early. Standing in my doorway was a neighbor named Eddie Rollo. I had not yet celebrated my 12th birthday. Eddie Rollo was about 16 years older than me, which made him 27 at the time. He had been an outstanding 3-sport athlete at Southie High a couple of years before that day. He was actually drafted as a pitcher by the Milwaukee Braves, but an irregular heartbeat dashed his hopes of a major league pitching career. He was a great guy who always went out of his way to be friendly. This was the first time, however, that he had ever knocked at my door. By the time I arrived downstairs, my mother and Eddie were in deep conversation.

"Brian, Mr. Rollo has 1 ticket for today's baseball game at Fenway Park," my mother said.

"Mom, it isn't a baseball game, it's a Yankee' game," I said, apologizing for my mother's baseball ignorance. Eddie shyly held up something in his hand.

I just asked your mother if you could go to the game," he said. My heart skipped a beat.

"I don't know if he can go over there by himself, Mr. Rollo, but I know he appreciates the offer."

"Whoa, whoa, whoa," I interjected.

" I explained to him that you have never gone to Fenway Park by yourself. She was half- right. Sully and I had been regulars on Lansdowne street for two years, which she had no idea about.

"Come on ma , I'm be 12 in a couple of weeks, and this is the New York Yankees, Mantle, Maris, Yogi Berra, Moose Skowron, Boyer, Bauer, Richardson, Kubek, Whitey Ford, "

"I guess you've heard of them Eddie Rollo laughed. I took the ticket and studied it. It was not only a ticket to the Yankees game, it was a BOX SEAT to the Yankees game. I had never sat in a box seat legally in my life. I had never sat in a box seat for more than an inning. Sully and I had tried, every game, but the same usher would always throw us out before we managed to become too comfortable.

"I probably should call your father," she said as I continued to study the ticket.

"No way ma, this is a box seat and I'm going." I said as I grabbed the ticket with one hand and my official score book, with the other, and I was out the door, before either my mother or Eddie Rollo had time to react. I yelled my thanks to Eddie Rollo as I headed for the bus stop and Fenway Park and a day I will never forget.

I kept thinking about the Bronx Bombers. I was a die- hard Red Sox fan but the Yankees were special; even I had to admit that. Especially in 1961 when both Roger Maris and Mickey Mantle were taking dead aim at the Bambino's single season home run record of 60 round- trippers. Even their manager Casey Stengel was bigger than life. I was the first one at the Park that day. I waited patiently for the doors to finally open. When they did I dashed to the Box Seat area and found my seat. Unbelievable. I was going to sit directly behind the Yankees dugout. in the first row. Now for an 11 year- old baseball junkie, life just doesn't get any better than that. The Yanks were already on the field taking batting practice as I entered the venerable park, and headed for my seat and began looking for him. He wasn't on the field. Finally he came out of the dugout #7 Mickey Mantle. A big smile on his handsome Oklahoma face and shaking hands with everyone who had gathered around the dugout , drawn to the Yankees like Don King to controversy.

Before I knew what was happening, I heard a strange voice call out, "Hey Mick," and I realized it was me. He turned and looked right at me. I was only about 12 feet from him.

"Can I have your autograph?" I asked quickly. He smiled that famous smile.

"Well I think I can arrange that." He walked slowly over to the edge of the dugout and reached for my extended score book, which had magically appeared hanging over the roof of the Yankees dugout. He took the book and my pen.

"What's your name son?" he asked in that slow Southern drawl.

"Brian," I managed to remember. He began to sign and stopped.

"Who you - all rooting for today Brian?" he asked.

Before I knew what I was saying, "The Red Sox," I said without thinking. Now that was stupid, I thought to myself.

He looked down and continued writing. When he was finished he handed me the now valuable, score book.

"Good boy, you always have to be loyal to your team, right Brian."

"Yes sir," I smiled, I still couldn't believe I was actually having a conversation with Mickey Mantle.

"I'll tell ya'll what though," he smiled "I have a feeling that I'm gonna catch one today." At first I didn't know what he meant. And just as he said that, he turned and pointed to #9, who just happened to be Roger Maris.

"And if I don't catch one, I know he will," as he pointed to Maris. This was a bit too much for me. I was so close to Mantle and Maris that I could reach out and touch them.

"Hey Rog," Mantle yelled out. Maris walked over to where Mantle and I were.

"I suppose you want his autograph too?" Mantle said, taking my scorecard and handing it to Maris.

"Yes sir," I managed to get out. Maris signed it and they both walked to the batting cage and put on a hitting clinic. They both also "caught one," as Mantle said, that afternoon. That year Maris went on to break Ruth's record as he hit 61 home runs, one better than the Bambino. People forget that Mantle hit 54 home runs that year while leading the league in runs scored with 132.

Mantle drove in 128 runs and batted .317 that year. Not bad numbers. Some people remember Mantle for the 565 foot home run he hit on April 17, 1953 in Yankee Stadium. Some people remember Mantle for his 3 MVP Awards or the 3 home runs he hit on May 13, 1953. While still others remember the slew of World Series records he holds, including most home runs(18), most runs scored(42), most runs batted in(40). I'll always remember Mickey Mantle for being nice to a 11 year- old bespectacled Southie kid, one hot July afternoon in the summer of his life. And I'll always remember the Mick for something he said in 1963.

"When I hit a home run, I put my head down and run around the bases as fast as I can so that I don't ever embarrass the pitcher." Now that was class. That was Mickey Mantle. God rest his soul. They just don't make players like that anymore.

Brian P. Wallace

Chapter 27 – An All Star Game To Remember

O sure I loved Ted Williams and Jackie Jensen and I loved Jimmy Piersall but there was something very special about those guys from New York. Mickey Mantle, Yogi Berra, Roger Maris, Hank Bauer, Moose Skowron, Tony Kubek, Bobby Richardson, and Casey Stengel. I never missed a Yankee game at Fenway. I never rooted for the Yankees but I did love to watch them play. We would get to the park real early for batting practice and stay real late for autographs. More than a couple of times we followed some of the Yankees to the nearest tavern after the game and talked to them, as we walked. The Yankees were like the Celtics. They were the class of the field. I really loved baseball and I really loved Fenway Park. One of my favorite Fenway Park memories occurred during that same summer that Mantle and his buddy Maris chased the Bambino. All my life I had read about and heard about Willie Mays, Warren Spahn, Ernie Banks, Duke Snider, Eddie Matthews and Stan Musial, but I never had the opportunity to see them because they were in the National League and the Red Sox were in the American League. The only time that an American League city entertained the National League teams was during the World Series and the Sox weren't usually invited to that party. When those invitations went out, every year, the Yanks were always first in line. There was, however, one other time when the National League players would come and play before American League fans, it was called the All Star game. And on July 31, 1961 the All Star game was played At Fenway Park. And if Spahn and Mays and Banks and the rest of them were going to be there, well so was I. I called Sully bright and early that July morning in 1961. No answer. His father's car was nowhere around. I called Knuckles. He wasn't home either. I called Ridge. His father said that he was visiting his grandmother in Gardner Mass.

This day wasn't turning out as I had planned. I was all- alone, without a ticket for the game. I did had two bucks and I was determined to see the game. I grabbed the bus in front of the club and headed over to Fenway. I had no idea what I was going to do once I got there but I had to be there. Even if I just saw Warren Spahn and Willie Mays I would be happy. It was still about three hours before game time, so I stood by the player's parking lot and waited for them to come to the park. A couple of players had arrived, but none of the future Hall of Famers. I heard a booming voice.

"Hey kid you can't stand there." I turned and saw a huge Boston cop walking toward me. I had always stood there before and nobody ever bothered me. But Willie Mays and some other guy had just pulled into the parking lot. I had a real dilemma on my hands. Do I move and miss my chance at Mays, or do I get arrested? Not much of a choice in my mind. I stayed put. I called out to Mays, he smiled and gave me a big wave, just as the big cop put his huge hand on my shoulder.

"Didn't I tell you to move?" he barked.

"Yes," I said. "But that was Willie Mays."

'I don't care if it was Babe Ruth, I told you to move and you disobeyed me," he snapped.

"I'll move now," I weakly said. "Too late, he barked. Come with me," the cop said. I couldn't believe this. Where was Sully when I needed him? I was too stunned to say anything. He still had his hand on my shoulder, so I wasn't going to try to run. There was about twenty other kids standing there, I thought, why did he pick on me? He led me out of the parking lot and through a door and into the park. This was weird.

"Now you can't stand in the parking lot but you can stand right here," the cop said. Right here, was INSIDE Fenway Park. I was dumbfounded. I heard everyone yelling. I turned around and I was staring right into the faces of Warren Spahn and Eddie Matthews. Before I had a chance to say a word, the big cop who just had my by the neck said, "excuse me gentlemen, would you mind signing an autograph for my son's friend." I looked at the cop. It was Knuckles's father. I almost fainted. I had never seen him in uniform before and I realized I had never actually looked at his face, just his badge, which was enough. I hadn't recognize him at all. He knew it, and had a good laugh at my expense.

"Sure," said Spahn, "We have a special place in our hearts for Boston kids, right Eddie?" Eddie Matthews laughed.

"Yeah, but I think this guy was a little too, young to see us play in this town." He was right. I hadn't seen the Braves play, in Boston, before they moved to Milwaukee but I knew everything they did. I was in heaven.

"You going to be all right here?" Mr. Mc Grath asked.

"Fine," I said as I spied Ernie Banks coming in the door.

"I wish Knuckles was here," I said to his father.

"I do to," he said. "Can you get him a few autographs?" he asked.

"I'll get him a ton" I said. And I did. After all I had the best spot in the whole park. Every player, who played, had to walk past me to get into the clubhouse. I pulled a Sully that day. Every time I asked for an autograph, I put on a sad face and asked if they would sign one for my little brother. Worked every time! I had 41 autographs. Knuckles got 39. Spahn and Matthews were mine and only mine. It was one of the best days of my life, thanks to Mr. McGrath. Sometimes it's better to be lucky than good.

A few years ago the Boston hosted the Major League All Star Game again. It was the first time, it has been held in Boston, since 1961. I took my little guy, Cullen, who was 9 years old at the time, to the Fan Fest, which was held at the Hynes Convention Center. During the course of the afternoon, I spotted a whole room that was called the "Collectible's Corner. There were collector's from all over the country at the Hynes that day. One of the booths was called "My mother threw out all of my baseball cards Inc." I laughed and went over to the guy who was operating that booth. I asked him how much a program from the 1961 All Star game, signed by almost every player on both teams would be worth today. The guy's eyes bugged out.

"Do you have it?" he asked in disbelief.

"No. my mother threw out all of my baseball stuff when I went to College, but I thought I would ask," I said. The guy looked defeated. He thought a minute, as I mentioned some of the autographs that were on my program.

"Fifty to a Hundred thousand," he said, "If all the signatures were in good shape and all of them were on the original program." I thanked him and left, almost sick to my stomach. I told Cullen, on the ride home, to hang on to his baseball cards. You never know.

Chapter 28 – Joe Crowley, Ray Flynn and Pat Flaherty

We had some great times at Fenway the most memorable however were not Red Sox games but Patriot games. The Boston Patriots began, as a franchise in 1960. We had never seen professional football before, except on TV, so this was a real big deal to us. We went to every game whether at Boston University, Boston College, Harvard or Fenway Park. Having no permanent home, the Patriots moved around a lot in those early days. They were new and fledgling but it was pro football. They played most of their Fenway Park games on Friday nights, which was fine with us. Southie High played most of their games on Friday afternoons at White Stadium. We would go directly from White Stadium to Fenway Park without stopping at go and without going home for supper. My parents weren't crazy about this Friday schedule, but they knew how much sports meant to me and they relented. I looked forward to our Friday football doubleheaders. It was just one non-stop madcap adventure. From White Stadium to Fenway Par. All we did was laugh. There was one day that stands out above all others, and of course Sully was right in the middle. It was my freshman year in high school and earlier that Friday, Southie High had beaten a good Charlestown team. What was even better was that one of our best friends was the star of the game. His name was Pat Flaherty and we didn't even know he played football. Actually, he had never played organized football before he went to Southie High. Pat was a quiet kid, who studied a lot. He was a great basketball and baseball player but had never strapped on pads before. He came down the cafeteria one day, and told us he was going to try out for the football team. We all laughed at him because we knew how good the team was, and we figured that Coach Crowley wouldn't even give him a uniform. Great call. Well, Pat did go down to practice that day and signed up for the team. Pat was a great kid but he was as quiet as a church mouse, which didn't fit the stereotypical high school jock mold. Coach Crowley was one of the top football coaches in the state. Ever since Crowley took over the head coaching job, from Southie legend Steve White, his team would roll through every other teams in the City. A bad year for a Crowley coached team was one loss. Two losses during the course of one year was unthinkable and rarely happened. And Crowley was tough as nails.

Brian P. Wallace

He didn't take any shit from his players and he never babied them. Crowley knew what it took to win and he wasted no time getting there. The problem with Crowley was that you were only as good as your last game. Not many football players, at least the good ones, flunked off the team, during football season. A straight D student would somehow get all C's during the football season and then return to his all D status once the Southie - Eastie Thanksgiving game was played. Imagine that. All the football players somehow passed all their subjects from September to November. After that, they were on their own. That was Joe Crowley. If he could use you he would. If you couldn't help him then he most certainly wouldn't help you. The worst part was that he was guidance counselor my senior year. A lot of guidance I got that year. I received a few basketball scholarships that year and went to talk to Mr. Crowley about which ones he thought I should explore. He laughed in my face.

"Listen Brian you're not one of the best players in the city. Go to whichever school will give you the most playing time on the basketball court." Great guidance, huh.

But, I guess the best story about Joe Crowley happened in the fall of 1958 and is legendary in Southie. Crowley's football team was, again, loaded. They had compiled back to back undefeated seasons, and were heading for another one. They were led by a talented d quarterback, who had a rifle arm, and good if not great, speed. One of the top coaches in the country, a guy named Ben Schwartzwalter, who coached Syracuse University was interested in this young quarterback. Schwartzwalter coached some of the greatest players in the game and knew talent when he saw it. Jimmy Brown, Ernie Davis, Floyd Little, and Larry Csonka. ere just some of the players that Ben Schwartzwalter had recruited and coached at Syracuse. He was so interested in Southie's quarterback that he made the trip from upstate New York to South Boston to see the kid play. He was very impressed with the young signal caller, and was prepared to give him a full football scholarship to Syracuse University. Before he did, he asked Coach Crowley about the senior quarterback who had led Crowley's teams to 27 straight wins. Crowley listened to Coach Schwartzwalter, but interrupted him before he had a chance to finish.

A Southie Memoir

"Listen, Crowley said, "The kid can throw the ball pretty well, but he doesn't have a brain in his head. He'll end up a truck driver or down the docks, like his old man. "Don't waste a scholarship on him," Crowley concluded. Schwartzwalter was stunned and left Southie High and never to return. The young quarterback graduated from South Boston High that year and went to prep school the following year. He did receive a full scholarship, but not for football. A basketball legend named Ron Perry Sr. had seen the former quarterback play basketball and he loved what he saw. He called a friend of his down in Providence Rhode Island and told him all about this kid. The coach, whose name was Joe Mullaney, also liked what he saw and gave the kid a full scholarship to Providence College to play basketball. The former quarterback went on to win the Most Valuable Player Tournament in the National Invitational Tournament in Madison Square garden in 1963. He was selected to the first team Academic All American squad and led the entire country in free throw shooting, both his junior and senior years at Providence. After graduation he came back to South Boston, married and began to raise a family. He entered politics 6 years after graduating from Providence. He was elected to the Massachusetts House of Representatives on his very first attempt at public office. From there he went on to become a Boston City Councilor and Mayor of Boston in 1984. He was appointed Unites States Ambassador to the Vatican, by President Clinton on July 12, 1993. The kid, who was going to end up driving trucks or unloading ships became one of the highest- ranking members of the Clinton White House team. His name is Ray Flynn. Great call Joe. Someone told me that Crowley also picked Germany to win World War II. So you see the reason we laughed at Pat Flaherty is because we knew what kind of barracuda Crowley was. We also didn't think Pat could play football.

Brian P. Wallace

Chapter 29 – Hold Deese Line

We were as wrong about Pat Flaherty as Crowley was about Ray Flynn. Pat became an All State halfback and one of the greatest football players ever to come out of South Boston. But that day that me, Sully, Knuckles and Dukie Buckley went to White Stadium, before we headed for Fenway, was the first time we had ever seen Pat play. He only scored 4 touchdowns and had over 200 yards on the ground. Not a bad introduction to high school football. So as we took the subway to Fenway that memorable night we were really psyched. We snuck in, no problem and headed for the bleachers, which was not a bad spot to watch the game from, unlike baseball. The football field was set up so that the bleacher seats were actually very close to the action, and we loved the action in more ways than one. We sat down and couldn't stop talking about the game that Pat had played earlier that afternoon. It wasn't too long before we noticed a guy, sitting all by himself, who was acting very strangely. The guy was screaming and yelling, which is fine in and of itself, but the game hadn't even begun yet. I snuck a quick look at Sully and his eyes were lighting up, which wasn't necessarily a good sign. It was a pretty cold and windy that late September night and this guy, who was acting up, only had on a thin, white Navy issued T-shirt. He must have been freezing. He did have some liquid fortifications however, which he had already ingested. By the look of him, he had ingested a lot of those liquid fortifications already. Like a moth drawn to a fire, Sully was off. The minute I saw this guy, I knew that Sully was going to do something. What, I never knew. We followed, as usual. When we got closer to the guy we could see that he had his name stenciled on his shirt , in back, right near the collar of the white T-shirt. It just had one word; CARTER.

One word is all that Sully ever needed. I was a little leery of the guy because of the strange way he was acting. Not Sully. He sat right down beside the guy. There were a bunch of seats around the guy, since anybody, who was sane, and was sitting near him had got up and left a long time ago. I never said Sully was sane.

"Carter," Sully screamed, scaring the guy a little. The guy quickly turned around. It was hard to tell how old he was. He was a black man who looked to be in his early 30's. He had a mustache and a huge smile, which showed all of his big white teeth, when he flashed it. As Carter turned around, Sully had his hand outstretched, waiting for Carter to slap him five. Carter did just that, and then with a puzzled look on his face, he looked at Sull.

"You know me, man?". Carter asked, a bit puzzled.

"Come on Carter, you don't remember me?" Sully looked hurt.

"No man," Carter said still puzzled. "Should I?" Sully, now knowing that this guy's name really was Carter, as it said on his shirt, pressed on.

"You're putting me on man, right?" Sully shot back.

"Now way Jose," Carter responded. "How you know me man?" Sully's mind was racing. He knew that the guy's name was Carter and he knew that he was wearing a Navy shirt. And with Sully, that was all he needed. He had his ammunition and now he went on the offensive.

"What are you drunk or something man, I can't believe you don't recognize me," Sully said, acting mad this time. Carter softened a bit.

"Well I did have a couple of drinks tonight, man, maybe that's it." I couldn't believe this. Sully had given the guy a way out and he took it. He was a long way from being out of the woods though. Carter's few seconds of indecision had given Sully all the time he needed to compute all the facts into the little computer that acted as his brain. And like a cat, he pounced.

"I went to boot camp with you," Sully said to a tipsy Carter.

"You were in Norfolk?" Carter shot back. I could see exactly what Sully was doing. He was throwing out a blank sheet of paper and letting Carter fill in the blanks. Now Sully knew that his real name was Carter. He was, in fact, a sailor and he trained in Norfolk Virginia All in the matter of a few seconds.

"You were one crazy dude at Norfolk," Sully laughed. Again not a bad deduction.

"Still am," Carter said. "Crazy Carter," that's me." He went into a fit of laughter that Richard Pryor would have been proud to have induced. It was a weird, crazy laugh. I could see why they called him crazy Carter. People, who had made the mistake to sit close to Carter, were all now moving.

"I never called you that," Sully said. "I always called you by your first name." Carter stiffened. What's he doing? I thought.

"You know my first name?" Carter said surprised.

"Of course, it's Joe," Sully said very convincingly.

"Damn straight," Carter laughed. "now I thinks I member you" he said , slapping Sully five. Game, set and match, to Sully.

"Where did you go after Norfolk?" Sully inquired.

"AWOL," Carter laughed so hard I thought he was going to pass out. "I'm AWOL now man," he said loudly. Sully looked around.

"Why don't you say it a little louder so all the cops in Boston can hear you." Sully said Carter looked around and began that laugh again.

"Ya man I sees what ya mean." And he shut up as quickly. This guy was a lot more than just drunk, he was crazy. All, of a sudden he went for that maniacal laugh to being real serious.

"Where'd they send you after Norfolk?" he asked, now having bought Sully's story completely.

"Boston," Sully said.

"Ain't that a bitch," Carter replied. "I ain't never going back man," And then he brightened up.

"Shit man enough of this swabbie bullshit, How you be man, I haven't seen you in," and he hesitated. Sully filled in the blanks, again.

"A long time man."

"Aint that a bitch,"Carter laughed, "Ain't that a bitch. You really had to see this scene to believe it. In 3 minutes, Sully , all of 15 years old and looking all of 13 years old, had this AWOL sailor totally convinced that he was one of his best friends from boot camp, In that short space of time, Sully knew his name, first and last (I still didn't have a clue as to how he knew his first name) he knew where he was stationed in boot camp, he knew he was AWOL and he knew he was a little bit crazy. All in 3 minutes.

"I forgot yo name," Carter said.

"Man you are drunk," Sully admonished him. "It's Sully."

"That's right man, Sully, I knew it was something like that," Carter said, again slapping Sully five.

"Hey man this here's a party, why ain't you drinking?" Sully quickly said.

"You ain't gonna believe this man, but I don't have my Navy ID and the guy in the beer booth said I look to young too drink, ain't that a bitch."

Carter started to laugh again, as if Sully had just told him the funniest joke he had ever heard.

"Man you do look like young, I know dat. I always sayed that" Carter laughed. Sully just shrugged. Carter then smiled this huge smile and said very conspiratorially.

"Buts Crazy Carteeer can fix dat." He then jumped up and was gone.

"Man you are too much for words." Dukie Buckley said to Sully, shaking his headWe all started to laugh like little kids in a class -room, afraid the teacher would catch us. I still had a question.

"How did you know his name was Joe?" I asked Sully.

"I didn't," but I figured that was his jacket on the ground," he said , pointing to a windbreaker type jacket , that I didn't even see. Sully went on to explain his split second logic.

"On the sleeve of the jacket are the letters JC, I knew his last name was Carter and I figured his first name had to be either John, Joe or Jim and I went with Joe." Sully laughed.

"Here he comes," Dukie said, as we saw our new friend Joe Carter struggling up the stairs with four cups of beer. Now, they'll only let you buy two beers per customer, but things were different back then, in more ways than one. Carter kept two beers for himself and handed Sully the other two beers.

"Just like the old days," Sully said, and saluted Carter. They both took a big gulp of beer. Dukie Buckley grabbed the other beer.

During the first half, alone, Carter bought us at least six beers and he had six beers himself. He was getting out of control. The more beer he drank the more he believed Sully's stories about their time together in the Navy, all of which Sully was making up right on the spot. Carter was really starting to act up and I was getting a little bit uneasy, as a few more cops came over to our section and began to watch us. After all I was only thirteen. Knuckles was fourteen and Dukie and Sully were fifteen, and we already had split six beers, well Dukie and Sully had anyway. They were also starting to get a little tipsy. Things were starting to get out of hand , as Carter continued to get louder and louder. The cops were paying no attention to the game. All their attention was now riveted to our section and more specifically to a guy named Joe Carter.

Brian P. Wallace

Carter was now cheering louder than the Patriot cheerleaders who, unfortunately for them, were cheering directly in front of where we sat. More people were watching him than were watching the game. His T-shirt was now off and he naked from the waist up, The temperature, was probably in the low 40's, but the wind made it seem a lot colder. Carter was also chanting and dancing suggestively to each of the Patriot cheerleader routines. Every time the cheerleaders would begin a new cheer, Carter would stand up, face the crowd, with his back to the game, and lead the cheer. The funny part was he knew every single cheer. Sully said to him.

"Were you a cheerleader in high school, or something?" Sully asked Carter.

"No but I could have been." Carter laughed that crazy laugh.

"You ain't shitting," Sully said, as we all laughed. The game was now secondary. We were pissing our pants laughing and the more we laughed the more outrageous Carter behaved. Everyone was laughing, except the cops and the cheerleaders. They saw nothing funny about Carter's performance. The Patriot's defensive team took the field, in what I think was a close game. We had totally lost track of the score by then. The cheerleaders began a familiar chant. "Hold that line, hold that line." What happened next was totally unexpected and went right into the Sully Hall of Fame.

Carter, once again, stood up faced the crowd, with his back to the cheerleaders, who were being upstaged by this AWOL sailor. He began to chant, in unison with the cheerleaders.

"Hold that line, hold that line." Since he had been acting this way most of the second half we kind of ignored him.

Sully nudged me. "Check this out." Carter had changed the words of the cheer. Instead of saying hold that line, Carter was saying hold DEESE line. Hold DEESE line. And while the Patriot cheerleaders were talking about the Pats defense, Carter had pulled out his Johnson Bar, as he called it and was waving it in the cold New England breeze.

"Hold DEESE line, hold DEESE line" he would yell as he yanked his now unexposed Johnson Bar. We were hysterical and not even egging him on. It got worse or better depending on which side you were on. Carter was now gyrating around, holding his dick, which made all of our little Irish dicks look tiny in comparison. He had already taken off his shirt, a long time ago. Now it was time for his pants. He now was clad only in his Navy issued underwear. with his large black dick in his hands. Everyone, except the cheerleaders weres pointing and laughing at the gyrating Carter. We started our own chan.

"GO CARTER, GO, GO CARTER GO," and he did. Out of the corner of my eye I saw the cops beginning to descend to our section. Carter wasn't through though. I turned to check on the progress of the cops and when I turned again I almost had a heart attack. Carter still had his very large Johnson Bar and was still swinging it in the breeze. I guess it was true what they said about black men. I had only seen two black men's Johnson Bars' in my life,Carter's and Wilt Chamberlain's, and boy did I feel inadequate. He continued to swing his now frigid Johnson Bar, which only hastened the police intervention. They quickly converged, grabbed Carter and hustled him out of there. The whole time they were giving Carter the bums rush, the crowd had picked up our chant, and was saying "go Carter go. go Carter go." And that is exactly what he did. He went, right out the door, to thunderous applause. The Patriots probably thought that the applause were for them. Now that would have been something different. Two cops came over to us and took a look at all the empty beer cups.

"Are you kids drinking?" They asked.

"No sir, those were all his beer."

"Do you know that guy?" one of the cops asked Sully.

Sir I never saw that man before tonight." It was the first truthful thing that Sullyhadsaid all night. The cops said that we should be very careful as to who we associate with and left. Poor Carter. I wonder whatever happened to Mr. "Hold DEESE line." He could have had a career in pornographic movies or cheerleading.

Chapter 30 – Meet The New Boston Patriot Ball Boys

The next Friday night we were right back at Fenway and raring to go. This was the infancy of the American Football League and there really wasn't a whole lot of structure or security on the field, like it is today. Nobody knew who belonged and who didn't. Shit, half the players didn't know who their own teammates were going to be until the National Anthem. But once the game was about to get started, they cleared the field and made us go into the stands to our seats, which we really didn't have either. The Patriots, like the Bruins, never sold out, so finding a seat was always easy. But Sully didn't like easy things. He always had to push everything to the limited. We were sitting in the stands watching the game, which had just started, and Sully became all excited.

"I got it, I got it," he jumped up, like some roly poly jack in the box, Dukie Buckley and I just looked at him, having no idea what he just got. He didn't care, he kept right on talking.

"What are those ball-boys wearing?" he asked.

'Blue sweatshirts," we answered in unison.

"And what else?" he went on like some frustrated teacher.

"Red sweatpants," I answered.

"What's the big deal?" Dukie asked.

"There's no team logos on their clothes, it's simple." For a moment I thought the only thing around us that was simple, was Sully. I still didn't get it.

"What did we wear on the Celtics bench?" he asked.

"We wore white pants and a white sweatshirt."

"Great," he said being very sarcastic. "But what was on the sweatshirt?"

"The Celtics logo," I answered, now understanding where he was going with this. He immediately saw the gleam in my eye.

"Get it?" he asked. I shook my head in the affirmative. Poor Dukie didn't have a clue as to what we were talking about.

"Those are just ordinary blue sweatshirts, no team logo, no nothing, just blue sweatshirts, Sully laughed" The very next day, Sully and I went to

Gorin's on West Broadway and bought blue sweatshirts and red sweatpants. They were identical to those worn by the Patriots ball-boys.

The very next Friday night we arrived early at Fenway and found the window already open as two kids from the Club had already snuck in and had, as a courtesy, left the bathroom window open for those of us who would follow. There is honor among sneaks. We had on windbreaker jackets, which we quickly hid, and just as quickly, we were Patriot ball boys. We ran from the bathroom and jumped onto the field and started acting like we belonged there. The Patriots franchise was in such a state of disarray array that nobody knew who was who and more importantly they were afraid to ask. The players didn't even know each other, so who was going to question the appearance of two new ball boys. Simple, but masterful. Actually one of the ball-boys, and they only had two, one working the Patriots side and the other working the visitors side, asked us who we were.

"We're from the Boys Club," Sully answered. I didn't know if the kid was going to question us further or if he was going to create a problem. I soon found out.

"Thank God," he said, "It's about time they got me some help. There is no way I can handle this alone." I looked at Sully and smiled. We had done it. We were now Patriot ball The kid was from Newton and his father was connected somehow to the Sullivan family. He didn't have a clue as to what to do. We were veterans. Our Celtic training paid off big time, as we took right over. I thought the kid would be mad, but he was happy as hell, and he let us do whatever we wanted. He had been overwhelmed the week before and was ready to quit. We convinced him to stay because we didn't want anyone checking into the ball boy situation. We did all the work, so he readily agreed. We did the next five home games and not one person asked us who we were, or what we were doing there. We even started walking through the player's entrance with our blue sweatshirts and red sweatpants on. Today you would go to jail for something like that. But back then, they were just glad to have the help. The funny part was the player situation. With the Celtics you dealt with the same player's game after game. The Patriots locker room was like a revolving door. Week to week the names, faces and numbers changed. After a while we forgot we were impostors. We had become familiar with the coaches and some of the mainstay players. They knew us by our first names and we were doing the job, so who cared how we got the job. By the second game we were even going onto the field and in the huddle with water, during time outs. One game, against Oakland, it was really pouring out. The Patriots called a time out and the coach, Lou Saban, waved me on to the field with the water. As I was passing out the water, I looked across the huddle and Sully was passing out towels, we both cracked up. WE had made it to the AFL.

After the game we would get to the locker room before the players, as we did at the Garden. The main difference was the size of these players. The Celtics were tall but these guys were huge. They had muscles on top of muscles. One night, our friend from Newton didn't show up, I was asked to work the visitor's bench, by the Patriots assistant coach. That is how mixed up things were back then. Before I knew what happened I was heading across the field to the San Diego Chargers locker room, as their new ball boy. As I walked in to the Charger locker room, I just stopped dead in my tracks. There was a guy in front of me who was the biggest man I had ever seen. He had his back to me as I entered. His name was Ernie Ladd. I couldn't believe that someone had to block this guy. Then I thought about a saying my mother always used, "I'd rather clothed him than feed him." This was the guy, that my mother's saying was talking about. No doubt. The guy sitting beside him was no midget either. His name was Earl Faison. That was quite a defensive line. And then way over in the corner I spotted a guy who I thought was a trainer. He was tiny, compared to Ladd and Faison. I was busy with the many things I had to do before a game and I forgot all about the little guy in the corner. By the time I had gotten back to where he was sitting he had put on his game pants and cleats. I then thought that maybe he was a kicker. He took one of those great San Diego shirts out from his locker and pulled it over his head. I almost had a heart attack. I instantly knew the number. As he lifted #19 over his shoulder pads, I just stared in amazement. The little guy I thought was the trainer was the best pass receiver in the league. His name was Lance Alworth. He was nicknamed 'Bambi' because he ran like a deer. I continued to stare, not really aware of how long I had been staring. He must have felt me staring at him.

"How ya doing son? "

"Fine Mr. Alworth," I stuttered.

"Mr. Alworth is my father," he laughed, "my name is Lance," he continued, as he extended his hand, which I quickly shook.

"Yours," he smiled.

"Oh, Brian" I managed to get out.

"Nice to meet ya Brian," he said and went back to his locker. He wasn't much bigger than me. But boy could he play. He scored two touchdowns that night as the Chargers crushed the Pats. After the game I went over to him.

"Great game Mr. Alworth."

"Thanks Brian," he said, remembering my name.

"But the name is still Lance," he smiled. "The Patriots secondary should call you Mr. Alworth," I joked. He started laughing his head off and made me tell some of his team mates what I had said. On the way out of the locker room he slipped me $10. Now you don't forget a guy like that. Lance Alworth was bad. The next game, which was a couple of weeks later I was back on the Patriots side. It was again raining and the Pats were again losing. The Patriots all wore these long full- length parks with the Patriot logo on the back. They were beautiful. I was standing on the sideline when the Patriot coach yelled.

"Bellino get in there." The crowd went wild. Joe Bellino was a local kid who made good, very good. He played for Winchester High School and went on to play football at Annapolis where he won the Heisman Trophy Bellino, like Lance Alworth, looked more like a trainer than a player. He was about 5'9" and weighed about 170 pounds. But don't let that fool you. Joe Bellino was all football player. He was also one of my boyhood heroes. The first book, actually the only book, my father bought me was a book called "Navy's Joe Bellino." It was made up of a lot of pictures of Joe, at Annapolis and at Winchester High, doing what he did best, carrying a football. If he had entered pro football right after his senior year at Annapolis he would have been an outstanding professional running back. But part of the deal when you go to Annapolis is that you go right into the Navy, for four years, active duty after you graduate. By the time Bellino finally got to play at the pro level, he had lost a step and a little quickness, which was his only advantage against the big guys. But, in Boston, he was still Joe Bellino and as he threw off his parka, that rainy night, the fans went wild. The fans were expecting Bellino to create the kind of magic he did at Annapolis. It never happened, unfortunately.

I was really rooting for Bellino to do something when he got in. The field was pretty chewed up and the footing was terrible. He just couldn't get started and when he got the ball, the huge defensive linemen and quick linebackers killed him. I was so enthralled watching Bellino that I completely forgot that I was a phony ball boy. The two- minute whistle blew and I just stood there. One of the coaches tapped me. "Anytime tonight," he sternly said. I quickly realized that I had the water at my feet and it was supposed to be in the huddle. I ran onto the slippery field hoping that I wouldn't lose my footing in front of 20,000 fans. I wasn't even thinking of Sully, who I figured was already in the huddle passing out towels.

By the time I got into the huddle the quarterback, Babe Parilli was really mad.

Where are the towels?" he yelled at me. The towel that the center had tucked into the back of his pants for Parilli to use to dry off his hands was now totally soaked and caked with mud.

"There not here?" I asked. I could see through his face- mask that Parilli was really mad. I turned around, ran to the sideline, grabbed a bunch of towels and headed back to the huddle, fell flat on my ass, got up and made it to the huddle just as the ref was blowing the whistle for play to resume. Parilli grabbed a towel, wiped his hands, and threw it at me. I picked up the water and headed back to the sideline, embarrassed and humiliated. Then it hit me. Where the hell was Sully? With only two minutes left in the game, I scooped up all the stuff I had to and ran to the locker room. The players came trudging in about ten minutes later, defeated, and soaked. I got busy real quick and again I forgot all about Sully. When it quieted down I realized that he was never in the locker room. I started to worry a little. I thought that something might have happened to him. I cleaned up very quickly and headed toward Kenmore Square Station. As I got closer to the station I saw him huddled in a doorway directly across from the entrance of the MBTA station. I felt a whole lot better. I started to get a little mad though, as I thought back to myself lying on my ass in the middle of Fenway Park with 20,000 people laughing at me.

He was all smiles as he spotted me. He was sitting on something, which I couldn't make out and he never moved as I got closer.

"What the hell happened to you?" I said angrily.

"I had to bring your towels into the huddle and I fell on my ass and I had to clean up the locker room by myself and on and on and on. He just looked at me never even getting up from where he sat and whatever he was sitting on.

"I left," was all he said.

"That's pretty obvious," I shot back. "But why?"

He then got up from what he had been sitting on. "This is why." He then proceeded to produce one of those beautiful parkas that I had talked about earlier. I was stunned. He turned it around and instantly a name on the jacket jumped out at me. BELLINO. I wasn't mad anymore.

"How'd you do that? When did you do that?" I stammered.

"Take it easy," he said, "As soon as Bellino was called in the game I went over to where he stood and he handed me this parka and ran into the game," he very calmly said.

"Then what happened?" I asked. "I just rolled it up and walked away," he said. "I walked out of the Park and came here waiting for you." He then threw the parka at me.

"Now you can pretend you're Joe Bellino." He knew how much I admired Joe Bellino, much the same as he knew how much I admired Jerry West. He saw an opportunity and went for it. Much the way he lived his life. He didn't even do it for himself. He did it for me. He took all the risks and I got all the benefits. He was a little crazy sometime, but he was as good a friend as you could find. We worked the next game and it was never mentioned. I'm sure they had no idea what equipment they had or didn't have. As I mentioned earlier, we really weren't into stealing. God knows we had the opportunity, especially with the Patriots. They didn't even know who we were. The Celtics at least paid us and had our names, addresses and social security numbers. The Patriots didn't even know our names and we never got paid for working the sidelines for them. So one parka isn't really wasn't that bad, I said to myself. And once in a while, the opportunity was just too great to pass up. That was definitely one of those times. I still have that parka in my cellar.

Chapter 31 – Navy's Joe Bellino

A couple of years later we were playing basketball at Murruay Hall, which was located in the Fargo Navy base in South Boston. It was used as a recreation place for enlisted Naval personnel and former Naval officers who wanted a steam bath or to play some basketball or lift weights. It was a huge facility and there was always a basketball game going on. The guy who worked at the door was my father's friend. He had let us in one day and we never stopped going down there. We got to know all the sailors and all the people who worked there, so getting in was never a problem. One day, there was a new guy at the door and he wouldn't let us in because we had no naval ID Sully spotted one of the Colonels who always played on our team and yelled to him. The Colonel came over and asked the enlisted man what the problem was.

"They don't have ID's sir," he said.

"Well they're my guests, is that all right?" he barked at the guy.

"Yes sir," the enlisted sailor said, as he stepped back and handed us towels. We never had a problem after that. The Colonel wasn't that good of a player and I couldn't understand why Sully asked him to be on our team. We played games of eleven with each basket counting as 1 point. The first to get eleven baskets won and kept playing. The losing team sat down and had to wait to play again. Sometimes if you lost you never got a chance to play again. I remember saying to Sully one day.

"That guy, isn't that good, he could cost us the game." I said to Sully one day. I had no idea he was a Colonel. Everyone looked the same with sneakers, shorts, and a T-shirt on. I just knew that the guy wasn't a basketball player.

"Trust me," Sully said. He was already thinking ahead to when the guy could be useful to us. I should have known, and he was right So the guy played on our team with me, Sully, Ridge and a big kid from Southie, who dominated the boards, named Gerry Nee. We won seven games in a row. The Colonel, who was used to playing one game and sitting down, was ecstatic.

"You guys are great, that was the best workout I've ever had since I've been in Boston," he excitedly said.

"When are you guys coming back" he asked.

"Tomorrow at 1," Sully quickly said.

"I'll be here" the full- blown Colonel said. Ridge and I still had no idea who the guy was. We showered and started to get dressed and I thought Ridge's eyes would pop out when the guy put on his uniform complete with full Colonel bars.

"See you tomorrow," he said as he left the locker room.

"Did you know he was a colonel?" Ridge asked me.

"No, but he did," I said pointing to Sully He played on our team from then on and we were treated pretty well from then on, by everybody. It's kind of nice having a Colonel as your friend. Sully was thinking ahead, way ahead of me. He was unbelievable.

A couple of weeks after we enlisted the Colonel, I was on the court shooting and Sully came running up to me.

"You'll never guess who's in the locker room?" he said. I didn't know if this was a joke or not.

"Bob Cousy!" I said. He laughed and said.

"Close," he said, laughing. I continued shooting. A few minutes later a guy came walking out of the locker room. I would know that walk anywhere.

"It's Joe Bellino," I said to Sully.

"No shit," he laughed. Being a former Naval officer he could use Murruay Hall anytime he wanted. He played against us and he was damn good. We won by a couple of points. He hung around and played against us again about a half an hour later. This time he beat us. I introduced myself, later in the steam bath. We told him we worked as ball boys for the Patriots when he played. He was polite enough. I just couldn't believe that I was sitting next to Joe Bellino, even if I couldn't see him through the steam. I asked him about a game in which he played in 1956 against South Boston High School. The game was played at Boston Garden in the quarterfinal round of the Tech Tourney, which is the Eastern portion of the State basketball tournament. Bellino was playing the backcourt for Winchester High School against a Ray Fynn led South Boston High School basketball team. Ray Flynn scored 26 points and Southie went on to win the State title that year. Bellino remembered the game very well. We talked a little bit about Ray Flynn who went on from there to be an All American at Providence College and later Mayor of Boston and he is presently the United States Ambassador to the Vatican. I also asked him about certain games he played in College. He laughed.

"You know quite a lot about me, don't you." He couldn't see me blush in the steam room, as Sully answered his question.

"He knows everything about you." I blushed even more. I was really enjoying this moment, with my boyhood hero, but I was also getting pretty dehydrated in the steam room. I was starting to get a little dizzy but I wasn't about to leave, just yet. He asked us how we liked working for the Patriots and Sully, all of a sudden, had to pick this moment to confess all our sins.

"We didn't really work for them, we kind of made it look that way" he said. Bellino was confused and asked us what that meant. Sully told him the whole story about sneaking in and buying the blue sweatshirts and red sweatpants. Bellino started laughing. "You guys are too much." Bellino was really enjoying our talk. Sully loved a good audience. Some other guys came in the steam room so we left. I was about ready to pass out anyway. I guess I never learn my lesson. About 12 years after our steam room chat with Joe Bellino I actually did pass out after leaving a steam room.

It happened down the Boston Athletic Club, which ironically enough was built next to the rubble of old Murruay Hall, after it was torn down It was an unseasonably warm early June day and I had spent about five hours down Pleasure Bay working on an early summer tan. I was just going down the Athletic Club to take a nice cold shower. As I entered the locker room I spotted a friend of mine named Michael McDonough. Michael, at that time, was the State racquetball champion and was ranked in the top ten in the Country. I had played Little League with Michael and I don't think he ever said more than 25 words to me in his entire life. He was one of the quietest but most talented kids I have ever known. He seemed a little angry as I approached that hot afternoon. It seemed that his racquetball match canceled on him so he was left with a full hour court charge and nobody to play.

"Ya want to hit for a while Brian?" Michael asked. Now you have to understand, me playing Michael McDonough in racquetball is equivalent to the Romans facing the lions in Rome. But I also felt that the only way to improve is to play somebody who was better than me and Michael

Brian P. Wallace

McDonough certainly fit that bill We ended up playing the entire hour and I even got a few points, very few.

By now I was totally drained from the sun and the workout. All I wanted was a cold shower. As I went back into the locker room another friend Willie McDonough, who was a famous sports writer and my first football coach was just getting undressed. We started talking.

I'm going to take a quick steam, come on in." Willie said I always liked talking to Willie because he had such great stories about athletes and about sports in general. I wasn't going to stay in there long because I knew I was pretty dehydrated. Willie and I were in there alone for a minute, or two, when the door opened and in walked my old boss, Red Auerbach. This was about two weeks before the NBA draft and Willie, being a reporter, quickly jumped on the chance to get a little inside information.

"What's the draft look like, Red?" he immediately asked. Red was always cute and wasn't about to answer Willie with a definitive answer. Instead Red gave a rundown on the top five or six players, and how each would look good in a Celtics uniform. This was good stuff and there was no way I was leaving that steam room because I knew Willie would persist until he got a more definitive answer. After Red went through his litany of top players, "I know all that Red, what I don't know is which of those players you're interested in?" Willie finally said. Red took his time, as my head started getting light.

"Personally, Will I like the kid from Minnesota." Red quietly said.

"McHale?" Willie asked. And Red just nodded his head. I got a scoop but more importantly Willie had a scoop. By that time I was cooked. I walked out of the steam room and before I could even make it to the showers I was out cold on the floor. I came to about thirty seconds later. I was totally dehydrated and totally embarrassed. I had a cold compress on my head and about a dozen guys staring down at me. I was naked and semi- conscious, sunburned and utterly embarrassed on the locker room floor. I got up and did my best Inspector Clousseau imitation, as if nothing had happened, got dressed and got the hell out of there as quickly as I could. And by the way, Kevin McHale became a Boston Celtic two weeks from that day and Willie broke the story. I on the other hand almost broke my neck when I fell against the whirlpool.

A Southie Memoir

So I was very glad, that day, when Joe Bellino decided it was time to get out of the steam room and hit the showers. We finished showering, and were in the locker room getting dressed. Bellino was really getting a kick out of Sully, who was telling him about some of our friends and our experiences. We were really hitting it off quite well. As we were just about to leave, two good size officers came in and sat down. Joe put on a Navy sweatshirt from Annapolis. One of the guys, the bigger of the two, said to Joe.

"Did you go to Annapolis?" Joe told him that he had gone to Annapolis.

"What year did you graduate?" he politely asked.

"1960," Joe replied. The guy got all excited.

"Did you know Tommy Webster?" one of the big guys asked Joe.

"No, sorry I didn't know him," Joe replied.

"He's my cousin," the big guy said. Sully interrupted.

"You guys don't sound like you're from around here, where are you from?"

"Texas, son," they said in unison.

"Longhorns," I said, as they both smiled approvingly.

"Yes sir, from deep in the heart of Texas."

"You guys are pretty big, Did you play any ball?" Sully very nicely asked. Their faces lit up.

'University of Texas," they again, said in unison.

"What sport did you play?" Sully asked. They looked at Sully as if he were crazy.

"What do you think we played son? There is only one sport in Texas, football."

"Excuse me," Sully said very sarcastically. Then Sully pointed to Joe.

"Joe was a football player." The two Texans looked at the size of Joe and laughed.

"What you play Pop Warner?" Joe laughed. Sully didn't.

"He won the Heisman Trophy," Sully shot back at the two, as if they would be to stunned to talk. Instead they began to laugh.

"Ya son," the littlest one said, "And I'm OJ Simpson." (Simpson had just been awarded the Heisman a few weeks before). I had a feeling we would hear Simpon's name again. Sully was pissed.

"He did win the Heisman," Sully said, as the guys continued laughing.

"When did you win the award, Mr. Heisman" they asked very sarcastically.

"It's no big deal," Joe said, trying to end the conversation.

"I think it is a big deal Mr. Heisman." The guy now sounded mad.

"I think it's a very big deal. You telling these kids lies like that and filling their heads with all kinds of bullshit, some great football players won the Heisman Trophy, and you couldn't hole their jock straps." Now Joe was getting mad.

"You Texans think that you're the only ones who ever played football," Joe shot back. "We played Missouri in the Orange Bowl and they had the same attitude as you two, when the game started, they didn't when the game was over." Joe angrily charged.

"Now you played in the Orange Bowl too, Mr. Heisman, this is getting even better."

"It's not worth it," Joe said as he started to leave. Our Colonel friend, however, would, once again, come to our rescue. He entered the locker room just long enough to hear Joe being challenged by these Texans and he was pissed. He ran over to Joe and hugged him. The Navy's secret weapon, Joe Bellino," he said, as he pumped Joe's hand until I thought it was going to come off. The two Texans said nothing. It was Sully's turn.

"Colonel these two guys," he said pointing directly at the half-dressed Texans, "Called Joe a liar." the Colonel's face became very red and he walked over to where the two of them stood.

"Is that true?" he asked the bigger Texan.

"No sir, we just didn't think this shrimp," he pointed to Joe, "Should be filling these kids heads full of lies." "

What kind of lies?" the Colonel asked.

"He told those kids that he won the Heisman Trophy," they looked at each other and laughed. The colonel, feigning disgust.

"He said he won what?" The two big blowhards now figuring they had offered.

"Can you imagine that colonel, that little guy telling everyone he won the Heisman Trophy, at Annapolis, now don't that beat all." Joe just stood there with a slight smile on his face. Now it was the Colonel's turn. He turned to face the two Texans.

"Boys I've been in this man's Navy for 18 years and I know a little bit about Its' history. I know only one man from the United States Naval Academy has ever won the Heisman trophy"(Roger Staubach would be the second). He paused for effect and then he said to the Texans.

"Do you know who that football player was?"

"No sir," they both said.

"Well," he said very slowly, "His name was Joe Bellino. He was from Boston and he could run like the wind." He wasn't through.

"Bellino ended his career in the Orange Bowl by scoring three touchdowns against Missouri, in one of the greatest victories that Navy has ever had, on land, and he did it in front of the brand new President John F Kennedy who was also from Boston. Now gentlemen you two idiots have insulted the greatest running back in Naval history and I want you to apologize to our Heisman Trophy winner Mr. Joe Bellino." The two Texans were in shock.

"You're Joe Bellino," the big one said, pointing to Joe.

"In the flesh." the Colonel replied. 'Oh my Gawd,' the other one said, as he went over, shook Joe's hand and apologized profusely.

"Forget it," Joe said humbly.

"I certainly am not going to forget it," the Colonel sternly said, as he eyeballed the two jerks. Now it was Sully's turn. "

Did you guys say something about jock straps, you know neither one of you could hold Joe Bellino's jock strap." He knew the colonel was right behind him when he said it. He might have said it anyway, who knows. "Sorry again, Mr. Bellino," they both said as they left the locker room. They probably would have liked to kill Sully. As they walked past Sully, he smiled and yelled.

"See ya later OJ." Bellino really cracked up. He looked at me.

"Where did you get this guy," pointing to Sully, the baby-faced assassin. Even the Colonel knew about Sully. He was laughing as well.

"Sully if they get you out on the court they'll kill you."

"No way," Sully smiled "I know a Colonel down here." Now everyone laughed. As we were walking out of Murruay Hall some guy called Sully over to the side, pulled out his wallet, and started giving Sully money. Joe and I kept walking.

"What's he doing now?" Bellino asked me.

"Who knows," I said as we walked out the door. Bellino was laughing again.

"Is he always like that?"

"Always" I said.

"I've never met anyone like him," the former Heisman Trophy winner said.

"Most people haven't" I laughed. Joe got in his car and was just pulling out as Sully reappeared, counting his money. Joe waved and shook his head. That was the last time we ever saw Joe Bellino because they tore down Murruay Hall not long after that. Just another day in the life of Sully.

Chapter 32 – Sully Takes On Jerry Williams

I had another friend named Avi Nelson, who like Joe Bellino asked me, "Who is that guy." Avi, at the time, in 1975, was the host of the top rated radio show in Boston. He was on WHDH and was a big hero in South Boston because of his opposition to forced busing. Avi was, and is, one of the most intelligent people I have ever met. I was then working for State Representative Ray Flynn, and we became very friendly with Avi. We would bring him pies from the Supreme Diner a s he was finishing his radio show at WHDH on Morrissey Boulevard in Boston. We would talk for hours once the show had ended. We also had a lot of the same interests. Avi, like Ray and myself, was a baseball junkie We would sometimes talk just about baseball but most often the subject would get back to politics which was also fine with us. I got a call late one July morning in 1975 from Avi. He asked me what I was doing for lunch. I had no plans, so Avi said he would pick me up. Just before Avi showed up my doorbell rang and it was Sully. He was married now and I hadn't seen him in a month or so.

"What are you doing?" he asked.

"I'm going to lunch with Avi Nelson," I told him. He looked a little sad, so I asked him if he wanted to go. He brightened up.

"Sure is he paying?" Some things never change, I thought. When Avi arrived I told him that Sully was going with us. I introduced them, and we were off. Avi, when he called, did not tell me where we were going for lunch. In the car, he told me that he was taping a television show at Channel 5 and he wanted me to accompany him. The show was called "A left and a right. It was a 30- minute show in which Avi debated longtime Boston radio personality Jerry Williams. I use that word personality with a grain of salt. I had never met Jerry Williams, before that day, and I didn't care if I ever met him again. He turned out to be a real jerk, at least that day, he did. The topic of the show was the CIA.

"I want you to ask Jerry Williams a question on the CIA."

"I don't know anything about the CIA," I told Avi. He threw me a little book as we headed to the television studio.

"Read this and you will." When the time came I stood up and asked my question and Williams answered it. I forgot what I asked and what he answered. I do remember that Avi kicked his ass. Williams wasn't too happy once the show was over. He had an ego as big as Donald Trumps wallet.

Channel 5 had put out a nice spread for all of us after the show. We went back to the room, with Avi, and made a sandwich, or two, and just made small talk with the channel 5 staffers. Jerry Williams came in and the whole atmosphere changed. He was really obnoxious and he was making some pretty fresh remarks to Avi's secretary. She was a very tall, beautiful black girl who was doing her best to ignore Williams.

"Hey Avi where did you get such a tall drink of water for a secretary?" William laughed. Nobody else did. It was clearly out of place and rude. Before anyone had a chance to say anything, Sully bolted from the back of the room and grabbed Williams by the neck. He proceeded to throw the task show host against the wall. Nobody moved.

"It isn't that she's such a talk drink of water, it's just that you're a fat little roly poly." Sully said to a frightened Jerry Williams.

"What is that mans name?" he yelled. Nobody said a word.

"I want to know who that man is," he literally yelled. Sully spun and went back at Williams who scurried behind a channel 5 executive.

"You want to know my name you ignorant jerk?" Sully yelled at Williams. Williams said nothing.

"My name is Peter Hawkins, did you get that Peter Hawkins, Sully shouted. I cracked up and so did Avi. We left shortly after that.

"Does he do that all the time?" Avi asked me.

"Only to conceited little jerks" I laughed, as we headed home to Boston.

Chapter 33 – Johnny Most

Another guy that Sully didn't really hit it off with was Johnny Most. I don't know why. Johnny and I had become very good friends when I worked at the Garden. I would get him his coffee and coke's before the game. I never saw anyone drink so much coffee or smoke as many cigarettes as Johnny Most. I admired Johnny Most. A lot of people, including Sully, thought he was abrupt and had no personality. But that was his personality. I thought he was a genius. He used to tell me about poems he wrote and stories he wrote. He was a lot deeper than most people saw. And Johnny Most had a good heart. If he liked you, he liked you forever. On the other hand if he disliked you, watch out. He was a very complex man and one that I always enjoyed talking to. I wrote a poem about Johnny, which I gave at the World Trade Center shortly before his death. He was really moved when I finished.

"Not bad for a Southie kid" he said to me when I finished, as only Johnny Most could say. He had a tear in his eye and he knew, as did I, that death was around the next corner.

"Make sure you get me a copy of that poem," he said in his raspy voice, after the speeches were over.

"I will John," I said, "And I want it on your wall." He smiled and laughed.

"Hey kid, don't get carried away. It wasn't that good," and we both laughed. It was good to see him laugh again. He was in a wheelchair and had oxygen tubes up his nose. He never looked particularly good but that night I had never seen him look so bad. I sent him my poem but I never heard from Johnny again. He died a few months later.

I entitled my poem "HIGH ABOVE COURTSIDE".

> He sits high above courtside in no man's land
> An ever present coffee and a mike in one hand
> From Rough House Rudy LaRusso to Big Wayne the Wall
> He has seen, called and nicknamed them all
> From Philly to New York and out in L.A.
> 76'er, Knick and Laker fans just wish he's go away

Brian P. Wallace

    But for 36 years he's remained in one place
Screaming things like "Russell just put it back in Wilt's face
He sits here tonight looking so calm
Dying to yell out "Barkley almost took off Bird's arm"
He sees only one color of course which is green
He's called plays at the Garden that only he's seen
Once labeled by Johnny that nickname you marry
From Jarring John to Wide Clyde over to Leaping Larry
But the thing that I remember the Most about John
Was a warm March night in an era long gone
The leprechaun on the rim was smiling and alive
When the ball hit the wire, the seconds left were five
The Celtics were in trouble, their crown was about to fall
As Greer inbounded Oh my God, "Havlicek stole the ball"
Johnny Havlicek stole the ball, "it's all over" screamed Most
A play of which Celtic fans to this day still boastSo from KC to Satch and Jungle Jim too
We say thank you Johnny, Boston loses you.

To us, Johnny Most was, and always will be, the greatest announcer ever. I remember being down the Boys Club and everyone listening, at the front desk, as Johnny described the action as only he could. I loved the nicknames he gave everyone, some of which I mention in my poem. And I loved to hear him talk about the villains. From Rough House Rudy Larusso to McFilthy and Mcnasty. If you somehow got yourself in John's doghouse there was no way out. And he pulled no punches when it came to the villains. I remember listening to John, kind of late in his career as Jerry Sichting and big Ralph Sampson squared off. Ralph had about a foot and a couple of inches on Sichting. Johnny described the action.

"Ralph Sampson a gutless coward goes after little Jerry Sichting." I knew, at a very early age, that what John was describing, didn't necessarily mean that it was happening quite that way on the court. Anytime the Celtics were on television, we would shut off the sound on the TV and listen to Johnny, on the radio. Being a sports announcer now, I guess that is the ultimate compliment anyone can pay to an announcer. One of the very first games that I watched on television, as I listened to Johnny call the game on the radio, I saw how Johnny called games that only he's seen. The Celtics were playing the San Francisco Warriors. Everytime these two teams played the writers would compare Cousy to the Warriors little guard Guy Rodgers. This drove Johnny crazy. He felt that Cousy was a far superior player to Rodgers, and he was. But Johnny was going to make sure every Boston fan knew this. Rodgers, like the Cooz, was a great ball handler. This particular game, was a very close one. Both teams were trapping and pressing all over the court. The Warriors scored and Sharman threw the ball, in play to Cooz. Rapid Robert, another Most nickname for the Cooz, proceeded to go behind his back, once left and once right and then between his legs to break the trap press. It was vintage Cousy. Johnny in describing the moves by Cousy said something like this: Sharman throws the ball into Cooz. Rodgers in his shirt. Cooz tricky dribbling goes left. Cooz goes behind his back. Cooz tricky dribbling now goes right and behind his back again. What a move by Cousy. Cooz approaches the ten second line and goes between his legs. What a dribbling exhibition. Most was screaming now. The master just gave the pupil. a lesson in dribbling. Cousy took Rodgers to school. You won't see a finer dribbling exhibition than that in this league. Bob Cousy just made a fool out of Guy Rodgers who just stands there shaking his head." Heinsohn, while Most was praising Cousy, hit one of his patented line drive shots and the Warriors were putting the ball in play. Most call went something like this.

"OK Attles puts the ball in play over to Rodgers. Celtics pressing." Now Rodgers, probably on purpose, did the exact same moves that Cousy had just done on the Celtics last possession. Rodgers went left and then behind his back. Rodgers then went right and again behind his back. Rodgers then went between his legs as he reached the half court circle. It was the exact same series of moves that the Cooz had just pulled off only seconds before. There was, however one difference. Johnny Most. Here is how Johnny called this series. "Rodgers goes left and starts showboating. This guy is nothing but a hot dog. Now Rodgers again showboating. There's no need of this stuff in basketball. Rodgers is a clown. He should stay and work for Barnum and Bailey when the circus comes back. Still showboating he gets over half court. What a hot dog this guy is. He couldn't hold Cousy's sneakers. Now I was watching the whole thing on TV and listening to Johnny. Guy Rodgers did exactly what Cousy did. Exactly. That was how I saw it. Not John. As I said in my poem, he sees only one color, of course which is green. He calls plays at the Garden that only he's seen. That was my introduction to Johnny Most. I was probably 10 years old. I never forgot that incident. It was pure Johnny Most.

Johnny Most was the original homer. He didn't care what he said, or did, as long as the Celtics won. If he helped in any way, even better. He hated going to St. Louis and Philadelphia. He used to call Philadelphia the "City of Brotherly Hate, He absolutely hated a guy named Dave Zinkoff who was the Philly public address announcer. The guy was obnoxious if you weren't a Philly fan. If you were a 76'er fan, you loved the guy, much like Johnny Most to Celtic fans. Zinkoff would stretch out a player's name for as long as his big lungs would let him. When a Philly player scored a hoop, he would stretch out the name until the other team was already over half court. If Wally Jones scored, Zinkoff would yell, "Basket by Waaaaaaaaaaaaaaaaaaaaaaaaaaaaallllllllll llllllllllllllllllllyyyyyyyyyyy Jones. or if and when Wilt scored it would be basket by Chamberererererererererererer erererlain. He would drive Most crazy. Johnny even had a nickname for him. He called Zinkoff "Hysterical Harry." When Johnny would return from trips to St. Louis it would take him a day just to settle down. Sully would ask him how it went and he would go off into a diatribe about St. Louis, the City, the team, the fans and on and on. I knew what Sully was doing but Johnny never did. Another place he hated was Detroit, not so much when we were working at the Garden, but later in his career. The bad guys, back then, were St. Louis and New York. But as the league changed and teams like the Pistons, who were always fair but never good, started to emerge and the St. Louis franchise moved, so did Johnny's dislike for thenewer teams on the rise. And right at the top of that list were the Pistons. And at the very top of that list was one. Bill Laimbeer. The Pistons through the draft and some trades had become a very good basketball team as Johnny's career began to wind down. He might have been winding down but he was as vitriolic as ever. Bill Laimbeer was a villain of the first order and his team mate Isiah Thomas was not far behind. Laimbeer, it seemed, would commit these very flagrant fouls which drove Most wild. One time I was driving in my car, listening to John on the radio, when he described this play.

"Bird gets a pick doesn't use it , now Bird goes left, sees an opening and drives strong to the hoop." And then John's voice would completely change.

"Oh my God Laimbeer just took off Bird's arm. I don't believe it. Bill Laimbeer just took off Bird's arm." if you were a young kid listening you probably thought that Larry Bird would have to play the rest of his career with only one arm. In actuality Laimbeer slid off the pick and fouled bird. No big deal. Except if you listened to the game on the radio That was the thing about John, he had all different ranges in his voice. He would go to a higher octave depending on the importance or the sheer brilliance of the play. His highest octave voice was reserved for "Havlicek stole the ball" plays or "Bird steals over to DJ, who lays it in" plays. Bird, probably more than anyone, could raise Johnny, literally off his seat. He saved a particularly sinister, angry voice when talking about Laimbeer, Rough House Rudy LaRusso, Chamberlain or Rodgers. I asked Johnny one night why he hated Chamberlain. He went off on me about Wilt having no class and Russell was a much better player and Wilt being a loser. I told him that Wilt was a great guy to all the kids who worked the Philly bench, but he didn't want to hear it. Johnny also hated whiners and there were more than a few of those in the league. He especially disliked Rick Barry, Oscar Robertson and Isiah Thomas, all of whom he considered as cry babies. And they were.

He really hated Rick Barry and for good reason. They were also great players, but that didn't matter to John. He absolutely hated cry-babies. If you looked up the definition of a cry baby in the dictionary, it probably has Rick Barry's picture next to it. Barry was a great player, who would have been a lot greater if he learned to keep his mouth shut, but he never did. Even in College, he was a whiner. Barry wrote a book called "Confessions of a Basketball Gypsy," and I hope this book sells more copies that that, or I am in serious trouble. In the book, Barry wrote about one of the biggest games of his College career. It came oddly enough against my good friend Ray Flynn, who was the Captain of Providence College in 1963. The game was played in Madison Square Garden, and it was in the semi-final round of the National Invitational Tournament. Ray was having a career game in front of a packed Garden and a

Brian P. Wallace

large television audience. With just over a minute to play, Providence led Miami, who Barry played for, by 1 point. Barry had the basketball, and was backing in against a defender named Kovalski, from Providence. In a flash, Ray Flynn came from the weak side and stripped Barry of the ball. Ray went the length of the court and scored on a layup. Barry fouled Ray, as he put the ball of the glass and in the hoop. It was Ray's 36th point of the game. Ray hit the fouls shot for his 37th point and a four point Providence lead. Barry, furious that Ray stole the ball in the first place, said something he shouldn't have said to the referee. He was immediately signaled for a technical foul. Ray calmly stepped to the line, again, and swished his 38th point, which gave Providence an insurmountable five point lead, with less than one minute to play. Ray went on to win the Most Valuable Player Award, and a place in Barry's book. According to Barry, of course, Ray fouled him, when he stole the ball that day. Barry wrote that Ray should have been charged with the foul and not him. I expected nothing less from Mr. Whiner. Providence went on to win the NIT Title the next day. Barry went on to a great NBA career. Ray went on to become Mayor Of Boston and the United States Ambassador to the Vatican.

Chapter 34 – Confirmation Debacle

A funny thing happened to me the next day, as Ray played for the National Title against Canisius. I lived in a triple-decker in South Boston, and for some reason, our 3rd floor television could get the Providence station that televised the Championship game. We must have had 60 people, from Southie, crammed in to my tiny little third floor parlor. Ray had another great game and Providence won their second National Championship in three years. That was the good part. The bad part was that I was scheduled to make my Confirmation that same afternoon. The Championship game started at 1:00 PM. My Confirmation was scheduled to start at 3:00 PM. I figured that I could watch the game and still be on time for my Confirmation. My parents weren't as sure as I was about that. But, they knew how much that game, especially with Ray playing, meant to me. At 2:30 my father climbed the stairs to our third floor and told me it was time to go. The game, at that time was extremely close, and there was no way I was going to leave, at that point.

"It's OK, Mr. Wallace, I'll drive him to the Church, as soon as the game is over," one of my brother's friends named Skippa King said.

"How much time left," My father asked. "Only nine minutes," I pleaded. My father didn't know that nine minutes, in basketball, is not the same as nine minutes in the real world. He agreed, but he warned me, not to be late. He and my mother drove to St. Peter and Paul's Church, and I stayed glued to my televisions set. Canisius began to foul and they began to use all their time outs. I looked at my new watch, which was a gift for my Confirmation, and saw that it was fast approaching 3:00 The game ended at 3:10 as I. I put on my cap and gown and got set to hurry to the Church.

"Hold on, Skippa said, "Let's see if Ray gets the MVP." I was all for that, except that they announced the All-Tournament team first. They gave out all of the individual trophies, and finally at 3:30 p.m. they announced that Ray Flynn was the Most Valuable Player. I was thrilled, until I looked at my new watch. It was 3:37 p.m. and I knew I was approaching deep trouble.

"Come on Skippa lets' go," I screamed. We all flew down the 3 flights of stairs and piled in to Skippa's car. We got three blocks and the stupid car ran out of gas.

"You've got to be shitting me," my brother said to Skippa.

"When was the last time you put any gas in to this pig?"

"Last week sometime," Skippa said, shaking his head, as if he couldn't figure out what had happened.

"Last week," Tommy Conley said, "When you put in a dollar's worth of gas?"

"Yeah, a buck doesn't buy it what it used to," Skippa exclaimed, as I bolted from the car and began running the six blocks to the Church. I must have looked great running down Broadway, holding my cap, and wearing my red gown. I arrived at St. Peter and Paul's Church just in time to see my classmates exiting the Church.

"Shit," I yelled, as two of my friends, spied me, all out of breath, with sweat pouring down my, now worried face. I stopped in my tracks, and watched the whole procession walk down the stairs and across the street to Cardinal Cushing High School hall. Finally I saw my parents come out of the Church, and you didn't have to be a rocket scientist to tell that my father was not a happy camper. My father looked around and spotted me. He was so mad, he just walked away, got in to his car and drove off with my mother. I didn't know whether to shit or go blind. (another of my mother's famous saying) I did neither. I walked in to the Church, all by myself, and went up to Sister Superior, which took balls, believe me. She was pissed.

"Mr Wallace, nice of you to join us," she said icily.

"I'm sorry sister, I started to say, but she cut me off in mid-sentence.

"Save it," she barked, "Go tell Cardinal Cushing that you're sorry that you embarrassed him." Cardinal Cushing, I thought to myself, he's right up there next to God. I was scared shit, but I approached the legendary priest warily.

"Your Emminence, I am truly sorry, but I missed my Confirmation today." I had never been that close to him before, and I could literally feel myself shaking. He waited a few seconds.

What is your name son?"

"Brian, Your Emminence, Brian Wallace." I stammered.

"Can I ask you why you missed such an important day in your Catholic upbringing?" There was no way I was going to lie, to a guy who was on a first name basis with God. I was in enough trouble already without adding any more offenses.

"I was watching a basketball game," I whispered.

"A what?" he asked, almost unbelieving.

"A basketball game your Emminence," I shyly said.

"Son, do you think a basketball game is more important than God?" No matter what I thought inside, I wasn't stupid.

"No, Your Emminence," I managed to get out. Cardinal Cushing looked away with a disgusted look on his face and he turned to Sister Superior.

"Sister has this ever happened at Monsignor Patterson's before?'

"No your Emminence, not to my knowledge," she sadly said.

"Where are your parents?" the Cardinal who just three years earlier stood on the stage next to another pretty important figure, President Kennedy, as he was sworn in. That is some ty big time company.

"They went home, I think, Your Emminence," I said.

"I'm sure they are very disappointed in you, Brian" he stated.

"I know," I said sadly, not looking up.

"Sister what are we going to do with our little basketball fan, here?" the Cardinal asked, She just shrugged. He looked at me.

"What do you think we should do with you?" I had one shot, and humor had always worked for me in the past, so I went for it.

"Well your Emminence they were two Catholic schools I was watching," I smiled. Wrong answer! His face became bright red.

"He's all yours sister." He said as he turned to leave the venerable old Church, which is now condos like everything else in Southie Not what I wanted to hear.

I got one month's detention at school and I had to stay in my house for the same period of time. I also had to take the subway over to Lake Street in Brighton, where the Cardinal lived, to make my Confirmation by myself. When I got there I told the lady who answered the door, asked who I was and why I was there. She was an old Irish lady who reminded me of my Grandmother. She ushered me in to a little sitting room.

"The Cardinal will be right with you." Great, I thought to myself, I don't think he's a very big fan of mine. Twenty minutes later he appeared.

"Come this way Brian," he instructed, and I followed the former son of South Boston, whose picture hung in every house in Southie right alongside President Kennedy's. I went in to a little chapel and he motioned for me to kneel down. He put on his robes and began to the confirmation process. He asked me what name I chose.

"Patrick," I responded.

He then said a few more prayers and slapped me across the face, which was part of the Sacrament of Confirmation, but I had never seen anyone get slapped that hard before. It was a little payback, I guess. I was a little stunned. He had a big smile on his face, as he finished the Sacrament. He turned and left the room, as I continued to kneel. I didn't know what to do. The Irish lady came in and rescued me.

'Would you like as piece of cake," she asked. I was starving.

"Yes please, I offered, and she sat me back in the same small sitting room. She came back with a delicious piece of cake.

"Are you the little boy who told the Cardinal that you shouldn't be punished because you were watching 2Catholic teams play football?" she asked.

"Basketball, I said. And yes, I am, but they were playing basketball.

How did you know?" I asked. A beautiful smile came over her Irish face.

"Oh the Cardinal got quite a kick out of that one. He has been telling that story for weeks now." He had a sense of humor after all, I thought to myself. But that didn't help much with my parents or the nuns. I ate my piece of cake and thanked the nice lady and started to leave. As I got to the door, I heard his unmistakable voice.

"Brian, where do you live in Southie?" he asked.

"West Fifth Street," Your Emminence, I answered.

" A lower ender, huh," he smiled. I just nodded my head.

"How are you getting home?" he asked.

"I'm taking the T," I said.

"If you want to wait around, I'm going over to the Cathedral in about 40 minutes, I'll drop you off," he offered. I thought about it, but I wanted out of there.

"Thanks, Your Emminence, but I have basketball game, and I'm never late for my games," I said. There was a moment where what I said, just kind of hung in the air, and then he started tosmile. Thank God.

"Get out of here," he laughed. As I was closing the door, I heard him say, "Southie kids, ya gotta love em," and he did. He just shouldn't have slapped me so hard.

Brian P. Wallace

Chapter 35 – Where Is The Catholic In Catholic Schools

I don't know what it was about the Sacraments and me, but we just didn't seem to get along. I don't' remember much about my Baptism, but I trust everything went fine with that, at least I never heard otherwise. The first Sacrament that I actually remember making was my First Communion, and I would love to tell you that everything went along without a hitch, but I can't. I was attending Monsignor Patterson Grammar School and my nuns name was Sister Regina St. George. To this day, I wonder how and why she had that word Saint was in between her two other names. She was tough, and I being the class clown was not one of her favorite targets. The pastor at St. Vincent's, where we were to make our First Communion, was Father Gross, seriously, that was his name. He, like Sister, did not suffer fools gladly and that is putting it as nice as I can put it.

There are a couple of things that I will never forget about First Communion, Sister Regina St. George or Father Gross. It was a Friday morning, a week and a day before we were to wear our dress whites and receive the Sacrament. Sister told us that we were going to be getting out of school at 12:30 p.m., that day and that we were to get to St. Vincent's, on our own, for practice at 3:00 p.m. Father Gross, we were told, would be waiting for us at that time. This was unusual because we usually practiced during school hours, which was fine with me. Practicing after school created a slight problem for me. I had been asked to pitch for my brother's softball team that same afternoon, at, you guessed it 3:00 p.m.

Pitching, that day, was my big chance. I was five years younger than my brother's gang and I had been the bat- boy, all year, for their team. I hounded them to let me play, but they laughed and said I was too small. But, a funny thing happened the night before the game against the Lancers. Their regular pitcher Skippa King got appendicitis, and they asked me to pitch. I was so excited, all day in school, that Friday that I could think of nothing else. Then the bombshell about First Communion practice hit, and it hit hard. Getting chances like that didn't come around every day and I knew it, even at seven years old. I had one of the first major decisions of my life to make, other than avoiding Sully. If I didn't go to First Communion practice, I would have to deal with Sister and Father Gross, a pair that could beat a full house, any day. If I didn't go to the soft ball game I would blow my chance to play with the big kids, probably forever. I ended up pitching a complete game and got the win. I also ended up pitching every single game that summer. No wonder Skippa King never liked me. The next day, I saw my friend Ozzie Orton, who was in my room at Monsignor Patterson. Ozzie couldn't wait to tell me how much trouble I was in.

"Father Gross called your name three times," he said, "Boy was he mad." Great, I had two days to live. To say that weekend was ruined would be the understatement of a lifetime. I even tried to play sick that Monday morning, but my mother would have none of it.

"Get your books and get to school," was the last thing I heard as I headed out the door to my imminent demise.

My friends, in the school-yard, were waiting for me as I arrived, like a bunch of ghouls waiting for the hangman.

"You're in trouble, you're in trouble," they chanted. Some friends, huh? As the bell rang for us to go in to our class-room, I was scared to death. I didn't think that being 1-0 in my brief pitching career was worth it then. All eyes were on me as we waited for Sister to storm in the room. I knew that whatever Sister did to me was not going to be half as bad as what Father Gross was going to do to me, so I waited. But something was different about Sister that morning. She sat down and didn't say a word for about five minutes, which was extremely unusual. Finally when she did speak she did so haltingly.

"We will all pray for Father Gross who passed away this morning," she managed to say. I was in shock. I never knew anyone, personally, who died before. She had completely forgotten about my transgression. The incident about my missing Communion practice was never brought up again. I made my First Holy Communion with no problem after that initial bump in the road, and my parents never found out about the incident. I finished the year with a 12-0 pitching record, but it was the first game that I will never forget.

What I remember most about that day had nothing to do with me being let off the hook. It had more to do with me being placed on another kind of hook, by who else, Sister Regina Saint George. After we did our morning prayers she asked me and a friend named Travers to come to the front of the room. I was convinced it had something to do with me missing First Communion practice, but why was Freddie Travers there?

"Boy's I need you to go to St Vincent's Church and see if they need you to do anything to help Father Buck. Father Gross will be lying in state at the Church tonight and tomorrow and I think it would be nice if you helped," she said as nice as pie. Who was this lady and what state was he lying in. Talk about confused? But, getting out of school is a bonus on any day so Freddie and I headed the two blocks to St. Vincent's Church to meet up with Father Buck. The first thing we noticed as we entered the church was how dark it was.

"Let's look around," I said to Freddy, who by the look on his face wanted no part of that plan.

"Are you shittin me, this place is scary as hell," he managed to say as he looked, bugged around the drafty old church. It must have been the Sully effect on me, but I told Freddie I was going to look around. I could tell that Freddie was torn. He didn't want to go into the church but he didn't want to be alone either, so he followed me in and we began to check things out. Bad move.

I had always wanted to check out the altar and the sacristy and even, if I was brave enough, the chalice. We never knew when Father Buck would show up so we moved with a little bit of speed and our shoes echoing off the marble floor didn't help, but we managed to get everything in. This, like the smoke bomb, was a huge adventure for a second grade kid.

"You all set now?" Freddie asked in a whisper.

"I guess," I said. "Why don't we go in the back of the church and wait for father," I said, looking around the huge edifice.

"The closer to the door, the better," Freddie said as he wiped off some sweat on his face. We walked to the back of the church. Our eyes were now much more accustomed to the dark than when we had first walked in.

"What is that over in the corner?" I asked Freddie.

"I didn't notice it when we came in," he said a little uneasy.

"Let's check it out," I said in my best Sully imitation. Freddie wasn't as adventurous, but he followed me to whatever was in the corner. As we got closer we could see that whatever it was draped in church vestments.

"What do you think it is?" I asked Freddie, who was backing up as I was going forward. It was still too dark to see what I was looking at. As I got closer to what was now, I could see, a bed or something like it, I picked up part of the vestment and it was the dead body of Father Gross staring back at me. Freddie was already out of the church and I was following as fast as my feet would allow me. I had never even seen a dead person before. I was so scared I almost pissed my pants as I took the church steps three at a time until I hit the pavement. I couldn't believe I had touched Father Gross and he was as dead as a haddock. Freddie kept blessing himself over and over.

"What are you blessing yourself for," I said "You screwed, I'm the one who touched him." That brought about another round of blessings from Freddie.

"You actually touched him," he asked with a little hint of admiration in his voice. We both pondered our situation for a while before either of us spoke again.

"Wait until I tell the kids at school that you actually touched Father Gross and he was dead," he said as we saw Father Buck walking down the street towards us.

"Please don't tell Father Buck or Sister," I pleaded with Freddie.

"Of course not," he smiled. "But the kids are going to love it, and they did. Brian Wallace the dead priest toucher. It still freaks me out today when I think of that moment when I pulled back the vestments.

Chapter 36 – Hanging With The Mafia

Even after we stopped being ball boys we still went to most Garden events. We had made a lot of friends there, and we always felt at home in that atmosphere. It really was a great place to grow up and believe me we grew up very quickly. Our parents would have had collective heart attacks if they knew the people we called friends or some of the people we knew in the North Station area. They never knew the stunts we pulled, the places we went or the people we hung around with. From perverts to gangsters, and everyone in between. As long as we were together we were all right. I wouldn't want to be alone with some of the characters that frequented those areas, however,. Some of our best friends were scalpers. They were all from the North End and they started very young. Some of the kids were our age, 15 and 16 years old. Some of them had one foot in the Mafia, and the other foot in High School. Then there were the big time scalpers. Those were the guys that the young guys looked up to and wanted someday to be like. We hung around with them and did some small errands for the big time scalpers. One time a guy named Jimmy asked us to go uptown to a store on Washington street and get him a box of cigars. It was about four blocks away. He had written down the name of the cigars on a racing form and had given me a hundred -dollar bill. Sully went with me. We told the guy behind the counter that the cigars were for Jimmy and he treated us like we were big shots. I kind of liked that respect. We brought the cigars back and gave him the change, which was $21. Jimmy thanked us and told us to keep the change, which we gladly did. I used to love to just listen to those guys. Scalpers and big time gamblers had their own language. It went something like this : Tickets were called dukes which is short for ducats, No looks were obstructed view seats, which again was indigenous to the Garden. Buyers were called pigeons. Ten dollars is called a saw or a sawbuck. Twenty dollars is a double saw. A hundred dollars is a C note. A thousand dollars is a G note or just one large. If a guy bet three thousand dollars on a game, they would say that he was in for three large. Over and under meant the number of points scored in a particular game. Say the Red Sox were playing the Yankees. There would be a line set, by the bookies, on the number of runs they felt would be scored in that game. Say they set the runs line at nine. And you wanted to bet a hundred dollars on the under. Bet made. Now the Red Sox win the game by the score of 6 to 4. You add the total number of runs scored, which is 10. You lose. Now you owe the bookie the one hundred dollars, you bet, plus the vig, which we'll get to. If you had bet the over and the Sox and Yankees combined for 10 runs, you would have won your bet. Get it. A tease bet, which the bookies called a suckers bet, is when you bet more than one team on a given bet. They call it a tease because they will give you six points on a football or basketball game and both teams, you bet in your tease, must win outright. Let me explain. The Patriots are playing the Giants and the Patriots are 3 point underdogs. The Cleveland Browns are playing the Philadelphia Eagles and they, like the Patriots are also 3 point underdogs. You call the bookie and say you want a hundred -dollar tease and you want to tease the Patriots and the Browns. Now both teams get 6 points. So the Patriots and the Browns, who were 3 point underdogs are now 9 point underdogs. The catch is that they both have to cover, in order for you to win the tease bet. That is why the bookies love these bets. The Patriots play a great game and lose by the score of 21 to 14. They have only lost by 7, so you have covered the first half of your bet. The Browns play a decent game but lose by the score of 24 to 14. You lose that game by one point and you lose the entire bet because both teams have to cover, ergo the tease There are also 3 team teases, which the bookies absolutely love. In a 3 team tease you choose 3 teams and you get 9 points with each to play with whichever way you want. If the Pats are a pick, then you take them in a 3 team tease and all of a sudden they are a nine point underdog. The Browns , on the same bet, are favored by 10 points. Combined with the Pats you take the Brownies in a 3 team tease and they are now a 1 point favorite instead of a 10 point favorite. On the third bet of the 3 team tease you take the Giants who are underdogs by 15 points and you apply the last part of your 3 team tease which makes the Giants a 24 point underdog with you 9 points. Sounds too good to be true?. It is, take my word for it and a lot of bookies are driving new Cadillac's with the license plate TEASE. Then there are bets called bird cages and action reverse bets, which are way to elaborate to even try to explain.

    A gambler is called a player. A bet is called action. Paper means counterfeit money or counterfeit tickets. A big gambler is called a high roller.

Brian P. Wallace

Or whale. C's meant the Celtics. B's meant the Bruins. One man is a police officer. This is indigenous to Boston and needs a little explaining. The Boston Garden lies in the area that is patrolled by the District One Police Station. The only cops, who were assigned to patrol the Garden area, were police officers and detectives from Area One, hence the one man. Simple. Mafia guys were called wise guys or made men. I never once heard the term Mafia or Costa Nostra. Everyone knew what and who a wise guy was. Those were people that you didn't mess with, under any circumstances. A runner was usually a young kid who carried money back and forth to the bookies or the scalpers. All the scalpers were high rollers. Those guys lived to gamble. And they gambled on everything. Didn't matter if it was football, basketball, baseball, hockey at every level of competition, they bet on it. Sully and I were hanging around with these nuts, one night before a Celtics game and I asked a guy named Toggy if he had a line on the South Boston-Charlestown basketball game, that was I was playing in the next day. I was kidding. He wasn't.

"I don't gut a line but I could make one for ya," he said very seriously.

"That's all right," I said as I quickly walked away. He really meant it. Betting on High School games? But these people lived for the track. Dogs or horses, it didn't matter. These guys were always talking about this dog or that horse. It was constant. Another thing I liked about them was their nicknames. They all had nicknames. Tough Tony, Fat Tony, Frankie the Wretch, Big Johnny, Little Johnny, Jimmy the Man, Large Anthony, Frankie the Wolf, Vinny the Squid, Tommy Muscle, Whitey, Tommy Gat, And each nickname had a meaning behind it. Large Anthony weighed close to 400 pounds. Frankie the Wolf was a ladies man. Whitey had blonde hair. Tommy Gat always carried a gun or a gat. Vinny the Squid always ate fish rather than pasta. Tough Tony was just that. Frankie the Wretch would beat up his mother if she screwed him out of a double saw. Jimmy the Man was the head scalper and bookie. Jimmy the Weasel was a weasel. Tommy Muscle was a gang enforcer It sounds crazy but all the nicknames fit. I never knew anyone's last name, which is exactly the way they wanted it, When someone asked, "Have you seen Jimmy the Man?" everyone knew who he was talking about. No need for last names. What was really funny though was listening to one of their conversations, or better still one of their arguments. It would go something like this.

"Hey Whitey you see Tommy Gat around?" Jimmy the Man would ask.

'Yeah he's over Hanover Sreet," Whitey would say.

"That somma ma bitch owes me four large" and he's ducking my ass."

"I saw him blowing some serious scratch last night with the Wolf," Whitey replied.

"That rat bastard," Frankie the Man would say. (A 'Rat Bastard could be anybody or anything. A snitch, an enemy, a friend, a horse, a dog. 'Rat Bastard' was a catch-all phrase that encompassed everyone one and everything.)

"The Gat is walking around in a dead man's suit," the Man would say as his face began turning colors.

"The Gat is made, Frankie forget about it" Whitey would counter.

"I don't care if he's a don. I'll call the Muscle right now and end his show." Whitey would eventually calm him down and life would go on. But for people who might happen to be listening, like the FBI, they might not have a clue as to what was just said. Here's what happened. Tommy Gat owed Jimmy money and he and the Wolf were out wining and dining a couple of ladies, with Jimmy's money or at least he felt it was his money. Jimmy then threatened to have Gat killed by Tommy Muscle. Whitey, however, intervened and reminded Jimmy that Tommy Gat was made, which means he was Mafia or Costa Nostra, and killing a made man was a no no in their ranks, even if he was a 'Rat Bastard'. These arguments happened constantly and were usually just talk. Usually. I think the most arguments were over the races.

Somebody always had a hot tip. Always. It would go something like this.

"Hey wolfman I gotta pony off at Pimlico at a dozen to, the horse is a gimmeeI'm laying 3 large to carry you wanna piece?" That would be how Large Anthony would pproach Frankie the Wolf and tell him that he was betting three thousand dollars on a horse, to win, who was going off at 12 to 1 at Pimlico Raceway. Anthony wanted to know if his friend wanted to get any action on this race. This was usually where all the arguments stemmed from. The race would be run and the horse, which Large Anthony said couldn't lose would do just that. The Wolfman would check the papers the next day and get all over Anthony for his bogus tip.

"Hey wadda ya want from me I lost three large on that 'Rat Bastard'," Anthony would counter, and they would go on like that all day long or at least until the next bogus hot tip came in. It never changed. They would win 1 out of 10 but they never stopped trying, and they never stopped bitching. If I had a dollar for every time I heard one of them say.

"My horse was in like Flynn but the 'Rat Bastard' died on me in the stretch." Another one was, "I should have bet the 3, I knew the 3, (pronounce tree)was gonna win," or "My horse was this close." All of these conversations, accusations, threats, stories, and bragging always took place over or around food. These guys could do some serious eating. Everything revolved around eating. There was always a pizza or half of a pizza on the table at all times. They would pour over the scores of all the games played the night before and would memorize the stats. If these guys did that much studying in high school they would all have graduated from Harvard. That's assuming they went to high school. The reason they went over all the games was because they bet on most of them or they took action on most if not all of them. The first thing they would do was to go over the money they made, or the money they lost the night before. It was very rare that they went over the latter. And no matter how much money they made, it was never enough. Someone always beat them out of money, at least in their minds. We used to have a game to see who had the best hard luck story of the day. They would have killed us, figuratively speaking, if they knew we were poking fun at them. If Jimmy the Man made $20,000 the night before, it shoudda been $21,000. This was where the 'top this hard luck' stories would come into play.

"I should'a had the Knicks game too," Jimmy the Man would say, "But," and there was always a "but," "

West hits a 20 footer at the buzzer and I'm a dead man." Yeah a deadman with 20,000 new bills in his kick. The Squid would then say "You dink dat's bad, I'm holding four large in my hand and Oscar Robertson nails a fifty footer with two men on him. He kills me." Another dead man albeit a rich one. This would go on for quite a while as they each tried to top each other's stories on how they lost money, when in actuality none of them lost a dime. It was all part of the ritual. Before the 9:00 AM. bell sounded at St. Leonard's, in the North End, they knew every score of every game in the World. I don't think they knew what an editorial was but they certainly knew what a box score was, and what a large double cheese was. They also knew what dog was running, in what race and what the odds would be at Wonderland. They could tell you about every horse at Suffolk who the jockey was and what he weighed, and which ones would look the other way if the right amount of money was on da table. They knew the point spread of every game being played that night in every sport and in every town. They knew in an instant if a line was dirty. They could tell in a millisecond if the odds at the track were suspicious. And they were always right, That was their business and they were good at it.

The average 'Joe fan' would never beat these guys. He might have a winning streak and do well for a while but he would, as they would say, "Come back to da pack." That was why they were driving Cadillacs and wearing diamond rings and flying to Vegas every time they got a little bored. But they always came back with some great stories. Some stories were so good that they were constantly told, adding just a little more each time until you could hardly recognize the original story after a few months. Some needed no embellishment, they just got better with age. My favorite was told by Tough Tony. Tony's best friend was a guy by the name of Joe "The Animal" Barboza. If you saw Joe Barboza you would instantly know that the nickname was justified. The first time I saw him in the restaurant he scared the shit out of me and he hadn't even opened his mouth. He just looked bad. And looks in this case weren't deceiving. And when he finally did open his mouth, his vocabulary was somewhat limited to four letter words. If Hollywood wanted a stereotypical gangster they need look no further than Joe Barboza. He would gain some notoriety, later in life, as, of all things, a stool pigeon. He was the last guy in the world that I would pick as a stool pigeon. He was later killed in San Francisco for his loose tongue but that was still years away as we sat in the restaurant that first time I met Joe 'The Animal' Barboza. He and Tough Tony liked Vegas and were constantly taking trips to the gambling capital of the World. Tony was no slouch in the gangster looks department either. He was about 6'2" and he weighed about 275 pounds. He had arms like leg and hands like catcher's mitts. His nose had been broken a couple of dozen times He had a large scar on the right side of his face and a constant scowl on that same face. Meeting one of these guys was scary. Meeting both of them together was downright frightening. The story, according to Tony, goes like this. Tony and Joe Barboza were in Vegas for the weekend. It was after 2 O'clock in the morning and they had just dropped a bundle at the crap table. They were staying in the Penthouse of the hotel, which I think was Caesar's Palace, and they decided to go up to the room, freshen up and come back down. The elevator arrived at the Lobby and the two gangsters got on. They were the only ones on the elevator. Barboza pressed the button for their floor, and started their ascent. The elevator stopped on the 5th floor and a lady, who had a good package on (which means she was drunk) got on the elevator. She looked at the two gangsters and began to tremble. The doors closed, and she continued to look straight ahead, afraid to look at them.

"The lady was frozen," Tony said. "So's we waited for her to press a Goddamn floor and she becomes a statue." Tony goes on to describe the scene.

"Now I had just dropped some serious money and I was in no mood for this kind of shit, so I yells at her, HEY LADY HIT THE GODDAMN FLOOR. Next thing I know the broad's laid out on the floor, saying take my money but please don't hurt me." The lady thought that Tony meant for her to hit the floor literally. What he meant was for her to hit the floor button that she was going to.

"We both starts laughing," Tony says, "Then the goddamn elevator stops at the 8th floor and there are three more people waiting to get on. They see this lady lying on the floor, dey take one look at me and the Animal and dey begin to scream." 'The Animal 'says to the lady, who thinks we're going to kill her, rob her or rape her.

"Lady we don't want your money we just want to get the hell off this elevator before we get arrested." The lady was still quivering on the floor and never looked back. When their floor came they stepped over the lady and went into their room.

"I sees this same dame two days later, as I'm checking out and I gives her a big smile," Tony told us, "But the bitch turns red, and beats it outta dere, how'dya figure." The story was legendary and they all had stories like that. It was one of the reasons it was so enjoyable to be in their company, It was exciting and a little on the edge.

We didn't, at that age, see the bad. We knew that some of these people were very bad people and that some were probably hit men for the Mob. But, for a brief period in our lives, they were our friends. Many of them were killed and many of them were jailed for various crimes from murder to extortion. I read about a lot of them, years after we stopped hanging around the Garden. We were never in any danger, I don't think. We were just there for the ride. Growing up in South Boston, Sully and I had many friends who turned out to be murderers, drug dealers and drug users. Don't get me wrong, not all our friends or acquaintances turned out bad. There were a lot of teachers, policeman, policewomen and firefighters a few priests and nuns who we knew growing up in Southie. Two of my good friends, John Clogherty and Leo Paulsen became Doctors. Dr. John was a Boston Firefighter until he was 35 years old. One day, after a very bad fire, John decided he wanted to change professions. He enrolled in Med School and 7 years later he became a Doctor. My brother Eddie did the same thing, only he went from being a Firefighter to being a Boston Police Officer and he retired as a Boston Police Captain. Can you imagine going from firefighter to Doctor. Another one of my closest friends growing up was Tommy Frane who became Police Commissioner in Quincy Mass. Paul Evans and Mickey Roache, both two good friends of mine from Southie were both Boston Police Commissioners. They just don't make the front page of the Globe and the Herald on a regular basis, unless they do something radically wrong. But that was part of growing up, where we did. Sully and I knew that, it was no problem. It is called a street- smart education. You don't get one at some fancy finishing school. You get it by seeing what goes on around you and adapting to that situation and nobody adapted better than Sully.

Brian P. Wallace

Chapter 37 – Flirting With Danger

We knew some very crazy people growing up and a lot of them aren't around any more. We couldn't help where we grew up, but we always tried to avoid putting ourselves in bad situations and we usually succeeded. Usually. About a year after Sully had moved from E street to the Old Harbor project we found ourselves in China Pearl Restaurant late one Friday night after a Chippewas game. We were about 16 or 17 and we thought we were pretty bad. That particular night there was me, Sully, Ricky Calnan, Bobby Gibbons, Jimmy Ridge and Jackie Cherry. We were acting up a bit, as everyone, it seems, did when they went into Chinatown. The owner was a guy named Billy Chin. He was a good guy but usually people who went into Chinatown, late on a Friday or Saturday night, and were half drunk or totally drunk and they always gave the Chinese people a hard time Billy Chin would become one of my dear friends later in life, but we didn't really know each other that night back in 1966. He thought my name was O'Brien. He came over to our table a couple of times and asked us to be quiet which we paid no attention to whatsoever.

"Come on give us a few beers," Bobby Gibbons said to Billy Chin. He laughed knowing how old we were. But Gibbons kept it up. Finally Billy came over to our table and said in a heavy Chinese accent.

"You kid too young to drink, now you behave yourself and Mr. O'Brien you stop your dancing." I had been showing off my latest moves to four girls who weren't the least bit interested in me, my moves, or my friends. We kept making noise and Billy kept telling us to quiet down. I felt a hand on my shoulder and I turned around. There was a guy standing there, who I had never seen before, and he had his hand resting on my shoulder.

"That's enough guys now behave yourself."' this guy said in a very controlled voice. I had turned to face the guy so I had my back to all my friends.

"Screw, before we knock you out," I said. Go back over there and eat you chop suey before I take you outside and make chop suey out of you," I said.

A Southie Memoir

"That's not nice. You guys should learn some respect." he said very slowly and deliberately.

"Mind your own business, I said. "We weren't bothering you. Now beat it, before I take you outside and kick the shit out of you." I laughed. I'm not usually that fresh nor that brave but a few beers will work wonders for a 16 year-old kids courage level. He smiled.

"Southie punks, I used to be a Southie punk once." I jumped in.

"Now you come to Chinatown late at night by yourself looking for faggots. Screw." This time there was no smiling from the stranger.

"I'll be back for you in a little while," he said, and he turned and walked away. I thought I was bad. I turned around quickly expecting to see all my friends smiling. They weren't. I had no idea what was going on. I thought I had been pretty cool and very funny. I looked at Sull, his face was white. I looked at Ricky and he avoided my eyes. I quickly looked at Ridge and Cherry they weren't smiling either. Bobby Gibbons broke the ice.

"Do you know who you just called a fag?" I was starting to worry a little.

"No," I replied.

"That was Whitey Bulger," Gibbons said softly. I almost fell out of my chair.

"Why didn't you tell me?" I asked. "

"You didn't give us any time" Sully replied in hushed tones. Whitey Bulger had served 15 years in prison for bank robbery and was at Alcatraz when they closed the place. I obviously had never seen him before. Sully, Ricky, and Gibbons knew him because they all lived down the Mary Ellen McCormick project where Whitey lived with his mother. Ridge and Cherry knew him from L Street where they lifted weights together. I was the odd man out Whitey was a mystery man but had a very serious reputation. I was dumbfounded. I had just called Whitey Bulger a fag. To his face.

Our table became deathly quiet as our food came. I couldn't eat, knowing that I would soon have to face Whitey Bulger. I had embarrassed him, in public, which was probably the worst thing someone could do to a guy like that. Sure enough, just as we were finishing, or more appropriately, they were finishing, Gibbons pointed.

"Here he comes." He said. I thought my heart was going to drop out of my chest and roll right across the floor. Nobody said a word as he approached. I was scared to death. He pulled up a chair and sat very very close to me. He was so close I could smell his breath, which was bad.

"You got something to say smart ass?" he said, only inches from my face.

'"No sir," I blushed.

"Oh it's sir now, huh hotshot, what happened to Mr. faggot?"

"It was a mistake," I said very quickly.

"You ain't shitting it was a mistake, it was a big mistake." His face was now getting red and his blue blue eyes looked into my soul. I had heard the expression, "Eyes cold as ice." Whitey Bulger's eyes that night were colder.

"You know who I am now hot shot?" he asked, already knowing the answer.

"Yes sir," I said, again, very quickly. He moved back a little but was still very close to me. I could smell the gum he was chewing.

"Ya know smart ass, one thing you always have to do is to know who you're talking to, before you open your mouth. Do ya know what I mean hot shot?" I didn't answer.

"I was a Southie punk just like you guys, when I was you're age, and you know what it cost me?" he asked.

"No sir" I said.

"It cost me fifteen years of my life," Now he looked at all my friends. He took his time and looked at every one individually.

"You guys wouldn't last fifteen minutes in prison. Not one of you." Nobody said a word. He looked directly at me. "You still want to take me outside, hot shot? We'll see who makes chop suey out of who?"

"No," I said looking down.

"You bet your ass, no" he said. And then a funny thing happened. He smiled this incredible smile like he had just won the lottery, pun intended, and said to me.

"Lesson learned?" as he stuck out his hand for me to shake. "Learned," I said, as I quickly shook his hand, before he changed his mind again.

"Now how many beers do we need here?" Whitey asked, looking at all my friends many of whom averted his eyes. I should have been so smart.

"Six, seven if you want one," Bobby Gibbons answered." I couldn't believe he said that after what I just went through. Whitey began to laugh.

"You kids are too much." He then got us all beers. I had survived. barely. But it was a good lesson and one that I have practiced ever since. I had to laugh, however, at the Chinese guys, who were so adamantly refusing us any beer just twenty minutes before, were now tripping over each other opening the beers they had placed in front of us. Whitey certainly carried some weight even back then. It was a night I'll certainly never forget but unfortunately it would not be my last run in with Whitey.

He and I became pretty good friends after that night. He had a fascination with politics, and he was brilliant. We would always talk politics every time I would run into him in a bar somewhere in Southie. He was very well read and very charming. I was quoted in a Boston Magazine story about the Bulger brothers Whitey and Billy.

"They both were very charismatic and if you were in a room and closed your eyes you wouldn't know if you were talking to Billy or to Whitey". A pretty tame quote. About a month after that story was written in the Boston Magazine, I was going to meet a friend of mine named Frankie Noonan in Triple O's, which is a bar on Broadway in South Boston, owned and operated by an associate of Whitey's. As I opened the door, I felt someone move in quickly and place a gun behind my ear. It was cold, hard and scary and it was almost touching my ear. Before I even had time to turn around I recognized the voice from Chinatown.

"I'm glad you finally had some nice things to say about me," the voice, belonging to the number one Mob man in New England, whispered in my ear. It was chilling. I'm quite sure that, voice was the last voice a lot of people heard before they met their maker. Not me thankfully.

I never thought that there would be another run in with Whitey, but I was wrong. And strangely enough Sully was on the scene that day as well. It occurred the same day that Sully was putting Jerry Williams in his place. Avi Nelson dropped me and Sully off at my house after the TV show. Sully and I talked for a while and he got in his car and went home. While we were talking,

Brian P. Wallace

I noticed a blue car going by us a couple of times but I didn't pay a whole lot of attention to it. I said good bye to Sully, and went into my house to get ready for supper. I hadn't been in the house a minute when the phone rang. My mother answered it and handed me the phone.

"Who is it?" I asked.

"Someone named, "Jimmy" was all she said. I knew a ton of kids named Jimmy, so I didn't think anything of it as I spoke into the phone.

"Brian this is Jimmy Bulger." That same monotone voice that had scared me years before in China Pearl, did the trick again.

"We have to talk," he said very seriously.

"When?" I asked.

"Right now, I'm sitting outside of your house in my car." If I was scared before I was petrified now.

"Sure," I said as I hung up the phone.

"Who was that?" my Father took one look at me and asked.

"Whitey Bulger," I managed to say "And he's waiting for me outside in his car." My father was a pretty street -smart guy, and I could tell from the look on his face that he wasn't too keen on me going for a ride with Whitey Bulger. My mother heard the word Bulger.

"Oh isn't that nice, does he want to talk about the campaign." She immediately thought it was Senator Billy Bulger, Whitey's brother, and I secretly wished it was as well. I got into the blue car that had been circling my block while Sully and I were talking, and oh how I wished Sully was with me now. We drove for 20 minutes, I could tell because there was a clock on the dashboard. He said absolutely nothing for that whole period of time, which didn't do much for my state of mind. He finally came to a stop. He turned. To me.

"I was going to hit you last night." Now let's get one thing straight. When Ted Williams hits a home run he knocks the ball out of the park. When the Beatles had a hit it meant one of their songs was at the top of the charts. When Whitey Bulger hits someone, they are usually dead. It took me a few seconds to comprehend what he had just said. Only a few. Then the fear took over, and with it came a surprising calmness, and then I actually got mad. I know it sounds strange, but who can predict how one would react in a situation like that. I know most people will never be placed in a situation like that, but believe me, this was kind of new to me as well. It was kind of surrealistic, actually. I was speaking, but it seemed that I was speaking from somewhere off in the distance.

"Why?" was all I could manage to say.

"For a couple of reasons," he said, in that cold and calculating voice that cut through me better than any stiletto could ever do. One wasn't bad enough. He had a couple. I was a little but overwhelmed. I didn't travel in his circles I wasn't a wiseguy. What possible reasons, could he have to kill me.

"You and some of your friends at the Bay View Pub have been saying that I killed Eddie Connors," he said matter of factly. Eddie Connors was a local bookie, who was a member of a private club I belonged to called the 487 Club. It was located at 487 West Broadway, directly across the street from the Bay View Pub, where I and a lot of my friends hung out. Eddie had made the cardinal sin of being too predictable in a profession where predictability can often mean a sudden death. And that is exactly what happened to Eddie. Every night, Eddie would go to a phone booth on Morrissey Boulevard and call in his night's earnings. He figured this isolated phone booth was not bugged, so it was a safe place to use to avoid the law. Eddie avoided the law all right, but that turned out to be the least of his troubles. One night in May of 1975 Eddie went into his phone booth, and while he was talking on the phone one or two guys approached with guns drawn and ended Eddie's life in a hail of bullets. There was a lot of speculation as to who actually killed Eddie Connors. There was also a major gang war going on at the time Eddie was hit (there's that word again). People were getting killed left and right. I knew a lot of them. I had played second base six years before, on the Pleasure Bay softball team and the team, which I didn't know when I agreed to play, was made up of a lot of wiseguys. On any given night we would have half the top wiseguys in Boston and Somerville watching us play, while the other half was on the field playing. Nobody ever messed with that team, believe me.

Chapter 38 – Get A Hit Or Get A Casket

One night I was home watching TV when Jimmy Ridge rang my bell. He was all dressed up in his PBL softball uniform and looked agitated.

"Bri we need you to play second base for us tonight," he said. "Our second baseman didn't show up. I didn't know it at the time but Jimmy played on a team of wiseguys and a lot of them weren't showing up for their games or anywhere else for that matter, This was right in the middle of the gang wars in Boston and people were dropping like flies.

"Jimmy I can't hit those fast pitch softball pitchers. They are way out of my league," I said. I had seen them pitch and they were awesome. Guys like Chicka Noonan, who thank God pitched for Ridge's team. He was almost unhittable. He had a pitch called the riser which started at your ankles and exploded to your shoulders. I still don't know how he did it. He was great and the other pitchers like Bobby Lancioni, Dicky Devin, Weasel O'Neil, Tubba Pierce, Mikey Sheehan, Jim Williams and a guy named Mickey Roache, who would later become the Police Commissioner of Boston. How ironic is that? Mickey Roache pitching to a team full of gangsters, led by his brother Buddy, who would later be shot in the back and paralyzed for the rest of his life in a gangland shooting.

`That was what I was facing as Ridge anxiously stood in my doorway that day. He was unrelenting.

"Brian, we don't need you to hit. We just need you to turn a double play now and then. You could always do that when we played down D Street," he implored.

"But I will look foolish against those pitchers," I said, still not convinced.

"You'll be in good company. They make everyone look foolish. Don't worry about it. We have Bobby Dunkle, Satch Crowe, Tommy Gun, Buddy Roache, me, Ozzie, Bobby Monteith, Jackie Connolly, Hoppa Prendegas, Chicka Hillt and Chicka Noonan. They all can hit. We just need you for your fielding, honest to God,"

"All right, I'll play but I hope your regular second baseman shows up next game. This isn't my sport." I said to Ridge. He threw me a PBL shirt and hat and I was officially on the filled with gangsters and their supporters in the stands. I didn't want to think about that then.

The guy I was replacing never did show up again, anywhere Whitey Bulger killed him and two of his other family members. I played the remainder of the schedule and behind the team that I just mentioned, we won most of our games. Ridge was right. The pitchers were overwhelming and most games ended with a 1-0 or 2-1 score. They really never said anything about my lack of hitting, at least not to me. I was 0 for the month of August. I did play pretty well in the field and they seemed happy with that. That all changed the night we were playing for the league championship. The series was tied at 1 game apiece in a two out of three series. We were behind 2-1 with runners on second and third and two outs in the last inning. And guess whose turn it was to bat. You guessed it, mine. It was about the most nervous I have ever been in a game and to make matters worse one of our players, who also happened to be a hit man for the Irish mafia, approached and called me over to the on deck circle.

"Listen, we have no pinch hitters left on the bench, so you are it. You haven't got a hit all season and if you don't get a hit now, you just might get hit on your way home tonight. Do you understand me," he asked looking directly into my eyes. I knew exactly what he was saying. I also knew I was facing Bobby Lancioni, the second best pitcher in the league. I had faced him three times before that night and didn't even get as much as a foul ball off him. He struck me out on three straight pitches, three straight times. Now I was facing him with the Championship and maybe my life on the line. I slowly walked to the plate as the crowd noise was deafening. I actually managed to fouled Lance's first pitch off, which gave me a little confidence. I missed his second pitch by a few feet, which took back my confidence. The season and maybe me, were down to one pitch. He teased me with a curve that was a little outside. I didn't bite. He teased me again with a low pitch, again I didn't bite. Two balls, two strikes, not dead yet, literally. His third pitch got away from him and sailed way outside. Three balls and two strikes. Maybe I could get a walk and let Ozzie, who was up next, win or lose the game for us. No such luck. As soo as it left his hand I could se it was straight, fast and right down the middle. This was no tease pitch. This was a pitch to strike me out. I don't know why I saw the ball better this time, but I did. As it approached I swung and hit a little dribbler through the infield and both runners scored. The crowd went wild. Ridge and Ozzie ran out and carried me on their shoulders. I looked at the hit man who had threatened me and he just smiled. One hit all year was enough o make me a hero.

After the game went back to the Mullen's club on O Street. There were more gangsters piled in there than there were on the Sopranos. Southie wiseguys, Charlestown wiseguys, Somerville wiseguys were all drinking and having a good time. In a few weeks they would be killing each other. On the bar there was a huge candy dish that wasn't filled with candy. There was any kind of amphetamine in there that I had ever seen.

"These guys don't need amphetamines," I said to Ridge who reached in and grabbed a handful. I was sticking to beer and it was flowing pretty good. I must have had five beers already in front of me and they were all sent over to me by the same guy. I asked my hit man friendwho was sending us all the beers.

"Oh, they are all from Howie Winter," he said.

"Howie Winter?" I managed to get out. Howie Winter was the head of the Winter Hill gang from Somerville and they were about as bad as they came. I looked over at the guy with sunglasses and a scaly cap on his head. I had never seen the guy before. I waved one of the beers at him and he waved back and headed over to where me, Ozzie and Ridge were sitting.

"Thanks for the beers," I said.

"My pleasure, you guys played a great game tonight and your hit won me $25,000," he said pointing at me." I almost fainted. Maybe I was naive, but I had no idea these guys were betting that kind of money on our games. I never only played another game after that night. All the fun had somehow disappeared. I retired from fast pitch softball a hero. A live one at that.

Chapter 39 – Getting Back To Whitey

That day in the car in 1975 in the car with Whitey I don't know where I got the guts, but I looked into his eyes.

"Well did you?" I asked.

"Did I what?" he asked.

"Kill Eddie Connors?" Again the icy stare.

"It's none of your fucking business," he said. There was a moment of complete silence in the car, which probably lasted about 5 seconds, but it seemed like 5 minutes, to me.

"That's not my style," he stated, quite emphatically. I just stared at him, not really knowing or caring to say anything. He took a package of gum out of his black leather jacket.

"Want one?" he offered. My mouth was way too dry to attempt to chew, I declined.

"What does it matter to you what people say, if you know you didn't do it," I asked, surprised at my boldness.

"It's a matter of respect," Whitey said. Honor among thieves and all of that stuff, I guess.

"Well I'm sorry, but Eddie was a friend of ours, and we just assumed you hit him."

"Didn't we have this conversation before about you opening up your mouth," he stared back at me.

"And what about the other thing," he said. I had no idea what the other thing was and I must have looked it because he went on.

"What about Ray Flynn."

"Ray Flynn, I said loudly, "What does Ray Flynn have to do with Eddie Connors?" At that time, in 1975, both Ray Flynn and Billy Bulger were talking about running for Mayor of Boston. I had no idea what that had to do with Eddie Connors. Whitey quickly filled me in.

"Some Flynn people are saying disrespectful things about my brother." Now this really floored me. Sure, there had been some bad blood between the two camps, but I certainly was not part or parcel to that. I totally admired Billy Bulger. So I had no idea what the Whiteman was talking about and I told him.

"Now you're really off the deep end," I said getting the courage from some unknown place.

'Don't piss me off tonight, or I'll whack you right where you sit" he yelled. I've killed twenty six people in my life Brian and I would walk in the Bay View Pub on a Saturday afternoon with Leo Mahoney and Scoop Canavan and Satch Crowe and Chrissy Connolly all in there and put a bullet behind your ear And do you know how many witnesses there would be"? I just shook my head.

"None. That's how many there would be," said. And a strange thing happened, which I'll never be able to explain. I called his bluff. I still can't believe I did it, but he really pissed me off. He was taking me for a ride because of some stupid allegations that I had nothing to do with and the Southie in me came out.

"Go ahead then." He looked kind of stunned.

"What?" he asked.

"If you're going to kill me then do it, otherwise I'm outta here" I said as I reached for the car door handle. He reached over and grabbed my hand. Now, that scared me.

"It's all about respect Brian" he said, but in a much different voice. "I can't let you or anyone else disrespect me, or my family. Do you understand? It's the same on Alcatraz as it is in Southie. If you don't have respect, you don't have nothing. Southie is my town and that is all I have." In that instance I actually felt sorry for him. He was right, that was all he did have, and that was pretty sad. I was speechless.

"I never said anything about your brother," I softly said.

"I know," he said.

"So why are," I caught myself. "So why were you going to kill me" I asked.

"I can't hit Ray Flynn," he said, "But if I hit you, they would get the message." Great. Now I was mad again, and I reached for and opened the door. We were down on First Street and there was absolutely nobody around. I began walking, my head spinning. He pulled up next to me.

"Get in." he said as he rolled down the window.

"Fuck you," I said, as I kept walking.

"You're disrespecting me again," he smiled. And I started laughing. He did too. I got in, and we talked for about an hour. We talked about the upcoming Mayor's race and about Kevin White. He didn't like Kevin White, and that is putting it as mild as I can. Years later I read that White was petrified that Whitey was going to, hit him during the busing crisis. We talked about his brother Billy whom he greatly admired and loved, and we talked about Southie, a town that he also greatly admired and loved. And then he drove me home, much to the great relief of my parents who were outside hoping that I would return. It was a very interesting day from Jerry Williams to Whitey Bulger. I have only told a few people about that day with Whitey. I learned my lesson about opening up my mouth, the hard way. We never had any more dealing after that day on First Street, Thank God. We were always friendly though. If I walked into a tavern or restaurant where Whitey was, I couldn't pay for a thing. He always made sure of that. One night I was at Amrheins restaurant and when I got finished with my meal I asked the waitress for the check.

It's all taken care of." she said.

What do you mean?" I asked.

"Whitey picked up you tab," she said.

"I can't let him do that," I countered. She laughed.

"Well you tell him, because I'm not" and she walked away. I hadn't even seen him that night. He certainly was tricky. I just wish he never got involved in the drug business. For a guy who loved our town he certainly didn't do right by it.

Chapter 40 – Meet Chuckie Fuller

Actually Whitey Bulger was quite tame compared to a kid that Sully introduced me to back when we were 13 years old. His name was Chucky Fuller, and he was the craziest person that I have ever met, by far. He started to hang around down E street with us, and nobody really objected, at first. I don't know how or where Sully met him but I always assumed it was up the Club. He lived on West 6th street, which was only a block from Sully's house. He seemed OK, at first,. I mean I wasn't a psychologist and I wasn't looking for anything bad. He was just another kid, who started hanging out down the corner. The rites of the corner are actually quite simple. A kid, like Chucky, would one day be introduced and then he would just start showing up more and more until his appearance was more or less accepted. There were no initiation rights or anything that exotic. I wish there had been in Chuckie's case. Within a month he had become part of our gang. And at first, he was fine. But the minute he was accepted we saw the real Chucky Fuller. And that was very scary. It started slowly. He robbed a Pepsi truck that was making a delivery to Pete's variety store. We thought it was funny at first. We weren't into stealing, or any of that stuff. We played sports all -day and chased girls all night. It was simple but nice. Next he came by the corner with a brand new car. Now he was only 14 years old, so there was something amiss here. A few of the guys got into the stolen car and went on a joyride with him.

I, to this day, have never knowingly gotten into a stolen car. Knowingly, is the key word here. Sully, like me, didn't want any part of this type of behavior. But Chucky was converting some of the younger kids to his way of life. The more kids he converted, the bolder his actions became. We were sitting on Sully's stairs one night when Chucky jumped up, picked up a huge rock, ran into the middle of the street, and threw the rock right through the windshield of a police car that was coming down E street. I couldn't believe it. Neither could the cops, who were stunned. Chucky took off like a bat out of hell up West 6th street with the wounded police car, giving chase. The car cut him off, before he got to the corner of F Street and West 6th Street. The cop, who was riding shotgun, jumped out of the car. He was a young cop who looked to be in pretty good shape. Chucky kept right on running right around the cruiser and the young cop who pursued him on foot. We were obviously as close as we could get. They ran up 6th Street, past the Boys Club and onto Dorchester street. We ran down F Street toward the Gavin School. Chucky took a right onto Tudor street, as we watched the young cop close the gap between them. Tudor street is a small, side street, which is in some disrepair, and there was glass lying all over the street. It's not a street that the street cleaner ever goes down, and the cop, who was getting closer and closer as Chucky began to tire, at least that is what it looked like to us.

"He's dead meat now," Sully whispered to me. I just shook my head in agreement. The cop was now so close he could touch Chucky, and he did finally reach out to grab his coat. As he did, Chucky fell to the ground, as if he had eyes in the back of his head. The cop, whose momentum was leaning, forward skidded face first over Chucky and onto the glass filled street. When he finally got up Chucky was long gone and hard to find. The cop's face was all cut and scraped. It looked like he had been through a war. The police car had arrived by then, as did 3 or 4 other police cars. They took the cop to the hospital, as we watched. As he was getting into the ambulance he looked over to us.

"Tell Fuller I owe him one." We went back to E street, stunned at what we had just witnessed. Within 10 minutes Chucky came running up Bowen Street with a big smile on his face. Some of the kids laughed. Sully didn't. He told Chucky to get lost.

"Make me," Chucky said, turning on Sully. Sully went after him like a madman and Chucky was on the ground before he knew what hit him.

"I was only kidding Sully, come on I was only kidding," he kept saying. Sully finally let him up, and Chucky tried his best to make a joke out of the incident. But we didn't buy it. He continued to hang around down E street, but Sully and I didn't have much to do with him, after that night.

I do remember one hot Saturday afternoon when we were all sitting on the Dhimitri's stairs.

"Brian let's go watch the Red Sox game up your house," Sully said. He knew that my parents weren't home. There were 6 of us there that day, Bobby Donnelly, Tommy Frane, Joe Pano, Chucky, Sully and me. It was an uneventful day, as days with Sully usually went, but something happened which has always stayed with me. The game was almost over when my parents came from home from a wedding. My father watched the last inning with us and then he went upstairs to bed. The Sox lost, as usual, and all the kids went home. At dinner that night my father asked me who the new kid was.

"His name is Chucky Fuller." I said.

"I don't want him in this house again," my father said. Now Chucky was a bad kid, but my father had never met him before and he was a perfect gentleman when he met my parents that afternoon.

"Why?" I asked.

"I just told you I don't want him in this house, and I don't want you with him" was all he would say on the subject.

"You don't even know him," I said.

"I know his type," my father replied. "Now Case closed," he said, as we went on to other subjects.

I told Sully about our dinnertime conversation.

"Your father is a smart man." Sully said. It's kind of funny how it takes others to pointout.

our parent's strengths. It's only years later that we see what others had seen all along. In this case, Sully and my father were both right. My father never again mentioned Chucky Fuller's name, nor did he ever say "I told you so." It was, however, a great lesson on the perception parents have about their kids. And Fuller just kept getting wilder and wilder. One night we went down his house, because he had taken our stick ball bat. He invited us in. It was the only time that I was ever in his house. For good reason. If Chucky was bad, his mother was worse. When we knocked on the door, that night, we interrupted a very important family meeting. It was not like any family meeting that my family or probably any other family in Massachusetts had ever had. Chucky's mother was running the meeting. Sitting at the kitchen table were Chucky, his younger brother Frankie and his younger sister, whose name I forget. The subject of the family meeting was a robbery. Mrs. Fuller had diagrams and maps all laid out on the kitchen table, and she was detailing the plans to rob one of the many factories that were located on A Street in South Boston. Each of the kids had a specific role, and was expected to know that role inside out.

She had been casing this particular factory for a month, and she had listed on her plans, the exact time the guard would come by, the way they would get in and out and how long that should take them. It was like a scene right out of the movies, but it was real. Their father was in the other room watching TV, while his family planned their robbery. The family that robs together hobnobs together, I guess. It was an incredible night and one Sully and I will never forget. We sat, mesmerized, as she methodically laid out the plans and grilled each of her three young kids on their role in the robbery. Two nights later the factory was hit and the police had no leads. We did. Not much chance of a future with a mother like that. Sully and I called her Ma Barker after that night. They continued to rob the factories and the trains that pulled in down A street. One time Chucky broke into a factory warehouse and stole the watch-dog, a beautiful German Shepherd. The police knew who was doing all the robberies, they just couldn't catch them. This went on for over a year but they finally made a mistake and they were caught. Chucky went to reform school while Frankie and their sister, who were only 12 and 13 years old, received probation. When Chucky came out of reform school he was 10 times worse than when he went in. He began robbing liquor stores and was basically out of control. He was arrested for a double murder on G Street but no witnesses were willing to testify. He was, however, convicted, on a bunch of armed robbery charges and sent to Walpole State prison for a long stretch. After six years he was out again. He had, conned the penal authorities that he had found God. He became an ordained minister and was back in Southie preaching the Bible.

  Sully and I ran into him on Broadway in 1976. I was running for State Representative in South Boston, and he was standing outside the Supreme Market with his robes, flaming red hair and of course his Bible. He even tried to con Sully and me. We didn't buy it. Sully said to him.

  "Come on Chucky don't bullshit us, we know you just became a minister to get out of jail." Sully said to him. He denied it, and told us that he had really found God. Yeah and I found James Michael Curley's desk. Well it didn't take long for the real Chucky to emerge. He began dating a very young girl. I think she was 14 or 15 years old. He was 28, at the time. The girls older brother found out, and told Chucky, in front of witnesses, that if he ever saw

Brian P. Wallace

Chucky with his sister again, he would kill him. Well the kid never did see Chucky with his sister. In fact the kid never saw anything ever again. His body was fished out of Houghton's Pond with his neck cut from ear to ear. The police had only one suspect. They also had no witnesses. About a month, after the killing, the girl found out that Chucky killed her brother and she confronted him with it. They fished her body out of Houghton's Pond the very next day. Her neck had also been slit from ear to ear. This time there was one witness. Guess who? Ma Barker AKA Mrs. Fuller. It seems that Mrs. Fuller had renounced her marriage to Chucky's father and was now a full -fledged lesbian. Wait, it gets better. She and her female lover were in the house the night that Chuck's girlfriend's brother was murdered. Mrs. Fuller testified that she and her lover saw Charles, as she called him in court, come into the house dripping wet with blood on his sneakers and pants. She also testified that Charles, once again, came into the house in much the same condition, the night his girlfriend was murdered. That testimony was good enough for the jury to send Charles to jail for life, without parole. It gets even better, still. Chucky, according to friends, was one of the toughest and craziest inmates in the entire prison. Neither black, nor white, nor Hispanic prisoners ever messed with him. But things began to change for Chucky. His cell mate was a kid I grew up with in Southie, his name was Robbie Rakes. Rakesie was a bank robber and had a heroin habit. He was never violent. Raksie got caught up in drugs and robbed banks to pay for his habit. He was Chuck's room -mate in Walpole for 6 years.

When Raksie got out of jai he came to see me about a job. I was the Executive Director of the Southie Boys and Girls Club, at the time. I talked to his parole officer and some of the counselor's at Walpole and Norfolk Prison who all said he was totally rehabilitated and needed a break. I gave it to him. I hired him as a custodian at the club. He told me that one day Chuckie started acting weird around the beginning of the 6th year they had roomed together. He started dressing differently and hanging around with the fags and the transvestites. One night, Raksie told me, he came into the cell and Chucky was lying on the bed crying. Raksie asked him what was wrong and this was the reply he got from Chucky.

A Southie Memoir

"I keep having these weird dreams and I think I'm going out of my mind."

"What kind of dreams?" Raksie asked.

'Sexual dreams," Fuller responded.

"Oh about girls," Raksie said, a bit relieved.

"No, that's just it," Fuller said "They're not about girls, they're about guys." Raksie said he was too stunned to say anything so Chucky did.

"Remember when I first came in here how I would kick the shit out of all the black guys?" Fuller asked and Raksie nodded.

"It's different now, when I see the black guys in the showers I don't know whether to kill them or to kiss them."

"What did you say?" I asked Raksie. He laughed, remembering the incident.

"I told him to please kill them." Well, Chucky didn't take Raksie's advice. He began to kiss them and to do other things which I won't go into. He began to wear a blonde wig with high heels and short, short tight cutoffs and stockings. They now called him Chuckles and he was as gay as Truman Capote. Mike Barnicle, a Boston Globe reporter, wrote a story about Chuckles one day in the The prison officials took away some of his more provocative apparel such as his bras, panties and lingerie. Chuckles AKA Chucky sued the prison for the return of his clothing. He lost.

I got a call a couple of months ago from my cousin who is serving time in a place called Bay State Prison in Norfolk Mass. He told me that he was standing by the door of the canteen and in walked Chucky AKA Chuckles. My cousin said he almost died. Chuckles walked right up to the head guard.

"I want to know right now, what items of woman's clothing am I allowed to were here and what items I'm not allowed to wear here. "A couple of the black kids started to make fun of him and started calling him names. Chuckles simply walked away. The next day they found one of those black - kids lying unconscious in a pool of his own blood. They didn't know who was responsible. My cousin did. I do too.

Chucky's younger brother Frankie moved to California when he was about 20 years old. One day, he got in a cab and asked the driver to take him to a particular address. The driver agreed. On a deserted street Frankie shot the cab driver in the back of the head, killing him instantly. He then took his wallet, and watch, and put the dead driver in the trunk of the cab. That's bad enough, but he proceeded to pick up fares in the cab. While pretending he was a cab driver he got pulled over by the police for running a red light. They became suspicious right away when they looked at the picture of the guy who owned the cab. The picture looked nothing like Frankie Fuller. They searched the car and then the trunk and found the dead body. Frankie denied any knowledge of the body, even though he was wearing the guys rings, watch and had his wallet in his back pocket. He was tried, convicted, and executed. I have no knowledge of what happened to Chucky's sister, mother, or father. I did, however, meet his two kids, I was running the South Boston Boys and Girls Club in 1990 and one of the staff members told me he was having a problem with one of the kids and he asked me to talk to this particular kid. I agreed and asked the staff member to bring the kid to my office. I was writing something, and when I looked up my heart almost stopped. The kid standing directly in front of me was Chucky Fuller at the age of 13 years. I did a double take.

"Your name's Fuller, right?"

"How did you know?" he asked.

"Just a lucky guess," I lied. Actually he was a good kid. He was no angel, but what did you expect? His father was a serial murderer who dressed like women. His grandmother was a lesbian and his uncle I a cold- blooded killer. Not a great start for any kid. We had it tough growing up, but nowhere near that tough., And don't get me wrong for every Chucky Fuller there were three Doctor John Cloherty, Doctor Leo Paulsen's or Bishop Hennessey. We certainly had quite a mixture, but we enjoyed growing up in Southie and I wouldn't have changed that experience for anything in the world. But as Chucky Fuller went off the reform school and my brother went into the Army and off to Vietnam, time was quickly passing by, and Sully and I were changing and everything around us was changing just as fast.

It is so funny how things have a way of coming around. When I hired Robbie Rakes, who was Chucky Fuller's cell mate, at the Club to be a custodian, I never envisioned so many paths would cross. Robbie's brother Stephen owned a local sub shop on East 8th called Stippo's. A few years later

Stephen AKA as Stippo got in to real estate in South Boston and ended up buying a liquor store on Old Colony Ave. Soon after he opened the store he got a visit, at his house, from Whitey Bulger and Kevin Weeks who told Stippo that they wanted the store. Stippo balked until Whiter put a gun on the kitchen table and sat his little daughter on his lap.

"It would be a shame for this beautiful little girl to grow up without a father now, wouldn't it?" Whitey said as he kept his right hand on the gun. Stippo sold. The details are a little cloudy but in the end Whitey owned the liquor store and Stippo kept his daughter. Many years later Stippo was scheduled to testify against Whitey during the Bulger trial. He was on the news every night telling how Whitey put the gun on his kitchen table and extorted he and his wife out of their liquor store. To testify against Whitey, with the whole world watching was the vindication that Stippo had long asked for and long needed. The day he was to testify, he was told by the prosecution that they didn't need his testimony. Crestfallen, Stippo left court that day and met one of his business associates, a guy named William Camuti who had done time with his brother Robbie. Camuti owed Stippo a lot of money and they agreed to meet at a McDonald's in Waltham. When Stippo arrived at McDonalds, there was a large ice coffee waiting for him. Stippo had no idea that Camuti had laced the coffee with cyanide. He drove the lifeless body of Stevie Rakes to Lincoln Mass where he dumped it on a walking trail. When the body was found everyone assumed it was done by friends or colleagues of Bulger. The same day a nude woman's body washed uo on shore at M Street beach in South Boston and the speculation and conspiracy theories began to spread like the cocaine Whitey sold. Neither case was connected. Robbie Rakes, who introduced Stippo to Camuti, also died from an overdose. The circle was complete. Stippo never did get his day in court and he died before Whitey. Isn't that ironic. Camuti was arrested for murder and will be back in jail with Chuckie Fuller for the rest of his life. The girl who was found naked on the beach had also overdosed, but people will believe ehat they want to believe and the conspiracy theories will go on long after Whitey is dead.

Chapter 41 – The Boys Club And The End Of An Era

The Boys Club, much like any society, had its own caste system. As you grew older you advanced in that system. It was much the same way as high school where seniors are granted the best tables in the lunch-room. It's just an unwritten law that is observed by all parties. At the Club the seniors, who were the oldest kids in the club were the highest ranked. Next came the Intermediates then the juniors while the midgets took firm control of the bottom rung of the ladder. The intermediates and seniors had the entire second floor of the club to themselves. The juniors and midgets had one big game room on the first floor. I can remember how great I felt the first time I legally walked upstairs and into the Intermediates room. I really felt like a big kid. The best part was that it was air- conditioned. We spent many summer days up in that room just cooling off. It was always tough getting the pool table because so many club members wanted to play. There were 3 tables but one was much better than the others. It was a very expensive table and the kids really took good care of it. We didn't get much of chance to play on that particular table because the older kids were always using it. They were always playing for money too, which really left us out. Losing a couple of bucks was no big deal, to them, but to us it was a weeks allowance. I had better things to do with my money than waste it on some stupid game of pool. I have to agree with my man Forrest Gump, "Life is like a box of chocolates, you never know what you're going to get." That was especially true when you hung around with Sully. You never knew what you were going to get. That was also the exciting part about hanging around with Sully, the thrill of the unexpected. I knew him better than anyone else and I honestly never knew what was going to happen next, whether at the Garden or school or the Club or just walking down the street.

We were walking up Broadway one day and this kid who Sully disliked was, for some unknown reason, walking on the sidewalk with his coat pulled over his head. We were very young, maybe 8 or 9 years old and this kid was a year younger than me, so he was probably 7 years old. I just noticed some kid approaching us with his coat over his head. I didn't have a clue as to why or even who the kid was. I guess he was playing a game and was trying to simulate being blind. Sully recognized the coat but didn't say a word. The kid had his hands outstretched in front of him trying to feel if anything was in his path. As he got abreast of us Sully hit him in the head with a right hand. The kid instantly hit the ground. I was as stunned as the kid on the ground. Sully just kept walking as if nothing had happened. The kid never knew what hit him. By the time he got up to we were already around the corner and out of sight. I'm relating this story because even just walking down the street with Sully was an experience. One other time we were hanging up Bent Court with Bubba Cahill and his friends. Bent Court was at the very end of the Old Colony project. I was 16 at the time. One of the kids who hung up there was Bobby O'Keefe. He played fullback for us in the Park League and was a very good football player. He also was the starting fullback for Southie High. I got along great with him, Sully not as well. Sully thought he was kind of a phony. This particular night one of the older guys had just made the run to the package store for us. We would buy one of the older guys a six pack, if he went into and got us beer, because we were to young to get served. Neither Sully or I were drinking but Bobby O'Keefe was. And as usual Sully was right. O'Keefe was putting on a show for the girls. He said, loud enough for them to hear.

"I got caught drinking last week by the cops and they made my mother come down to the station to get me." Sully said that O'Keefe made up the story.

"I'm afraid if I see that cop tonight I will yell something at him."

"Don't worry," Sully said "I won't let you yell anything." We went right on with what we were doing and forgot about that weird exchange. O'Keefe had downed about 4 beers and was acting drunk.

"Here comes the cops," Sully yelled and he hit O'Keefe with a wicked right hand which landed on the right side of his head. O'Keefe went down and out. I looked quickly to see where the cops were. They were a good 7 blocks away and heading in the opposite direction. We were standing on the corner of Old Harbor and 8th street. The cop car was at I street and was heading away from us toward City Point. O'Keefe woke up about 30 seconds later and asked what the hell happened.

"I saw a cop car and I didn't want you to yell at the cop and get arrested so I hit you to make sure you didn't yell." I was speechless. I was even more speechless when O'Keefe shook Sully's hand and thanked him. Now that took the cake. Going home that night I laughed.

"I don't believe that you suckered O'Keefe and you got thanked for it." He smiled.

"Be careful what you say it just might come back and bite you in the ass" He had used O'Keefe's own words against him. O'Keefe never did ask how far away the police car had to be. and Sully never volunteered the information either.

Years later I was having a few beers up a New Hampshire chalet with some guys and girls from Southie. One of those guys was Bobby Doherty who was a good kid. He grew up around the Dorchester Heights area and was a decent baseball player, which was about all I knew about him until that day. We were swapping Southie stories and I happened to mention Sully's name.

"Do you mean Sully from the Club," Doherty asked.

"Yeah, do you know Sully?" I asked Doherty.

"Know him? He suckerd me three different times," he said. I started laughing.

"Three times? How the hell did you let him do that?" I asked.

"I didn't, he's just good at it," Doherty said.

Some of the stuff Sully planned, like the incident with Charlie the popcorn man or jumping out a window in high school, but most of his stunts were spontaneous and happened very quickly. This next incident was an important one in that it signaled the end of an era at the Club and a realization that times were, in fact, really changing. It happened in the intermediate room and on that beautiful pool table that I alluded to earlier. I usually didn't know when he was going to do something. It was strange, that day, because the minute we walked into the Intermediates room I knew, somehow, that something was going to happen. I had an eerie feeling race through my body. Sully didn't seem to notice. He was too busy watching one of the local tough guys beat a scared, young kid out of his allowance money. The tough kid was named Ronny and he was 4 years older than Sully, which made him 19 at the time. He was a real jerk and a bully who constantly picked on younger and weaker kids. We both hated him with a passion. Everyone, except his gang members, hated him. He and all his buddies were, what we called 'Rats.' 'Rats' were individuals who wore their hair slicked back with a pound of grease in it. They all had DA's, or Duck Asses. DA's were a style of hair similar to what Fonzie wore on Happy Days. Actually these guys were the original Fonz. They all wore leather jackets with their gang emblem emblazoned on the back. They all smoked, and had their cigarettes rolled up in their sleeves, when their black leather jackets weren't on. They all had large combs, which they continually raked through their greasy hair. They all seemed to be characters out of the play Grease, which I saw many years later, and which instantly transported me back to that particular day in the Intermediate room. They all thought that they were the cats ass. They intimidated everyone, including the club staff. There was no smoking in the club but that never stopped these jerks from lighting up the minute they entered the intermediate room. One night a new guy was working on the floor, and he told one of them to put out the cigarette. They all laughed at him. He was a pretty big guy, who was a student at Harvard, and had played football there that year. A lot of Harvard and BU kids worked at the Club for a semester. They received credits for their work with us inner city kids. That night the kid from Harvard literally picked up the smoking 'Rat' whose name was Flabbo, and carried him out of the room, down the stairs and out the door. We loved it. That night, however, as he waiting for the bus, outside the club, he got beat up pretty bad and he never returned to the club. Nobody was ever charged, but everyone knew who did it. The guys who worked at the club were only human, and they were all well aware of the incident. They all looked the other way from then on when Ronny and his gang began acting up, in the Club. Gambling was another thing that wasn't allowed in the club but Ronny, and his boys made a mockery of that rule. Nobody ever said a word about it, so it just became an accepted practice. It also became an accepted practice that once a kid put his money on the table, it was as good as in Ronny's pocket. It was like stealing the money. They made suckers bet, knowing full well that once they bet, their money was gone. It wasn't as humiliating as having the money just taken from you and it wasn't a crime either. But in all that time, I never saw one kid beat Ronny. it wasn't that he was that good. He won by intimidation. When that didn't work, he won by outright cheating. More than once I saw Ronny put one of his balls in the pocket when his scared opponent wasn't looking. If he was looking he still didn't have the nerve to say anything to Ronny. If the Club staff wasn't going to say anything they knew a scared 13 year -old kid wasn't going to either. Sully really disliked Ronny. He got along with some of his gang members, but Sully and Ronny were akin to oil and water. That afternoon we arrived just as Ronny was polishing off another pigeon. The kid looked grateful just to have the game over so he could get the hell out of there. They would grab a kid in the intermediate room and say, "how much you got on you?" If the kid said a buck, Ronny would smile.

"Ok a buck it is, put your money on the table," The kid, at that point had no alternative. If the kid said "I don't have any money," they would frisk him and if they found any money, they would take it and give the kid a beating for lying to them. You couldn't win. As Ronny finished off a kid named John Cobb, his pals already had another sucker waiting on the wings.

This time the sucker was a good friend of ours. His name was Billy McCormick, whose nick- name oddly enough was 'Itchy Balls., if you can believe that. That day Itchy Balls had 2 bucks on him, which is exactly what the stakes were. What a coincidence! Sully was pissed, but he said nothing. As I watched Ronny play I realized that he really wasn't good at all. He missed many easy shots that Sully or I would make 9 out of 10 times. He also put 2 balls in the side pocket when Itchy wasn't looking. Itchy came from a very poor lower end family, and two bucks was an awful lot of money to him. As Ronny put the second ball in the side pocket, Sully stood up and took it out of the pocket and placed it back on the table.

"Do you have to cheat to beat a kid a kid 5 years younger than you?" he said to Ronny. You could hear a pin drop, and my stomach as well. Ronny spun around facing Sully.

"What did you say fat boy?" Ronny smirked.

"I said, that you can't beat anyone without cheating?" Sully very plainly said.

"Are you calling me a cheater?" Ronny said indignantly. Nobody had ever called him a cheater, at least to his face.

"Everyone knows that you're a cheater that's the only way you win," Sully said, standing right up to Mr. Big. There was a moment of indecision in the room, as if everyone was deciding if what they heard was actually what they heard.

"Are you crazy?" was all that Ronny could come back with.

"No just truthful," was Sully's excellent response. Poor Itchy balls stood in between Sully and Ronny. He was just holding his pool stick looking back and forth at them like he was watching a tennis match. Sully was too far in now to get out. I looked around the room, real quick, and sneaky-like, there were exactly 12 people in the room. There was me, Sully, Itchy, Ronny, and 8 of his gang members. Not great odds and not a great time for Sully to pull this kind of a stunt, I thought. The two combatants stared each other down before Itchy broke the silence.

"Is it my shot?" he weakly asked.

"No it's not," Ronny barked.

"This game is over It's me and fat boy, now," Ronny said as his minions screamed their approval. We were in deep trouble and only getting deeper by the second. Itchy didn't know whether to laugh or cry.

"Take your money," Sully said to him. Again, there was that long moment when Itchy walked over and took his two dollars off the pool table. That had never happened before! Once a kid put his money on the table it was as good as gone. A precedent had now been broken and a lot more were about to be broken before this day was through.

Itchy still wasn't sure if he would get a beating if he actually took the money. He hesitated and looked at Ronny, who now had other, bigger fish to fry.

"Take it," Sully said defiantly. Itchy still hesitated, fearful of Ronny's friends.

"Go ahead," Ronny said, "I'll make it up on brave little fat boy, over there." Itchy grabbed the money, and was out of there in a millisecond. Great, now it's only me and Sully against nine of them. What I didn't know, at the time, was that Itchy ran straight to our corner and explained that Sully was into it with Ronny.

"How much ya got fat boy?" he mockingly said to Sully as his troops began laughing and carrying on. This was starting to get out of hand. Now don't get me wrong, Sully could really handle himself but this kid was 4 years older than Sully. Four years difference may not seem like a lot when one guy is 70 and the other guy is 66. But when you're 15 and the other kid is 19, four years is an awful lot, believe me. Even today when I'm at a re-union, or a get together, and I introduce one of my brothers friends I still say, "He was one of the big kids." There was no doubt that Ronny and his gang, were the "big kids." I had one last chance. I grabbed Sully.

"Come on, he's not worth it." He was having none of that however.

"I'm sick of his shit," was all Sully said, in response to my plea to get out of there while we still could. Sully walked over to the stick rack, took his time, and pulled out a cue stick. Ronny and his boys watched every move he made.

"You didn't answer my question, fat boy, how much money ya gut on ya."

"A double saw, can you match it?" Sully said very calmly, as if he did this thing every day. Ronny was a little flustered.

"I gut fifteen but I'm good for it," he said very quickly. Sully laughed right in his face.

"The only thing you're good for is cheating scared little kids out of their lunch money." Ronny was boiling mad.

"Who gut five bucks?" he demanded, as he stood before his gang.

"I gut two bucks," a skinny kid with very greasy hair and a face full of pimples piped up.

"Save it and buy some Clearasil," Sully said. I had to crack up, even though I knew I was severely increasing my chances of getting a beating.

"Keep it up fat boy and I'll just take that 20 bucks from you after I kick your ass," Ronny said.

"At least I have 20 bucks, and I haven't taken a dime from any scared little kids today," Sully shot back. He was good. Finally, Ronny came back to the table with his 20 dollars.

"Here's my 20," Ronny said trying to regain the upper hand, but Sully wouldn't let him.

"Who counted it for you?" Sully laughed. "I counted it," Ronny said, falling right into Sully's trap.

"You couldn't have," Sully said. "Why?" Ronny asked. Sully waited a second. "Because you still have your boots on." Ronny didn't get it for a second and when he did he exploded.

"You think I'm stupid don't you, ya punk ass little shit." Sully wasn't intimidated.

"I never said you were stupid, I just said you couldn't count to 20." One of Ronny' gang members laughed, and Ronny shot him a look that might have killed a lesser man. The kid shut right up. A little break in the ranks, I thought.

"Put your money where your fat little mouth is," Ronny smirked. Sully hesitated.

"Brian holds the money," he said, quite emphatically. Nobody ever held the money before. Nobody could be trusted, was the main reason. The money was always placed at the end of the pool table. Always.

"What are you friggin crazy," Ronny yelled.

"Just protecting my interest," Sully calmly asserted.

"It's in your best interest to put your friggin 20 bucks on the table, fat boy," Ronny said for the benefit of his gang.

"Listen, I don't trust you and I trust your boys even less, now if Brian doesn't hold the money there is no game," Sully said, all in one breath. I was stunned. First because he never even talked to me about holding the money and second because he was pulling it off. Ronny wanted Sully's money so bad he could taste it.

"OK give the runt with the glasses the money," Ronny said after thinking it over for a few seconds. It was a weakness and the first he had ever shown us before.

Sully was already winning, whether Ronny knew it or not. His gang started to murmur amongst themselves. A few kids, that I knew, walked into the room, curious as to what all the mystery and shouting was about. They took their place at the far wall as far away from Ronny's gang as possible.

"Can we play now, fat man," Ronny taunted. Sully did not respond or look Ronny's way. He had his cue in his hand as he walked to the table.

Brian P. Wallace

"I break,' Sully said and proceeded to break before Ronny had a chance to object. He is really pushing it, I thought to myself. Usually the two players flipped a coin to see who got the advantage of the break. Not this time. There was almost total silence in the room as Sully broke. I remember I could plainly hear the bus pulling up to the stop outside the club, which was quite unusual because of the constant level of noise that is ever-present in the intermediate room. Sully sunk the 6 ball. The stage was now set. I had no idea how the final act would turn out, but I would soon find out.

"Not bad fatty, did daddy buy his little fat boy a pool table for Christmas," Ronny mocked as his troops howled with derisive laughter. He was totally misjudging Sully. He had no idea what kind of a heart was beating inside that pudgy little body. This was also a basic part of Sully's strategy. People were always deceived by his altar boy looks, like Bobby Doherty. Once they had fallen into that trap, it was too late. That was his game, but this was the biggest game that Sully had ever set out to trap. I also knew how much Sully hated to be called fat or pudgy. But he acted, that day, as if Ronny were complimenting him every time he called him fat boy or fat man. He never showed any sign of a weakness or a chink in his armor, which is kind of a racist term in and of itself, isn't it. Actually I don't think I've ever seen a chink in hisarmor. Anyway, Sully lined up his next shot. He really took his time which was infuriating Ronny.

"Today, fat boy," he finally said. Sully never looked at Ronny. He continued to stare at the table. He finally shot and sank the 4 ball in the corner pocket. A few more kids straggled into the room.

"Go Sully," one of them cheered as all of Ronny's boys stared him down and the kid quickly left the room.

"Not bad for a fat little roly- poly dirt ball," Ronny cracked as his gang laughed as if what he said was the funniest thing they had ever heard. Sully acted as if he were deaf and dumb. Again he studied the table and again Ronny was getting madder by the second. Sully knew exactly what he was doing. Sully reminded me of Art Carney in the Honeymooners. He would act as if he were going to shoot and stop. He would then go to another position, act as if he were going to shoot, and stop.

By now the room was starting to fill up. Word had, no doubt, filtered throughout the entire club that there was a $40 game going on. That was pretty high stakes. Still none of my gang had shown up, which worried me. Sully shot and missed. Ronny's peanut gallery cheered as if the Red Sox had just won the World Series. All their cheering really accomplished was to bring more kids into the room to see what all the commotion was about. As soon as Sully missed, he turned to Ronny.

"Your shot Elvis." A few kids in the crowd cracked up at Sully referral of Ronny as Elvis. We had never heard anyone speak that way to him before. I knew that something was changing , even as I stood there, I just didn't know what. Ronny lined up his shot, as his gang encouraged him. He fired, and put the 9 ball in the side pocket. They cheered wildly. He quickly moved around the table, lined up his shot, and sent the 11 ball into the other side pocket. Now his gang could be heard three blocks away cheering.

"How'dya like that fatso?" Ronnie asked, looking directly at Sully. Sully showed no emotion.

"If I'm correct "I don't think you win the game until you sink the 8 ball, Elvis." Now the crowd that was continually pouring in, was totally behind Sully and they began to laugh.

"You call me Elvis one more time and I'll kick your fat little ass," Ronny growled.

"Just shoot and shut up, Elvis" Sully shot back. All the kids, our age, were shocked at the way Sully was talking to Ronny. He was actually calling his bluff. I think his gang was a little shocked as well, but they never let on. Ronny lined up his shot and sent the 12 ball into the corner. On the way into the pocket it grazed the 2 ball, and missed. The crowd behind me, which was now solidly on our side, began to cheer. Ronny's gang tried to stare them down. Sully, like a master chess player looked at every angle of every conceivable shot. The whole time Ronny was ranking him, Sully never even looked at him or gave any impression that he heard him, which infuriated Ronny even more. Sully finally shot and made a beautiful combination into the far corner pocket. The room erupted in cheers. The room took on an electric quality, much like a Celtic 7th game. It's a feeling that is very hard to describe but I knew everyone, in that room, felt that something was somehow different that day. I think even Ronny felt it. I heard a commotion behind me and when I turned around I never felt so relieved. About 15 members of our gang came in together, led by Itchy Balla McCormick. If Sully noticed he didn't let on. There were now about 75 people in a room that held 50 comfortably. The odds were steadily increasing in our favor. Sully calmly sank the next shot in the same corner and the crowd erupted.

"Well looky here the fat boy has his own cheering section," Ronny mocked. Before Sully lined up his next shot, Ronnie stood in front of him.

"OK fatso you have all your boys here now, why don't we put the money on the table, or are you afraid I'm going to take it in front of all your little faggot friends." I knew that my holding the money was bothering him. Sully looked at me and nodded. I walked over and put the 40 dollars on the end of the pool table. Ronnie was trying his best to gain back some control.

"What the hell is going on?" Knuckles whispered to me, from behind.

"What you see is what you get," I laughed.

"I know he has a lot of balls, but I don't know about brains," Knuckles whispered, as Sully lined up his next shot. The crowd was eerily quiet as Sully pumped and shot. He missed. An audible gasp went up from our side. Ronnie's boys, who hadn't been heard from in quite a while, began to go crazy.

"Poor little fat boy," Ronny cowed, "The little fat boy with all his friends watching is going to lose."

"Just shoot Elvis and shut up," Sully said as he sat down. Ronnie made a move like he was going to go after Sully. Sully never flinched. Knuckles leaned over to where I was sitting.

"He's calling him Elvis? What is he gone soft?"

"He knows what he's doing," I said in return. And God, I hoped I was right. Ronnie sank a ball in the corner and then missed. You couldn't fit another person in the room, which was beginning to get very hot. This was a happening. Nobody had ever challenged or spoke to Ronny like that before in or outside of the Club. Sully took a really long time before his nextshot.

"Want another twinkie, fatso" Ronny said, as his boys went crazy laughing. I finally knew what Sully was doing. He was studying the placement of every ball on the table. He would know, instantly if one were moved intentionally or unintentionally. He was way ahead of Ronnie. Sully missed badly.

"Too much pressure fatso?" Ronny asked. Sully said nothing and sat down next to me.

"Are you all right?" I asked, very concerned.

"He's dead meat," Sully shot back in whispered tones.

Ronnie missed as well as his minions groaned their disapproval. Sully made his next shot as a roar went up from our crowd. Ronnie stood and turned around. He slowly pannedeach kid as if he were memorizing every face. A few kids turned away but most didn't. I watched this drama unfolding in front of me. I knew that something big was taking place and I was trying to appreciate it, if I knew what it was I was supposed to appreciate. Both Sully and Ronnie took a time out to have some tonic. The room had become oppressively hot. One of the Harvard guys who was running the Intermediate Room walked in.

"You guys aren't playing for money are you?" he asked.

"Get the fuck out of here one of Ronny's Lieutenants yelled and the guy flew out of the room, no doubt aware of what happened to one of his classmate earlier that year.

Before play resumed Ronnie very deftly moved on his balls to a set up position, when Sully wasn't looking. He was very good at it. He faced the crowd and had his back to the pool table. All in one motion he swept the ball a few feet toward the side pocket as if by accident and then he walked over to his gang. Sully did have his back turned when he did it. I saw it immediately but this wasn't my call. Sully turned around and took one look at the table. He looked at Ronnie who was laughing and joking with his friends. Most kids had no idea that Ronny had even moved the ball. He was that good at it. I could see how he won all those other games and it wasn't through skill.

"Put it back." Sully said to Ronny in a very strong and demanding voice. Here we go, I thought. This is where we get our asses kicked. Ronnie turned around quickly. He looked puzzled as if he had no idea what Sully was talking about.

"What are you babbling about now fat man?" he asked.

Brian P. Wallace

"Put the 13 ball back where it was" Sully said, again, very forcefully. Sully was now staring at Ronnie for the first time all day. Up to that point Sully had only looked at the pool table and a few quick glances at the crowd. He acted as if Ronnie was not even in the room. Now it seemed as if he and Ronnie were the only two in the room. Sully was now staring a hole through Ronnie. I had never seen him so focused.

"Put back the 13 ball and we'll finish the game," he said directly to Ronnie. Ronnie looked around as if Sully were speaking to somebody else.

"Are you saying I'm cheating?" he asked, as if the implication hurt him. I think Ronnie expected the usual cop out that he was so accustomed to. He didn't get it this time. Sully put his stick on the pool table. The room was as quiet as a tomb.

"I'm saying that you moved the 13 ball that is all I'm saying." Sully seemed to be shrinking from his previous condemnation. But I knew better. He had this play fully scripted even before he picked up the cue stick.

"Did you see me move the 13 ball?" Ronnie asked.

"No," Sully replied, "But I know that you moved it."

"Now you're calling me a liar, and a cheat, fat man? Ronnie asked playing to his gang. Sully didn't back down.

"I didn't call you anything. I said that you moved the 13 ball, which makes you a cheater. You also denied moving the 13 ball, which also makes you a liar. Is that clear enough for you" Sully finished. I couldn't believe he said those things to Ronnie. Either could Knuckles, who wasstanding beside me.

"Uh-oh" Knuckles whispered. The die was certainly cast now, no doubt about that. Ronny walked over to Sully and put his stick on the table. His gang all stood up, in one motion, as if controlled by some unseen remote control switch. Sully stood his ground. The crowd fidgeted and murmured, expecting an imminent confrontation and not really believing what they were seeing.

"Put it back or this game is over," Sully stonily replied.

"You're damn right this game is over, fatso, and you lose," Ronny laughed. Now what is he going to do?" I thought. But before I had time to get scared, Ronny walked past Sully and reached over the table to grab the forty dollars.

"This game is history," Ronnie said. As he leaned over the table, Sully spun around and hit him with one of the best uppercuts I had ever seen, It all happened so quick. As Ronnie hit the floor Sully reached down and grabbed the 40 dollars, which had fallen on the floor.

"No, you lose, Elvis," Sully said as he walked over the unconscious gang leader.

At first there was an audible gasp in the room and then one person began to clap, I don't know who it was, but another and another and another until the whole room was clapping wildly. It was very strange but gratifying. Ronnie was just waking up. His gang, now leaderless, looked pitiful and scared. They huddled around their fallen hero, not really believing the circumstances, which brought them to this point. Sully never looked back, as Ronnie was hoisted onto the pool table by his gang. A lot more than Ronnie's pride was hurting that day as his minions administered to him. The kids behind us continued to clap and slap five, in a scene somewhat reminiscent of the Wizard of Oz. The wicked witch, in this case the wicked warlock, was dead, and the Munchkins behind us were letting loose a lot of pent up and hidden emotions that they, until that afternoon, would not even think, less Ronnie knew what they were thinking. They let it all out that day, however. As Sully and I began to walk out, the crowd simply parted, reminiscent of Moses and the Red Sea. Kids, who we didn't even know, began to pat Sully on the back and shake his hand. Others were still to shocked to actually believe what they had just witnessed. They just stared at Sully, as if he were some kind of super hero and in a way he was. That day he stuck up for all the little kids who couldn't stick up for themselves. But more than that, Sully had struck back, at what for a lot of these kids was a way of life that they were forced to adhere to. Many of the kids, in that room, that afternoon, had very tough home lives. Their fathers, at least a lot of them, were alcoholics and would take their frustrations and unfulfilled ambitions out on their kids. It happened a lot, people just didn't talk about it much back then. Then these same kids would come to the Club to escape their abusive father, only to be further abused by people like Ronnie and his gang. This was a first for many of those kids who stood cheering that hot afternoon, in the intermediate room. For many, if not all, of those kids, this was the very first time that their abusers had to gotten a taste of their own medicine. Although that taste might not have agreed with Ronnie, it certainly tasted pretty sweet to those kids. It was also a changing of the guard. In that split second an era had ended and a new one had begun, even without our knowing it at the time. The 50's or the products of the 50's were fast becoming as obsolete as DA's, leather jackets and Doo Woop. Ronnie, in the eyes of all who witnessed the pool game that day, was dead, as sure as if he had been shot through his unfeeling heart, and a new order was being formed as quickly as the old one lay unconscious on the club floor.

Ronnie, or his boys were never the same after that day. Ronnie kept telling anyone, who would, listen that Sully was a dead man. But the people who listened became fewer and fewer, and even Ronnie didn't believe his own story after a while. After a few weeks he seemed to forget all about Sully, despite all his macho boasting of what he was going to do to him when he saw him. Pretty soon, Ronnie and his gang, sensing the lack of respect they were now shown by those that once cowered in their wake, came to the club less and less. After a couple of months it was if they never existed. Time marches on and waits for no man, even those clad in leather jackets and Elvis hairdo's.

Word, however, about Sully's triumph spread like wildfire. Good gossip, like a well planned fire, is hard to stop. Likewise, both have the innate power and appetite to destroy. Respect, I found out is something that cannot be forced upon people, it has to be earned. Ronnie thought that intimidation bred respect. He was wrong, it bred contempt and resentment. Ronnie and his gang, soon after, went into the Marines. They tried to be macho to the very end, I'll grant them that. A couple of years flew by and I had completely forgot about Ronnie, his gang, and the incident in the intermediate room. It's funny how life has its own agenda and things that were earth- shattering one day, are merely trivia the next day. We all manage to go on with life no matter what kind of pitches we are thrown. I don't mind the fastballs, it was always the curves that got me. Ronny, however, was just a memory of something that had happened hundreds of years ago, or so it seemed. Sully and I were playing basketball one Saturday afternoon, I guess it was about three years after Sully had rocked Ronnie's world. A kid came into the gym and said that a former club kid had been killed in Viet Nam. I immediately stopped the game and went over to find out who had gotten killed because we had a lot of friends over there.

"Some greaser named Ronnie, why did you know him?" the kid asked.

"Yeah, in another life," Sully said, and I realized how right Sully was. It did seem like another life, even though it was only a couple of years. The kid said his last name, but I am leaving out of the book, for a number of reasons. First of which, his family still lives down the street from me and I know his wife very well. Some things are better left unsaid, especially after a person dies. I felt pretty bad that day.

"Ya know he really wasn't that bad, he was just playing a role," I said to Sully.

"Brian, he was an asshole," he said, walking away shaking his head. It's funny how we forgive all past transgressions once a person had died. Well, almost all of us do.

I remember the very next year, Mr. Ray told me that I was going to be singing a solo in our Class Day Production. I couldn't carry a tune if I had a bucket. But Mr. Ray would have none of it. We were doing Oklahoma and I was penciled in to sing a song called "Poor Jud is Dead" The song was about a guy named Jud Fry, who everyone in the town hated, until he died. Once he had passed away his neighbors talked only of how good he had been while he was alive, which was stretching the truth more than a little bit. But I certainly could relate. So it was with Ronnie. Nobody ever again talked about the money he extorted from younger kids, or all the kids he and his gang had beaten up. In death he had found dignity, something that had alluded him the 20 years he was on this earth. From that day on, " "Ronnie the Bully" would forever be known as "Ronnie the hero," and life went on. His life was now just a memory on a black granite wall with 58,213 other names of young kids like himself who would always stay young. His death had become a symbol of patriotism. His sins in life forever absolved.

About ten years after Ronnie was laid to rest I was elected Chairman of the South Boston Community Health Center. The night of the new Board's very first meeting I was all dressed up in my new 3- piece suit, lucky Sully wasn't around. I had a new briefcase and a brand new gavel that my mother and father had given me for my birthday. I must admit, I thought I was pretty cool. Ray Flynn was running for re-election to the House of Representatives, that year, and I left his headquarters, that night and headed tp the Health Center, which was a couple of blocks away. As I passed Thornton's Flower Store, on Dorchester street, I heard a voice and I froze. The voice, from my boyhood days, instantly transported me back to a warm July day in the Boys Club's Intermediate room. "Hey mister can you spare a quarter for an old vet." The voice was unmistakable. It was also unmistakable that the voice belonged to a very sick man. It was the voice of a street person, a bum. It was also the voice of Ronnie's top lieutenant. I never knew his first name, everyone just called him Flabbo, which meant that his last name was probably Flaherty. Most kids, in Southie whose names were Flaherty, were at some time called Flabbo. I hadn't seen this particular Flabbo since the day Sully had knocked out his fearless leader Ronnie. Flabbo, like Ronnie, had joined the Marines and had gone off to fight in that place called Viet Nam. He had survived Viet Nam, psychically, that is. The Flabbo that came back from Viet Nam was not the Flabbo who had gone to Viet Nam. Whatever happened to Flabbo, in Nam, we'll never know. What horrors he saw there did not die like his friend Ronnie had. Flabbo was a casualty of VietNam as surely as Ronnie was. The only difference was Ronnie died quicker than Flabbo. Not all the casualties, of Viet Nam, I found out, came back in body bags. There were thousands of men like Flabbo who died a much slower, torturous death. But make no mistake about it, they were all casualties of Viet Nam, even if there names were not placed on the Viet Nam memorials. A lot of men came back in name only and Flabbo was one of those men. He now slept in hallways or on the sidewalk, bummed change and drank cheap wine or anything else he could afford to buy. We, as a Society, have become so complacent that we walk right past these poor souls and don't really bother to take the time to look past the dirty clothes or the whiskey breath. We pay no attention to these poor souls, whose lives have taken a wrong turn somewhere along the road of life and it's too bad. I had seen people, like Flabbo, my whole life, but until that night I didn't really know any of them personally. Those bums, as we called them, were faceless, nameless human beings, who were to be mad fun of, rather than pitied. They had no bearing on my life and I none on theirs. Until that night. This bum was a person I knew. I knew his story. I knew him when he was on top of the world. I knew him when he had a girlfriend and drove a convertible. I knew he would soon be dead, as well, and that bothered me. He had no gang now to look out for him. He had no girlfriend and no car. All he had now was his wine bottle, and his life revolved around how fast he could get to the bottom of that bottle every day. What a horrible existence. The voice came back again, and shook me out of my daze.

"Hey mister can you spare some change for a veteran." I looked down, and at first I didn't recognize him. I recognized the voice but not the man. I knew he didn't recognize me. It was Flabbo however, or more appropriately what was left of Flabbo. There was no mistaking that, even in those tattered clothes. Flabbo was always Ronnie's top guy. I had never seen him fight, but word on the street was that he could really handle himself. This was actually the very first time that I had seen Flabbo without Ronnie standing beside him. I looked into the bloodshot eyes that I had once feared and now pitied. I reached into my pocket and pulled out a dollar bill. Flabbo brightened, and for a brief moment I thought I saw a faint glimmer of recognition. But, I was wrong. His tired eyes showed a lot of mileage and the remnants of too many forgotten days and night, but not of recognition. I was a little disappointed that he had no idea who I was. But, by that time, he didn't even know who he was anymore. I handed him the dollar and he quickly grasped it less I change my mind.

"Thanks pal," he said in a hoarse, whiskey soaked voice, with visions of a new bottle of cheap wine dancing in his head.

"You have a nice night" he muttered, as he tried to stand up. I extended my hand to help.

"You too, Flabbo" I said quietly and walked away.

'You know me?"

"In another world my friend," I said, as I walked the half a block to the Health Center. As I got set to chair my first meeting at the Health center, I couldn't help but reflect back on that day, a hundred years ago, in the intermediate room. The day the music died for Ronnie and Flabbo.

Brian P. Wallace

The day that Sully knocked out Ronnie changed a lot of things. It proved to be the demise of Ronnie's gang and the beginning of our puberty. We quietly and without fanfare, inherited the pool table, which was a symbol, if nothing more. Even if we didn't know it, we were growing up. As Ronnie and the older kids moved on with the rest of their lives whether it was the Marines or work or marriage, we took over their domain. The rights of manhood are passed down without so much as a blink of an eye or the utterance of a single word. It just happens. The strong, in all societies, survives. And we survived, especially Sully. The legend of Sully was actually growing larger than life. He was becoming kind of a folk hero at the Club, especially after he KO'd Ronnie. Down the club, there is a sign at the entrance to the gym, which says "A quitter never wins and a winner never quits." There probably should be one painted next to it that said "For every Ronnie, there is an Sully" Now that would have been appropriate.

Chapter 42 – Who Was Sully And Where Did He Come From?

Where did he come from and how did he survive? Right now you're probably saying to yourself, in the immortal words of Butch Cassidy, "Who is this guy? Well, Thomas Patrick Sullivan was one of 3 children born to Thomas Sullivan and Mildred Callahan Sullivan. Their eldest child was a girl, named Donna. Then came Thomas Patrick, forever to be known as just Sully. The youngest of the 3 Sullivan children was another boy named Michael. That is where he came from. How he survived is still a mystery to a lot of people. Not me. Sully simply fooled people. He was a pudgy little kid with an altar boy face and a 3- stooges approach to life. He saw a joke in everything and he was afraid of absolutely nothing, from cops to priests to adults to his parents. Swanny, his dad and Millie did their best to control their eldest son and sometimes he even let them.

His family was a lower middle class hard working family who moved as much as Casey and Hayes. His father Swanny worked for the City as well as a myriad of other part and full time jobs. As I mentioned the Sullivan's were quite nomadic. I met him when he lived, for the first time on E street. He lived in a wooden three -decker. His mother, like most mother's back then, took care of the family home and the Sullivan children. If Sully was "The Beaver" then I most certainly was Eddie Haskell. Sully's mother used to always say.

"Brian, why does my Thomas always get in trouble?" or "Brian, why does my Thomas always do such crazy things?" Sometimes she would say to Sully, in my presence.

"Thomas why can't you be more like Brian?" that drove him absolutely insane. But he always had a comeback. When she would ask him why he didn't act like me, he would say.

"Maybe if you weren't so cheap and gave me an allowance like Brian's mother maybe I would act like him." At times, however, he would act as angelic as he looked, once in 1965 and once in 1966. Milly Sullivan was not the disciplinarian in the Sullivan household. The task of adminstrator of discipline fell squarely on the rounded shoulders of one Swanny Sullivan. Swanny would lecture Sully incessantly. Sully would listen politely, and then go outside and do the exact same thing that he had just been lectured about not doing. I asked him, one time, why he even listened to Swanny's time - consuming talks if he had no intentions of heeding them. Sully said because it made Swanny feel like he was in charge. Now that was said when he was 12 years old. Sully always knew who was running the show, make no mistake about that. He just wanted them to think they were in charge.

Chapter 43 – Sully's Dad - Swanny Sullivan

Swanny Sullivan was born in South Boston. I don't know much about his early years and he never volunteered much either. All I knew was that he was Sully's father and that was enough for me. He was never home. He worked about four jobs back then and come to think of it he worked about four jobs his entire life. I really got to know Mr. and Mrs. Sullivan when I was about 12 years old. By that time I was an unofficial member of the Sullivan family. I didn't know, however, if that was good or bad. There were a couple of things that stood out about Swanny. The first and most glaring, was his speech pattern. It was endless and non- stop. Swanny could talk a dog off a meat truck. The second was how he talked. Swanny talked faster than any human being I had ever met at that time in my life. He was a great guy, with a heart of gold, but he most certainly qualified as a character. His main job was working for the city of Boston, but he had so many other jobs I literally lost count. His other steady gig was working, part time at the Supreme Diner on Southampton Street. Swanny not only worked at the Diner, he also hung there. And if you thought Swanny was a character, a night in the Diner, would leave you shaking your head and questioning your sanity. The thing I remember most about the Supreme Diner was its baseball team. The Supreme Saints played in the Senior Park League in Boston. There were some mighty good players competing in that league, A lot of former and would be major leaguers played in the Senior Park League. It was top- notch baseball, long before the TV was swamped with ESPN games and ESPN 2 games or NESN games. Back then the Park League was the only game in town, and the crowds reflected that sentiment. The owner of the Saints was a guy named Frank Passinessi. He was a good enough guy who loved baseball and lived for the Supreme Saints. Swanny didn't know a whole hell of a lot about baseball, but he, like Frank Passinessi lived for the Saints as well. He was what you would call an all- purpose man. He was the batboy, at 42 years of age. He collected money in a hat, each game, after the 6th inning, and he made sure there was water for the players to drink. He chased foul balls that went into the stands, and he collected all the equipment and he argued every call that went against the Saints. All of these tasks gave Swanny a place of honor on the Saints bench.

Brian P. Wallace

He would take me and Sully to the games and he would be as nervous as a rookie pitcher facing Ted William's for the first time. At least once on the ride over to the game, Sully would say to his father, "Relax, you're only a batboy." Johnny would explode, which is exactly what Sully knew he would do.

"I'm no god damn bat boy" he would scream, "That team needs me."

"Yeah to wipe their asses," Sully would counter with, and they would continue to argue all the way to the game. It was a ritual and it happened every single game. Sully never got tired of this ritual and I loved every minute of it. Some nights when we got home early, Sully's mother would be waiting for us and she would ask Sully how the game went.

"Not bad, Dad was 3 for 5, he dropped one bat and spilled 1 glass of water." Sully would say and again Swanny would explode. He fell for it every single time, it was hilarious. Actually I liked going to the Diner after the games, more than I liked going to the games themselves. Sully and I would get a piece of pie and sit in a back booth and watch the floor show, of which Swanny was a major part. When the Saints won, everyone would be in a good mood and the banter would be light and humorous. When they lost it was the complete opposite. That was the most fun. If Norman Lear had ever walked into that Diner after the Saints lost, his show 'All in the Family,' might just as easy have become 'All in the Diner'. They even had their own newspaper, called the Supreme Diner Digest. It was a newsletter printed once a week. On the back page of the newsletter was a feature called "Saying s from Swanny." They were hilarious. Swanny fractured the language so bad not even William F Buckley could put it back together again. I know that growing up, Norm Crosby lived only three miles from the Supreme Diner. I've always had a sneaking suspicion that he might have eaten a few times there, and built his act on the clientele at the Supreme Diner. He could have written an entire act on the malapropisms that were spewed in the course of one sitting.

Swanny's rival, on the bench and for Frank Passinessi's affection, was a guy named Yogi. He, unlike Swanny, was a baseball man. He was a former catcher who, looked, played, and talked like Yogi Berra. His baseball arguments with Swanny were classic. Swanny would argue about anything, regardless if he knew anything about the subject or not. He was so good at arguing that he would convince anyone listening that he knew everything on the subject they were arguing about. Swanny had taken the art of arguing to a higher level. Sully and I would sit out in center field during the saint's games. It was hilarious to watch Swanny and Yogi, two grown men, chasing after a foul ball, or both rushing to get the Pitcher's jacket so they could bring it to him on second base.

"Look at those two horse's asses," Sully would say and we would laugh like hell. Sully Anytime Sully wanted to get Swanny going he would say.

"Well at least I'm not Frank Passinessi's gopher." The first time Sully said that to Swanny, we were riding home from a Saints game. They began bickering andarguing over some stupid thing, and the subject, as it usually did, after a game turned to Swanny's role as Ball-boy etc.

"You're nothing but Frank Passainnisi's gopher," Sully said, to a confused Swanny.

"That makes no sense at all," Swanny countered. "Why would you call me a gopher." Sully had him, "Because Frank Passanissi tells you to go for this and to go for that." Swanny went into a tirade, He knew his son had won yet another round. Swanny never wavered, he always believed that he was the man who made the Saints go. Just ask him, and you'd had better pack a lunch because you were going to be there for a while. Swanny's arguments and nonstop talking was legendary. Years later Swanny got thrown out of an old age home for talking too much. Can you imagine that? The residents got a petition and brought it to the manager of the nursing home asking him to ask Swannny to leave due to his incessant talking. The family called me and I got him in another home. I thought it was the funniest thing in the world. Getting thrown out for talking to much, but it leads right into my next Swanny story, which had to do with hisfamous Sunday day-trips.

As I said Swanny always worked at leastfour4 jobs, and because of that he never had time to take his family on a real 2- week or even a 1 week vacation. The Sullivans would take day trips usually on Sunday when Swanny had an infrequent day off. Now if Swanny knew nothing about baseball he knew even less about cars. Sully said his father knew where to put the gas in and that was it. But, if you talked to Swanny about cars you would come away feeling that he was pretty knowledgeable about them, which was far from the truth. He did know the names of certain parts of the car and he could fool anybody, who didn't know about cars, into thinking that he did. He did this quite often and always on those famous Sullivan family day trips. When Swanny had a day off, he would pack the car, early, and head for the down to the Cape or up to New Hampshire or down to Houghton's Pond for a relaxing day with his family. More often than not, however, the family never arrived at the intended destination or they arrived too late to enjoy their family day off. As I mentioned, Swanny had a heart of gold and would do anything for anybody, especially stranded motorists. If the family was driving down the Cape and Swanny spotted a disabled motorist, off to the side of the road, he would cut through lanes of fast moving traffic, and pull up behind or in front of the stranded motorist. The motorist would be thrilled that a good Samaritan had pulled over to help them out They would figure, as would I, that the person who fought through lanes of traffic to get to the side of the road, did so because so he knew something about fixing cars. That's a logical assumption, right? But , they had never met anyone like Swanny before. Why else would someone jeopardize their safety, and their families, when they spotted a stranded motorist. In Swanny's case, to talk.

  I found it amazing after listening to one of Sully's famous day trip stories about how many people really know very little about their cars. They got in, turn the key and they expected to go and they expected that to happen every time they turned that key. People didn't put oil in. They never had a tune up. They got the wrong gas. And they knew absolutely nothing about the names of certain parts of the car, which brings me to one of the funniest Swanny stories about a stranded motorist, who he pulled over to give assistance, usually only the verbal kind. He was talking to the stranded motorist who finally got fed up with Swanny.

  "Do you know anything about cars?" the guy finally asked after baking in the sun.

  "I know a lot about cars," Swanny shot back.

  "OK what do you think is wrong with this car. Why won't it start"?

  "It needs a new Otto Preminger," Swanny said with all the conviction of a judge. An Otto Preminger? Last time I looked he was directing movies in Hollywood, but it sounded good. I asked Sully how he knew what his father told the guy and he said they drove him to the nearest restaurant, and when the guy got out Swanny yelled, "Just tell the mechanic you need a new Otto Preminger." I wonder what the mechanic said when he heard that?

As I said before, Swanny knew absolutely nothing about cars. He did know, however, that a stranded motorist was a very captive audience, with no place to go. There were no cell phones, or I Pads or I pods back then. When you were stuck, you were stuck. The poor motorist, however, had no idea what he or she was getting in to. They already had the misfortune to break down, and now they had the double misfortune to have Swanny as their new best friend. And Swanny would, then, do what he did best. He would talk. He would talk as the weather, his family as the unfortunate motorist all grew increasingly hot, literally and figuratively. Sully told me that a prospective one hour trip would often turn into a 3, 4, 5 or 6 hour trip, depending on how many motorists had broken down on the Sully family's day trip. Sully said the motorist's smile would quickly vanish into a frown and then a look of bewilderment as Swanny kept on talking, never once inquiring about the broken down vehicle. Sully's favorite was a trip in which Swanny talked to a stranded motorist for 2 hours. The motorist began to cry and told Swanny he would give him money if he just left. The guy was actually crying, Sully said. My favorite was a guy, who after an hour and a half, chased Swanny into his car with threat of bodily harm if he didn't leave. The Sullivan family, having gone through these breakdowns many times, would bring cards and other games to play as Swanny was doing his talking. I once asked Sully what Swanny would talk about during one of these pit stops.

"He would talk about the Supreme Saints, the Chippewas, his job, his relatives, my Yogi, his mother" Sully would laugh. He would laugh, now, that is. Back then during those long hot summer days, it wasn't always that funny. Sully said, oftentimes, because of those delays they would get to their destination, stay for an hour and head back home because it was getting dark and Swanny hated to drive in the dark. I always waited for Sully to get home from one of those day trips because he always had a new Swanny story for me. I would go home that night and laugh to myself all the way home. My father was actually a bigger Swanny fan than I was. He would laugh so hard when I would tell him Swanny stories that I really worried about his heart. My father's face would turn beet red, he would start coughing, and laughing at the same time, which made some weird hybrid laugh come out of his mouth. My mother would invariably come running into the room with a worried look on her face. After a while she would look at me and say "Swanny?" and I would nod my head, as my father, with his hand, implored me to continue. One day Swanny barged into my house, he never rang the bell, and began a rambling speech about teenagers. My father was sitting in his favorite chair, and was having a grand time just listening to Swanny. Swanny would ask a question and answer it himself before the other person has a chance to answer it. This particular day he was on a tirade about teenage girlfriends. I was sitting on the couch with my teenage girlfriend, Anne Marie, who I had been dating for over a year. I was 16 at the time of Swanny's tirade.

"They're too young to have girlfriend's, they have no money, no responsibilities, no work ethic. They want to take them to the movies, where do they get the money, from the father, that's where" Swanny said, as we all listened. He spoke for a good fifteen minutes about why Sully and I shouldn't have girlfriends at our age. When he finally finished he looked at me for the first time. It was as if he never noticed that Anne Marie and I were in the room.

'Who's this?" he asked, looking at Annie for the first time.

"This is my girlfriend," I said. Swanny looked at her, looked at me, then looked at my father, and then went over to where Annie sat on the couch. She was scared to death, having just sat through fifteen minutes of Swanny's monologue on girlfriends.

"You're Brian's girlfriend?" She weakly shook her head.

"Well, let me tell you one thing, you got a nice kid there, of all Sully's friends he's the best." He reached out his hand and shook Annie's hand, turned and left. It was unbelievable. It was also vintage Swanny. My father loved every minute of it. He thought Swanny was the funniest man on this earth and never tired of Swanny stories.

Swanny loved his family very much, almost as much as his car. Swanny's car was his prized possession. It also was the place where I had one of the funniest days of my life. Sully knew how much Swanny loved his car. Sully also knew how much he wanted to get his drivers license. Therein lay the dilemma. In order to get his license, Sully had to have some sort of driving experience, and he didn't have money to go to driving school. He studied the learners permit book and got his learners permit on the first try. He was really excited when he pulled the folded pink piece of paper out of his battered old wallet.

"Guess what I got?" he asked me, as he began to pull the wallet out.

"I know it's not money," I replied.

"Better" he said, as the learners permit appeared.

"That's great," I said, "But who's car are you going to drive?"

"Swanny's," he quickly said. Acting as if I hadn't heard him, I said.

"Whose car?"

"You heard me," he said.

"I heard you but I don't believe you," I shot back. He didn't say anything and I felt a little bad because I knew how much he wanted to get his license.

"I'm sorry," I said "But we both know how Swanny is with his car."

"Yeah, I know, but I have to try" Sully said, already acting as if he lost.

"Well let's go ask him," I said grabbing his arm, swinging him around and heading toward E street and Swanny. I had never seen him so nervous.

"Take it easy, all he can say is no," I told him, finally able to use that line myself after having it said to me for my entire 16 years on the earth. "Bullshit," Sully said "We're talking about Swanny here, the words all he can say don't apply to Swanny." He did have a point.

"Well, all we can do is try?," I said.

"Any more clichés," he asked.

"That's all I gut," I said as we headed towards a showdown with Sweany We were in the house for fifteen minutes before Sully got up the nerve to ask. He pulled out his wallet and the newly acquired learners permit and put both on the kitchen table. The moment had arrived.

"Dad, do you know what this is?" he politely asked.

"If it's a summons Sully, I'm not going to court," Swanny said. I thought to myself that I wished my father were here for this. Sully got really mad. His altar boy makeover didn't last very long.

"No it's not a summons," Sully said angrily.

"Good," Swanny murmured. "I hope it's not a report card either."

"Forget it," Sully said, as he began to walk away. His mother intervened.

"You sit right down here, young man, and you tell me what you have" Millie said, knowing that Sully was very upset. He turned and sat down.

"He's a jerk," he said, looking at his father.

"I heard that," Swanny said, in between swigs of milk out of a carton.

"You were meant to," Sully said angrily.

Millie again intervened. "What is it that you have there?" she asked.

"I got my learners permit ma," Sully said, unfolding the document. Millie wasn't expecting it, and her immediate glance at Swanny gave herself away. But like all mothers, she rallied.

"Oh good for you honey. I'm so proud of you." Swanny who had not heard the word "proud" very much in regard to Sully, spun around.

What'ya got there? A draft notice I hope," Swanny laughed. Sully didn't.

'What do you care?" Sully said. "It's his learners permit," he said to Swanny. He started laughing, which really pissed Sully off. I could tell that he was really pissed off, by the look on his face.

"Let's go," he said, turning to me. Millie jumped up.

, "Now that wasn't very nice. You apologize to your son." Swanny mumbled something and headed into the living room.

"I should just steal his car," Sully whispered to me. I knew that he was mad enough to do just that, so I quickly talked him out of it. Millie wasn't through with Swanny though, and we followed her into the living room where Swanny sat watching the news. He took one look at Millie and us trudging immediately behind her and yelled, "What now?"

"I think you ought to teach your son how to drive" she said matter of factly. Swanny looked astonished.

"Are you crazy?" he literally yelled.

"You taught Donna," she said, not backing off.

"That was different" Swanny said, not backing off.

"Why?" Millie asked.

"Because Donna isn't him," Swanny replied pointing to an angelic looking Sully. Millie walked over to Swanny, in one of those parent moments and began to talk real low so that Sully couldn't hear, but I did.

"Look how disappointed he is," she whispered to Swanny.

"How many times has he disappointed me?" Swanny asked in return.

"He's only a kid," Millie said.

"He was never just a kid," Swanny said, and for once I had to agree with him. Then Millie said something that shocked everyone in the room. She looked straight at Swanny.

"It's your choice, you either teach him how to drive or he'll steal the car and teach himself." I was totally shocked. This was totally out of character for Millie, but she knew what buttons to push on Swanny, and that was the right button. Most fathers would have taken that as a joke, but Swanny knew his son and he knew what he was capable of. He looked at Millie and then over at Sully.

"Meet me at the car., I'll be down in five minutes. Millie hugged him, which was the only outward sign of affection I ever witnessed in all the years with Sully. Swanny rebuffed the advances, and began mumbling something under his breath, as he headed to his room to get his shoes on.

"Thanks ma," Sully said, genuinely excited at the prospect of driving. We ran out the door, down the one flight of stairs and out onto E street in a few seconds. I had never seen him so excited. Swanny, on the other hand, looked as if he had just been condemned to a death sentence, as he walked out the front door.

"You don't have to get so excited dad," Sully said, as Swanny approached us and the car. He looked at his car as if it were a beautiful woman he was having a romance with.

"I'm not going to total your precious car," Sully madly said, as he interpreted the look in Swanny's eyes.

"I'll never put anything past you," Swanny said, in his fast talking manner. Sully just shook his head and headed to the car I followed, not knowing where this would all lead but dying to find out.

We waited at the car as Swanny, walked over, as if he were heading toward the electric chair, instead of giving his son a driving lesson.

"All right son, we're going to start at the very beginning," Swanny said. He stood next to his car, patted the hood.

"OK now what is this? "You've got to be shitting me," Sully said, as he stared at his father.

"There's no need for blasphemy here" Swanny fired back. Sully was just shaking his head. "Now son it's either my way or the highway," Swanny said, as he again patted the hood of the car.

"At this rate I'll never see the highway," Sully responded.

"We'll start all over," Swanny replied. "Now what is this?"

Sully, embarrassed, softly said, "It's a car."

"Whose car is it?" Swanny asked.

"It's your car," Sully said, with his head down.

"That's right and I want you to always remember that," Swanny said, smiling. He really enjoyed having the upper hand, for once.

"Next question. What are these?" Swanny said, holding up a set of keys.

"This is ridiculous,"Sully said, as he stared at his father.

"My way or the highway," was all Swanny said.

"Those are keys, dad." Sully said, defeated.

"WRONG." Swanny screamed. Sully and I looked at each other. "They're not just any keys, they're CAR keys. See, you think you know everything , don't you?" Sully was somehow holding back his temper. Swanny kept on.

"What do these CAR keys do? " Sully looked as if he was ready to walk away.

"They start the car," he replied.

"WRONG" Swanny shouted again "These CAR keys only fit into the ignition,"

Swanny was on a roll.

"Who starts the car son?"

"I start the car dad," Sully sarcastically replied.

"That's right, you start the car" Swanny said and then he stopped. He was quiet for about 20 seconds, which was an eternity for him. Then he exploded.

A Southie Memoir

"Son, you can start it, BUT CAN YOU STOP IT' he yelled. As if to reemphasize his point he again yelled, "You can start it, BUT CAN YOU STOP IT?" He kind of scared us with all the yelling, and the way he emphasized the words BUT CAN YOU STOP IT. He then went on a 5 -minute tirade about teenage kids and car accidents and drinking and driving and on and on. By this time all our friends had joined us at the car, which made absolutely no difference to Swanny. I actually feel that he liked the audience. And just as quickly as his tirade started, it stopped. Sully was steaming.

"All right son, you want to drive let's drive," Swanny said, as he threw the car keys to Sully.

Sully jumped in behind the wheel, and I jumped into the back seat Swanny was riding shotgun. I couldn't believe that this was really happening.

"Remember son, anyone can start a car, but can they stop it?" Swanny reiterated. That wouldn't be the last time I would here that phrase, not by a longshot. By this time, Sully had literally shut out the sound of his father's voice, which made absolutely no difference whatsoever to Swanny. Finally we were on our way. Sully sitting behind the wheel for the first time in his life, and Swanny flapping his gums non- stop all the way down Old Colony Ave. Sully, at first, was extremely cautious. The more he drove the more he became relaxed and the faster he went, which drove Swanny absolutely bonkers.

"Pull it over, pull it over," Swanny screamed, as we passed the Boston Globe. He kind of startled Sully who was in the middle of traffic and kind of panicked.

"Over, over, over," Swanny yelled at the top of his lungs. Sully, after a short time, was able to guide the car up onto the shoulder of the road just beyond the Globe.

"Son you're too fast on the gas, way too fast on the gas." Swanny was talking so loud, I think people who worked in the Globe could hear him. Swanny then went in to a veritable plethora of all his sayings combined. "Sully, I told you anyone can start it but can they stop it, and when you're too fast on the gas, the answer is no, you can't stop it."

"Dad I was only doing 30 miles an hour," Sully disgustedly said.

"That's too fast Sully, way too fast." Sully looked back at me.

"Brian and I do faster than that on our bikes." Swanny pounced.

"But, they're you're bikes, this is my car Sully, do you understand, this is my car, and we'll do it, Sully then said before Swanny could get it out.

"I know my way or the highway." I was trying to disguise my laughter in the back seat, much like in school, when the teacher is in class and you try to keep you're laughter as quiet as possible.

"Can I go now?" Sully said as he turned the CAR key.

"You can go Sully but you'd better no be fast on that gas." Sully behaved himself for the next half -hour as we drove around Boston. He was doing very well for a first time driver as far as I was concerned, but not Swanny. He complained about everything. He was watching the speedometer, like a hawk, and anytime that Sully went over 35 miles per hour, he would scream.

"There you go again Sully, too fast on the gas." I could tell that Sully was getting very frustrated with this constant complaining and non- stop jabbering. We passed our favorite spot, the Garden, and headed over the bridge into Charlestown. Sully had been driving for at least an hour, and he was really getting the hang of it. We went up Bunker Hill street and a little kid, chasing a ball, ran in front of the car. Sully stopped in plenty of time but I thought Swanny was going to have a coronary.

"Jesus Christ, you almost killed that kid, you almost killed that kid," he screamed. In actuality, Sully never even came near the kid, but it was too close for Swanny none the less. He kept it up all the way up Bunker Hill street, and into Sullivan Square.

"I knew this was a bad idea, you're just not stable enough to drive a car Sully." Sully slammed on the brakes in the middle of the Sullivan Square rotary, as the car behind us almost crashed into the back of Swanny's precious car. Swanny almost flew through the windshield.

"I'm not stable?" Sully yelled, as he faced Swanny. "I'm not stable?" he yelled again at Swanny. The severity of Sully's screams, and the fact that only Swanny's seatbelt saved him from lying on Main Street in Charlestown, totally unnerved Swanny. He was looking at the cars behind us, now all beeping their horns as our car, now in the middle of the rotary ,was blocking traffic.

"I'm not stable, you're a Goddamn lunatic," Sully yelled as the cars continued to beep, and a trickle of sweat ran off Swanny's bald- head and on to his precious cars' upholstery.

"Come on son, this is not the time to fool around, come on, you're holding up traffic," Swanny, who was now on the defensive, said. Sully pulled the keys out of the ignition, and held them up in the air.

"Now where do you stick these?" he asked Swanny.

"For Christ sakes, this is no time to play games," Swanny pleaded. Sully acted as if he didn't even hear him. 'Where do you stick these?" Sully again asked, as more sweat began to trickle down Swanny's bald- head.

"No time for games son. No time for games." The cars were now going crazy behind us. Sully never blinked.

"You know where you can stick these?" Sully said, as he, again, held the keys before Swanny's eyes. Swanny never answered, so Sully answered for him. "You stick these keys right up your ass." Swanny, for the first time in his life was speechless. Sully looked back at me, opened the driver's side –door.

"Let's go." We jumped out of the car in the middle of the rotary, with horns blaring and Swanny scrambling over to the driver's side to get the hell out of there. He was having trouble starting the car, because in all his haste he had flooded the engine. It was unbelievable, and to make matters worse, some guy who was two cars behind Swanny's car, yelled.

"What the hell is going on?" Sully in an instant changed demeanors and yelled.

"That guy tried to kidnap us." That was it for me, I totally lost it. I fell on the grass, on the rotary, and just laughed until I couldn't laugh anymore. The absurdity of it all hit me and I just couldn't get a grip. People were yelling out the windows of their cars at Swanny. The guy in the second car was yelling for someone to get the cops to arrest the kidnapper, and Sully was smiling as he surveyed his handiwork. Finally the motor caught and Swanny left rubber getting out of there. I was still laughing. Sully said to me.

"How much ya gut." "Nothing," I said. He put his hands in his pockets and came out with 1 dime.

"Great," I said sarcastically. I really had no idea where we were, but he did. I never knew how he knew these things but he always did.

Brian P. Wallace

"That's Sullivan Square Station over there, let's go." We snuck into the station with no problem, and headed back home. Needless to say that was Sully's first and last driving lesson in Swanny's car. It was very interesting that Sully somehow got the money to enroll in driver's school the very next week. It was undoubtedly the wisest money that Swanny ever spent By the way Sully did get his license not long after that. And no, he never did get Swanny's car to drive ever again.

Chapter 44 - A Pimple Ball And City Games

Sully's mother was a real nice lady. I really liked Millie who was a very good mother and did everything to make her children happy. How or why she got Sully is something that I'm sure she asked God more than once. She tried everything with Sully but nothing worked. What it basically came down to was, she just couldn't control him, he knew it and she knew it. It was really that simple. She did her best to keep him in line at least until Sully wanted to step out of that line, which he did with great frequency. It wasn't as if she was embarrassed that she couldn't control her eldest son, nobody could, so why should she be any different. She would tell people, "Oh you know him, he's just sowing his wild oats," she would tell people. If that were the case, he had enough wild oats to start his own cereal brand. One particular incident, I remember very clearly and was vintage Millie and Vintage Sully. I lived on West 5th street and Sully, as I told you, lived on E street. Oftentimes he would walk up West 5th street to my house and we would go from there. One of the kids who lived about 8 houses down from me was a kid named Paul. I liked Paul, Sully did not. I could tell, just by his mannerisms, that he disliked this kid. He never said a word about him. But I knew. One day we were playing tag football on West 5th street. We played right in the middle of the street and our time-outs were necessitated by the amount of vehicular traffic that day. One of the things that city kids, at least poor city kids, had to do was to invent games or at least make due with what you had, which was usually pretty minimal. We used a 15 cent pimple ball so often that the pimples came off. For only 15 cents we could keep occupied for a couple of days, unless someone hit the ball up a particularly challenging roof. Whether alone, or with a group of kids, that pimple ball became the hub of our universe. I wish I had a dollar for every hour I threw that white pimple ball against my house, all by myself. at least to passer byes it looked as if I was throwing that ball against the brick front of my house, by myself. In my mind I was always in Fenway Park and always right in the middle of a game winning situation, which I usually won for the Red Sox. I drove my parents absolutely crazy with the constant pounding of that little ball against the front brick facade of my house. My father once told a neighbor that he was so used to the sound that it didn't even bother him anymore. My mother never quite got that used to my imaginary Fenway playing days. My brother thought I was absolutely crazy.

"Nobody plays that much baseball, why don't you go out and get laid," he once said to me.

"Because I'm, only nine years old," I shot back. A good pimple ball could last me a good three weeks to a month. And I knew a good pimple ball. I was the neighborhood expert on pimple balls. It was a pretty big acquisition for any nine year - old kid. I would have kids knock on my door when they were going to shell out the cash for a new pimple ball. I was the official pimple ball expert, even at such a tender age. When they were going to buy a new ball, they called me to escort them to Pete's store to make sure they got the best ball available. Fifteen cents was a lot of money, for us, and I was the pimple ball guru. I never had one dissatisfied customer. I would always get at least a couple of pieces of candy for my expert opinion. It was a good deal all around. The kid got a good pimple ball and I got my candy. Everyone was happy, except Pete.

Pete was the guy who owned the corner store. He would cringe when he saw me walk in with another prospective pimple ball buying kid, at least at first. He kind of got a kick out of it sometimes when he wasn't too busy. He was a character. He loved to bet. Pete would bet on anything and often did. One day Sully and I walked in his store to get our regular devil dog and Pepsi. There was a well-dressed guy in the store that I had never seen before. Boy did Pete set that pigeon up. They were having a heated discussion about who was a better hitter Musial, Mays or Williams. No contest in my mind, but I was hungry and I wasn't there for sports trivia. But Pete wasn't about to let us get out of that store that quickly.

"You don't know what you're talking about," Pete said in a very loud voice.

"Musial or Mays couldn't hold Ted Williams Jock strap." The other guy was starting to take the heat, his face was getting redder by the minute, and his voice was getting louder and louder.

"Williams had a few good years," the well-dressed guy said. "Mays and Musial have had all good years."

"What?" Pete screamed, "Now I know you don't know anything about baseball." The guy took the bait.

"I've forgotten more about baseball than you ever knew," he screamed back in Pete's face.

"I bet any kid in this store knows more about baseball than you do" Pete said very calmly.

"What are you crazy?" the guy looked at Pete, who was smiling behind his counter.

"No, I'm dead serious, and I'm willing to put up twenty five dollars to prove it." The guy, I could see, thought that Pete had flipped. He also saw a way to pick up a quick twenty- five bucks.

"Any kid in this store, that I pick will know more about baseball than me?" he again asked.

"Any kid," Pete would say to clarify the bet. The only two kids, in the store were me and Sully, and Sully had his head inside the tonic chest when the guy turned around, just as Pete had planned. The guy immediately pointed to the skinny bespectacled kid who was halfway through his devil dog.

"Him," the guy yelled pointing directly at me.

"You're on," Pete said. Pete looked directly at me.

"What's your name son," Like he didn't know. I went along.

"Brian, why?" Pete kept up the charade.

"OK Brian we have a little contest going here can you help us out."

"What's in it for me?" I asked. City kids are a lot of things, but stupid is not one of them.

"That devil dog that you're eating is free, if you help us with our contest" Pete said getting a little mad. He hated to give anything away for free. I knew I had the upper hand.

"And the Pepsi too?" I asked, already knowing what he had to say.

"Yeah and the Pepsi too," he mocked.

"Cool, what do I have to do," I said in a very innocent way.

"Just stay there for a minute while I get my baseball book" he said as he scurried into the back room.

By now Sully had gotten his tonic, and he asked me what was going on. The guy, who Pete bet, was watching us like a hawk, as I explained to Sully what I thought was happening.

"Pete is having some kind of contest and he wants me in it," I said to Sully as the guy beside me beamed with delight, I'm sure already debating on where he was going to spend his twenty five bucks. Pete was back. He had a huge maroon colored book opened and was reading to himself when the guy spoke.

"All right Mister know it all, let's begin." Pete looked at the guy.

"What is Stan Musial's lifetime batting average?"

"Within how many points?" the well- dressed guy said.

"OK ," Pete said, "Within 5 points." The guy's face broke into a huge grin."325." He immediately blurted out. Pete looked very impressed.

"Not bad," Pete said.

"You bet your ass, not bad" the guy smiled. Now Pete looked directly at me.

"Do you know who Stan Musial is?" he asked. The guy behind me Laughed.

"Yeah he's a frigging school teacher." "I turned to the guy.

"No he's not, he plays for the St. Louis Cardinals and his lifetime batting average is.331." I thought the guy was going to faint.

"Absolutely right," Pete said as he turned the book around so the stunned gentlemen could see for himself.

"That was a lucky guess," the guy screamed. "The bet is the best of three questions."

"Since when?" Pete asked.

"Since right now," the guy stammered.

"I'm not losing twenty bucks on some wild guess." Pete was very calm.

"OK here's the next question."

"How many RBI's did Ted Williams have last year?" The guy looked at me, before he answered.

"Ted Williams had 121 RBI's last year," he said confidently.

"Wrong," I said "he had 127 RBI's last year." Pete began to laugh, as he held the book out for the angry better to see.

"You lose, Mr. Baseball," Pete said as he held out his hand for the twenty- five big ones.

"Something's wrong here," the guy screamed. "Something is definitely wrong here."

"Don't be a sore loser," Pete said with his hand still extended.

"I told you any kid in here knew more about baseball than you, and I was right, you lose"

"How does that little four eyed urchin know so much?" he asked.

"It's not just him they all know more than you," Pete laughed, with his hand still extended. The guy was really pissed off now.

"I was set up," the guy yelled.

"Pay up, Mr. Baseball," Pete said again. "These kids know everything about baseball, don't feel so bad," Pete said trying to soften the impact.

"They know everything?" the guy asked, seeing a way to get his money back.

"Just about," Pete said and knowing he shouldn't have said it."

"How about double or nothing?" the guy said looking to take Pete down.

"No way," said Pete, "You lost fair and square."

"I'm not so sure of that," the guy said. "How bout I chose the topic and the opponent this time?" Pete was trying his best to weasel out of the situation.

"We're done for the day," he said, and he started to go back behind his counter.

"If we're done, so is the last bet," the smiling better said. "No bet this time, no bet last time."

"OK," Pete finally said, "It's your question." The guy walked around the store for over a minute before he finally spoke.

"Take a pimple ball out of that box," he said to Sully."

"Take it out yourself," Sully said, "Who the fuck do I look like?" Pete began to laugh, like hell, behind the counter.

"Smart and tough," he said in between laughs. The guy proceeded to go behind the counter, and he stick his hand inside the glass counter. He pulled out a snow- white pimple ball.

"Now I have a question" he said, "But not for Einstein, this one is for fresh mouth, over there," the guy said pointing to Sully. Pete's face drained of all color.

"This is crazy," Pete said, "I have as store to run, no bet."

"What's the matter Pete, I thought these kids knew everything about baseball," the guy smiled. The well- dressed guy then turned quickly to face Sully.

"OK Mr. wise guy, tell me how many pimples are on this ball?" I took a quick look at Pete, he looked as if he had just lost his last friend. The other guy was already laughing, at his brilliant strategy. He turned to Pete and held out the ball for us all to see. In that instant I saw my opportunity and I took it.

"Seventy three," I said to Sully, in a very low whisper, that I wasn't even sure he heard. Sully played it to the hilt. He walked over and asked if he could feel the ball.

"Each ball is different," Sully said, going in to his act. Pete didn't know whether to laugh or cry. He looked over at me and I gave him a wink. The smile, which had disappeared a few seconds earlier, had now reappeared, brighter than ever. Pete was back on his game, knowing from my wink that we had his back covered.

"Hold it right there," he yelled, as everyone in the store stopped and looked at him.

"You asked the question, I make the bet," Pete said to the well -dressed guy. I was only 9 years old, but I knew that was a great move by Pete.

"The bet is 5 dollars." Pete said. The guy looked at Sully, his face all covered with the chocolate from a devil dog, and he laughed.

"I knew you were a coward Pete," he laughed. "My Albanian friend has no balls, ladies and gentlemen," he said loudly, so that everyone in the store could hear him. Pete acted as if he was furious.

"All right, you asshole, the bet is $100. Pete yelled. A hundred dollars was a lot of money, back then in 1959, and everyone, who was in that store, let out a gasp.

"Pete, what are you crazy," I yelled. "Every ball is different, that's not a smart bet Pete."

"Too late, the guy jumped on it.

"You gut yourself a bet, Pete," he laughed, as if he had already won. The tiny store became packed, as word about bets, and deaths, spread like wildfire in an Irish community, even if the guy making the bet was Albanian.

"Can I feel it," Sully, now onstage, asked, as he stuck out his devil dog, covered hand.

"Just for two seconds," the guy said still looking at Pete, and laughing at his own brilliance. Sully twirled it around, threw it up once and before the ball landed back in his hand

"Seventy three." Sully proclaimed The guy was still laughing. Pete looked at me, and I gave him another wink. He looked as if he had just won the lottery, which back then was called something completely different. Suffice it to say that it was called two words and the second word was pool. Enough said.

"You heard the boy," Pete screamed. The guy stopped laughing, as quickly as he had started.

"What?" Sully nonchalantly said.

"There are 73 pimples on this ball." Sully said calmly.

"No way," the guy yelled, "No way in hell."

"Count them," Sully said.

"That is exactly what I'm going to do," he said as he took off his coat and began to count the pimples on the ball. He marked each pimple with a pen mark, as he counted. Pete was right behind him as all the customers waited. Sixty six, sixty seven, sixty eight, sixty nine, seventy, seventy one, seventy two and with only one pimple was left to be counted, the guy threw the ball about a hundred miles an hour against the wall.

'You're a cheat" he yelled at Pete.

"Cheat? You made the bet," Pete laughed, "How could I be a cheat?" Pete laughed as the guy forked over five twenty- dollar bills and rushed out of the corner store. Pete was smiling like he had just won Megabucks.

"Did he pay you for the first bet?" Sully asked. I didn't even think Sully knew there was a first bet. He had his head stuck in the tonic chest as the bet was made.

"Holy shit," Pete yelled and got the guy before he got in to his car. The guy was livid, but he forked over the other twenty five dollars. I had never seen Pete so happy in my entire life. He danced with his wife and sang some Albanian song. Sully and I were laughing, as well. The other customers thought we had all gone crazy. Finally Pete came over to us and said to Sully, "How did you know how many pimples there were on that ball?" Sully laughed.

"I didn't even know the ball had pimples. Brian told me." Pete actually hugged me. "My little genius," he said "I knew we you would get the baseball questions right but how did you know about the pimples?"

"Simple," I said "They all have 73 pimples." He hugged me again only this time he shoved a ten-dollar bill into my hand.

"Go buy yourself a year's supply of pimple balls," he said, as he went back to his singing.

"Pete you can't sell that ball that he marked up with his pen, can I have it?"

"You gonna be a lawyer, I know you gonna be a lawyer," he laughed, as he threw me the ball with the 72 marks on it. I had a great morning. Life was good in America, especially when you were nine years old and had a free Pepsi and devil dog, money, friends and a brand new pimple ball in your pocket.

Chapter 45 – Too Much Meat

Sully and I took off with our new-found fortune. We found out later that the guy was a small time bookie who was always taking Pete's money, well almost always. As we left Pete's that day, Sully headed up E Street and away from where we usually hung out.

"Where you going?" I asked.

"Come on there's a new spuckie shop up the street." New stores were no big deal, but new spuckie stores were a big deal. I had no idea that one had even opened, but Sully somehow knew everything that went on in the town. The store was located on the same street as Pete's, but it was one block on the other side of Broadway, which was only five minutes from where we had just come into our new found riches. The store, had three customers already inside as we entered. The sign out front said 'Jerry and Phil's Sandwich Shop.' There was only one guy behind the counter. He was taking the orders, and making the sandwiches, and he looked pretty beleaguered as we walked in. He was a small man about 5'1" tall and he weighed maybe 120 on a good day. Sully watched him intently as he made sandwiches for the three people in front of us, and made small talk, as he did. The three people, who were together, left and we stepped up to the brand new counter.

"Are you Jerry or Phil?" Sully immediately asked.

"Jerry's the name, what's your game," he said. I could feel it coming. This guy was going to be no match for Sully.

"Oh great," Sully smiled "I was hoping you were Jerry," Sully said in a tantalizing way.

"Now why would you be hoping I was Jerry, if you never met me before," he asked puzzled.

"Reputation," Sully said. Both Jerry and I waited for him to say something else but he never did.

After a kind of a pregnant pause, the little guy behind the counter said, "Reputation?" Now Sully was back on stage, for the second time in the last half-hour. Here we go again, I thought.

"Yeah, my friend Johnny Britt was in here yesterday and he was telling everyone that some guy named Jerry made him the biggest and best Italian spuckie that he ever had in his life." By him saying that his friend was Johnny Britt, he gave me the only clue I needed to know that he was scamming. Sully hated Johnny Britt. But Jerry didn't know that, and I could see Sully slowly reeling him in. I had no idea where he was going with this, but I never did anyway, so why should this time be any different.

"Yeah, he said that?" Jerry asked. "Absolutely, he was telling everyone, I figured this place would be mobbed by now." Sully said, looking around as if he expected a hundred people to storm through the door.

"Well we have been pretty busy," Jerry said, falling in even deeper.

"No wonder," Sully went on "Johnny said you actually put ten pieces of ham , ten pieces of capicola and ten pieces of salami in his Italian spuckie. Now that is a real Southie sandwich, wait until word gets around, you're going to be very rich."

"Well I don't know if it was ten pieces now," Jerry stammered trying to backtrack a little.

"Yeah, yeah,ten0 pieces that's what Johnny said, he counted them," Sully said as if it actually happened.

"That's a lot of meat," Jerry said, "ten pieces is a lot of meat."

"Yeah, that's why we're here," Sully kept right on going. He was absolutely amazing. He had this guy by the balls, and the guy didn't even have a clue.

"When I woke up this morning I called Brian," he said pointing to me. Jerry gave me a cursory glance, "And I told Brian. as soon as I get my allowance I'm going down to that new store and get on of those ten piece special Italian spuckies. Isn't that what I said Bri?" I just nodded. Jerry never looked at me anyway. "That's what I'm going to have Jerry ,the ten piece Italian special from my new favorite spuckie shop." Sully seemed so excited that the guy had no alternative. He never even asked me what I wanted. He began to make Sully his ten piece Italian spuckie. I couldn't believe that Sully had talked this guy into making him this huge sandwich and believe me it was huge. And Sully counted, as he laid each piece on the bread.

"All right here goes the salami. one, two, three, four, five, six, seven, eight, nine, and ten. all right." He did the same for the ham and the capicola.

That sandwich must have cost about eight dollars to make. Jerry never even looked up.

"Anything on it?" he asked. There was really no room to put anything on it. Leave it to Sully.

"Everything, " he said. I had to get out of the store, I was laughing so hard. That sandwich was enormous.

"All right," Sully said "Johnny Britt was right." He gave the guy his two dollars and got a quarter back. There was enough meat in that sandwich to feed an entire family for a week. I was outside, catching my breath, and he kept motioning me to come in to the store. Finally I had my composure back and I went in. He had been eating for a good five minutes and hadn't made a dent in the sandwich.

Just as I sat down the door opened and this huge guy came in. He must have weighed about 350 pounds. We were still the only two customers in the store. The guy looked at me and then at Sully, and then he looked at the sandwich, and his face became so red thought he was going to have a heart attack.

"Gerry," he screamed. All of a sudden Gerry came out from the back room, and his face took on a similar color. He looked at the big guy, who was watching Sully trying to finish his spuckie.

"Hi Phil, back early," he said weakly.

"Did you make that sandwich?" the big guy roared.

"Yeah," Jerry managed to say. "Well he wanted a ten piece special and I made him one." Phil cowered.

"There is no such thing as a 10 piece special," he said as he chased the little guy into the back room. All we heard were slaps.

"Don't you ever make a sandwich like that ever again," followed by a loud slap. "Do you hear me?" he again roared and another slap. Then we heard the little guy's voice.

"OK, OK but you don't have to hit me." That was it for me, I was out of that store and halfway home, followed by Sully, who was still eating.

About three months later we were coming out of St. Vincent's CYO, which was diagonally across the street from the spuckie store. Father. Lincoln, who was the Priest at St. Vincent's, was with us as we finished our class.

Brian P. Wallace

"Oh look that spuckie store must have gone out of business, it only lasted a couple of months." I looked at Sully.

"I knew it Father, they put way to much meat in their sandwiches." I cracked up and we left Father Lincoln on the corner of E and West Third Street, thinking about that one for a while. Now you have to remember both these incidents happened on the same day in the span of less than an hour, which incredibly enough, was not unusual with Sully. Some days you just knew were going to be better than others. I never knew where we would end up, but I knew it would be pretty funny by the time we got there. And he was far from through on that memorable day.

We walked up E street after leaving the spuckie shop and headed to my house, which was a block past Pete's store. On the way to my house we saw a bunch of kids playing tag football. It was late August and the new professional Football team in town, the Boston Patriots had brought a new sense of excitement to all the kids in my neighborhood. Usually nobody picked up a football until well after Labor Day, but here it was still August, and a tag rush game was already in progress.

'Want to play?" Sully asked.

"Looks like they already have sides," I answered.

"So what," he said, and proceeded to go into the middle of the street and convince the six kids who were already playing that the game would be a lot better if eight kids played. He even somehow managed to get both of us on the same team. I remember there was Tommy Gailunas, a big heavy kid who thought Sully was completely out of his mind. Tubby weighed a good 250 pounds and was one of the fastest runners on the block. That combination always made Tommy a first round pick in any pickup tag football game. Sully somehow even managed to get Tommy on our side as well. Amazing. Tommy was a great kid, who both Sully and I liked very much, even though Sully intimidated him. He was the same age as Sully and had been in Sully's class since the first grade. He could probably write a book as well. He used to say, "Come on Sully, don't frig around, come on Sully don't frig around." Secretly Tommy Gailunas loved the danger that Sully presented he just didn't want to get too close to the flame. Tommy became a starting lineman for Southie High and he was a good one to. He used to ask me, what it was like to always be with Sully. He would listen to Sully stories until the cows came home. He just didn't want to get to close.

Another kid playing that day was a kid who was almost as big as Tubby and almost as fast, his name was Quinn and for everyone who loved Tubby Gailunas there was an equal number, who hated Jimmy Quinn, especially Sully. He saw Quinn as a bully, always picking on smaller kids and he had the personality of a rock, which did nothing to endear him to anybody. He was obviously on the other team. The other kids playing that day were Paul McDonald, who Sully disliked, who was on the other team. John DiPerri, who Sully liked, was on the other team. I told you earlier about 'Dibs'. 'Dibs' were what you called if you wanted a drink of someone else's tonic or a bite of their spuckie. The rule was the first one to call 'Dibs", automatically got a bite or a swig of the desired item, be it tonic, ice cream or a sandwich. It was strictly up to the kid who bought the ice cream or tonic, as to whether anyone else, who called 'Dibs' would get a bite or a swig. Sometimes, the kid who bought the tonic, ended up with only two swigs, after everyone got their 'Dibs." But, John DiPerri was smarter than us all. John was an Italian in an almost entirely Irish neighborhood, which was tough enough. His father was a fish-cutter, and the DiPerri's didn't have a lot of money, not that any of us did, but they had even less than us, which was really bad. I remember playing a softball game against the kids from D Street one scalding hot summer day. The game was tied after nine innings and we played another eight extra innings before they eventually beat us. We dragged our little asses to Pete's and we found out that none of, except John DiPerri, had any money. He bought an ice cold Pepsi, and he got the first swig, which turned out to be his last swig. DiPerri was bullshit, and he stormed off after calling us all kinds of names, some even in Italian. About a week later, the same thing happened. DiPerri and Wally DiReeno went in to Pete's and each came out of the store with an ice-cold tonic. Wally DiReeno had a Pepsi, and DiPerri had a Moxie. Now I don't know if you have ever tasted a Moxie but if you have even tasted cold cough syrup, you have tasted a Moxie. It was much more like medicine than tonic. I didn't know 1 kid who drank Moxie. Actually I don't know 1 person who drank Moxie, other than John DiPerri. It was awful. John took a huge gulp.

"Anyone want dibs?" he asked holding out the dreaded Moxie bottle. We all drew back reminiscent of Superman when in the presence of Kryptonite. We all turned and attacked Wally DiReeno's Pepsi, as DiPerri leisurely drank his entire Moxie without interruption. Every day after that day, John DiPerri drank Moxie, and nobody ever called "dibs' again on John DiPerri. One day we were playing stickball in the Gavin Schoolyard and we sent a little kid to Tily's store for us. He returned, and handed me my Pepsi and he handed DiPerri his Moxie.

"John how the hell can you drink that stuff, it sucks." I said. He laughed.

"I know I hate it, but you don't see anyone calling for 'Dibs' anymore do you?" He was smarter than all of us. Another kid who played that day was a kid named George Seeley, who Sully and I both liked, but who was picked by the other team. Our fourth player was Paul McDonald's visiting cousin, named George , who is now a dentist.

Those were the sides that day as we got set to play our first football game of the season. The game was going along all right when in the corner of the end zone, which was the front of the 1960 Chevy, Sully and Paul McDonald started to push each other. Before we had a chance to break it up they were in a pretty good fight. Good, anyway, from Sully's vantage point. Sully basically kicked his ass, and he had wanted to kick his ass for a long time. That ended the game and we headed back to E street to Sully's house. Sully told me that he had hoped that Quinn would have jumped in because he wanted to kick his ass too. That came a few months later. But we were relaxing in Sully's parlor when we heard a loud knock at the door. Millie ran to get the door and we heard voices and shouts in the hall.

Next we heard, "Mr. Sullivan you come right here." Trouble. Standing in Sully's doorway was a battered and bruised Paul McDonald, and his mother. Mrs. McDonald went into a long dissertation about what Sully had done to her son, and how her son never did this and never did that. Sully listened intently for a couple of minutes and didn't say anything. Finally when Mrs. McDonald was through, Millie turned to Sully.

"Is all that true?" Millie asked.

"I guess," Sully replied.

"Did you do this to him?" Millie asked, pointing to a battered and bruised Paul McDonald.

"Yes I did." Millie was caught off guard for a second. "Why?" she asked. He took his time and started to speak as if McDonald weren't even there.

"Ma, the kid is an asshole, I know it, he knows it and even his mother knows it, nobody likes him, and he's just lucky I didn't kick his ass years ago." That was it for me. I had to get the hell out of there. I was trying to keep a straight face, but I wasn't succeeding. I thought my heart was going to explode.

The last thing I heard was Sully's mother saying to Mrs. McDonald, "See I can't do anything with him." Next, I heard the door slam and the McDonald's retreat back to West Fifth street without much satisfaction. At least Sully never kicked his ass again. I remember Millie asking Sully after the McDonald's left, why he has to beat people up. Sully was indignant.

"Ma how many people have come up this house, like tonight, and said that I beat them up?"

"Maybe four or five," she said.

"Yeah but those were all asshole, name one good kid who came up here and told you I kicked his ass?" I couldn't believe the conversation She thought for a couple of seconds.

"Yeah, maybe you're right." Millie said.

"Thanks," Sully said. He had done it again. Unbelievable. Millie was a nice lady but certainly no match for her eldest son. I looked at the clock as we were leaving the house that day and it wasn't even 2PM yet. Pete's store, Phil and Jerry's store, and Paul McDonald's beating all happened in less than three hours. Another day in the life. Only the Beatles said it better.

Sully had two other siblings to pick on as he was growing up. Donna was the eldest of the three Sully children and Jackie was the youngest. They both deserve some sort of a medal for just getting through puberty alive. There were times when I didn't think they were going to make it. It was constant bedlam in the Sullivan house when Sully and his brother and sister were all in the house together. Poor Millie. I would just sit there and watch. It was better than anything on television.

Brian P. Wallace

"Come on let's go tease my sister Donna." Sully would say when he got bored He loved teasing Donna, although I'm sure that Donna wasn't quite as thrilled with the teasing as Sully was. If Millie Sullivan had received a dollar for every time she said, "stop picking on your brother" or "stop teasing your sister," she would have been a very rich woman. I wish they had camcorders back then. It would have been absolutely hilarious. Sully would create total havoc, in the house, for about twenty minutes, then tire of it.

"I've had enough of this let's go outside," he would finally say as Donna, Millie and Jimmy counted their blessings. We would then leave the Sully's house and go to our corner where he would instantly create more havoc. One particular incident comes to mind, which has to do with Donna.

Chapter 46 – Donna's Boyfriend

I was about 13 years old and Sully called me at home, and asked if I would like to come up to his house to watch the Red Sox game. I agreed and I picked up some popcorn, potato chips and other assorted goodies at Pete's on the way to Sully's house. Everyone was gone except Sully, and the house was nice and quiet. The Sox were up a couple of runs in the third inning when Donna and her boyfriend, Tony, came in. Sully wasn't very fond of Tony and that is putting it mildly. Tony felt the exact same way, and did nothing to hide his feelings, which really put poor Donna in the middle all the time. Tony and Sully, in the same room, was an accident waiting to happen, and on this particular day, it did. Tony was five years older than Sully, which is a lot when you're fourteen. They were constantly arguing. They argued over everything. Tony was a lot bigger than Sully, but he, or his size never intimidated Sully. That day, as the Sox were getting ready to bat in their half of the third inning, was a day I'll never forget. Donna went into the kitchen to make a sandwich for Tony. Tony came in to the living room, plopped down in the recliner.

"Are you two watching these bums again? When will you ever quit."

"We're not quitters, like you" Sully shot right back. This was even a record for these two. Less than two seconds before they were arguing. The room became very quiet, which worried me. Nobody said a word for about five minutes as we watched the Sox go one, two,three, in the third. Donna entered the room with a big sandwich for Tony and a glass of milk. She misinterpreted the silence as a sign of reckoning.

"Glad to see you all getting along so nicely," she smiled. Nobody said a word in response. Tony wolfed down the sangy, and turned to Donna.

"Do we have to watch this shit, it's boring." Again Donna was in the middle.

"We can go out the kitchen," Donna replied.

"You go out the kitchen," Tony ordered. I could tell that Sully was boiling mad. The White Sox second baseman, Nellie Fox was up to lead off the top of the fifth inning, when all of a sudden, Tony jumped up, and changed the channel. I was stunned. Sully was taken aback as well, because it took him a couple of minutes to react. When he did, he like Tony, jumped up and put the Sox game back on. Before he had gotten back to his seat, Tony had jumped up and changed the channel again. Sully was furious as he changed the channel back, again, to the Red Sox game. Something had to give. This time Tony waited until Sully was fully seated before he got up and changed the channel. Without hesitation, Sully jumped up, changed the channel back, and looked directly at Tony.

"Change that channel again and I'll knock you out," Sully said very matter of factly. This time Sully did not sit down. He stayed there for at least a minute, as I sat watching him watch Tony. Finally he went back to his seat. Nothing happened for a couple of minutes, and I thought this craziness had passed, but I was wrong. Tony got up very slowly. I was hoping he was going to go out to the kitchen with Donna, but I was wrong again.

"You little jerk," he said, and proceeded to change the channel, once again, He then turned and headed back to his seat. He never made it that far. Sully threw a right hand punch from the floor, which caught Tony flush on the right temple. There were two distinct sounds, Sully hitting Tony and Tony hitting the floor. Tony was out cold. It was one of the best sucker punches I had ever seen, and I have seen my share believe me, and I have seen more than my share.

"Let's go," Sully said to me. I was still in shock, like Tony.

"What about him?" I asked, pointing to the prone figure of Donna's boyfriend.

"Screw him," he said as he stepped over the body and out the door. I followed, as usual. I had to actually step over Tony, who as they say in boxing, was on queer- Street. We were halfway down the stairs before Donna discovered that her boyfriend had just been knocked out by her little brother. We heard an ungodly scream.

"Mom, look what your son did to my boyfriend." I always wondered how that scene unfolded. A couple of hours later we went back up Sully's house, Tony was long gone, but Swanny was waiting and he was mad. Donna was standing right behind Swanny as we entered the house. Swanny tore into Sully, who just stood his ground without saying a word. The more Swanny chastised Sully the more I realized that he really wasn't all that mad. This was more of a show for Donna. I had seen Swanny really mad before, so I had some basis of comparison. He was screaming and yelling at Sully, but it was a show and Sully knew it as well. He actually listened politely until Swanny was finished and then he turned and walked out the door. Swanny followed us down the stairs, and out on to E street. Sully turned and began his own tirade.

"Dad that jerk, walked into our house like he owns it, he makes Donna get him a sandwich, then tells her to get out in to the kitchen and then he changes the channel on the Sox game that Brian and I were watching." Swanny stood erect, listening.

"What would you have done, dad?" Swanny was between a rock and a hard place, but he said nothing. Then the old Sully took over.

"I'll tell you what you would do, if you were any kind of a man. You would do exactly what I did, knock the bastard out cold." I actually thought I saw a little smile cross Swanny's face.

"Don't swear at me. Don't you dare swear at me," Swanny yelled. Then Swanny looked directly at me.

"Brian is that what happened up there," he said, pointing to the second floor, where they lived.

"Yes sir, it happened just like he said it did." I said. Swanny softened.

"Sully you can't be going around beating up Donna's boyfriends, she's not that good looking in the first place" he said, without cracking a smile. It took me a second to comprehend what he said, and when I did I just burst out laughing, as did Sully. Swanny did the right thing that day. I respected him for that and I know Sully did as well. He put on a show for Donna, which he had to do, but he knew that Sully was not entirely wrong, this time. Then I saw Swanny do something that I had only seen him do one other time in my life. He reached into his pocket and gave Sully a dollar bill.

"Go buy something for yourself and Brian," he said to Sully, as if he had given him a hundred. Sully looked down at the single dollar.

"Thanks dad, do you want the change?"

"No you keep it all", Swanny said, not knowing that Sully was being facetious. We laughed like hell. Sully and Tony never spoke after that incident. A couple of months after Sully knocked him out, Donna threw him out, and both Sully and Swanny seemed relieved. Donna met a great guy and believe it or not he and Sully got along great. Donna got married and had a bunch of kids. I would see Tony around Southie once in a while, he never acknowledged me, nor I him. I wonder what he told his friends about his shiner? I doubt he told them that a 15 year- old kid decked him. Sully never told anyone either. I did though.

Chapter 47 – Sully's Brother Jimmy

Sully's younger brother was named Jimmy. He was the complete opposite of Sully. He was very quiet, easy going, somewhat lethargic. I never understood how Jimmy and Sully came from the same parents. Sully, like almost all older brothers, spent most of his time harassing Jimmy and making his life miserable. If I were in Sully's house for an hour, at least half of that hour, I would hear Millie.

"Leave your little brother alone." Jimmy was a skinny little kid, while Sully was more rotund, which drove Sully crazy. When Jack was about 14, he shot up like a tree. He towered over Sully, which made teasing him all that more worthwhile. Jimmy went from 5'3" to 6'3" and from 130 lbs. to 220lbs. It seemed that overnight he became huge. He never seemed to get accustomed to his new body. I gave him the nickname 'Tornado Jim' because he was constantly breaking things. He would sit in a chair and it would collapse under his size. He would lean against something and it would come crashing to the ground. I one time saw him lean against a railing on a porch. The next thing I knew both the railing and 'Tornado Jim', were lying in the front yard. Thank God it was on the first floor. I really liked Jim, he was a good kid who, despite all the teasing, idolized his older brother. Poor Jim had to live in the shadow of his infamous brother, which I'm sure wasn't easy. He went to the same schools as Sully.

"You're not related to HIM are you?" the teachers would eventually ask. They didn't have to explain, whom the HIM was. Jim would shyly nod his head and the teacher would slowly lower theirs. People just assumed that because he was Sully's brother, he was like Sully, which he wasn't. God only made one of those, believe me, and there were a lot of Boston Public School teachers who were certainly glad about that.

After Sully went into the Marines I kind of lost track of Jim. Sully was visiting one day and he told me that Jim had recently become engaged. He said nothing more about it and I didn't ask. I was at a party at Sully's house a couple of months later when I saw Jimmy walk in the front door. I was in shock. He stood about 6'4" tall and he must have weighed well, well , well over 300 pounds. Sully saw my face and he came right over to me.

Brian P. Wallace

"You ain't seen nothing yet," Sully smiled that same conspiratorial smile that I had seen throughout my childhood. I had no idea what he meant, but I soon found out. The girl that Jim was engaged to, came in a few seconds behind him. Now I really was in shock, and Sully loved every minute of it. She was as big as Jim. I congratulated Jim on his engagement, and we talked a little about old times. I wasn't invited to his wedding, but Sully was the best man. There is something about Sully and weddings, which brings out the absolute worst in him, which isn't hard to do. I will tell you a couple of Sully wedding stories right after this. But the day Jimmy was getting married, Sully I'm told, was on his very best behavior. He was a model of decorum at the Church, and the receiving line, and for the picture taking festivities. He told me a day or two before the wedding, however, that he was really afraid about giving the toast.

"I hate speaking in front of crowds," he told me over the phone. I was very accustomed to public speaking and I gave him a few hints to calm him down. The day of the wedding he called me again.

"I wish you were going to be at the wedding," he said.

"Why I can't make that speak for you," I laughed.

"I know, but you always calm me down" he said in a very agitated manner. Then I made a big mistake.

"Listen if you are that nervous, just have a couple of drinks to loosen you up." I Instructed.

"That's a good idea," he said, and he sounded relieved.

One of 'Tornado Jim's' friend, who was at the wedding, told me the story of how Sully's speech went. It seemed that the first drink did nothing to calm his nerves, nor did the second or third drink. By the time Sully had inhaled his fifth drink he was relaxed, good and relaxed. When it came time for him to give the toast, he strode up to the microphone like Johnny Most. He looked out at the crowd and then looked down at his brother who now weighed in excess of 360 pounds, and his new sister in law, who was in the 260- pound range, and he changed the speech that I had written for him. He lifted his glass, as everyone except the bride and groom stood.

"Ladies and Gentlemen when a couple gets married they dream about buying a nice house where they can grow." Nice so far.

A Southie Memoir

"Well, after looking at my brother Jim and his wife Helen, I realized that they should buy a restaurant rather than a house." There was total silence in the hall. One guy who had already begun to drink the champagne toast almost choked to death, while another simply dropped the toast glass on the floor shattering the all-encompassing silence. Then someone laughed. Then someone else laughed, then another, and another and another, until the entire room had completely lost it. People were keeling over with laughter. Jimmy and his new wife were pissed, as was Swanny, but everyone who was in attendance that day still talk about that toast. It was classic and vintage Sully. Always expect the unexpected.

Brian P. Wallace

Chapter 48 – Bubba Cahill – A Car And A Wedding

Our good friend Bob "Bubba" Cahill was getting married, and both Sully and I were ushers. Mistake. The wedding reception was to be held at Florian Hall, the Firefighters Post. Bubba was a fireman, and from a long line of firemen. He was marrying a great girl named Karen Lydon, who came from Gates street. The Wedding, at St. Augustine's went off without a hitch, as did everything else. We finished the pictures, and the band leader came over, and lined us up according to how we was going to call our names Sully and I were old pros at this by now. Sully came over to where I was standing, with my wedding partner, and grabbed my arm.

"Come here, I have to talk to you," he said urgently.

I knew that the guy would be calling us to take our seats, at the head table, any second. "What?" I said impatiently. "He's going to call us in a second."

As I turned to face him he had that look on his face. It was the exact same look, I had seen some 25 years earlier as he reached in his pocket, way back then, and produced a smoke bomb. This time out of his pocket magically appeared two Groucho Marx disguises, complete with the black glasses, big nose, and trademark black bushy mustache, and eyebrows.

"What the hell is this?" I asked, as I heard the band- leader begin the introductions in the background.

"Come on we'll both wear them, it'll really be funny," he laughed.

"Get away from me," I said as I handed him his disguise and headed back into the line of march.

"What's wrong with you? Bubba will get a big kick out of this," he persisted.

"You're crazy," I said, which wasn't any news to anyone in that hall.

"Come on I already have it arranged," he implored as he held out the disguise, once again for me.

"Arranged with who?" I asked.

"The photographer is in on it, and the band is in on it too," he said excitedly. I was thinking. "The band is going to play that Groucho Marx song, you know Lydia the tattooed lady," he quickly said, as the couple in front of me were called and headed into the overflowing hall.

"Come on Bri, don't screw this up, everyone is in on it." I took the stupid disguise, just as I heard.

"And our next couple is Mr. Brian Wallace and Miss Nancy Cahill" I reacted quickly and put the Groucho disguise on and headed into the hall.

Silence. The Band even stopped playing, and nobody laughed because nobody was in on it.

Nobody clapped, they just pointed. I never felt so out of place in my life. I wanted to hide under the nearest table. My only salvation was when they called Sully, and people saw that he too had on the disguise, then they would get the joke and laugh. I hoped, as the longest walk of my life was coming to a close , Thank God. Sully will make them laugh, I thought to myself, I know he will. Next, I heard, "Ladies and Gentlemen Mr. Thomas Sullivan and Miss Colleen Lydon." I stared at the door as he finally entered. My heart almost stopped. In walked Sully, a huge smile and no glasses, no bushy mustache, no bushy eyebrows, no big nose, nothing. I knew how all the other felt. I had been had. After all these years I still fell for it, even though I had seen him pull this kind of stunt a hundred times on other unsuspecting kids. He got me. He got me good, and he was delighted with himself. I couldn't believe that I had fallen for one of the oldest, you go first and I'll follow right behind you," routines. As he was walking toward the head table he looked directly at my, now beet red face, and winked. Nobody was safe. Nobody. As he passed Bubba and Karen he said, loud enough for me to hear.

"What the hell is wrong with Brian, this was no place for that stupid disguise." Talk about rubbing salt in the wound. I cringed and looked the other way. There was nowhere to hide. Sully strikes again. Only this time I was the victim.

Every time he went into that pocket, I got in trouble. Age made no difference. He got me at 6 years old and he got me at 31 years old. I can laugh about it now, but it wasn't so funny as I sat at the head table, and people were pointing at me, like I was in some circus. One of the guys, who was at that wedding, still, to this day, calls me Groucho. Another time we were with Bubba, long before he got married, and it of course was at the Garden. Bubba

Brian P. Wallace

had just gotten his license, and he borrowed his father's new car for the night. We were Seniors at South Boston High at the time, and about seven of us piled in to Mr. Cahill's car and headed over to North Station. We had about $15 between all of us, so there was no way we were going to pay to park. We drove around for a long time and Sully told Bubba that we had better find a parking spot quick or we were not going to be able to sneak in. With an added sense of urgency, Bubba saw an open spot, and floored the car to get there, before any other cars beat him to it. Sully saw where Bubba was heading and screamed.

"No way Bubba, you don't want to park there." Bubba was getting madder by the minute.

"For Christ sakes Sully make up your mind, you just told me I had to find a spot quickly, and I just did."

"Believe me Bubba," Sully said, "You really don't want to park here."

"Give me two reasons why not," Bubba shot back, as he eased the car in to the spot.

"I'll give you three" Sully replied, "birds, birds and more birds."

"You're crazy Sully," Bubba said as he turned off the ignition.

"I might be crazy," Sully said, "But you're the one who's going to be sorry." Having said that, we all alighted from the car and headed toward the back of the Garden and up the ramp.

Once the game was over we walked out the front door. We might enter through the back but we always exited through the front. We headed to Bubba's car. Sully was being conspicuously silent as we walked to the car. I looked at him and he just smiled, but there was a lot hidden behind that devious smile. We walked in the direction of the car, but we couldn't find it.

"I swear I parked it around here," Bubba said, with a look of confusion on his face. Sully was standing next to an old junk box with that smile on his face. Bubba was now panicking.

"They stole my father's car," he said to Raymond Linnell.

"No they didn't," Sully said. "It's right here." Everyone looked at the old junk box that was covered in about five inches of bird shit.

"That's not my father's car," Bubba said, dismissing Sully.

"Yes it is Mr. Know it all," Sully smirked. We had walked by the car at least six times, but it looked as if it had been abandoned, for at least a month. I began to laugh as I realized that Sully was right. That was the car. There wasn't one part of the vehicle that was visible. Every single piece of the car was covered in bird shit, at least three or four coats of it. As soon as I began to laugh it became contagious. I had never seen a car with more bird shit on it in my entire life. Bubba was in shock.

"I told you not to park there," Sully said, as Bubba examined the car.

"How am I going to get in," he said, as if in a daze. I said.

"Very carefully" I said, as Ricky Calnan hit the ground. I had never seen Ricky laugh so hard in all the years that I had known him. Next Ray Linnell hit the ground, then Jimmy Ridge. It looked like there was a sniper on the roof of the Garden. I was next and then Sully. We were all on the ground, holding our stomachs and laughing hysterically. Bubba was bullshit. No make that Bubba was bird shit. He didn't think it was one bit funny. He had managed to scrape off enough bird shit to get in the car, and he tried to put the windshield wipers on, but there was too much shit on the window. The wipers wouldn't even work, which made us all laugh even harder. I actually began to throw up from laughing, as Bubba got out of the car, and just stared in amazement at his father's pride and joy.

"You guys are all assholes," Bubba said, as he began to wipe the shit off the wind- shield, but nothing was happening. The windshield was literally caked with bird shit.

"I'm going, are you guys coming or not?" We all staggered in to the car, careful not to get any of the offending bird shit on our clothes. Bubba was livid, and didn't say a word as we got on to the expressway.

"Hey Bubba lets' go pick up some chicks, they'll love this car," Sully laughed as everyone started laughing once again. Everyone, that is except Bubba. He got off the expressway and went in to a car wash near Andrew Square in South Boston. The guys in the car wash took one look at the car and walked away.

"If you want that car cleaned," the boss said to Bubba, "you are going to wash it yourself." Bubba stormed out of the office and we went to one of those mechanical car washes, where you sit in the car as the car is sponged, wiped, and washed. It took us seven times going through that car wash before the car was clean. Seven times, and we were laughing harder each time. I had never seen Bubba so mad. Sully said.

"Hey Bubba it would have been a lot cheaper to park it in a lot," Sully said but Bubba did not respond. It was one of the funniest nights we ever spent at the Garden, although Bubba doesn't agree. Every time I see a car with bird shit, I think of that night and Bubba's car. He should have listened to Sully, for once.

Chapter 49 – Chumpy's Wedding

I told you about Southie and nicknames. One other wedding that I have to tell you about was in 1972. My good friend Jimmy Chumpy Dolan was marrying Janet McNeil at St. Monica's church. I actually introduced Jimmy to Janet, one night, down the Andrew Square VFW Post. One of the best moves I ever made, and most certainly the best move that Jimmy ever made. Janet was perfect for Jimmy, and they have had a nice life together with two lovely children. Jimmy is a retired U.S. Marshall and a great guy and a great friend, even after what Sully and I did to him on his wedding day. Jimmy and Janet were to get married on a Saturday. The night before, we had the wedding rehearsal in St. Monicas, and the wedding rehearsal party back at Janet's parent's house. I don't know whose idea it was, but it seemed a good one, at the time. One of my friends was waiting to get into the bathroom and walked into Janet's bedroom where Jimmy's tuxedo, shirt, tie, cumber bum, and shoes were all lying on the bed. Most people wouldn't have given it a second thought but my friends were not most people. The next thing I knew, Joe Maury Flaherty was assigned the job of keeping Dolan preoccupied. Nobody did it better than Maury. We tiptoed into Janet's bedroom closed the door and went to work. Out of nowhere, it seemed, a bottle of white shoe polish appeared. I grabbed the shoes that Jimmy Dolan was going to where to get married in, the next day, and we began to write on the bottom of both shoes. When we were finished with our work we went back, and joined he party, and nobody was the wiser and nobody, thanks to Maury, had even missed us. The next day we all arrived at St. Monicas all decked out in our rented tuxedos and began the task of escorting the guests to their seats. Before too long, Fr. Murphy appeared on the altar, the music started, and Janet, looking absolutely beautiful, was escorted down the aisle. Jimmy met her at the altar. I looked over at my friends, and they were all trying to stifle their laughter, without much success, I might add. Everything was going along great until Jimmy and Janet knelt down. We were sitting in the front row so we had the perfect vantage point. At first you could hear a murmur, and then some muffled laughter, and then Jimmy and Janet stood up and the Church was again quiet, except for Fr. Murphy's voice. The next time Jimmy knelt down, the laughter started almost immediately. We were trying our best to keep our composure, without any luck at all. Fr. Murphy seemed stunned as he looked out at the congregation. The laughter was now unabated and very loud. We had hoped for a response, but not this much of a response. Jimmy and Janet didn't have a clue as to why all their friends were suddenly laughing at this very solemn ceremony. I quickly glanced over to where Jimmy's mother, Mae, sat and I could see the fire in her eyes. She was not taking this well. Everyone in the Church, now, was laughing except Fr. Murphy, Jimmy's mother, Jimmy and Janet. Even Janet's family was laughing. Jimmy was still in the kneeling position, the bottom of his left shoe had the words HELP on the sole. The bottom of his right shoe had the word ME on its sole. So when Jimmy knelt down, all the people in the Church could see were the words HELP ME staring back at them. We had no idea that the white shoe polish would show up so well. It looked like a neon sign. I honestly thought that only the people in the first few pews would be able to see our message. Wrong. Everyone in the Church, from the first row to the very last row, could very plainly see our handiwork. We were in trouble and we knew it, but it did nothing to quell our laughter. The look on Fr. Murphy's face was priceless. Obviously this had never happened to him before, and he didn't have a clue as to what was wrong or what to do about it. The whole ceremony had stopped. I had never heard people laugh in Church before, and that in some way made it even more hilarious. It was like being a kid again in grammar school and getting away with something. If looks could kill, Jimmy's mother's looks would have killed all of us who sat in that front pew. None of us looked across at her. I just wanted the ceremony to start up again. The more the wedding was delayed the more trouble I knew we were in. Finally one of the altar boys went up and whispered something in Fr. Murphy's ear. Uh-oh. We held our breath and waited to see what his reaction was going to be. The altar boy pointed to his own shoes and continued to whisper into the priest's ear. There was no mistaking what he was telling him. Finally Fr. Murphy shook his head, and bent over to talk to Jimmy and Janet. I kept thinking that this had somehow gotten way out of hand, just like five years before , when Sully, Ricky, Maury and I were in this same Church, one Saturday afternoon waiting to go to confession.

Chapter 50 – Confessions With Fr. Maury

Confessions started at 4O'clock and they continued until there were no more people left to confess their sins that day. Ricky kept looking at his watch.

"Ya gut a date?" Sully asked.

"As a matter of fact, I do" Ricky said, shocking all of us. Sully was all over him.

"Who is she, where is she from, when did you meet her, where did you meet her." Sully was like the National Enquirer and Ricky knew it. Sully was getting absolutely no information from Ricky, on that day.

"I have to get going," Rick said, again looking at his watch, "I wonder where the priest is?"

"Maury you should hear the confessions, after all you are the President of the CYO." Sully whispered.

"Some real good logic there" I said to Sully.

"Ya, come on Maury, you're a lot bigger than all the priests."

"Some more irrefutable logic," I said to Rick. Maury was only 16 years old but he stood 6'4" and weighed 230 pounds. It was now ten minutes past four and still no priest.

"Come on Maury, it'll be funny," Sully laughed. Maury didn't say anything. For once I was being the naysayer in this situation.

"The people will see him go in," I said to Sully, but he was, as usual, way ahead of me.

"We'll use the confessional way down the other end of the Church," he said, having already, in the span of a minute, thought out a plan. Finally Fr. Murphy came out, and went into the confessional. I felt a little better. Sully was determined though. He kept talking to Maury until finally Maury said, "Let's go." I watched as the two of them walked out of the pew, and down to the opposite end of the Church. Nobody except me and Ricky paid any attention. They made as if they were lighting a candle, and when I next looked there was only Sully at the alter, near the candles. Maury had disappeared. Sully waited a minute or two, and then slowly walked up the aisle to where about 50 people were waiting to have their confessions heard. I scurried over to the other side of the pew so I could see what he was going to do. He walked to the first pew and announced.

"Confessions will also be heard by Fr. Flaherty in the last confessional on the left." Immediately, about 12 people got up. and hurried down the aisle to tell their sins to this new priest, who happened to be 16 years old. I was in shock. Ricky was laughing so hard, he had to walk out of the Church. Sully walked slowly down the aisle and sat in back of the people who were going to tell Maury their indiscretions. I knew about five of the people, which made it even worse. They all went in and in a few minutes came out, and went to the altar to say their penance. But instead of hearing only a few confessions, more people continued to enter the Church and head down to Maury's confessional. He was now in there for over an hour and his line was getting longer than Father. Murphy's. I panicked.

"Sully he's going to get caught, Father. Murphy is almost through." I told the lookout named Sully, who quickly glanced around and saw that only two parishioners were lined up outside Father. Murphy's confessional, while there were six lined up outside Father. Maury's. I had to hand it to Sully, he had balls. He jumped up and went to the pew in front of the six waiting confessors. I had no idea what he was going to do next, which is not unusual.

"I'm sorry to bother you, but Fr. Murphy will hear your confessions in the back confessional, right now." The six people never questioned him, they all got up and headed down to the back of the Church. Finally the last person came out of Maury's confessional. It was one of our baseball coaches. We both looked at each other and laughed. Sully waited about a minute and a half, and quickly and quietly, swept the big curtain aside and was in the confessional. Two minutes later he was out, and a minute after that Father. Maury was out and thirty seconds after that we were all out, on the street, that is. We couldn't wait to hear about the confessions.

"What did they say?" Sully eagerly asked Maury.

"Excuse me, what those people told me is strictly confidential." Maury said without any hint of a joke.

"You gotta be shitting me," Sully yelled.

"I told you I would hear the confessions but I never told you that I would tell you the confessions." Sully was bullshit. Ricky and I were laughing our heads off. Maury knew exactly how to get him and he just did.

"Sully you'll never know what they told me" Maury said. Another thing Sully didn't know was that someone saw he and Maury coming out of the confessional and told Father. Murphy. Boy did they get in trouble. They almost got thrown out of the CYO and Maury was the President and Sully the Vice President. Rick and I never got caught, which made Sully even madder.

This wedding ceremony, much like the confessional, wasn't what we thought it was going to be Father continued to talk to the Jim and Janet and finally he straightened up and a big smile washed across his face, and I was able to breathe a little. I thought that Father was going to be really mad, he wasn't. I guess he knew us pretty well by then. Dolan pretended to be mad, but we knew he wasn't. His mother was. She wouldn't talk to any of us that day. She was livid. She came around a couple of years later. We buried Maury from that same Church in 1994. I gave the eulogy and mentioned the time Maury got caught hearing confessions in the very same Church, where he was now being buried. Jimmy Dolan. Sully, Ricky and Knoxie were all pallbearers for our beloved friend. It was the toughest speech I ever had to give in my life. Fr. Murphy came back to St. Monicas to bury his old CYO President. Maury, by the way, never did tell Sully anything about those confessions, which drove Sully crazy, as only Maury could do. I miss him very much.

Brian P. Wallace

Chapter 51 – We Weren't Rich But We Got By

I mentioned earlier the importance of a 15- cent pimple ball, when we were growing up. You have no idea how many ways we found to use one 15-cent rubber ball. There is an old song that says, "City girls seem to find out early," well that certainly holds true for City boys as well. We weren't rich, but we didn't know what rich was, so it never bothered us. We had a very rich childhood, without money. We made the most of what we had, and we shared what we had. Take the pimple ball for example. If we had the price of a pimple ball, which we didn't always have, we were all set for a day maybe two or three depending on what we played and where we played it. With a pimple ball you could play, what we called whole ball, which could be played anywhere. We preferred to play whole ball in the Gavin school- yard because it had a fence and was enclosed, but there were drawbacks, like the roof. The Gavin roof was too high to climb and was basically unreachable, so one very long foul ball could end the game and cost us 15 cents. We also played whole ball in the middle of the street and used sewers and telephone poles as our bases. We would pick out certain objects as automatics. An automatic home run might be a ball hit, on the fly, past the 1962 Chevy and an automatic granny, or grand slam might be a ball hit, on the fly, past the new green dodge.

To play whole ball all you needed was the ball and an old broom stick or mop handle, which was the bat. Everything else could be made up, like the bases(sewers) the automatic hits(cars) etc. The only problem was the traffic, which created an inordinate amount of time-outs. A good whole ball game could last for a couple of hours. I played in a number of whole ball games in which the ball split into two pieces. Without missing a beat the game would change from a whole ball game to a half ball game, which required only two half- balls and the broom -stick or mop handle which we already had anyway. A lot of mothers, back then, would swear they had bought a brand new mop handle or broom only to have it constantly misplaced. Well, we needed it. A new pimple ball could always start a game of bar ball, which was usually played in the Gavin school yard, because only one or two kids were strong

A Southie Memoir

enough to hit the ball all the way from home plate onto the Gavin roof in bar ball. To play bar ball all we needed was the ball. In bar ball the player threw the ball in the air and hit it with his closed fist, as far as he could. In the Gavin, you could play the ball off the wall, which made getting a hit very difficult. I spent many many hours with a pimple ball, just throwing it off my house, all by myself, or at least until a friend showed up. Once I had a playmate we would use the ball to play off the curb. In this game you tried to hit the ball off the edge of the curbstone and try to hit it as far as you could and as fast as you could. while the opposing player stood in the middle of the street and tried to catch it. If it got by him on the ground it was a single on a fly a double, below the second floor, but off the house a triple and over the second floor, but off the house a home run. The guy in the street, however, could catch the carom off the house, before it hit the ground and that was an out. We would also use a pimple ball to play, "Off the stairs" which was the same as off the curb, except you hit the ball off someone's front stairs. If someone got a hard ball for his birthday, we would head down to Fifth Street park, where we would use that new ball until the cover came off and then we would use electrical tape and tape it up until it split.

Softball was played in the Boys Club yard. Tag rush football was always played in the middle of the street, where the quarterback would tell his receiver.

"Go down to the green car, cut left to the blue car and I'll hit you near the stop sign." Some of my most memorable games were after a big snowstorm. As if by magic, all the kids would gather at Fifth Street park and play tackle football in the snow, the deeper the better. But our games weren't limited to sports. One of my favorite games was a City game called "relievio." Relievio would start with two team captains. The captains, say, would be me and Sully, we would choose sides based on the number of players. We would buck up, which meant throwing fingers and picking either odd or even, to see which team hid first. Once that was determined we picked a, "Goolles" We would then choose boundaries, in which the teams could not go beyond. If we were playing down E street, our goolles would probably be Sully's doorstep and the boundaries would be from West Ninth street to West Fourth street and from Dorchester Street to D Street. Sully's team would get to hide first, they could hide anywhere inside the boundaries that we set. My team had a designated time, say 30 minutes, to capture all of Sully's team, or they would get to hide again. We would give them a 2- minute head start, before we tried to find them. One of my men, or women, this was a coed game, had to be stationed at the goolles. The rest of the team would go after Sully's team, who was hiding somewhere in that 6 block- area. Once we captured one of Sully's guys, we would place him or her in the goolles, which served as a makeshift jail. Once in the goolles, they were taken out of play. But, if one of Sully's guys managed to get to the goolles, and get by my goole keepers. They would say, "One two three relievio," and it was like a huge jailbreak. All of Sully's previously captured guys, were now free to hide again and the game went on like that for hours and hours, until we couldn't run anymore or it was too dark to play.

  Sully was, by far, the best relievio player in South Boston. He had the greatest hiding places of anyone who ever played. Nobody had the guts to hide where he hid. He would hide under cars by holding on to the muffler, or he would hide behind the statue of St. Joseph in front of St. Vincent's church. One time he actually hid inside the Laboure Center Convent. Since we played for hour upon hour we would often get new kids who would want to play. When that happened , whatever team was doing the capturing, would walk around the area yelling "Oellie, oellie entry, new cucumber." That would let the hiding team know that they had to get back to the goolles and start all over again. The process would continue all over again. Relievio didn't cost any money and kept us busy for hours at a time, which was a prerequisite of all City street games. It was a lot of fun and I have some great Relievio memories, most revolving around Sully, of course. Another City game was a bit violent it was called buck buck. This again cost no money, and was played for a couple of hours at a time, or at least until someone got hurt, and in buck buck someone always got hurt. I had a cousin who lived in Norwell, and one time my parents took me out of the big City to stay with my Country cousin in Norwell. Now Norwell, as the crow flies, is only 26 miles from Boston, but it might as well have been 2,600. This place, I soon found out was a different world. I was only 10 years old at the time when I first visited my cousin. We had made arrangements to stay with them for a week, it was the longest week of my life. Every day I prayed that Sully would mysteriously show up, and I could get back to the real world. But sometimes miracles never happen. I remember how excited I was about the Olympics that year. There were taking place in Rome and I couldn't wait to see John Thomas in the high jump. Now we weren't rich by any means, but we did have a television. My cousin did not. I couldn't believe it. I was stuck in this hick town, with no friends, and no television and the nearest basketball court was two miles away.

"This is supposed to be a vacation? I said to my father. It was the vacation from hell. And if it was bad for me. I can just imagine how my brother felt. He was 15 years old and had already discovered that girls were different than boys, that would come later for me. Poor Sully had no one to hang out with. I, at least, had a few kids my own age, at least chronologically speaking. My birth certificate said I was ten years old. Their birth certificates said that they were also ten years old, but believe me there was about four years difference between us. One kid's name was Watsie another was Ricky Roseback. They were nice kids but the difference in our street education level was akin to Bunker Hill Community and Harvard.

"What do you guys do for excitement around here?" I asked Watsie on my first day there.

"Well on July 4th they have a huge bonfire down the center of town," he smiled.

"Yeah, but this is only June 14th" I said in amazement.

"I know," he said "I can't wait." Neither could I, but I couldn't wait to get back home to Southie.

"Do you guys know how to play relievio?" I asked Ricky Roseback. In his best Andy of Mayberry voice he said, "Naw, but we know how to play hide and go seek."

"I do too," I said, "but I stopped playing it about five years ago."

"How about foxy?'" I asked, praying they would know that game. They both looked at me as if I was speaking another language.

"Is that like tag?" Watsie asked. "We know how to play that." I just walked away. Tag. I hadn't played tag since I was four years old. But they were really nice kids, who were just different than me, and I did learn some stuff from them.

Brian P. Wallace

They raised chickens and they grew crops and stuff like that, which I had never seen before, and which was pretty cool for a City kid. I remember every morning I would put my leg weights on, and run the two miles to the basketball court dribbling a basketball while I was running. The first time Ricky and Watsie saw me running up High Street with the leg weight strapped to my ankles, they thought it was the funniest thing they had ever seen.

"What are those things on your legs?" Ricky asked.

"They're leg weights," I replied as I ran past them.

"Why would you put weights on your ankles?" Watsie then intoned."

"To make me run faster," I said, and they went into gales of laughter and told just about everybody in Norwell that the dumb City kid wore weights on his legs and he thought they made him run faster. They thought it was the funniest thing in the world. I remember asking them if there was anywhere I could watch the Olympics. They looked at me as if I was an alien.

"What are the Olympics?" they asked. I just shrugged and said, "It's a long story." And it was a long week. I told my friends that I once spent a month in Norwell, one week. That week in Norwell, however, did teach me that City kids were, in fact, different and that our games, were just that, our games. They were invented by City kids, for City kids. Kids who lived in the Country, or suburbs did things completely different than we did in the City. Foxy was a City game as was buck buck and four corners. All were indigenous City games and a few were indigenous to South Boston. Those were all physical encounters in which more than a few kids ended up at City Hospital for a few hours, especially when you were playing buck buck against Tommy Gailunas.

We also had non- physical games like "Make Me Laugh," and my favorite 'Spin the bottle'. The first time I saw anyone play 'Make me laugh', I was only about eight years old. My brother's friends were playing on the stairs directly across the street from my house. My brother kept telling me to get lost, but I had never seen his friends make such fools out of themselves and I was really enjoying it. This kid named Skippa King, who was a con man, was up next. He disappeared into an alley, next to the Lecinskas house, and reappeared two minutes later completely nude. Right on West 5th Street, right in front of my mother and father, I couldn't believe it, but I laughed, boy did I laugh. He won. It was legendary and it was funny. Another thing we did, which was usually funny was mother ranking. Sully was one of the best mother rankers in Southie. If he remembered his homework as well as he remembered mother ranks he would have graduated from Stanford, Harvard, or Yale.

Chapter 52 – Paul Brack And Mother Ranking

    I don't know where he got his mother ranks because some of them were really unique and not many kids in Southie would dare start a mother-ranking contest with Sully. There was however one kid who could outranked Sully, even on Sully's best day and he did go end up going to Harvard. His name was Paul Brack. Paul Brack was a horse of a different color. He got 800 in Math and 780 in English on his College Boards. He went to Boston Latin and was first in his class. He wore glasses that were thicker than the thickest coke bottles ever made. He lived in a shack, directly across from the Gavin School that was about 600 square feet. He loved to play sports, especially hockey and baseball, His family was very very poor, so Paul had one glove, a goal tender's glove which he used to play goalie in the winter and first base in the summer. I had never met anyone like Paul Brack and I have yet to meet anyone like Paul Brack. He was the first nerd I had ever met, and talk about a stereotype. He had dirty black, greasy hair, black glasses with ever-present tape holding the frames together, and a dirty white shirt with ink stains and a pen and pencil holder hanging out of his shirt pocket. He was a nerd, before we knew what a nerd was. He was also a genius, which was another thing we were totally unfamiliar with. The first thing that struck me about Paul Brack was how poor he was. I knew I wasn't rich but I had never met anyone who was that poor. His house was a disaster area, with dog shit on the floor and dirt everywhere. I couldn't believe that anyone could live like that. It certainly made me appreciate my surroundings a lot more. Actually Brack wasn't a bad goal tender, but he had the worse temper of anyone I had ever met.

    When we played baseball, Sully would drive Paul Brack absolutely to distraction. Sully would throw two fast balls by him and Brack would be steaming mad.

    "Can't hit the fast one, huh four eyes," Sully would smirk. You could almost see the steam starting to fog up Brack's glasses. He would step out of the batter's box and try to compose himself, but Sully wouldn't let him.

    "What's the matter coke bottles, can't see the ball?" Sully would yell into Augie, which was his nickname. I would have my glove in front of my face trying to hide my laughter.

"Throw me one more fast one, fatso and see where I hit it," Brack would shout back at Sully.

"What happened to the two I just threw," Sully would mock They really went a long way, didn't they?"

"Just one more fast one, you impertinent slob," Brack would yell back at Sully, who knew he had him exactly where he wanted him.

"Wait until I get my dictionary four eyes" Sully would shoot back, and finally Brack would step back into the batter's box with a fierce look of determination on his face.

"Here comes the fast one asshole," Sully would say as he would begin his windup. Finally the pitch. Sully would lob a very slow change up, and Brack, expecting a fast ball, would miss the ball by at least three feet. We all knew what was coming next. He would let out a string of invectives that would make a longshoreman blush, at the top of his lungs. And then he would turn his anger on Sully and call him swears in 3 different languages. His vocabulary was truly amazing. I think he made up swears to call Sully. Sully just smiled, which made Augie even madder. It was priceless, every time. Paul Brack could not hit a fast ball nor could he hit a slow change up but he gave me and Sully more laughs than almost anyone we grew up with.

And I'll never forget the day Paul Brack went down. It was on one of those long hot summer days of our youth that the greatest mother- ranking contest ever held was precipitated by another Augie Brack strikeout. The pitcher of record was, who else, Sully, and once again Brack fell for the slow change up on the third strike. For a very smart kid, how could he be so stupid, I thought, that memorable day over 45 years ago.

"You're a motherless miscreant," Brack yelled out to the pitcher's mound. Sully had no idea what a miscreant was, but he knew it was something bad especially when it followed that hated word, motherless. Sully, this time, did not laugh. He spun, and ran in to where Augie had just shattered his bat into a thousand little shivers of wood. Sully went right for the jugular "Augie, your family is so poor when I asked your mother if I could use your bathroom, she said sure pick a corner." There was a moment of silence, and then the place erupted. Sully had to be holding that rank for the perfect time and place, and he determined that this was where he made his mother-ranking stance, against the very best in the business, one Paul Augie Brack. Brack was not ready for that one and it caught him like a slap shot in the forehead. He reeled, but came back firing.

"Sully your mother is so skinny her nipples touch," Brack spat out. He wasn't the king for nothing. Sully had that look in his eyes, and I knew he was ready for all of Brack's best. I started to write them down on our baseball scorebook, because I knew I would never remember all the ranks.

"Augie your mother is so fat she irons her clothes in the driveway," Sully said, as the crowd erupted into applause.

Augie didn't hesitate. "Oh yeah Sully, your mother is so fat, they had to baptize her at the aquarium." The crowd grudgingly applauded. Make no mistake about it, this was a Sully crowd.

Sully was ready. "Augie, Your mother is so fat she can't even jump to a conclusion."

Brack shot back,"Your mother is so fat she broke her arm and gravy poured out."

"Augie, your mother is so fat her blood type is Prince," which got a great cheer from the crowd.

Not intimidated Augie changed the subject. "Your mother is so dumb, she couldn't pass a blood test.

The crowd booed, not one of Augie's best and the crowd knew it. Sully, as all good rankers do, went right back to the fat ranks, which made it seem as if Augie was all out of fat ammunition. There was a science to this, you know.

"Augie your mother is so fat the Doctor put her on a light diet, as soon as it gets light she start eating." The crowd again erupted. Augie never changed expressions.

"Sully your mother is so cross eyed that when she cries the tears roll down her back," he deadpanned , as the crowd howled. Sully was again ready.

"Augie your sister is so cross eyed she can see her own ears." Again the crowd erupted. Sully was good. Nobody had gotten this far with Augie in years. He was the undisputed champ and he wasn't about to go down easily, if at all.

"Your mother is so old she was a waitress at the last supper," Augie said, again not one of his best. Sully had him unnerved. Without any hesitation Sully was right in his face and was starting to bring it on home.

"Your house is so small, (which it was,) that when you eat in the kitchen your elbows are in the living room." Augie flushed, hesitated, then went after Sully's sister Donna.

"Sully your sister is so ugly she went in to a haunted house and came out with a job application." Now it was anything goes. Now it was getting real personal and Sully was more than ready.

"Augie if ugliness were a crime, your mother would get the electric chair." I had never heard that one before, and I had to admit Sully was getting the best of the famous Augie Brack. But Brack was far from through.

"Sully, your father is so ugly he went to Friendly's and got punched in the face." That was another one I had never heard, as I quickly wrote down the word Friendly's on my rapidly filling piece of paper. I was waiting for Sully to start on all of Augie's weak points and he had quite a few. He had bad teeth, acne, he was dirty with coke bottle glasses and bad breath. As if reading my mind Sully hit him good.

"Augie your teeth are so yellow, cars slow down when they see you smile." Ouch. That one hit Augie where it hurt, as the crowd started to chant "Sully. Sully. Sully." Augie wiped some sweat off his face and went right back at Sully.

"Sully you're so fat your belt size says equator." A little to intellectual for this crowd, I thought. In Mother ranking or any offshoots thereof, the punch lines have to evoke instantaneous laughter. You can't make people think about what you had just said, and that is what Augie did with the equator rank. Sully had him on the ropes, and he went in for the kill.

"Augie your glasses are so thick you can see things that happened yesterday. Augie reeled. The chanting grew louder "Sully, Sully,Sully." Augie stepped back, he was losing, and he knew it. This had never happened before to Augie, and he was having a difficult time handling the pressure.

"Sully your ears are so big you can hear what I'm thinking," not bad but not great. Sully could feel it. He walked over to Augie and said 'Augie, your breath smells so bad that people on the phone hang up." Sully's material was getting to the crowd and to Augie because a lot of it was true and both Augie and the crowd knew it. Augie was going down quickly, his crown slipping away to his nemesis.

"Sully if ugliness were bricks you'd be the D street project." Original but Sully was going in for the kill.

'Augie you smell so bad you need right and left guard." Augie was almost down.

"Sully you're a clown" he said as he started to walk away. Sully had one left, as the dethroned king began to walk away.

"Hey Augie is it true that your mother has only one tooth and she snaps holes in doughnuts for a living." That was it, the coup de grace. The grand slam. Sully was the king and the crowd went wild. He had done the impossible, he had outranked Paul Brack. The kid who never ceased to amaze me had done it again. He had beaten the toughest kid in Southie, Paul Moore and now he had outranked a genius, who was never the same after that day. We walked home from the Gavin that day, and I asked him where he got those ranks.

"Oh I've been getting ready for Brack for quite a while," he said with very little emotion.

"He deserved it," I said, and again he surprised me.

"Naw he's not a bad kid, he really has nothing going for him. I kind of felt sorry for him," Sully said.

"Well it didn't look it this afternoon," I laughed, as we slowly approached his house.

"That was just a show, you know that," he replied and he walked into his house. That was also the last time I ever saw Sully get into a mother-ranking contest. He proved his point, and we were finally growing up. I hated the thought of that, not because I didn't want to grow up but because I didn't want to lose Sully, and I knew those things happen even to the best of friends when you grow up.

Chapter 53 - A Weekend At The Kennedy Compound

One of the last times we were together turned in to an incredible adventure. I was eating dinner, on a Friday night, when the phone rang. It was Sully.

"Bri I'm down the corner with Leo McCarty, do you want to go down the Cape?" he asked. I had just gotten paid and I had no plans for the weekend so I quickly agreed.

"I'll meet you in twenty minutes," I said, not knowing that this was going to be our last real escapade, before I went off to College and Sully went in to the Marines. I thought that Sully had a place for us to stay. He didn't. We all had our Southie suitcases, which are basically glorified garbage bags with, some clothes and some toiletries.

"Where are we staying?" I asked.

"Down your brother's cottage," Sully replied nonchalantly. I was kind of shocked.

"No way," I said quickly, "My brother will kick all of our asses, if we even get close to his cottage."

"How do you know?" Sully asked.

"Because I know my brother a lot better than you do, and I know what he will do to us if we knock on his cottage door."

"Well we'll find someplace else." he said. I was rethinking my decision to spend a weekend looking for a place to stay, down the Cape.

"I don't know," I said, "What if we can't find anyone down there that we know." Sully jumped in.

"We always find someone at the Falmouth Pizza Place, don't we?"

"Yeah I guess so," I said "I just don't want to spend a weekend sleeping in the bushes."

"Come on Bri," that'll never happen." He was right, we didn't spend that weekend in the bushes. We spent it in the biggest, most expensive, and most famous mansion on the Cape. How we got there is totally unbelievable.

We thumbed down the Cape that Friday night and we were in the Falmouth Pizza Place, which was in the center of Falmouth, looking around for any familiar faces. We found none, and it was starting to get late.

Brian P. Wallace

"This is great," I said to Sully. We had hidden our Southie suitcases in some bushes a couple of blocks from the Pizza Place.

"Looks like we'll be sleeping with our bags in the bushes," Leo said. I wasn't very happy about this turn of events and neither was Leo. Sully just kept looking around without saying a word. At around 10 O'clock a car, packed with kids, screeched in to the parking lot, and almost sideswiped me.

"Get out of the way four eyes," a kid yelled out the back window of the car, as it sped by.

"What did he say?" Sully yelled at me. I really didn't want a fight, especially one with a car full of kids.

"Forget it Sully," I said "it's no big deal."

"To me it is," he said, as he headed over to where the car was now parking. I looked at Leo and we both just shrugged our shoulders, and ran to catch up with Sully. I counted seven kids who piled out of the car. Not a good sign. Some of them were pretty big. Another bad sign. Sully had already taken his partial plate out of his mouth, which meant only one thing…a fight. Whenever Sully was going to fight, he would swipe his right hand across his mouth, like he was wiping his mouth. What he was actually doing was taking his partial plate out and putting it in his right hand pants pocket. He did it so quickly, however, that even if you were looking for it, chances are you would never see him do it. I knew better, and it gave me a few seconds to get ready to fight.

"Who yelled at my friend?" Sully said as he reached the car. The kids in the car looked at this little roly- poly kid like he was crazy. They were certainly on the right track. Nobody, from the car said anything.

"Which one of you said something to my friend?" I was hoping whoever said it would be one of the smaller kids, who had alighted from the car. No such luck.

"I said it," a kid who was about 6 '1" and about 200 pounds, said as he headed toward Sully.

"Here we go," I said to Leo, as we ran to be at his side.

"He's pretty big," Leo whispered, as the kid stood directly in front of Sully. He had a good five inches and about 20 pound of muscle on Sully, which was another bad sign. Sully quickly sized up the situation.

A Southie Memoir

"If you're so tough, why don't you say it to me," Sully said, looking around to make sure we were behind him. We were.

"OK shrimp," the kid laughed, "What do you want me to say." All of his friends were pissing themselves laughing. "That will do," Sully said and before anyone knew what happened, Sully had hit the kid with a sucker punch, and the kid was lying on the ground looking up. There was no laughing now, only shock. The kid was bleeding from the nose, and as he wiped his hand across his nose he seemed to go crazy, as he saw his own blood on his hand. He quickly jumped up, as his friends began to get brave again.

"Come on OD, kick his fat little ass," one of the kids, who looked vaguely familiar, yelled. The kid, whose name, we found out was Kenny, was so mad that he swung wildly at Sully. Sully was prepared for the wild punch, he ducked, and came up with an uppercut that laid Kenny on his back once again. Kenny's friends were in shock, as was Kenny, who was now looking up from the ground for the second time in less than thirty seconds. This time Kenny took his time getting up, as a nice shiner began to show itself under his left eye. Sully just stood there looking down. I looked at Leo, and then looked at the othersix6 kids, who didn't look too happy.

"Now we are really in trouble," I whispered to Leo. But the six kids made no move towards us. They were too busy looking down, at their fallen hero to care about us. Thank God. By now a pretty good crowd had come out of the pizza place, to see what was going on, which also meant that the Falmouth Police would be on the scene very quickly. By now, Kenny was back on his feet, hands up high, and circling left. You could tell that he had done some boxing before.

"He's a pretty tough kid," I said to Leo, who just shook his head in agreement. Kenny started to throw a few jabs at Sully, all of which connected. Every time one of his jabs landed his six friends went wild, and began to yell, which I knew would bring the Police even sooner They traded punches for about five minutes with neither fighter getting the best of the other.

"Come on O'Donnell," one of his friends yelled, as the two fighters circled each other. Kenny O'Donnell? Where have I heard that name before? The kid caught Sully with a great right hand, and Sully was hurt. His friends were screaming now. They wanted Sully's hide. All of a sudden it hit me. Kenny O'Donnell wasn't that the name of JFK's top aide? As quickly as it started it was over. Sully was acting as if he was really hurt, and O'Donnell fell hook line and sinker for the act. O'Donnell let his guard down, just for a second, and Sully hit him with a four punch combination, all of which found their mark and O'Donnell went down like a sack of potatoes. I knew he wasn't getting up. But his friends, who thought that O'Donnell had turned the fight around, couldn't believe that their fighter was again on the ground. The kid was tough. I'll certainly give him that. He tried to get back up but his legs were not working in concert with his brain. He got halfway up and crashed back to the ground. His friends looked on incredulously. They couldn't believe what they had just seen. I could, I had seen it my whole life. In all the years that I had known Sully, I had never seen him lose a fight, and he had more fights that Julio Ceasar Chavez.

"Let's get out of here," I said to Sully. I was worried about the cops and I still didn't like being outmanned by more than 2 to 1. It was obvious to everyone that the fight was now officially over. O'Donnell was helped to his feet, and was now leaning against the car that had only minutes ago, sideswiped me. We started to go. We walked out of the pizza place parking lot in the general direction of our expensive luggage. After we got about 25 yards the car was back. This time instead of sideswiping us, it came on to the sidewalk and blocked our way. Leo and I looked at each other with apprehension. We both figured that we would have to fight The rest of the kids in the car. "You still got a problem?" Sully said addressing the fallen warrior.

"No, you beat me. I just wanted to shake your hand" he said, as he extended his right hand.

"It's a trap," Leo said to Sully, "don't shake his hand." But Sully was not listening or he didn't want to listen. I was sure that O'Donnell was going to throw a sucker shot. He didn't. He extended his hand and Sully shook it.

"Nice fight," O'Donnell said, "Where are you from?"

"Southie," Sully said.

"Figures," O'Donnell laughed. "Where are you staying?" he said, in between wiping blood off his face.

"We don't have a place," Sully said.

"Hold on," O'Donnell said, and he went back to talk to his friends. We waited for about five minutes, and he came back to where the three of us stood.

"You can stay with us, if you'd like," he smiled, showing a rapidly rising shiner under his right eye. We all looked at each other.

"No thanks," I said quickly. Being a city kid, I immediately sensed a setup.

"Where are you going to go?" O'Donnell asked Sully.

"Can we talk this over?" Sully asked O'Donnell.

"Sure take your time." O'Donnell laughed, nor understanding why we would even hesitate at such an offer.

"Let's go with them," Sully said to me and Leo, as we huddled as if we were calling a play in touch football on E Street.

"This is a setup," I said, "They just want to get us back to their place and kick our asses."

"I don't think so," Sully said "These kids are different. I don't know what it is about them, but I know they are different." They're not city kids."

What do you think Leo?" we both asked.

"Ordinarily I would say no way, but I think Sully is right, these kids are different, I think we'll be all right."

"Two against one," I said, "You win." But Sully knew I wasn't comfortable with the situation.

"Look at it this way Bri, that kid probably was their best fighter right." I nodded. "If he's their best we don't have much to worry about."

"Yeah maybe you're right," I said "OK let's go with them." So we went. Where we went and who we went with is a different story.

It turns out that I was right. At least, I was right about the name. I was wrong about their motives. The kid Sully fought was the son of JFK"s top aide Ken O'Donnell. The other kids in the car were Kennedy kids and a few of their cousins. They had never met anyone like us, and we had never met anyone like them.

"Where are we going?" I asked O'Donnell.

"Just follow us," he said.

"We don't have a car," I said.

"How did you get here" one of the other kids asked.

"We thumbed," Leo said.

"What does that mean?" one of the Kennedy kids asked "You have no place to stay, and you have no car?"

"Right" I said.

"You guys are unbelievable," one of the kids in the car said. "Do you have any luggage?"

"Yeah, it's in the bushes over there," Sully said pointing across the street. When we retrieved our garbage bags, I thought they were going to pass out from laughing.

"You're serious?" O'Donnell said.

"As a heart attack," Sully said, as the laughter continued to come from the car.

"Pile in," they said, and we were off to Hyannisport and a weekend that was out of this world. I don't even know who owned the house we stayed in, but it was one of the nicest houses that I had ever been in. It was huge. There was more food in their refrigerator that I had ever seen in my life. We told them stories about growing up in Southie, and they couldn't get enough. These were little rich kids who had never experienced what we had experienced, growing up. They were good kids and we really got along very well. It turned out that Kenny O'Donnell was in fact the toughest kid in the group. He had never lost a fight, until that might in the Falmouth Pizza Place parking lot. He was an undefeated boxer in the fancy Prep School that he attended. They thought that he was going to kill Sully when the fight started. That is why they were so stunned when O'Donnell went down and kept going down. They were good sports though, especially Kenny O'Donnell. He thought Sully was great, and he kept asking us to repeat our stories, especially the ones at the Garden.

They were from one world and we were from another and for one strange weekend down Cape Cod the two worlds met and we were all better for the experience. At least I knew I was. I have no idea what happened to Kenny O'Donnell, but I hope he is doing well. I know what happened to some of the Kennedy kids. You can't pick up a paper, nowadays, without seeing them on the front page. I don't know which Kennedy's or Shriver's we were with that weekend, they all looked alike. A couple of their sisters came over and spent some time at the house. They didn't think we were as cool as their brother's did.

"He beat up Kenny," they laughed, pointing to Sully.

"You have got to be kidding" they said, when they realized that Sully had really beat up their poster boy. They didn't like us, from that moment on. They had a cookout and they had every kind of food imaginable.

"Great call Bri," Sully said in between bites of his sirloin steak.

"If we listened to you we would still be looking for a place to crash."

"Just shut up and eat," I laughed.

"Another steak Sully," one of the Kennedy's yelled to Sully who had taken on some kind of cult status with them.

"I don't believe you Sully" I said "I just don't believe you. You see, we weren't impressed with the fact that they were Kennedy's. Maybe that was why they liked us. We took them for who they were. We didn't care how much money they had or who their Father Uncle or Cousins were, and I think they liked that about us. The funny part was that I never saw an adult the entire weekend. They had one fridge filled with beer. They had another fridge filled with beer and not an adult to be seen. It was the only time that I lived the rich life and I liked every minute of it, even if we knew it was only going to last for a weekend. We never kept in touch and I kind of wish we had. But life goes on and so didn't our lives and they were about to change.

Brian P. Wallace

Chapter 54 – Time To Grow Up

    A couple of weeks after spending the weekend with the Kennedy's I was off to College in Montreal to play basketball and to do a little studying. Sully, Maury, Knuckles, Ricky, Ridge, Knoxie, and Dolan were all going into the service. I remember my first week at Loyola in Montreal. I was walking down St. Catherine Street and I was all- alone. For the very first time in my life, I was all- alone. I missed my friends, especially Sully, so much it hurt. For the very first time in my life I was unhappy. My girlfriend thought that I was unhappy because I missed her, and I let her think that, it was easier that way. I went home for Thanksgiving break, and I immediately went down to see Swanny and Millie to see how there little Marine was doing.

    "He's not one for writing much, you know him," Swanny said. Yeah I did know him. I knew a lot more about their son than even they did. But I didn't know when I would see him again, or if I would see him again, and that was unbearable. A few of my friends had already been killed in this place they called Viet Nam, and that scared the shit out of me. No not for me, I knew I was going to be in College for a while but I also knew that they don't train Marines for nothing.

    I went home and went to bed. I awoke the next morning to an incredible sight, a skin headed 150 pound Marine standing at attention over my bed. I couldn't believe it. There he was, fifty pounds lighter, with a huge grin on his Marine face. I started to cry.

    "Do I look that bad?" he said.

    "No, you look that good," I laughed between the tears and it felt good. No it felt great. I can't remember ever being as happy in my life to see anyone in my life. We talked non -stop, in my kitchen for an hour.

    "I have to go meet Nancy," he said.

    "Yeah I have to go meet Anne Marie," I said in return.

    I'll call you tonight," he said, as he ran out the door, Boy he looked great.

    "Yeah tonight," I said. I was up Anne Marie's house that night, when I heard him yelling my name from the street.

    "Gotta go," I said. She wasn't too happy about it.

"The master calls," she said, as I headed out the door. He had just dropped Nancy off and he had a double six pack of Schlitz in the shotgun seat.

"Where we going?" I asked.

"Let's have a few beers with Swanny," he laughed.

"Yeah let's," I smiled, and we headed to the Old Harbor project and the Sullivan's new Home. We were already sitting at the kitchen table with an open beer in front of us when Swanny came into the kitchen.

"What's this?" he said, as only Swanny could. I thought he was kidding. He wasn't. "Son, you're not drinking in my house, no way, not in my house."

"Dad I'm 19 years old and in the Marines for Christ sake. I'm going to Vietnam," Sully said.

"Son remember, drinking is a curse. You'll never take the second if you don't take the first," and he repeated it. "Son, listen to me. Drinking is a curse. You'll never take the second if you don't take this first." We both got up and took our beer across the street into Columbia Park, drank our beers, and we laughed as we never had before. Our childhood ended that night at Columbia Park, where we had shared so many great times together as kids. I watched him walk away, that night. as I had so many times before. But I knew in my heart that this time was different. He wasn't going to call me in the morning. We both knew it was the end of our friendship, as we knew it, but we were OK with that, finally. We would always be best friends but we would never be as close as we were all those days and nights we spent together as children, teenagers and young adults., at the Garden, at the Club, at the BC High dances, down E Street, on the basketball court, in the snow, in the heat, talking about girls, laughing together, crying together and always being there for each other, and we were for a while. I always thought that we would grow old together, and laugh about all the stories that you have just read, but God had different plans. I guess he needed someone in heaven to make him laugh, He took Sully five years ago, and now all I have are my memories, and as Simon and Garfinkel once said, "Preserve your memories there all that's left for you." And now you have my memories as well, I just hope you like reading about them as much as I liked living them.

Brian P. Wallace

WHERE ARE THEY NOW

Sully is in heaven telling God jokes.

Ridge is doing two life sentences for murder.

Maury died in 1994 from complications from Agent Orange.

Ricky just moved to Florida after a stellar career as a Boston policeman.

Dolan served as a US Marsha and recently retired.

Knuckles moved down South and became a successful businessman.

Peaches became a Lawyer after an unsuccessful run for Congress in 1976.

My brother retired as a Boston Police Captain.

Ray Flynn was appointed by President Clinton as US Ambassador to the Vatican.

Anne Marie got married and moved to Florida.

Bubba Cahill recently retired from the Boston Fire Department.

Red Auerbach recently passed away.

Jimmy Dolan retired from the US Marshall Service.

Leo McCarty had a hit record released in 1969 and sung at many clubs in the Boston area. He recently retired from the Boston Housing Authority.

Paul Moore was sent to jail as part of Whitey Bulger's gang. He served nine years and is out now.

Chuckie Fuller is still in jail and will never get out. He murdered about 5 or 6 people. He has changed his name to Chuckles and wars hot pants and bras around the jail.

Whitey Bulger you already know.

I was elected to the Massachusetts Legislature in 2002 where I served 4 terms. I am now a writer.

Made in the USA
Middletown, DE
23 July 2020